Reading *Fin de Siècle* Fictions

Longman Critical Readers

General Editor:

Stan Smith, Professor of English, University of Dundee

Published titles:

K. M. Newton, *George Eliot*

Mary Eagleton, *Feminist Library Criticism*

Gary Waller, *Shakespeare's Comedies*

John Drakakis, *Shakespearean Tragedy*

Richard Wilson and Richard Dutton, *New Historicism and Renaissance Drama*

Peter Brooker, *Modernism/Postmodernism*

Peter Widdowson, *D. H. Lawrence*

Rachel Bowlby, *Virginia Woolf*

Francis Mulhern, *Contemporary Marxist Literary Criticism*

Annabel Patterson, *John Milton*

Cynthia Chase, *Romanticism*

Michael O'Neill, *Shelley*

Stephanie Trigg, *Medieval English Poetry*

Antony Easthope, *Contemporary Film Theory*

Terry Eagleton, *Ideology*

Mark Currie, *Metafiction*

Geoffrey Holderness, Bryan Loughrey and Andrew Murphy, *Shakespeare's Roman Plays*

Brean Hammond, *Pope*

Lyn Pykett, Reading *Fin de Siècle* Fictions

Reading *Fin de Siècle* Fictions

Edited and Introduced by

Lyn Pykett

Longman
London and New York

Longman Addison Wesley Limited
Edinburgh Gate
Harlow, Essex CM20 2JE, England
and associated Companies throughout the world.

Published in the United States of America
by Addison Wesley Longman Publishing, New York.

© Addison Wesley Longman Limited 1996

First published 1996

ISBN 0 582 23392 5 csd
ISBN 0 582 23390 9 ppr

British Library Cataloguing in Publication Data

A catalogue record of this book is
available from the British Library

Library of Congress Cataloging in Publication Data

Also available

Set by 5k in 9/11.5pt Palatino
Produced by Longman Singapore Publishers (Pte) Ltd.
Printed in Singapore

Contents

General Editors' Preface   vii

Acknowledgements   ix

1   Introduction   1

2   NINA AUERBACH Magi and Maidens: The Romance of the Victorian Freud   22

3   SANDRA M. GILBERT Rider Haggard's Heart of Darkness   39

4   LINDA DOWLING The Decadent and the New Woman in the 1890s   47

5   STEPHEN HEATH Psychopathia Sexualis: Stevenson's *Strange Case*   64

6   RICHARD DELLAMORA Homosexual Scandal and Compulsory Heterosexuality in the 1890s   80

7   ED COHEN Writing Gone Wilde: Homoerotic Desire in the Closet of Representation   103

8   JONATHAN DOLLIMORE Different Desires: Subjectivity and Transgression in Wilde and Gide   127

9   DANIEL PICK 'Terrors of the Night': *Dracula* and 'Degeneration' in the Late Nineteenth Century   149

10   ELAINE SHOWALTER Syphilis, Sexuality, and the Fiction of the *Fin de Siècle*   166

11   PATRICK BRANTLINGER Imperial Gothic: Atavism and the Occult in the British Adventure Novel, 1880–1914   184

12   BENITA PARRY The Content and Discontents of Kipling's Imperialism   210

13   EDWARD SAID Conrad's *Heart of Darkness* and the Histories of Empire   223

Further Reading   232

Index   235

General Editors' Preface

The outlines of contemporary critical theory are now often taught as a standard feature of a degree in literary studies. The development of particular theories has seen a thorough transformation of literary criticism. For example, Marxist and Foucauldian theories have revolutionised Shakespeare studies, and 'deconstruction' has led to a complete reassessment of Romantic poetry. Feminist criticism has left scarcely any period of literature unaffected by its searching critiques. Teachers of literary studies can no longer fall back on a standardised, received, methodology.

Lecturers and teachers are now urgently looking for guidance in a rapidly changing critical environment. They need help in understanding the latest revisions in literary theory, and especially in grasping the practical effects of the new theories in the form of theoretically sensitised new readings. A number of volumes in the series anthologise important essays on particular theories. However, in order to grasp the full implications and possible uses of particular theories it is essential to see them put to work. This series provides substantial volumes of new readings, presented in an accessible form and with a significant amount of editorial guidance.

Each volume includes a substantial introduction which explores the theoretical issues and conflicts embodied in the essays selected and locates areas of disagreement between positions. The pluralism of theories has to be put on the agenda of literary studies. We can no longer pretend that we all tacitly accept the same practices in literary studies. Neither is a *laissez-faire* attitude any longer tenable. Literature departments need to go beyond the mere toleration of theoretical differences: it is not enough merely to agree to differ; they need actually to 'stage' the differences openly. The volumes in this series all attempt to dramatise the differences, not necessarily with a view to resolving them but in order to foreground the choices presented by different theories or to argue for a particular route through the impasses the differences present.

The theory 'revolution' has had real effects. It has loosened the grip of traditional empiricist and romantic assumptions about language and literature. It is not always clear what is being proposed as the new agenda for literary studies, and indeed the very notion of 'literature' is questioned by the post-structuralist strain in theory. However, the uncertainties and obscurities of contemporary theories appear much less worrying when we see what the best critics have been able to do with them in practice. This series aims to disseminate the best of recent criticism and to show that it is possible to re-read the canonical texts of literature in new and challenging ways.

RAMAN SELDEN AND STAN SMITH

The Publishers and fellow Series Editor regret to record that Raman Selden died after a short illness in May 1991 at the age of fifty-three. Ray Selden was a fine scholar and a lovely man. All those he has worked with will remember him with much affection and respect.

Acknowledgements

We are grateful to the following for permission to reproduce copyright material:

The author, Nina Auerbach for her article 'Magi and Maidens: The Romance of the Victoria Freud' from *Critical Inquiry* 8, 1981 (Pubd University of Chicago Press); Blackwell Publishers for the articles 'Psychopathia Sexualis: Stevenson's *Strange Case*' by Stephen Heath from *Critical Quarterly* 28, (1986), and ' "Terrors of the night": *Dracula* and "degeneration" in the late nineteenth century' by Daniel Pick from *Critical Quarterly* 30, (1988); Cornell University Press for 'Imperial Gothic: Atavism and the Occult in the British Adventure Novel, 1880–1914' (abridged) from *Rule of Darkness: British Literature and Imperialism, 1830–1914* by Patrick Brantlinger, Copyright © 1990 by Cornell University; Routledge and the author, Jonathan Dollimore, for his article 'Different Desires: Subjectivity and Transgression in Wilde and Gide' from *Textual Practice* 1, (1987); the author, Sandra M. Gilbert, for her article 'Rider Haggard's Heart of Darkness' originally published in *Partisan Review* 50, No. 3, (1983); The Johns Hopkins University Press for the essay 'Syphlis, Sexuality and the Fiction of the *Fin de Siècle*' by Elaine Showalter (abridged) from *Sex, Politics, and Science in the Nineteenth-Century Novel* edited by Ruth B. Yeazell (1991); the Modern Language Association of America for the article 'Writing Gone Wilde: Homoerotic Desire in the Closet of Representation' by Ed Cohen from *Publications of the Modern Language Society of America* 102, (1987); the author, Benita Parry, for her essay 'The Content and Discontents of Kipling's Imperialism' (abridged) from *New Formations* 6, (1988); Random House UK Ltd and the Authors' Agents for 'Conrad's *Heart of Darkness* and the Histories of Empire' from *Culture and Imperialism* by Edward Said, Copyright © 1994 by Edward Said, reprinted with the permission of Wylie, Aitken & Stone, Inc.; The University of California Press and the author, Linda Dowling, for her article 'The Decadent and the New Woman in the 1890s' from *Nineteenth Century Fiction* 33, No. 4, (1979), Copyright © 1979 by the Regents of the University of California; The University of North Carolina Press for the article 'Homosexual Scandal

Reading Fin de Siècle *Fictions*

1 Introduction

The approaching end of the twentieth century, accompanied as it has been by 'endisms' of various kinds – the end of history, the end of politics, the collapse of the grand narratives – has led to a renewed critical focus on the senses of ending that characterised that earlier turn of the century, the period between around 1880 and 1914 which has been labelled as the *fin de siècle*. Holbrook Jackson's pioneering study *The Eighteen Nineties*, a 'comprehensive guidebook to the region by a near-native'[1] has been reissued on several occasions since its first publication in 1913, and its appearance in a new edition in 1988 was part of the torrent of new books on the period which began to appear from the mid-1980s. Several of these new studies are indebted to Jackson, but all of them modify or challenge his version of the 1890s.[2]

The term *'fin de siècle'* appears to have entered cultural discourse in 1888, as the title of a play by F. de Jouvenot and H. Micard which was performed in Paris in that year. Five years later the term was so well established that one of the characters in George Egerton's story 'The Spell of the White Elf' could use it as a kind of shorthand to denote a set of values and a lifestyle that together virtually constitute a cultural formation:

> 'Larry Moore of the *Vulture* – he is one of the most wickedly amusing of men, prides himself on being *fin de siècle* – don't you detest that word? – or nothing, raves about Dégas, and is a worshipper of the decadent school of verse, quotes Verlaine, you know – well he came in one evening on his way to some music hall.'[3]

Egerton's story appeared in 1893 in *Keynotes*, a book produced by that self-consciously *fin de siècle* publisher John Lane. A year earlier the *fin de siècle* mentality had been anatomised at great length by the Austrian Max Nordau in *Degeneration*. This extraordinary diatribe, which was translated into English in 1895, was a psycho-social pathology of modern 'degeneration', a condition which Nordau represented as both a cause and symptom of contemporary moral, cultural, and aesthetic decline. For many of those who lived through it, whether they were cultural pessimists like Nordau, or the avant-gardists and prophets of a new world order against whom he raged, the *fin de siècle* was a time of great cultural ferment. It was the age of 'the Dusk of the Nations',[4] the rending of social, moral and aesthetic traditions, the growth of mass society, the spread of urbanism, the development of a consumer culture, and the physical and mental deterioration of 'civilised' man; in short, it was a crisis in civilisation.

The age of decadence and/or transition

In retrospect literary historians and critics equated the *fin de siècle* in Britain (and particularly in England) with yellow books and green carnations, and with the literary 'movements' of aestheticism and symbolism; the distinctive literary genre of the period (thus constituted) was poetry. For many later commentators the period could be summed up in one word, 'decadence', which Arthur Symons (who was both an advocate and practitioner of decadence) defined as a 'morbid subtlety of analysis ... [and] ... morbid curiosity of form'.[5] According to Holbrook Jackson, one of the first literary historians of the *fin de siècle*, the chief characteristics of decadence were perversity, artificiality, egoism, and curiosity. This equation of the *fin de siècle* with 'the decadence' has proved remarkably persistent in literary studies of the period. It can be traced in Barbara Charlesworth's *Dark Passages: The Decadent Consciousness in Victorian Literature* (1965), Ian Fletcher's *Decadence and the 1890s* (1979), R. K. R. Thornton's *The Decadent Dilemma* (1983), John Reed's *The Decadent Style* (1985), Linda Dowling's *Language and Decadence in the Victorian Fin de Siècle* (1986), and most recently in Murray Pittock's *Spectrum of Decadence* (1993) (see Further Reading).

One of the main claims made about the cultural significance of *fin de siècle* decadence was that it was a subversion of, or reaction against, Victorianism; a tendency which was judged deplorable or laudable depending on the critic's estimation of the Victorians. This view of the *fin de siècle* as a period of Decadent revolt was developed in Holbrook Jackson's *The Eighteen Nineties*, a book which was extremely influential in establishing the 1890s as *the* quintessential *fin de siècle* decade; a decade in which,

> for a few recognisably coherent years the artistic, literary, ideological, even religious strands in the Victorian revolt against Victorianism came together. Beardsley questions classical sexual morality *and* classical graphic conventions; Shaw gives recipes for a new drama *and* a new woman in the same breath; Wilde argues for art *and* socialism, and even, for a moment, believes in both.[6]

For Jackson, viewing the *fin de siècle* from the perspective of 1913, it was not simply a period of revolt, but also an age of transition:

> People said it was a 'period of transition', and they were convinced that they were passing not only from one social system to another, but from one morality to another, from one culture to another, and from one religion to a dozen or more.[7]

The transitional status of the *fin de siècle* was further emphasised in Jackson's preface to the 1927 edition of his book:

> It was not, primarily, a period of achievement, but rather of effort: suggestive, tentative, rather than formative ... an old civilization a little too conscious of itself and the present, and a little too much concerned for its future.[8]

As the *fin de siècle* became an increasingly distant prospect, and one, moreover, viewed from the perspective of Departments of English Literature in universities it was characterised, above all, as an age (perhaps *the* age) of transition; wandering between two worlds, one dead (Victorianism) the other (Modernism) waiting to be born. As Raymond Williams put it in 1958 in a verdict which echoes Jackson's, the *fin de siècle* was a 'working-out, rather, of unfinished lines; a tentative redirection'.[9] In short, the *fin de siècle* was a space between two literary and historical periods, and not a distinct literary or historical period; it occupied a borderland between two fields of study, rather than constituting an object of study in its own right.

The 'new' *fin de siècle*

Over the last twenty years or so we have seen the construction of a 'new' *fin de siècle*, a *fin de siècle* which is increasingly seen as a distinctive and diverse cultural moment rather than as a limbo-like 'age of transition'. At the same time critical attention has been redirected towards the genre (or more accurately genres) of fiction. The 'new' *fin de siècle* is, to a great extent, the product of new critical and theoretical perspectives and/or current political and ideological concerns. In the case of this period as in so many others feminist literary history and theory have provided a variety of revisionary perspectives. The post-Foucauldian interest in the histories of sexuality (and particularly of homosexuality), sexual science, and discourses of gender has also been particularly important in redefining the *fin de siècle*, as has the developing post-colonialist interest in the discourses of imperialism and the critique of the culture of Empire. The development of Cultural Materialism and the growth of an interdisciplinary Cultural Studies have also played important parts in shaping the new *fin de siècle*. Both of these Post-Structuralist approaches have redefined the relationships between literary and non-literary texts, and between texts and their contexts which had become established in literary studies as traditionally conceived. Roland Barthes' interdisciplinary concept of the text as a 'methodological field'[10] has provided one of the theoretical models for the new Cultural Studies. Another has been provided by Raymond Williams's rethinking of 'culture' as 'a general term to describe not only the products but the processes of all signification, including the signification of values'.[11] This new focus on signifying practices and on all of the components of a culture, and not just the (handful of) texts of what Williams has described as the 'selective tradition',[12] has been particularly important for re-reading the *fin de siècle*, which was a period of fierce cultural contest and a defining moment for observing the processes by which the boundaries between high culture and popular culture are established and policed. In addition to these theoretical and methodological engagements, current political engagements with sexual and gender politics, and, in particular, with issues of class, race, and ethnicity, have also opened up the *fin de siècle* to investigation in all sorts of new and interesting ways, as will be evident in the essays reprinted in this volume.

My aim in compiling this collection of essays about *fin de siècle* narratives has been to demonstrate something of the range and diversity of the newly constituted *fin de siècle*, and also to provide examples of some of the main lines of investigation which have brought it into being. I hope that the essays and extracts I have selected for inclusion, together with this introductory material, will form an introduction to *fin de siècle* cultural studies and also provide a commentary on important aspects of current critical debates. Three themes or topics have dominated recent studies of the *fin de siècle*: gender and sexuality, decadence and degeneration, and imperialism. I have organised this collection around these three broad areas, moving from a group of essays concerned with issues of gender and sexuality, to essays concerned with aspects of decadence and degeneration, and finally to a group of extracts dealing in various ways with the discourses of imperialism. In practice, as readers will soon discover, these three areas continually intersect and overlap, and each of the essays or extracts included in a particular grouping also ventures into one or more of the areas addressed by the other groupings.

Gender and sexuality

Theoretical and political engagements with issues of gender and sexuality have been of particular importance in the re-reading of the *fin de siècle*, and of *fin de siècle* fiction in particular. The impact of feminist scholarship and criticism has been extensive, contentious, and diverse. The second wave feminists of the 1970s (and after) returned to the various and competing feminisms of the *fin de siècle*, seeking a historical grounding for their own movement, and (perhaps) attempting to situate and understand their own dissensions by locating them in the turbulent and divided history of the women's movement of the late nineteenth century, from the social purity campaigns of the 1870s and 1880s – for example, on the sexual double standard, the social evil of prostitution and the Contagious Diseases Acts – to the increasingly militant struggle for the vote.

As late twentieth century feminists began to 'fabricate new mythologies commensurate with our growing belief in our strength' (Auerbach, p. 23 below) feminist literary critics turned their attention to the mythologies of the past, and re-examined and deconstructed some powerful myths of femininity in texts by late nineteenth-century male writers. The first two essays in this volume, both of them first published in the early 1980s, are examples of this latter approach. Both re-examine the *fin de siècle* preoccupation with the *femme fatale*. In the first essay Nina Auerbach re-examines what she describes as that 'alluring conjunction of women and corpses' (p. 23 below) in the literature and visual culture of the *fin de siècle*. She also reviews an important scene from the 1890s, a tableau in which three men (Du Maurier's Svengali, Bram Stoker's Dracula, and Sigmund Freud) lean longingly over 'three mesmerized and apparently characterless women' (Trilby, Lucy Westenra and Frau Emmy von N), and discovers in these prone women, not dispiriting victims but rather disturbingly powerful figures with a 'capacity for amazing and empowering transformations' (p. 31). In the second essay Sandra Gilbert revises Mario Praz's contention that in the nineteenth century, above all others, sex was the mainspring of imaginative literature, and argues that Praz's book[13] in fact demonstrates that it was 'the power of the female sex' that 'increasingly obsessed male writers' at the *fin de siècle*. Gilbert makes her case by means of what has become a much-imitated reading of Rider Haggard's *She* as 'a symptom of a complex of late Victorian sociocultural and sexual anxieties' (p. 40), and also as an early engagement with the phenomenon of the New Woman: the novel is 'a definitive *fin de siècle* embodiment of fantasies that preoccupied countless male writers . . . an entirely New Woman: the all-knowing, all-powerful ruler of a matriarchal society' (p. 40).

These essays by Auerbach and Gilbert both contain a number of elements which have been extremely important in the re-reading of *fin de siècle* fiction. Both look at best-sellers by male writers who were self-consciously committed to the project of producing novels that would convert men into novel-readers, and reclaim fiction from the process of feminisation to which it had supposedly succumbed. Like much of the more recent innovatory work on the period, both essays focus on popular culture and on genre fiction, and they also explore the links between different forms and genres: Auerbach compares the representations of male and female figures in fiction texts with the illustrations of those texts and with other magazine illustrations of the period; both writers make interesting connections between the forms of fiction and the early texts of psychoanalysis, and between the discourse of adventure stories and the discourses of anthropology, spiritualism, or popular science.

Freud is an important figure in both of these essays. However, rather than invoking Freudian psychoanalysis as a way of understanding *fin de siècle* texts, both critics, offer their readings of late nineteenth-century literary texts as a way of locating the historical and cultural specificity of Freud's narratives. This historicisation of Freud has been a particularly interesting aspect of recent work on *fin de siècle* fiction (see, for example, Stephen Heath's essay 'Psychopathia sexualis: Stevenson's *Strange Case*', reprinted below). Like much of the work on the *fin de siècle* undertaken in the last fifteen years, and in common with several of the other essays collected here, these opening essays not only foreground a network of anxieties which pervade the culture and which are articulated in a wide range of cultural forms, but they also suggest that these anxieties – among the chief of which are anxieties about gender, and especially about feminism, female power, and the female as primitive and pre- or non-rational – are key components of an emergent modernism.

Approaching the literature of the *fin de siècle* from a different perspective feminist literary historians, intent on rediscovering the women writers whose work had disappeared from view as part of the process by which the dominant literary tradition was constructed, have restored to critical view many long-neglected texts by *fin de siècle* women. They have also re-examined the processes of literary periodisation which have tended to consign women's writing to the interstices of literary history. During the last twenty years feminist critics have gradually reconfigured the map of literary history, replacing a *fin de siècle* which was defined in terms of decadence or symbolism in poetry and the New Realism in fiction (both definitions which tended to exclude or marginalise the contribution of women writers), with a *fin de siècle* which was defined as the age of the New Woman, and which thus placed women writers and women's issues centre-stage.

This process of reconfiguration began in the late 1970s with Elaine Showalter's pioneering reassessment of the New Woman writers in *A Literature of Their Own*, which brought to light and re-read a number of neglected or forgotten women writers of the 1880s and 1890s in its attempt to recover a lost or hidden 'female tradition' of fiction. This was followed by Patricia Stubb's and Gail Cunningham's reassessments of writing about the New Woman (by both men and women) in *Feminism and the Novel*, and *The New Woman and the Victorian Novel* respectively, and by Penny Boumelha's important chapter on the New Woman writers in *Thomas Hardy and Women*. Each of these books played an important part in rediscovering or reconstituting a cultural field – the New Woman writing and the female New Woman Writers – even if one of them (Showalter's) finds the achievement of the New Woman writers flawed by feminist anger and/or a retreat into the cul-de-sac of a 'female aesthetic':

> The feminists challenged many of the restrictions on women's self-expression, denounced the gospel of self-sacrifice, attacked patriarchal religion, and constructed a theoretical model of female oppression, but their anger with society and their need for self-justification often led them away from realism into over-simplification, emotionalism, and fantasy.[14]

The other books referred to above tend to see the New Woman largely as a subject for fiction (rather than as a writing subject), and to read the women's writing of the 1880s and 1890s mainly as a preparation for (what they see as) the more accomplished literary achievements of male writers. The perspectives on the New Woman writing offered by Stubbs, Cunningham, and Showalter are, to a great extent, products of their time; all three books were written when feminist literary criticism and literary history were in an emergent state. They are all examples of a 'compromise formation',[15] which endorses traditional conceptions of literary periodisation, and traditional standards of literary value. On the other hand, in *Rebellious Structures* (1987), the first full-length study of New Woman writing by women, Gerd Bjorhovde begins to revise traditional literary judgements, and to interrogate the settled views of literary history. Bjorhovde re-reads the New Woman writers in the context of what she describes as a 'serious crisis' of definition in the novel at the turn of the century. She claims them as 'pioneers . . . writers who were consciously trying out new things', and as oppositional writers whose rebellion was partly literary, and partly directed against social and political authority.[16] More recently Ann L. Ardis, in *New Women, New Novels* (1990) has re-read the New Woman novel in the light of later developments within feminist theory, especially Barbara Herrnstein Smith's critique of feminist criticism's failure to develop a 'non-canonical theory of value'[17] and Gayatri Spivak's contention that 'what is at the center [of our cultural narratives] often hides a repression'.[18] Ardis challenges dominant ideas of literary periodisation and, more particularly, questions the exclusion of New Woman novels from existing genealogies of modernism. Like other recent feminist literary historians Ardis develops a view of the New Woman fiction as both engaged and experimental, as both prefigurative of and, in its social commitment, an alternative to the aesthetic of high modernism.[19]

My selection on the New Woman is Linda Dowling's dense and suggestive essay which links the 1890s New Woman to the decadent. Dowling explores the way in which late-Victorian critics of the avant-garde persistently identified the New Woman with the decadent, and demonised both figures as 'twin apostles of social apocalypse' (p. 57), who threatened to make 'an anarchic chaos of the conventions of literary form' (p. 53) and to 'dangerously confuse established assumptions about class' (p. 53). Dowling anticipates the attempts of Ann Ardis and others to restore the New Woman writers to the genealogy of modernism, suggesting that their 'quarrel with established culture . . . was the first rebellious expression of that disenchantment of culture with culture that Lionel Trilling has taught us to recognise as "modernism" ' (p. 49). Dowling also focuses on the New Woman and the decadent as examples of that sexual anarchy which typified the *fin de siècle*.

The anarchy of *fin de siècle* sexualities has been subjected to intense scrutiny by recent commentators on the period. Since the 1970s feminist, gay and lesbian historians, and literary scholars have claimed the period as one of gender crisis, and have been exploring the implications of the crisis of gender definition at the *fin de siècle*. They have built up a substantial case for 'the critical importance of this period in the shaping of contemporary sexual discourses' and in the shaping of modern sexuality.[20] The theoretical framework for much of this scholarship has been provided by Michel Foucault's work on the discursive production of sexuality, and on the multiplicity and complexity of the forms by which sexuality is policed and by which gender norms are regulated and reinforced. Foucault's work on the production and circulation of discourses, and particularly his work on hegemonic and counter-hegemonic (or dominant and reverse) discourses, has also been particularly productive for literary historians and critics; it has been much in evidence in the considerable body of work that has appeared in the last few years on the contesting discourses on sexuality in the literary texts of the turn of the century. Indeed, as Jeffrey Weeks has pointed out, 'literary studies has become in recent years the radical cutting edge of the exploration of sexuality and gender'.[21] It is not difficult to see why this should be so when one considers the nature of some of the recent theoretical interventions in literary studies; for example, post-Althusserian work on ideology and various deconstructionist approaches which tend to focus on exposing and exploring conflicts and contradictions in literary texts.

Some of the most suggestive (and polemical) work on *fin de siècle* sexualities has come out of a new historicising of literary studies, which involves, as Eve Kosofsky Sedgwick has put it in *Between Men*, 'working on historical questions through the reading of literature'.[22] Sedgwick has been a dominant figure in this historicised, deconstructive re-reading of the literary texts of the *fin de siècle* in the context of, and as examples of, the contestation of historically specific discourses on sexuality. Sedgwick follows Foucault in arguing that the category of the 'homosexual' is a recent invention which became of central importance in organising gender and sexuality in the late nineteenth century. In her two important books, *Between Men* and the *Epistemology of the Closet*, Sedgwick undertakes a series of detailed analyses of a range of literary texts (pre-eminently, though not exclusively, from the *fin de siècle*) in which she re-examines patterns of relationships between men (which she terms homosociality) and also late-nineteenth century fears and fantasies about same-sex preference, in order to discover what they can tell us about modern definitions of masculinity in general and patterns of male domination in society in particular.

One of the texts which Sedgwick uses in *Between Men* to explore patterns of homosociality is Robert Louis Stevenson's *The Strange Case of Dr Jekyll and Mr Hyde*, a text which has received a great deal of critical attention in recent years (see Further Reading). For most late-twentieth century critics *The Strange Case* is, above all, a story about masculinity. The world of Stevenson's tale, as several recent critics have noted, is a masculine world, an enclosed world of middle-class male professionals (lawyers, doctors, men of science); it is a world from which the female has been excluded, or at least confined to the servants' quarters or the streets. Critical attention has also focused on *The Strange Case* as a story about male sexuality; a male sexuality, as Stephen Heath puts it in the essay reprinted below, which is 'taken for granted and repressed in the one operation' (p. 69).

Like the monster and his creator in Mary Shelley's *Frankenstein* (a critique of Romantic masculinity, among other things), and like the eponymous protagonists of those other popular *fin de siècle* texts which address the turn-of-the-century gender crisis, *Dracula* and *She*, Stevenson's Dr Jekyll and his alter ego Mr Hyde have acquired the status of a modern myth – in this case a myth about the primitive duality in man. These *fin de siècle* myths, like other mythic narratives, have been reworked in a variety of different forms and have been circulated widely in the culture, most notably in cinematic form. 'Mythicisation' has also been a feature of the critical circulation of these narratives; the formalist (i.e. proto-structuralist) work of Vladimir Propp on the morphology of the folk tale, Levi-Strauss's structuralist work on the transformations of myth, and Roland Barthes' post-structuralist work on the semiotics of myth have shaped many re-readings of these texts. However, some of the most interesting work, in my view, has been produced by the new cultural history.

In the case of Stevenson's tale, for example, some of the most interesting re-readings have been concerned to locate this modern myth in the specificities of its historical moment of production. Much attention has been directed at the way in which the text both reproduces and reworks late nineteenth-century discourses on gender and sexuality. Increasingly *The Strange Case* has been situated in the general discussion of sexual–social standards which pervaded print media in the closing decades of the nineteenth century; particularly the developing science of sexology whose founding texts tended to pathologise the sexual. Stephen Heath, for example, points out that Stevenson's *Strange Case* was published in the same year as those other strange cases in Krafft-Ebing's *Psychopathia Sexualis*, a text which, like Stevenson's, focused on perversions and the criminal–sexual. However, if *The Strange Case* is symptomatic of the late nineteenth-century medicalisation of sexuality it also participates in (even anticipates) the psychologisation of sexuality undertaken by Freud and others. *The Strange Case* is yet another example of those *fin de siècle* texts which have been thrown into new intertextual relationships with Freud. Not only does Stevenson's story of a day-time and a night-time personality anticipate Freud's theory of the unconscious, but the form of *The Strange Case* – a strange story in the form of a case history – is a mirror image of Freud's *fin de siècle* form – case histories which strangely keep turning into stories.

Hyde is, of course, one of those beasts in the closet which have preoccupied Eve Kosofsky Sedgwick and that growing band of critics who have been influenced by her work. Perhaps the most important aspect of Sedgwick's writing on late-Victorian sexuality has been the way in which it has brought homosexuality out of the closet of marginality into the centre of sex-gender discourse. The importance of the category 'homosexual', she argues, does not necessarily derive 'from its regulatory relation to a nascent or already constituted minority of homosexual people or desires, but from its potential for giving whoever wields it a structuring definitional leverage over the whole range of male bonds that shape the sexual constitution'.[23]

Sedgwick's work has clearly had a profound influence on the essays by Dellamora, Cohen, and Dollimore reproduced in this volume. Dellamora, for example, uses Sedgwick's work on the controlling and reinforcing of homosocial networks by homophobic mechanisms, and also Adrienne Rich's theorisation of 'compulsory heterosexuality' to explore the sexual politics of the 1890s and, in particular, the way in which gender roles are 'spectacularly encoded and enforced' (p. 81) in the 'public contest over the meaning of masculinity that takes place in the press and courts' (p. 81) during that decade. Dellamora is especially interested in developing Sedgwick's work on the processes by which the dominance of the bourgeois male in the late nineteenth century was secured by a 'double bind in which "the most intimate male bonding" was prescribed at the same time that "the remarkably cognate" homosexuality was proscribed' (p. 83). Dellamora's chapter is a good example of one kind of the new cultural history which examines the proliferation of a linked network of discourses in a range of cultural forms: homosexual scandal and the 'the sacrifice of the homosexual' are linked to the contradictions of the myth of the gentleman, the construction of the New Woman, and the theorisation of the lesbian, in literary texts, the critical discourse of literary reviewing, political discourse, the science of sexology, and the new journalism. As readers will see from Dellamora's discussion of Hardy's *Jude the Obscure* and its contemporary critical reception, one important result of this new cultural history is to complicate established readings of canonical literary texts, as well as bringing new texts into critical focus.

Ed Cohen's 'Writing Gone Wilde: Homoerotic Desire in the Closet of Representation' also looks at the journalistic representation of homosexual scandal in the 1890s as one of the key sites of 'the discursive production of "the homosexual" as the antithesis of the "true" bourgeois male' (p. 104). For Cohen, as for a plethora of recent critics, Wilde is the central figure and the Wilde trials of 1895 the defining moment in 'the Victorian bourgeoisie's larger efforts to legitimate certain limits for the sexual deployment of the male body and, in Foucault's terms, to define a "class body" ' (p. 104). Like many other critics working in this area, Cohen is indebted to Regenia Gagnier's reading of the Wilde trials as contests about textuality and cultural authority as well as about sexuality and morality. As Gagnier has argued, Aestheticism as well as homosexuality was on trial in the late spring of 1895:

> Wilde's trials confronted the public with an art that refused to say nothing but the truth, that refused to take its interrogation solemnly, and a sexuality outside of the rational demands of reproduction. Thus aestheticism came to mean the irrational in both productive (art) and reproductive (sexuality) realms: an indication of the art world's divorce from middle-class life.[24]

Cohen's conceptualisation of the Wilde trials as 'spectacle', like Dellamora's, is indebted to Gagnier's attempt to locate both aestheticism and the Wilde trials in the context of the modern development of the society of the spectacle; the mass society of late nineteenth-century capitalism in which the manufacture and proliferation of images, and particularly the images of advertising became increasingly important.[25] The main part of the essay, however, is an application to two of Wilde's texts of Sedgwick's suggestion that 'both the production and the consumption of literary representations depicting male interactions' should be situated 'within a larger social formation that circulates ideologies defining differences in power across sex and class' (p. 105). Cohen offers textual analyses of *Teleny* (a homosexual pornographic novel thought by some to have been partly written by Wilde), and the 'manifestly "straight" ' novel, *The Picture of Dorian Gray*, in an attempt to demonstrate how 'textual depictions of male same-sex experience both reproduce and resist the dominant heterosexual ideologies and practices' (p. 107). More importantly, Cohen assigns a disruptive role to the homosexual text, suggesting that, in the process of negotiating both the discourses of hetero/homosexuality and the dominant representational codes of the period, Wilde's texts came to problematise representation itself.

Cohen's essay, like the extract from Dellamora, situates itself as an example of a new cultural history; a post-structuralist cultural history which interrogates the background/foreground or texts/contexts model. Cohen cites the British cultural materialist critic Raymond Williams as his authority for approaching works of literature as complex cultural productions which do not simply reflect an already constituted external reality, but which are themselves constitutive of that reality; in other words as contexts as well as texts. Like Williams and other cultural materialists Cohen is interested in understanding the historical forms in which social relations have been put into discourse (in this case, relations between men) in order to begin to suggest other forms which those relations might take.

Jonathan Dollimore has been closely associated with the younger generation of British cultural materialists who have been concerned to re-read the texts of the past in order to appropriate their radical potential. In the essay reproduced here he explores the homophobia and homosexual panic, which preoccupy Sedgwick, from a different perspective, emphasising the radical potential of the transgressive, the perverse, the sexually dissident. Dollimore argues that Wilde's conception of individualism cannot be separated from either transgressive desire or a transgressive aesthetic, both of which necessitate the relinquishing of the idea of an essential self. He re-examines the individualistic philosophy developed in *The Soul of Man Under Socialism*, arguing that Wilde was interested above all in the 'dynamic social potential' (p. 131) of an individualism which generates (as Wilde puts it in that essay) a disobedience which is 'man's original virtue' and through which progress is made.

Dollimore's is a postmodern reading of the *fin de siècle* but one which also reads the earlier period as a key moment in the shaping of the modern and postmodern. He is not simply reading Wilde through the lens of contemporary theory, but as a way of advancing current theoretical debates. Dollimore explores the relationship of Wilde's transgressive aesthetic to three important aspects of those debates: the dispute over whether an inversion of binary oppositions subverts or merely reinforces the order which those binaries uphold; the question of the political importance (or irrelevance) of the decentring of the subject; the so-called disappearance of the depth model, especially the model of a deep human subjectivity in postmodernism. Moreover, in his discussion of two 1890 encounters between Wilde and André Gide which frame the essay Dollimore not only explores the construction of sex-gender identities at the *fin de siècle*, but also illuminates current debates within gay studies. In Wilde's attempt to 'demoralise' Gide, and in Gide's negotiations of the challenge of Wilde's transgressive individualism, Dollimore displays an engagement with what current theorists are now beginning to readdress: 'the complexities, the potential and the dangers of what it is to transgress, invert and displace *from within*; the paradox of the marginality which is always interior to, or at least intimate with, the centre' (p. 143).

Degeneration

While late twentieth-century Gay Studies has often been intent on recuperating the Wildean homosexual as a transgressive radical who challenges the established social order, for many of Wilde's contemporaries (as Dellamora and Cohen indicate) the homosexual was merely a degenerate who threatened both the natural and social order. The figure of the degenerate and its place in a wider network of ideas about degeneration have become increasingly important topics in the interdisciplinary, cultural history of the *fin de siècle*, as can be seen in recent books by Sander Gilman and Edward Chamberlin, Daniel Pick, and William Greenslade, as well as in a number of the essays reprinted here. Degeneration was one of the great organising ideas of the late nineteenth century – a heuristic fiction which had a profound impact on literary fictions. Theories of degeneration were first aired in specialist scientific journals in the 1860s. Summing up some of these theories in *Degeneration: A Chapter in Darwinism* Edwin Lankester suggested that natural selection far from being a progressive process which necessarily involved the development of an organism to a higher state of complexity, could just as easily involve degeneration, or a diminution in the complexity of an organism.[26] By the 1880s and 1890s the idea of degeneration pervaded the culture and was 'a major issue of social debate and political speculation' (see p. 153 below) in popular and serious journalism and in literary texts as well as in more specialised professional and scientific discourses. Theologians, natural scientists, social scientists, philologists and literary critics all saw their chosen field in terms of a model of degeneration: the moral and material universe, biological and social organisms, the human psyche, the language and literature of the nation, even the race itself were all thought to be subject to degeneration and decline. As several of the recent studies have demonstrated degenerationist thinking was fraught with contradictions, not least at the points at which the discourse on degeneration intersected with the developing sciences of anthropology and psychology. Late nineteenth-century anthropology, for example, conceived of non-European cultures as 'primitive' unevolved forms of cultural organisation. On the other hand, advanced or civilised European cultures (and especially English/British culture, the apex of civilisation) had evolved to their present state by repressing and controlling the primitive elements, although some primitive elements persisted as 'survivals'. Similarly the emergent science of psychology offered an evolutionary or developmental model whereby later stages of normal, healthy psychological development were represented as being achieved by repressing and controlling the primitive drives of the more primitive earlier phases of development. In these fields of enquiry, as in the biological sciences, there was much confusion about whether degeneration was a reversion to or a growth away from the primitive and the natural. Was degeneration a form of atavism or regression to an earlier primitive state – the Hyde waiting to reclaim every Jekyll, the savage beneath the skin of civilisation? Or was it the condition towards which civilised societies and the psychological subjects which they produced were tending – Hyde as created by the discontents of Jekyll's civilisation? Stephen Heath touches on this aspect of the degeneration debates when he reads Stevenson's *The Strange Case* alongside Freud's 1908 essay on ' "Civilized" sexual morality and modern nervous illness' (p. 69).

Recent reappraisals of the discourse on degeneration have also focused on its intersections with *fin de siècle* discourses on gender and sexuality. Some recent commentators have argued that the degenerative state is usually gendered female or feminine. Sandra Siegel, for example, has suggested that 'the later Victorians associated the idea of culture – civilisation was an interchangeable term – with "masculine force and masculine intelligence" '.[27] However, here as everywhere else that one touches down amidst the sexual anarchy of the *fin de siècle*, one is confronted by contradictions. In the last decade of the nineteenth century, civilisation and culture were just as likely (perhaps more likely) to be represented as feminine, or even effeminate, as masculine. Max Nordau's *Degeneration* and Edward Carpenter's *Civilisation: Its Cause and Cure* are just two examples of the contradictorily gendered discourse on degeneration: for Nordau modern civilisation is effeminately degenerate, for Carpenter (even more confusingly) it is both too feminine and not feminine enough).

Like *The Strange Case of Dr Jekyll and Mr Hyde,* Bram Stoker's *Dracula* has become one of the key texts in the current re-reading of the discourse on degeneration. (As the essays by Auerbach, Gilbert and Showalter indicate, *Dracula* is also a key text for recent discussions of literary representations of and responses to the New Woman, and also for discussions of the *fin de siècle* representation of sexuality.) I have included Daniel Pick's ' "Terrors of the Night": *Dracula* and "Degeneration" in the Late Nineteenth Century' as an example of an interesting attempt to read a literary text alongside a number of other degenerationist texts. Pick's essay implicitly invokes the dictum 'always historicise'. He self-consciously resists, and urges his readers to resist the temptations of falling prey to 'the mythological, folkloristic connotations of the vampire story and declar[ing] the novel merely a new twist to an old tale, the reiteration of antique taboos on death' (p. 152), and to concentrate instead on the significance of Stoker's transposition of the vampire tale to nineteenth-century London, a move which facilitates the articulation of 'a vision of the bio-medical degeneration of the race in general and the metropolitan population in particular' (p. 153). Pick historicises by placing Stoker's fiction alongside other contemporary narratives about degeneration and sexuality, and he also deconstructs, by exposing the silence of Stoker's text on issues which are articulated in those other texts. Pick argues that one of the most interesting things about *Dracula* is precisely that (*pace* some recent critics) Stoker is not telling the same story as Freud. On the contrary, in its efforts simultaneously 'to represent, externalise and kill off a distinct constellation of contemporary fears' (p. 149), *Dracula* seems to be 'frozen at the threshold between Victorian evolutionism and psychoanalysis' (p. 150).

Elaine Showalter, on the other hand, focuses on a very specific form of degeneration, syphilis. Taking her examples from medical texts, and advertisements, as well as from a wide range of *fin de siècle* novels, Showalter seeks to establish the existence of a pervasive discourse on syphilis in a wide range of cultural forms. As in the case of several of the essays reproduced here, Foucault's work on sexuality provides one of the obvious theoretical underpinnings for Showalter's project. The discourse on syphilis, she argues is 'part of what Foucault sees as the post-Darwinian theory of degenerescence, part of the new technologies of sex that opened up the domain of social control' (p. 167). More particularly (and more contentiously) Showalter is concerned to explore the gender distinctions of the 'iconography' of syphilis and also of 'the fantastic mode' which dominates turn-of-the-century fiction in England. Showalter's is a cultural history which plots yet another version of the separation of the masculine and feminine spheres. By the end of the nineteenth century, she argues, 'the imaginative worlds of male and female writers had become radically separate, and the sexual struggle between men and women had a counterpart in a literary struggle over the future of fiction' (p. 167). In this latter respect Showalter anticipates the sex wars metaphor that dominates Sandra Gilbert and Susan Gubar's massive study of turn-of-the-century writing, and which has come to dominate much recent feminist discussion of the genealogy of modernism (see Further Reading).

Imperialism

The discourse of degeneration also intersects with, indeed is an important component of, the *fin de siècle* discourse of imperialism. As Patrick Brantlinger has noted, fears that British institutions, culture, and racial stock were declining and degenerating constituted one network of 'the anxieties that attended the climax of the British Empire' (p. 185). The *fin de siècle* was not only a period of gender crisis, it was also as Daniel Bivona has argued,[28] a 'crisis of the civilized', a crisis which was in large part produced by Britain's role in 'the political game of empire' and the contradictions of the discourse of imperialism. Imperialism was a 'cultural metanarrative or mythology' which subsumed even its critics; it was the 'unconscious' of nineteenth-century Britain, 'lurking under the surface of a variety of discourses, conditioning the possibilities for emergence of some and precluding others'. In short the discourse of imperialism played a major role in producing *fin de siècle* self-understanding.

The complex and contradictory discourse of imperialism is another cultural field which has been opened up to investigation and critique by a politicised cultural history of the *fin de siècle*. Frederic Jameson's work on the political unconscious has informed several important studies of late nineteenth-century imperialism. Thus Patrick Brantlinger, who has made a major contribution to the analysis and critique of the discourse of imperialism, locates his own project in *Rule of Darkness* in relation to Jameson's contention that ' "the political perspective" is more than a theme and in terms of critical theory is also more than a mere "supplementary method . . . auxiliary to other interpretive methods current today"; such a perspective is rather "the absolute horizon of all reading and all interpretation" '.[29] Much of the recent work on *fin de siècle* imperialism has also been politicised in the sense that it involves a retrospective ideological critique of imperialism which is undertaken in an attempt to 'help change patterns of domination and racist thought in the present by revealing that the past is, for better or worse, our inheritance'.[30]

Foucault's theory of discourse as power has been another element in the historico-political cultural history of imperialism. Feminist work on the multiple forms of domination based on class, race, and gender has also been important in exposing and exploring the complex interconnections of sexism, racism and imperialism. The third world or post-colonial, deconstructionist critic Gayatri Spivak has been particularly influential in demonstrating the ubiquitousness of imperialist ideology in nineteenth-century texts. Edward Said, the author of the seminal study *Orientalism*, has also argued that imperialist ideology informs all nineteenth-century British culture, as it does all European and North American culture. Said's 'orientalism' is a specific form of the discourse of imperialism, 'a kind of Western projection onto and will to govern over the Orient'[31] which is dispersed throughout virtually all the productions of a particular national culture, from highbrow fiction to social science and from popular fiction to popular science. Said's suggestion that the western preoccupation with the orient in the nineteenth century was a form of writing the 'other' which was also a form of self-revelation has prompted a great deal of critical interest in the late nineteenth-century fascination with the alien other, as will be seen in the essays reprinted here.

The particular forms of the 'other' which Patrick Brantlinger explores in the extract reproduced here are the occult and the fascination with the barbaric and the primitive. Brantlinger identifies a fictional genre which is peculiar to the *fin de siècle*, which he describes as 'imperial Gothic' – a 'blend of adventure story with Gothic elements' (p. 185) – which has three main themes: individual regression or going native; an invasion of civilisation by the forces of barbarism; a decline in the opportunities for heroic action and adventure in the modern world. Brantlinger undertakes an historical analysis of this genre as a 'socio-symbolic message',[32] and considers it in relation to other manifestations of the *fin de siècle* discourse of imperialism, especially the fascination with spiritualism and the occult, and a network of 'anxieties about the ease with which civilisation can revert to barbarism or savagery and thus about the weakening of Britain's imperial hegemony' (p. 186).

Kipling's 'India' is the 'other' which Benita Parry examines in an essay which seeks to interrogate the recent critical 'rehabilitation' of Kipling. Parry offers a critique of Kipling as 'an exemplary artist of imperialism' (p. 222), who constructs the Raj as a text. Parry offers a political, post-colonial deconstruction of that text, arguing (in Said's terms) that Kipling's India is, on the one hand, romanticised and semiotically colonised 'as an object of sensuous and voluptuous pleasure to be enjoyed by Europe (p. 215), and, on the other, its otherness is demonised, and its differences are constituted as 'deviant, menacing, or magnetic' (p. 215). Like much recent politicised criticism, Parry's is attentive to the text's suppressions and omissions, and its strategies of marginalisation and exclusion.

While Parry's retrospective ideological critique sees Kipling as an exemplary voice of imperialism, Edward Said's post-colonialist reading of Conrad is interested in the self-consciousness which 'makes Conrad different from the other colonial writers who were his contemporaries' (p. 225); an historical and ironising self-consciousness by means of which Conrad allows the reader to realise that imperialism too 'was taking place in and was circumscribed by a larger history' (p. 226). Said is interested in the ideology of fictional form, and sees the 'complicated and rich narrative form' of *Heart of Darkness* as an example of an imperialist aesthetics: circular, self-enclosed, excluding non-imperialist alternatives. Unlike much of the work reproduced in this volume the extract from Said is frankly, but paradoxically, evaluative: he claims *Heart of Darkness* as a 'great novella', and proclaims Conrad to be superior to most of his contemporaries, as a writer whose 'genius' allows him to see things that they could not, but he also tries Conrad at the bar of his own politics and ethics. Said's is an historical but not an historicising criticism: Conrad is located in a specific historical situation (the contradictions of the late nineteenth-century discourse of imperialism), but is required to rise above it. Said praises Conrad for being ahead of his time, but in the end has to find him wanting, because he was merely 'a creature of his time', flawed by a 'tragic limitation ... that even though he could see clearly that on one level imperialism was essentially pure dominance and land-grabbing, he could not then conclude that imperialism had to end so that "natives" could lead lives free from European domination' (p. 229).

(Re)constructing the *fin de siècle*

If the *fin de siècle* was constructed as an 'age of transition' by the periodising and other cultural imperatives of a later age, this process of retrospective (re)construction is no less in evidence in the new *fin de siècle* which is (re)produced in this introduction and in the work which I have included in this book. As the editor of another book in this series remarks, 'every historical moment "writes" the literature it wishes to read',[33] and, one might add, every historical moment reads the past through the refracting lens of its own preoccupations. I should, perhaps, conclude by sounding a warning note against the perils of reshaping the nineteenth-century *fin de siècle* simply in the light of our own theoretical and political concerns, and claiming the writers of the earlier period as our own contemporaries. There has, perhaps, been something rather self-confirming in some recent re-readings of the *fin de siècle*. Some late twentieth-century cultural critics have revisited the turn of the century only to find their own questions and preoccupations mirrored in the cultural ferment which they 'discover'. Let me give two examples from quite different kinds of book. First, Murray Pittock explores the contexts of 'the literary culture of Britain in the so-called Decadent era of the Eighteen Nineties', and finds the origins of modern literary theoretical concerns in *fin de siècle* Symbolism:

> Symbolism was one of the chief aesthetic heralds of our modern ideological approaches to literature: Imagism, Formalism, Post-Modernism, Feminism, Structuralism, Deconstruction, the ubiquitous Marxism, and Modernism itself. The twentieth-century literary cult of the '-ism' is substantially foreshadowed in the central importance Symbolism accorded itself as a crusading ideology of interpretation . . .
>
> Since the end of the nineteenth century, our view of literature has continued to be similarly fragmented.[34]

My second example is from Elaine Showalter's fascinating and influential, *Sexual Anarchy*, which is concerned with the 'myths, metaphors, and images of sexual crises and apocalypse that marked both the late nineteenth century and our own *fin de siècle*'.[35] For Showalter the impending end of the twentieth century is a replay of the 1880s and 90s. 'From urban homelessness to imperial decline, from sexual revolution to sexual epidemics, the last decades of the twentieth century seem to be repeating the problems, themes, and metaphors of the *fin de siècle*.' In Showalter's account the main difference between the two *fins de siècle* lies mainly in the fact that the end of the twentieth century is a repetition; a kind of belated belatedness.

Of course, Pittock is right to insist that many of the recent theoretical developments in literary studies are (as one of his chapter titles puts it) 'The legacy of the Nineties'. However, it is a legacy which speaks a different language from that of the 1890s, and one which enables the modern critic to articulate the writers of the 1890s differently. Likewise, Showalter is right to insist on the similarities between the last *fin de siècle* and our own. However, it is important to remember that the late nineteenth-century preoccupation with 'borderlines', with sexual anarchy, and with gender, class, and race difference were not *the same as* our own, and that a properly historical understanding of the nineteenth-century *fin de siècle* will need to understand the difference of its preoccupation with difference.

Notes

1. CHRISTOPHE CAMPOS, Introduction to HOLBROOK JACKSON, *The Eighteen Nineties* Brighton: Harvester, 1976, p. 10).
2. The most obvious examples of this work include: BRAM DJIKSTRA, *Idols of Perversity: Fantasies of Feminine Evil in the Fin de Siècle* (New York and London: Oxford University Press, 1986), LINDA DOWLING, *Language and Decadence in the*

Victorian Fin de Siècle (Princeton, New Jersey: Princeton University Press, 1986), JOHN STOKES, *In the Nineties* (Hemel Hempstead: Harvester Wheatsheaf, 1989), MIKULAS TEICH and ROY PORTER, *Fin de Siècle and its Legacy* (Cambridge, Cambridge University Press, 1990), ELAINE SHOWALTER, *Sexual Anarchy: Gender and Culture at the Fin de Siècle* (New York: Viking, 1990 and London: Bloomsbury, 1991), JOHN STOKES *Fin de Siècle, Fin du Globe: Fears and Fantasies of the Late Nineteenth Century* (London: Macmillan, 1992).

3. GEORGE EGERTON, *Keynotes* (London: John Lane, 1893), pp. 88–9.

4. MAX NORDAU, *Degeneration* (New York: D. Appleton, 1895), p. 1.

5. 'The Decadent Movement in Literature', *Harper's New Monthly Magazine* (November, 1893), p. 867.

6. CHRISTOPHE CAMPOS, loc. cit., p. 6.

7. HOLBROOK JACKSON, loc. cit., p. 31.

8. Ibid, p. 12.

9. RAYMOND WILLIAMS, *Culture and Society* [1958] (Harmondsworth: Penguin, 1963), p. 165.

10. ROLAND BARTHES, 'From Work to Text' in *Image, Music, Text*, trans. Stephen Heath (London: Fontana, 1977), p. 157.

11. RAYMOND WILLIAMS, *Marxism and Literature* (Oxford, Oxford University Press, 1977), p. 70.

12. RAYMOND WILLIAMS, *The Long Revolution* [1961] (Harmondsworth: Penguin, 1965), p. 67.

13. MARIO PRAZ, *The Romantic Agony* (Oxford, Oxford University Press, 1933).

14. ELAINE SHOWALTER, *A Literature of Their Own* (London: Virago, 1978), p. 29.

15. ANN ARDIS, *New Women, New Novels: Feminism and Early Modernism* (New Brunswick, New Jersey: Rutgers University Press, 1990), p. 8.

16. GERD BJORHOVDE, *Rebellious Structures: Women Writers and the Crisis of the Novel, 1880–1900* (Oxford, Oxford University Press, 1987), p. 16.

17. See BARBARA HERRNSTEIN SMITH, 'Contingencies of Value', *Critical Inquiry*, 10 (1983), pp. 1–33, p. 7.

18. GAYATRY SPIVAK, 'Explanation and Cultural Marginalia' quoted in ARDIS, loc. cit. p. 2.

19. See also LYN PYKETT, *Engendering Fictions: The English Novel in the Early Twentieth Century* (London: Edward Arnold, 1995).

20. JEFFREY WEEKS, 'The Late-Victorian Stew of Sexualities', *Victorian Studies* 35 (1992), pp. 409–15, 410–11.

21. Ibid., p. 412.

22. EVE KOSOFSKY Sedgwick, *Between Men: English Literature and Male Homosocial Desire* (New York: Columbia University Press, 1985), p. 137.

23. Ibid., p. 86.

24. REGENIA GAGNIER, *Idylls of the Marketplace: Oscar Wilde and the Victorian Public* (Stanford: Stanford University Press, 1986).

25. GUY DEBORD, *Society of the Spectacle* (Detroit: Black and Red, 1977).

26. EDWIN LANKESTER, *Degeneration: A Chapter in Darwinism* (London: Macmillan, 1880).

27. SANDRA SIEGEL, 'Literature and Degeneration: the Representations of "Decadence" ' in J.E. Chamberlin and Sander Gilman (eds) *Degeneration: the Dark Side of Progress* (New York: Columbia University Press, 1985), p. 205. The interpolated quotation is from G.S. Fraser's *The Golden Bough*.

28. DANIEL BIVONA, *Desire and Contradiction: Imperial Visions and Domestic Debates in Victorian Literature* (Manchester: Manchester University Press, 1990), p. xi and viii.
29. PATRICK BRANTLINGER, *Rule of Darkness: British Literature and Imperialism, 1830–1914* (Ithaca, New York: Cornell University Press, 1988), p. 10. Brantlinger is quoting from FREDERIC JAMESON, *The Political Unconscious* (see below).
30. BRANTLINGER, op. cit., p. x.
31. EDWARD SAID, *Orientalism* (London: Routledge and Kegan Paul, 1978), quoted in PATRICK BRANTLINGER, op. cit., p. 10.
32. FREDERIC JAMESON, *The Political Unconscious: Narrative as a Socially Symbolic Act* (London: Cornell University Press, 1981), p. 141.
33. PETER WIDDOWSON (ed.) *D.H.Lawrence* (London: Longman, 1992), p. 11.
34. MURRAY PITTOCK, *The Spectrum of Decadence* (Routledge, 1993) pp. 2 and 181–2.
35. ELAINE SHOWALTER, *Sexual Anarchy: Gender and Culture at the Fin de Siècle* (London: Bloomsbury, 1991), p. 3 and p. 1.

2 Magi and Maidens: The Romance of the Victorian Freud*

NINA AUERBACH

Nina Auerback is a Professor of English at the University of Pennsylvania. She has written widely on the cultural situation of women in the nineteenth century. The present essay can also be found in her book *Women and the Demon: The Life of a Victorian Myth* (Cambridge, Mass: Harvard University Press, 1992). In this essay she analyses the late nineteenth-century construction of myths of womanhood in two 'middlebrow' fictional texts (Du Maurier's *Trilby* and Bram Stoker's *Dracula*), and in one of the founding texts of psychoanalysis, Freud's *Studies on Hysteria*. She also seeks to appropriate certain *fin de siècle* representations of femininity for feminism (see Introduction, pp. 5–6).

It is commonly assumed that Victorian patriarchs disposed of their women by making myths of them; but then as now social mythology had an unpredictable life of its own, slyly empowering the subjects it seemed to reduce. It also penetrated unexpected sanctuaries. If we examine the unsettling impact upon Sigmund Freud of a popular mythic configuration of the 1890s, we witness a rich, covert collaboration between documents of romance and the romance of science. Fueling this entanglement between the clinician's proud objectivity and the compelling images of popular belief is the imaginative power of that much-loved, much-feared, and much-lied-about creature, the Victorian woman.

Until recently, feminist criticism has depreciated this interaction between myths of womanhood, science, and history, seeing in social mythology only a male mystification which dehumanizes women: the myth of womanhood was thought to be no more than manufactured fantasies about woman's nature (inferior brain weight, educated women's

*Reprinted from *Critical Inquiry*, 8 (1981), pp. 281–99.

tendency to brain fever, a ubiquitous maternal instinct, raging hormonal imbalance) meant to shackle female experience to male convenience.[1] As feminist criticism gains authority, however, its new sense of power has resulted in an impulse toward rather than a denial of mythology.[2]

As we fabricate new mythologies commensurate with a growing belief in our strength, the time seems right to explore the mythologies of the past as well: they can tell us much about the blend of anger and awe men feel in our culture and much too about the secret victories of apparent female victims. When properly understood, the angel in the house, along with her still more passive and supine Victorian sisters, is too strong and interesting a creature for us to kill.

The myth I will look at here flourishes most obviously in popular literature of the 1890s, though its roots extend before and beyond that eccentric decade: the deliberate freakishness of nineties imagery illuminates both earlier ideals of respectability and later conventions of advanced thought.[3] A rich instance is the alluring conjunction of women and corpses, which has a resonance beyond both the titillating sadomasochistic vogue Mario Praz perceives and Frank Kermode's Romantic metaphor of art's self-contained detachment.[4] The female life-in-death figure may indeed be a metaphor for higher, or at least other, concerns, but if we look at her simply as a literal woman, her recurrent fits of vampirism, somnambulism, mesmerism, or hysterical paralysis illuminate powers that were somewhat fancifully, somewhat wistfully, and somewhat fearfully imagined in women throughout the century. The passage of our own century has not entirely dispelled the vision of these powers. Let us look at three of woman's best-known incarnations, both for the shapes they take on in the nineties and for their revelations about imagined womanhood in general.

In a key tableau of the nineties, we see first, as we often do, not women but men: three men lean hungrily over three mesmerized and apparently characterless women, whose wills are suspended by those of the magus/masters. The looming men are Svengali, Dracula, and Freud; the lushly helpless women are Trilby O'Ferrall, Lucy Westenra, and (as Freud calls her) 'Frau Emmy von N., age 40, from Livonia.' It seems as if no men could be more culturally and inherently potent than these, no women more powerless to resist. Svengali is not only a master mesmerist and musician – the vocal genius with which he endows Trilby is his alone, her mouth its mere monumental repository – but he brings with him incalculable inherited lore from his birthplace in 'the mysterious East! The poisonous East – birthplace and home of an ill wind that blows nobody good.'[5]

The master-mesmerist Dracula seems derived from Svengali, with his powers still further extended over time and space. The spell he casts on women – we never see him mesmerizing a man, though he captures several – includes the animal kingdom, whose power he draws to himself at will, and at times the elements as well. As he tells his relentlessly up-to-date antagonists, who destroy him with the modern weapons of committee meetings and shorthand minutes, his monstrous immortality aligns his power with time's: his memory encompasses not merely the primeval lore of the vampire but the military and political strategies of Hungarian nationalism through the centuries. Svengali and Dracula, then, are endowed with a magic beyond their own: they possess the secret traditions of their culture, while the women they captivate seem not merely enfeebled but culturally naked.

As a mere mortal and historical figure, Freud might seem out of place in this preternatural company, but in his case history of Frau Emmy von N., his first contribution to *Studies on Hysteria* (1893–95), written with Josef Breuer, there is delicious magic in his use of hypnosis, which he had not yet abandoned. After boasting that with hypnosis he can regulate Frau Emmy's menstrual periods, he revels in a psychic appropriation that is quite Svengali-like:

> I made it impossible for her to see any of those melancholy things again, not only by wiping out her memories of them in their *plastic* form but by removing her whole recollection of them, as though they had never been present in her mind. I promised her that this would lead to her being freed from the expectation of misfortune which perpetually tormented her and from the pains all over the body, of which she had been complaining precisely during her narrative, after we had heard nothing of them for several days.[6]

In fact Freud's promise was too sanguine, but the virtually limitless powers he arrogates to himself in this initial amalgam of science, myth, and magic give him access to our mythic pantheon in a manner A. C. Bradley had already foreseen in a prescient essay on the rise of social mythologies: 'Is not the popularisation of that science which is the most active dissolvent of old mythology, itself thoroughly mythological?'[7]

In these two popular romances and in the romantic beginnings of modern science, we seem to see the image of prone womanhood at its most dispiriting. Personal and cultural disinheritance, we feel, could go no further than these *tabulae rasae*, all selfhood suspended as these women are invaded by the hyperconscious and culturally fraught male/master/monster. But when we actually read *Trilby, Dracula*, or *Studies on Hysteria*, what strikes us is the kinds of powers that are granted to the women: the victim of paralysis possesses seemingly infinite capacities of regenerative being that turn on her triumphant mesmerizer and paralyze him in turn. Dispossessed and seemingly empty, the women reveal a sort of infinitely unfolding magic that is quite different from the formulaic spells of the men.

The put-upon heroine of George du Maurier's *Trilby* is not fragile, as her role in the plot would lead one to assume, but a virtual giantess. Her size is so great, in fact, that she can be parcelled into fragments with a self-contained and totemistic value of their own, such as her majestic (but not Cinderella-like) foot or the awesomely cavernous roof of her mouth. Like George Eliot's noble, outsize heroines, Trilby seems crammed by the very setting and action of her story; underlying her sacrificial destiny (like Camille, Trilby repudiates her true love at the instigation of his snobbish parent, and thus she falls under Svengali's fatal power) is the hint that the novel's world is simply too small for her to live in. Du Maurier's illustrations reinforce our sense of her stature: in all, Trilby towers helplessly over her interlocutors, like Lewis Carroll's Alice. None of the illustrations reflects the paradigm of prone victim and omnipotent devourer, though this tableau does appear in the text. When under Svengali's spell, the Trilby of the illustrations looms so monumentally over him that she seems about to swoop down and crush him.

Reinforcing Trilby's size is her seemingly boundless capacity for mutability. The great singer she becomes when mesmerized is only an index of her endlessly changing nature. From the beginning, her three adorers, Taffy, the laird, and Little Billee, see that she is a different woman in English and in French – as she will later have a tone-deaf and a singing self – and they await with awe each 'new incarnation of Trilbyness.' Falling in love is yet another metamorphosis, leading her to renounce all three men with the odd declaration: 'You have changed me into another person – you [Taffy] and Sandy and Little Billee' (p. 156). She does not need Svengali to incite her to new incarnations; her power of metamorphosis defines her character.

When she becomes a great singer under Svengali's spell, Trilby's metamorphic power enervates her master (he dies of a heart attack while trying to mesmerize her to new heights of genius) but takes possession of the novel. The essence of her singing lies in its seemingly endless variations. What dazzles is her 'slight, subtle changes in the quality of the sound – too quick and elusive to be taken count of, but to be felt with, oh what poignant sympathy!' (p. 250). These perpetual changes are not Svengali's endowment but Trilby's maddening essence. As simultaneous siren and angel, she haunts Little Billee as an image of infinite change: 'And little innocent, pathetic, ineffable, well-remembered sweetness of her changing face kept painting themselves on his retina; and incomparable tones of this new thing, her voice, her infinite voice, went ringing in his head, till he all but shrieked aloud in his agony' (p. 264). even before this most dramatic of metamorphoses, however, Trilby's love for Little Billee was only one component of a comradely *mariage à quatre* that included Taffy and the laird. Her endowed voice is an accidental index of the multiplicity which allows her always to be a new incarnation of herself.

Finally, the role of magus and mythmaker passes to her. Her ability under hypnosis to ring endless variations upon familiar tunes is the power of her character to transform itself endlessly and, in so doing, to renew endlessly the world around her. Her exquisitely lingering death licenses her to marry all three of the artists who love her: she bequeaths to each a wedding ring for his future wife. The myth at the heart of the novel comes not from Svengali's lore but from the capacious, regenerating mystery of its heroine, which awes and destroys both hero and villain: though Little Billee is supposed to be a great artist and Svengali a great musician, their artistry loses all meaning before the transforming bounty of Trilby's familiar presence. In drawing on ideals of the alluring vacuum of the uncultured woman waiting for the artist-male to fill her, du Maurier imagines powers that dwarf male gestures toward redemption and damnation.

The potent essence of each 'incarnation of Trilbyness,' counter-pointing her passive and stupefied role in the plot, is repeated in the characteristic patterns of du Maurier's drawings. In an illustration of one of the few episodes in which Trilby does not figure, captioned 'Darlings, Old or Young', the composition is such that she might as well be present: two giant, bedecked women tower over a huddled-up Little Billee, suggesting that the overpowering Trilby is not an anomaly but the quintessence of womanhood. The same pattern governs du Maurier's society cartoons in *Punch*. Typically, a bevy of large-bustled society women sweeps up and down the picture plane, taking to itself all available motion, while a few rigid young men stand immobilized and isolated. Du Maurier's women observe the proprieties with more demure compliance, less swelling fierceness, than those of his contemporary, Aubrey Beardsley, but like Beardsley's women, du Maurier's appropriate all available vitality, whatever the demands of the ostensible context.

Moreover, du Maurier uses the contemporary fashion of tight lacing and bustle for a significant reversal of physical fact. Though in actuality corsets and bustles transformed a woman's body to a construction of rigid, almost Japanese, angularity, as any fashion plate from the 1880s illustrates, du Maurier's women are creatures of active, curving lines. Their characteristic motion is a ceaseless, elegant swoop, while the men in their freer attire seem mysteriously hampered and inhibited. Du Maurier reverses the actualities of a Victorian ballroom to accord with the sexual dynamics we have seen in his novel: in both, despite the demands of probability and the plot, the women are free, mobile, and flexible, while the men appear by nature corseted and strangulated.

Despite the dominance of the wicked old count in the popular folklore Bram Stoker's novel inspired, in *Dracula*, too, women secretively take the novel away from the villain.[8] Early on in his traumatic visit to Dracula's castle, Jonathan Harker realizes that the sinister count is less terrifying than his three hungry brides – 'If I be sane, then surely it is maddening to think that of all the foul things that lurk in this hateful place, the Count is the least dreadful to me'[9] – and once the novel reaches England, it focuses on the vampiristic mutations Mina and Lucy undergo, of which the count is reduced to an increasingly immobilized catalyst.

Like Trilby, Lucy Westenra has two selves. She is all silly sweetness in the daylight, but as Dracula's powers invade her, she becomes a florid predator at night. Like Trilby, too, she longs to marry three men but can accept only one of them until death grants her wish: as Trilby bequeathed a wedding ring to each suitor, so the blood transfusions in which each suitor in turn pours himself into the dying Lucy provide the most convincing epithalamia in the novel (p. 158). Though Lucy does not meet the usual fate of English belles, she is not an aberration in nineties visions of femininity. Her fluctuations between virginal purity and bloody attacks link her to Thomas Hardy's dual-natured Tess Durbeyfield as well as to Trilby, and her penchant for somnambulism, trance, and strange physical and mental alterations, even before Dracula's arrival, would find her a place in either a romantic sonnet by Wilde or in Breuer and Freud's garland of female hysterics.

Stoker might conceivably have known of Freud's work. In 1893, F. W. H. Meyers reported enthusiastically on Breuer and Freud's 'Preliminary Communication' to *Studies on Hysteria* at a general meeting of the Society for Psychical Research in London. Stoker's alienist Dr Seward, indefatigably recording bizarre manifestations of vampirism, mentions the mesmerist Charcot, Freud's early teacher; Dr Seward's relentless attempt to make sense of his patient Renfield's 'zoophagy' is a weird forecast of the later Freud rationalizing the obsessions of his Wolf Man and Rat Man. Dr Seward's meticulous case histories of Renfield, Lucy, and Dracula's other victims introduce into the Gothic genre a form that Freud would raise to a novelistic art; his anguished clinician's record makes of Lucy both the early heroine of a case history and an ineffable romantic image of *fin de siècle* womanhood.

The word 'change,' sometimes modified by 'strange' and 'terrible,' almost always accompanies Lucy in the text; along with 'beloved,' it is her epithet. After her first transfusion, 'she looked a different being from what she had been before the operation' (p. 119), and in her fluctuations between passivity and prowling, consciousness and dreaming, innocence and experience, pallor and ruddiness, she can be said to be 'a different being' every time she appears. Though Dracula supposedly instigates her capacity for perpetual self-incarnation, he appears only in shadowy glimpses as Lucy passes into life-in-death. In fact, as women gain primacy, he withdraws increasingly except for intermittent stagy boasts; though he is the object of pursuit, Lucy, and then the vampirized Mina, are the objects of attention. His threat to turn London into a city of vampires is never as real as Van Helsing's ominous confidence to Dr Seward: 'Madam Mina, our poor, dear, Madam Mina, is changing' (p. 285).

By this time, we have learned that, unlike Lucy's and Mina's unpredictable changes, Dracula's powers of change are limited to noon, sunrise, and sunset. Moreover, as Mina's mind expands under hypnosis to meet Dracula's, his world contracts into the box of earth within which he is paralyzed. As the novel draws to a close, its 'good brave men' become more aimless and confused than ever. Heroes and villains recede as the metamorphosed Mina appropriates the qualities of all groups. As Van Helsing says of her: '. . . we want all her great brain which is trained like man's brain, but is of sweet woman and have a special power which the Count give her, and which he may not take away altogether' (p. 298). In Stoker's influential literary myth, the apparently helpless woman assumes male, female, and preternatural powers, taking away from the now paralyzed Dracula the magus' potency.

It is fashionable to perceive Dracula as an emanation of Victorian sexual repression. Despite Mina's pious disclaimer that she has anything in common with the New Woman, it seems more plausible to read the novel as a nineties myth of newly empowered womanhood, whose two heroines are violently transformed from victims to instigators of their story. Aggrandized by her ambiguous transformations, Mina, and by implication womanhood itself, grows into the incarnation of irresistible Truth: 'And I have read your diary that you have so goodly written for me, and which breathes out truth in every line. . . . Oh, Madam Mina, good women tell all their lives, and by day and by hour and by minute, such things that angels can read' (p. 167). In her many incarnations, Trilby also embodied Truth to her audience of reverent men: 'Truth looked out of her eyes, as it had always done – truth was in every line of her face' (p. 309).[10] By the end, these seemingly supine women assume the authority of personifications, the guiding spirits of their novels' action. The power of Dracula himself narrows to the dimensions of his vulnerable coffin, for, despite his ambitious designs on the human race, he seems to be the world's last surviving male vampire. Neither Renfield nor the Russian sailors Dracula attacked at sea are transformed after death; only his three thirsty brides, Lucy, and Mina rise into the Undead. Had Dracula survived the end of the novel, this army of women might indeed have devoured the human race under his generalship, for as far as we see, his greatest power lies in his ability to catalyze the awesome changes potential in womanhood, in those modest personifications of divine and human truth.

The implicit primacy of women in *Dracula* becomes explicit in Stoker's later romances, *The Lady of the Shroud* (1909), *The Lair of the White Worm*

(1911), and *The Jewel of Seven Stars* (1912). These novels contain sketchy
and desultory recapitulations of the myth that in *Dracula* is painstakingly
and elaborately documented, but in all of them, the Dracula figure
himself is missing: like a vestigial organ of waning patriarchal divinity,
he is displaced by a larger-than-life woman of a 'strange dual nature.' In
The Lady of the Shroud, Stoker's one Radcliffian denial of the supernatural,
the brave daughter of a Voivode nationalist disguises herself as an
Undead. Before she reveals her mortal nature, the hero, obsessed with
her as a lamialike vision, marries her in a secret ceremony. In this slight
story, a woman takes over Dracula's role as Voivode nationalist with the
powers of the Undead to transform and possess, but the rationalistic
political context alchemizes male demonism into female heroism.

In contrast, *The Lair of the White Worm* is Stoker's darkest myth of
womanhood. The book's Dracula figure, Lady Arabella March of Diana's
Grove, is in her true self a giant white worm older than mankind, living
at the bottom of a deep and fetid well that crawls with the repulsive
vitality of vermin, insects, and worms. From the mythic associations of
her estate to the vaginal potency of her true lair, Lady Arabella's
metamorphic power seems darkly intrinsic to womanhood itself. Lilla,
the pure heroine, is so passive and susceptible as to be virtually
nonexistent. Though she is recurrently mesmerized, she has no capacity
for transformation, suggesting that Lucy's and Mina's powers are
becoming divided: here the acceptable, womanly woman has renounced
access to the powers of womanhood. *Dracula's* women were poised
between angelic service and vampiristic mutation; here the lovable
domestic woman loses her strength, while the dark outcast woman alone
is equated with primal, self-transforming truth.

The Jewel of Seven Stars is a still more blatantly unresolved allegory of
female power. Its Dracula figure is the ancient-Egyptian queen Tera,
passionate and intellectual as Rider Haggard's mighty She-Who-Must--
Be-Obeyed. We see Queen Tera only through mysterious signs indicating
that she is about to be reincarnated in our strapping heroine, Margaret
Trelawny. The story builds ominously toward Margaret's amalgamation
with her potent and ancient double, but at the designated moment the
queen fails to appear: Stoker can no longer accommodate his noble
Victorian wives-to-be with his vision of primordial, transfigured
womanhood. Reigning without need of Dracula's catalyzing powers,
Stoker's later magus-women hover outside the gates, but they are
blocked from invading modern London. Efficient contemporaneity may
defeat an immortal foreign count, but it could not withstand the assault
of these dark and brilliant women.

The maimed females of Breuer and Freud's *Studies on Hysteria* seem
incapable of asserting power over their age. Like Dr Seward's possessed
inamorata, though, they are presented to us through that new medium of

portraiture, the case history; like that of Dr Seward himself, the
documentary rationalism of Freud's new science will be insufficient to
conquer Dracula, a Dracula sleeping in himself as well as in his patients.

Freud knew himself to be a believer in the myth of womanhood;
Haggard's She haunted his dreams as 'the eternal feminine, the
immortality of our emotions.' For Freud, however, myths bestow timeless
order on the confusions of the present; as Philip Rieff perceives, '[h]is
notion of myth is . . . basically anti-historical,' giving glimpses of a
deeper truth than history's.[11] Unlike Stoker's, then, Freud's female
hysterics are not directly associated with the assaults on family life that
were current in the nineties; he seems to have insulated his turbulent
consulting room from its adjacent, ordered, domestic kingdom. But
though Freud allows no topical validity to his female hysterics, he
accepts as wholeheartedly as du Maurier did the absolute authority of
performing womanhood. He wrote of Sarah Bernhardt in the 1880s: 'But
how that Sarah plays! After the first words of her vibrant lovely voice I
felt I had known her for years. Nothing she said could have surprised
me; I believed at once everything she said.'[12] This faith in 'Sarah' is a
surprising reversal of Freud's skepticism toward virtually all the
assertions of his female patients; his characteristic professional stance is
to translate their helpless deceit into his own impregnable truth. It seems
that only the controlled self-transformation of performance, rather than
the involuntary mutations of illness, could move Freud to believe, as
novelists did, that women and truth were one.

Though Freud's patients lack the immediate authority of du Maurier's
and Stoker's creations, they too are vehicles of incessant metamorphosis.
Their symptoms twist them into bizarre shapes: like Mina and Lucy, they
are prone to somnambulism, inability to eat or to stay awake through the
day; like Trilby, they divide into magnified totemistic parts of themselves,
as with 'Miss Lucy R., age 30,' who is troubled by a smell of burnt
pudding so overwhelming that she begins to disappear into her own
nasal cavity, or 'Katharina,' whose anxiety attacks throw each part of her
body into vivid relief:

> 'It comes over me all at once. First of all it's like something pressing
> on my eyes. My head gets so heavy, there's a dreadful buzzing, and I
> feel so giddy that I almost fall over. Then there's something crushing
> my chest so that I can't get my breath.'
> 'And you don't notice anything in your throat?'
> 'My throat's squeezed together as though I were going to choke.'
> 'Does anything else happen in your head?'
> 'Yes, there's a hammering, enough to burst it.' [*Hysteria*, p. 126]

Freud's prompting forces our awareness of the hallucinatory
consciousness that invades parts of her body in turn. He shows the same

anatomical fascination with the hysterical pains of 'Fraulein Elisabeth Von R.,' which he locates precisely in a 'fairly large, ill-defined area of the anterior surface of the right thigh' (*Hysteria*, p. 135). Like the discovery of Lucy's newly prominent teeth, these revelations that parts of a woman's body can become thus preternaturally animated make the reader uneasily aware of undiscovered powers.

Though Freud presents himself as a stabilizing presence, his actual task resembles that of Svengali, Dracula, and Van Helsing in that he strives to effect a further metamorphosis in his mobile victim. Katharina's cure is apparent in her speaking transformation, of which his interpretation is only a shadow: 'At the end of these two sets of memories she came to a stop. She was like someone transformed. The sulky, unhappy face had grown lively, her eyes were bright, she was lightened and exalted. Meanwhile, the understanding of her case had become clear to me' (*Hysteria*, p. 131). Changing womanhood is the vessel of scientific, as it was of supernatural, power.

Freud reminds us with some pride of the likeness of his case histories to short stories, and, as with so much contemporary fiction, the true theme of *Studies on Hysteria* is woman's capacity for amazing and empowering transformations. Here, though, Freud as narrator/healer/magus/master is always in control, as if to galvanize in anticipation the feeble magic of Svengali and Little Billee, Dracula and Van Helsing. Freud's own amalgam of mythic art and science, religion and iconoclasm, austerity and eroticism, combines the tools of all the men in romances who want to save and subdue mutable womanhood. The popularity of *The Seven Per Cent Solution* has allowed us to pair Freud and Sherlock Holmes instinctively in our imagination of the nineties. It may be more difficult for some to associate him with these darker, more complex literary figures, though Freud himself might not have repudiated the role of hero/villain in a quintessentially British romance. Like Svengali, Dracula, and Van Helsing, he was deeply drawn to the apparent rationalism of Victorian British civilization: in the last months of his life, he played out their role of exiled foreign wizard in his imaginative homeland. British romantic mythology was one of the staunchest loves in his life, but in his role as dark magician, evoking and controlling the secrets of womanhood, creation was sometimes at war with human reality. When a patient, now famous as 'Dora', wanted to take her life from the master's possession, the result was Freud's anguished account of a failed myth that also became a failed case history.

Unfortunately, the woman Dora cannot be separated in our imagination from the resonant name Freud gave her, her ever changing repertoire of hysterical illnesses, the verdict of one anonymous doctor that she was 'one of the most repulsive hysterics' he had ever met, and her stiff-necked persistence in saying 'no' to Freud. Despite his attempt to orchestrate her unconscious into agreement with his consciousness – at one difficult point, he invents a consoling aphorism of her infinite, if inaudible acquiescence: 'there is no such thing at all as an unconscious "No" '[13] – Dora met Freud's interpretations with a perfect symphony of nos until, on the last day of the year, she abruptly terminated treatment altogether. For me, at least, the facts of Dora's life and Freud's constructions explain her resistance perfectly: hedged by the pressure of authoritative men, she seems to have been fighting for her life.

Dora's parents were unhappily married. In writing of the family, Freud lays much weight on the mother's 'housewife's psychosis,' or compulsive domesticity, a disease he diagnoses more portentously than he does the syphilis Dora's father brought with him to the marriage. The father soon began a long-standing affair with one 'Frau K.,' who had befriended Dora as well; when Dora was fourteen, 'Herr K.' began to make violently sexual lunges at her. When she accused him, her father insisted that she had imagined these attacks, but her protests continued: as Dora saw the situation, her acceptance of Herr K. was meant to sanction her father's liaison with Frau K. It was then that her self-mortifying series of symptoms and depressions began and her father 'handed her over' to Freud.

Freud overrode Dora's father by accepting the truth of his patient's story. Incredibly, though, he insisted that any healthy young woman would become the sexual pawn her elders were trying to make of her. For Freud, her illness and her resistance were one: by his definition, her unconscious could not but respond to Herr K. Though Dora's resistance to a coercive father and a loathsome suitor was of the pattern of a British heroine Freud might have admired – her model could have been Richardson's Clarissa – he insisted that Herr K. was 'prepossessing' and her feelings aberrant: 'This was surely just the situation to call up a distinct feeling of sexual excitement in a girl of fourteen who had never before been approached. But Dora had at that moment [of Herr K.'s sudden embrace] a violent feeling of disgust, tore herself free from the man, and hurried past him to the staircase and from there to the street door' (*Dora*, p. 43). Surely, not only Victorian morality but the psychology and physiology of fourteen-year-old girls everywhere explain Dora's revulsion and fear. Yet Freud was so relentless in hammering at her repressed desire for Herr K. that even his most sympathetic commentators grow uneasy.[14]

As Freud writes about it, the case is reduced to a series of skirmishes in which Dora, refusing to transform herself under his touch as had Frau Emmy, Katharina, and the rest, meets his interpretative assaults as she did Herr K.'s: with a recurrent 'no.' The integrity of Freud's account lies not in his interpretations but in his fidelity to the intransigence of his experience with Dora and the Bartleby-like drama of her recurrent refusals. Freud's pained definition of the case as 'a fragment of an analysis' makes it for Steven Marcus a quintessentially modern document, great in its dogged truth to the impossibility of solution. For Marcus, Dora's desertion of the great man is sufficiently punished by the fact that all her psychiatrists found her 'an unlikable person,' though he does implicate Freud in telling, if unexplored, insight: 'Above all, he doesn't like her inability to surrender herself to him.'[15] For Freud, though, the loss of Dora seems to have inflicted a pain beyond modern malaise and personal dislike. What is lost, one feels, is the female capacity for metamorphosis without which male magic has no meaning.

The interpretations Freud thrusts at Dora are a pageant of symbolic transformations she will not enact. Not only are the objects and events in her dreams amenable to a boundless process of becoming something else but in Freud's vision her emotions are constantly mutating. He begins with her suppressed love for Herr K., then goes on to insist that she is in love with (of course) her father, with Freud himself, with the suitor disguised in her second dream, and finally and fundamentally, with Frau K. — in short, it seems, with everybody but her mother. Not only is Dora's inner life capable of seemingly limitless expansion but her very costume is alive with significant transformations. Her commonplace reticule becomes a speaking symbolic narrative: 'The reproaches against her father for having made her ill, together with the self-reproach underlying them, the leucorrhoea, the playing with the reticule, the bedwetting after her sixth year, the secret which she would not allow the physicians to tear from her – the circumstantial evidence of her having masturbated in childhood seems to me complete and without a flaw' (*Dora*, p. 97). Freud's gratingly censorious tone here is typical, but, as with Svengali and Dracula, his disdain for the woman he has captured is at war with his need for the gifts she brings.

Of all the predatory men in this story, it is Freud whose lust for Dora is fiercest, but despite the pyrotechnical transformation of her reticule into a vagina, her sexuality is incidental to him. The sexual connotations of a woman's reticule, which Freud was not needed to translate, were familiar comic staples of Victorian art and pornography;[16] the metamorphoses of the reticule is as commonplace as the linguistic metamorphoses scattered throughout the German text, in which such household objects as 'mother's jewel-case' or a 'box for keeping pictures in' translate themselves into crude symbols of female genitalia. A more valuable attribute than Dora's reticule or her 'jewel-case' is her capacity for boundlessly suggestive dreams, the essence of her transforming power which she withholds from Freud by leaving. Dora's case history, which was originally to be called *Dreams and Hysteria* and to be published as an outgrowth of Freud's *Interpretation of Dreams* (1900), is organized around two central visitations: 'The First Dream' and 'The

Second Dream.' Like Trilby's voice, like Lucy's and Mina's telepathic perceptions, Dora's dreams function in this case history as a token of a transforming power that enervates her increasingly paralyzed master. The note of frustration, of radical incompletion, pervading Freud's story seems less to signal Marcus' ache of modernism than the ache caused by loss of Dora and the powers she inadvertently brings. The central emotion of the case history is not Dora's 'penis envy,' as a vulgarizer of Freud might have it, nor, in Karen Horney's feminist inversion, Freud's 'womb envy,' but the teller's affliction, like that of an emotionally eroded Jamesian narrator, with what might be called 'dream envy.'[17]

Since in this case an imaginative myth played itself out in a real consulting room, Dora's story could not end satisfactorily. Freud makes several tentative and contradictory suggestions that she married, but these do not provide closure so much as further stabs in the dark. Later Freudians assert that she lived an appropriately miserable life,[18] but in fact Dora seems to have died querulously at a ripe age without any violent emotional or psychic upheavals. Life does not usually round things out: there was no last cry of '*Svengali* . . . *Svengali* . . . *Svengali*,' nor did anybody need to drive a stake through her heart. But in reading the transcript of her case history, where Freud obsessively explains her but where she is never allowed to explain herself, she seems as much a product of the mythmaking mind as were the popular romance heroines I have discussed, though as a real woman she was reluctant to the end. Insofar as Dora 'refused to be a character in the story that Freud was composing for her, and wanted to finish it herself' she both repudiated his projection and attempted to exercise the powers it allowed her.[19] Though she escaped Freud as she had her father and Herr K., she never wrested the role of magus from her possessive master. For us, at least, she is inextricably entangled in the myth Freud wanted to make of her; his mythmaking imagination took its final revenge when he imposed upon his recreant patient the name of Dickens' most fatally pliable and infantilized heroine. As with a character in a novel whose fate is muddied, we wonder how Dora would have named herself.

Freud's mythic and literary affinities are usually applauded, but their complex impact on his treatment of actual women has not yet been analyzed. From the beginning of his life to the end, though, his clinical work with women was intensely affected by an essentially literary mythology. As a young man studying with Charcot, he was so profoundly moved by a lithograph of Charcot in his clinic that he kept a copy all his life. The lithograph depicts a rigidly upright Charcot supporting a seductively supine patient, a tableau closer to the popular image of Svengali and Trilby than du Maurier's illustrations are. One suspects that the constant presence of this picture told more to and about Freud than he knew.

Freud's powerful mythic urge proved a professional triumph, however, in his treatment of a woman who shared his dream. Late in life, Freud analyzed the American poet Hilda Doolittle ('H. D.'). The analysis must have been successful, for H. D. wrote a rhapsodically affectionate tribute to her master (though his art collection seems to have impressed her more vividly than his interpretations). Since H. D. was not a desperate young girl but a successful poet in lifelong pursuit of her transfigured self, she approached Freud in the right occult spirit;

> 'By chance or intention,' I started these notes on September 19th. Consulting my 'Mysteries of the Ancients' calendar, I find Dr W. B. Crow has assigned this date to Thoth, Egyptian form of Mercury. Bearer of the Scales of Justice. *St. Januarius*. And we know of *Janus* the old Roman guardian of gates and doors, patron of the month of January which was sacred to him, with all 'beginnings.'[20]

Most Freudian analysts today would gleefully untangle these exuberant oracular connections, but Freud apparently let them stand. Whether or not he feared that Jungianism had tainted H. D.'s correspondences, they seem to have been at one in their central aim: to metamorphose the woman's selfhood into an infinitely shifting myth. In his foreword to H. D.'s *Tribute to Freud*, Norman Holmes Pearson quotes H. D.'s mythic creed: ' "For me, it was so important," she wrote, repeating, "it was so important, my own LEGEND. Yes, my own LEGEND. Then, to get well and re-create it." She used "legend" multiply – as a story, a history, an account, a thing for reading, her own myth.'[21] Though by the time of H. D.'s visit Freud was as surrounded by artifacts of old religions as 'a curator in a museum,' living as far as possible in a timeless atmosphere, one suspects that his central if unacknowledged faith belonged to the age that bred him. Long before, he had accepted with resignation that 'one still remains a child of one's own age, even with something one had thought was one's very own.'[22] As a child of his own age, he apparently approached H. D. with the same mixture of awe, horror, and reverence that infused Van Helsing's words: 'Madam Mina, our poor, dear, Madam Mina, is changing.' For in Freud's imagination, as in the fiction written during his life, the power of the magus is less than the self-creations of his prey.[23]

Realizing this dream in our own century, H. D. translated her analysis into an instrument of mythic self-creation. Her long autobiographical parable, *Helen in Egypt*, casts Freud in the ancillary role of the nurturing Theseus who enables the fleeing Helen to embrace her own grandeur. Though at first she shuns her transfigured self, asserting 'I am not nor mean to be / the Daemon they made of me,' Helen is soothed into power by Theseus' 'solution': 'All myth, the one reality dwells here.' H. D.'s narrative gloss makes it plain that the 'postanalytic' Helen is reborn into magic, not mere humanity: 'Was Helen stronger than Achilles even "as the arrows fell"? That could not be, but he recognised in her some power other than her legendary beauty.'[24] Like du Maurier's Trilby and like Stoker's Lucy and Mina, H. D. in her mythic awakening as Helen accepts possession by the magus as the crucible for her mighty self-apotheosis. In Victorian romances, in psychoanalytic documents, and in a modern poet's spiritual autobiography, the myth of the entranced woman is as covertly inspiring as it seems superficially enfeebling. The writers we have looked at and the readers who believe their visions imagine a Sleeping Beauty who only seems asleep, for her powers are secretly superior to those of the wicked witch who subdued her and the handsome prince who aroused her.

Notes

1. Kate Millett (*Sexual Politics* [New York, 1970]) sees myth exclusively as a male assault upon women. Elizabeth Janeway offers more subtle and sophisticated denunciations in *Man's World, Women's Place: A Study in Social Mythology* (New York, 1971) and *Between Myth and Morning: Women Awakening* (New York, 1975), though recently even Janeway has cautiously hoped for a new mythos; see her 'Who Is Sylvia?: On the Loss of Sexual Paradigms,' *Signs* 5 (Summer 1980): 589.

2. Sandra M. Gilbert and Susan Gubar's *The Madwoman in the Attic: The Woman Writer and the Nineteenth-Century Literary Imagination* (new Haven, Conn., 1979), a compendious anatomy of the wounded rage of nineteenth-century women writers, begins by echoing Virginia Woolf's exhortation that we kill the male projections of angel and monster, but it ends half in love with its antagonist's images, weaving them into a rhapsodic and sibylline myth of its own: woman's freedom is no longer simply initiation into historical integrity but the rebirth of mythic potential. Following this new impulse, two recent feminist critics appropriate to their own uses Erich Neumann's celebration of the mythic Psyche, on whom they project their own revisionist images of heroic womanhood; see Rachel Blau DuPlessis, 'Psyche, or Wholeness,' *The Massachusetts Review* 20 (Spring 1979): 77–96, and Lee R. Edwards, 'The Labors of Psyche: Toward a Theory of Female Heroism,' *Critical Inquiry* 6 (Autumn 1979): 33–49. Carolyn G. Heilbrun's *Reinventing Womanhood* (New York, 1979) is a call for an expanded female mythos incorporating characteristics that had been reserved for male heroes alone.

3. For a wonderful anatomy of the complex ethos of the 1890s, see Linda Dowling, 'The Decadent and the New Woman in the 1890s,' *Nineteenth-Century Fiction* 33 (March 1979): 434–53.

4. See Mario Praz, *The Romantic Agony* (Oxford, 1933), and Frank Kermode, *Romantic Image* (New York, 1957), pp. 49–91.

5. George du Maurier, *Trilby* (1894; New York, 1977), p. 337; all further references to this work will be included in the text.

6. Josef Breuer and Sigmund Freud, *Studies on Hysteria*, trans. and ed. James Strachey (1895; New York, 1957), p. 61; all further references to this work will be included in the text.

7. A. C. BRADLEY, 'Old Mythology in Modern Poetry,' *Macmillan's Magazine* 44 (May 1881): 29.

8. Recent vampire films are beginning to incorporate this underlying dynamic in Stoker's novel. In the most recent Hollywood *Dracula* (1979), directed by John Bodham, Frank Langella's count quite pales before the aggressive ardor of Kate Nelligan's Mina. In Werner Herzog's *Nosferatu, the Vampyre* (1979), Isabelle Adjani's Lucy takes the entire story into her hands, overriding the inscrutable passivity of hero and villain alike.

9. BRAM STOKER, *Dracula*, ed. Leonard Wolf (1897; New York, 1975), p. 38; all further references to this work will be included in the text.

10. ALEXANDER WELSH ('The Allegory of Truth in English Fiction,' *Victorian Studies* 9 [September 1965]: 7–28) discusses at length the hallowed iconographical tradition wherein Truth is represented as a woman. My own interest lies in the subversive implications within this conventional emblem.

11. PHILIP RIEFF, *Freud: The Mind of the Moralist* (New York, 1967), p. 181. For a provocative analysis of the congruence between Haggard and Freud, see NORMAN A. ETHERINGTON, 'Rider Haggard, Imperialism, and the Layered Personality,' *Victorian Studies* 22 (Autumn 1978): 71–87.

12. Freud, quoted in ERNEST JONES, *The Life and Work of Sigmund Freud: The Formative Years and the Great Discoveries, 1856–1900*, 3 vols (New York, 1953), 1:177–8.

13. FREUD, *Dora: An Analysis of a Case of Hysteria*, trans. Strachey (1905; New York, 1963), p. 75; all further references to this work will be included in the text.

14. See RIEFF's introduction to *Dora*, ibid., pp. 15–18, as well as his more general remarks on Freud's ideas of womanhood in *The Mind of the Moralist*, pp. 178–81.

15. STEVEN MARCUS, 'Freud and Dora: Story, History, Case History,' *Representations: Essays on Literature and Society* (New York, 1975), p. 309.

16. See ELAINE SHOWALTER, 'Guilt, Authority, and the Shadows of *Little Dorrit*,' *Nineteenth-Century Fiction* 34 (June 1979): 38–9.

17. On the face of it, Freud's actual achievements in these years are our clearest reminder that the myth is not true: his eleven-week analysis of Dora took place in 1900, by which time he had completed his laborious self-analysis and his seminal *Interpretation of Dreams*, using his own dreams as the primary source of both. But if we consider his ensuing drained depression, not to mention (dare one say it?) his essentially masturbatory role as both dreamer and interpreter, the anguished undercurrent of his failure with Dora, as well as his gleeful harping on her childhood masturbation, gain emotional if not objective coherence.

18. See, for instance, MARCUS, 'Freud and Dora,' p. 306, and FELIX DEUTSCH, 'A Footnote to Freud's Fragment of an Analysis of a Case of Hysteria,' *Psychoanalytic Quarterly* 26 (1957): 159–67.

19. MARCUS, 'Freud and Dora,' p. 306.

20. H. D., *Tribute to Freud* (with *Writing on the Wall* and *Advent*) (1956; Boston, 1974), p. 100.

21. Ibid., p. vii.

22. FREUD, letter to Wilhelm Fliess, Vienna, 5 November 1897, *The Origins of Psychoanalysis, Letters to Wilhelm Fliess, Drafts and Notes: 1887–1902*, trans. Eric Mosbacher and Strachey (New York, 1954), p. 228.

23. Freud's psychic recasting of ancient mythology lies at the heart of his 'new

science,' but we are just gaining perspective on his responsiveness to the mythologies latent in his own culture. LEE STERRENBURG's 'Psychoanalysis and the Iconography of Revolution' (*Victorian Studies* 19 [December 1975]: 241–64) traces Freud's appropriation of 'a nineteenth-century myth of our cannibalistic and revolutionary origins' which now 'lives on in the guise of psychoanalytic discourse' (p. 264). More recently, FRANK J. SULLOWAY's *Freud: Biologist of the Mind* (New York, 1979) analyzes the degree to which Freud's interest in magic and mythmaking has affected our understanding of his role in the history of science. Like Sterrenburg's intellectual tapestry of science, myth, and magic, Sulloway's conclusion that 'myth rules history with an iron grip' (p. 503) recovers A. C. Bradley's apprehension in 1881 that mythmaking lies at the heart of scientific modernism.

24. H. D., *Helen in Egypt* (New York, 1961), pp. 113, 161, 260.

3 Rider Haggard's Heart of Darkness*

SANDRA M. GILBERT

Sandra Gilbert is Professor of English at the University of California, Davis, and is best known for her collaboration with Susan Gubar on a series of massive books on women's writing and the situation of the woman writer in the nineteenth and twentieth centuries. In the essay reprinted here Gilbert undertakes a reading of Rider Haggard's *She* as a paradigm of a masculinist mythology of the *fin de siècle* which, she argues, was an important element in the formation of literary modernism. In this essay Gilbert begins to think through the argument that she and Susan Gubar develop more fully in the 'Feminism and Fantasy' section of *Sexchanges*, the second volume of their *No Man's Land* trilogy (see Further Reading); namely that modernism was a reaction formation against the power of the female and against a concept of history that was figured as feminine, and that in a number of popular fantasies and romances written by male writers at the *fin de siècle* we can observe the operation of the same sexual imperatives that shaped the writings of Freud, Conrad and the other major male modernists (see Introduction, pp. 5–6). For an alternative view of Haggard's romance see Laura Chrisman, 'The Imperial Unconscious? Representations of Imperial Discourse', *Critical Quarterly* 32 (1990), which reads Ayesha not as a misogynist image of female power, but as an orientalist fantasy which exposes the 'bad faith' or 'negative self-knowledge' of imperialism.

More than fifty years ago, Mario Praz wrote about the nineteenth century that 'In no other literary period . . . has sex been so obviously the mainspring of works of imagination.' In his groundbreaking study of *The Romantic Agony*, however, Praz amassed evidence to demonstrate, almost

*Reprinted from *Partisan Review*, 13 (1983), pp. 444–53.

overwhelmingly, that as the century wore on it was not just 'sex' but specifically the female sex, and even more specifically the power of the female sex that increasingly obsessed male writers in France and England. It should not be surprising, then, that one of the major bestsellers of the period was a novel whose terse title was an unadorned female pronoun, suggesting that the book might be an abstract treatise on the female gender or a fictive exploration of the nature of womanhood. Published in 1887, Rider Haggard's *She* sold a nearly record-breaking thirty thousand copies within a few months, and most of its charisma seems to have come from the regal radiance of its heroine.

The formal title of this woman (whose 'real' name was Ayesha) – She-Who-Must-Be-Obeyed – was hardly less shocking than the title of the novel in which She starred, yet it was as crucial to the book's power as it was in representing Her power. For Haggard's heroine was in many ways a definitive *fin de siècle* embodiment of fantasies that preoccupied countless male writers who had come of age during a literary period in which, to go back to Praz's remark, the (female) sex had been 'obviously the mainspring of works of imagination.' Unlike the women earlier Victorian writers had idealized or excoriated, she was neither an angel nor a monster. Rather, She was an odd but significant blend of the two types – an angelically chaste woman with monstrous powers, a monstrously passionate woman with angelic charms. Just as significantly, however, She was in certain important ways an entirely New Woman: the all-knowing, all-powerful ruler of a matriarchal society.

It is especially because of this last point that Haggard's portrait of Her was so popular (and so popular with male readers in particular). In addition, Her story was both a summary and a paradigm of the story told in a number of similar contemporary tales, all of which were to varying degrees just the kinds of fictive explorations of female power that Haggard's title promised and his novel delivered, and many of which solved what their authors implicitly defined as the *problem* of female power through denouements analogous to – perhaps even drawn from – the one that Haggard devised for *She*. Both the fascination of Haggard's semidivine New Woman and the compulsiveness with which he and his contemporaries made her 'the mainspring of works of imagination' were symptoms of a complex of late Victorian sociocultural and sexual anxieties that have until recently been overlooked or even ignored by critics and historians alike.

At first, of course, as Haggard's hero Leo Vincy, his aggressively misogynistic guardian Horace Holly, and their servant Job begin their journey toward Herland, they may not seem to be adventuring into a realm whose strangeness rests primarily in its femaleness. The African coast on which they are shipwrecked, for instance, seems a standard adventure story setting, complete with wild beasts, fever-inducing mists, and mysterious ruins. As they travel inland, however, through vaporous marshes and stagnant canals, the landscape across which they journey seems increasingly like a Freudianly female *paysage moralise*. When they are finally captured by a band of fierce natives whose leader is a biblical-looking Arab called 'Father,' our suspicions are confirmed. Lifted into litters, the explorers yield to a 'pleasant swaying motion' and, in a symbolic return to the womb, they are carried up ancient swampy birth canals into 'a vast cup of earth' that is ruled by She-Who-Must-Be-Obeyed and inhabited by a people called 'the Amahaggar.' About her people they soon learn that

> in direct opposition to the habits of almost every other savage race in the world, women among the Amahaggar live upon conditions of perfect equality with the men, and are not held to them by any binding ties. Descent is traced only through the line of the mother, and . . . they never pay attention to, or even acknowledge, any man as their father, even when their male parentage is perfectly well known.

Given the brief appearance of Leo's ancestor, Callicrates, in Herodotus's history of the Persian Wars, it is notable that there is an eerie correspondence between the strange land of the Amahaggar and the perverse Egypt Herodotus describes as a country whose people

> in most of their manners and customs, exactly reverse the common practice of mankind. The women attend the markets and trade, while the men sit at home at the loom; . . . women stand up to urinate, men sit down.

In each case the country is described as uniquely alien, and alien in particular because relations between its men and women inhabitants are exactly antithetical to those that prevail in 'normal' civilized societies. Thus both Egypt and Kôr, as Haggard's explorers learn the Amahaggar land is called, are realms where what patriarchal culture defines as misrule has become rule.

She, Herself, however, manifests the severity of Her misrule only after some delay. At first, it is Her subjects who enact and express the murderous female sexuality that She herself tends to deny. Thus we learn before meeting Her what it means for Her to be the queen of a people who, bizarrely, 'place pots upon the heads of strangers,' for shortly after the explorers arrive in Kôr they are invited to a feast at which a group of the Amahaggar try to kill the Englishmen's Arab guide, Mahomed, by putting a red hot earthen pot on his head. This astonishing mode of execution, a cross between cooking and decapitation, which seems to have had no real anthropological precedent, is such a vivid enactment of both castration fears and birth anxieties that it is hardly necessary to rehearse all its psychosymbolic overtones.

She is absolutely identical with the Byronic femme fatale who haunted nineteenth-century writers from Keats and Swinburne to Pater, Wilde, and Macdonald – so much so that Her character in a sense summarizes and intensifies all the key female traits these artists brooded on. Having lived under the hill of ordinary reality since classical antiquity, She chats familiarly about Greek and Arab philosophers with the bemused Holly; clearly, like Pater's Gioconda, She has 'learned the secrets of the grave.' Wherever She studied, moreover, She has strange herbal wisdom, esoteric healing powers, and arcane alchemical knowledge. She condemns men casually to death by torture and is capable of 'blasting' those She dislikes with a Medusan glance.

She is not merely a destroyer; because She is a combination of Persephone and Venus, She is a destroyer *and* a preserver. Perhaps the most peculiar feature of Haggard's discussion of Her kingdom is his ruminative, obsessive, even at times necrophiliac interest in the mummies that surround Her as well as the embalming techniques through which they have been preserved. The Englishmen are shown a 'pit about the size of the space beneath the dome of St Paul's' filled with bones; they regularly dine in a cave decorated by bas-reliefs that show it was used for embalming as well as eating; and they are invited to a ceremonial feast at which the torches are flaming human mummies as well as the severed limbs of those mummies.

The literal as well as metaphorical piling up of all this dead flesh reminds us, of course, that the womb of the Great Mother is also a tomb. But such mysterious preservation of the flesh also implies other and perhaps more uncanny points. In fact, the way in which the very idea of embalming is dramatized throughout *She* suggests that, for its author, this practice paradoxically evokes anxieties about both the ordinary world the Englishmen represent and the extraordinary realm She rules. With their perpetual repetition of the same character and the same message, for instance, the mummies evoke the dullness and dread associated with the imagined persistence of the self through history and thus the patriarchal horror of belatedness. At the same time, however, the practices that have preserved the mummies evoke an alien culture – Herodotus's peculiar Egypt as well as the strange Egypt that was being diligently studied in the nineteenth century. More than two thousand years old, She has not only been embalmed, She has been embalmed alive. Both destroyer and preserver, She has been, if not destroyed, at least spectacularly preserved. Significantly, however, She lacks the crucial third ability of creation, and just as significantly, She lacks the ultimate power of *self*-preservation. Implicit in such deficiencies, moreover, is the spectacular moment of Her destruction, a sexual climax that can be defined as a sort of apocalyptic primal scene.

She is destroyed, of course, by the very flame of life that has heretofore preserved Her (and which at one time presumably created Her). She is

quite unexpectedly annihilated by the 'rolling pillar of Life' that has kept
Her alive. The 'rolling pillar of Life' that brings Haggard's romance to its
apocalyptic climax is an almost theatrically rich sexual symbol. At
regular intervals, it appears with a 'grinding and crashing noise . . .
rolling down like all the thunderwheels of heaven behind the horses of
the lightning' and, as it enters the cave, it flames out 'an awful cloud or
pillar of fire, like a rainbow many colored,' whose very presence causes
Haggard's narrator to rejoice' in [the] splendid vigor of a new-found
self.' Such celestial radiance and regenerative power suggest that this
perpetually erect symbol of masculinity is not just a Freudian penis but a
Lacanian phallus, a fiery signifier whose eternal thundering return
bespeaks the inexorability of the patriarchal Law She has violated in Her
Satanically overreaching ambition.

As Henry Miller notes further, however, Ayesha's death is not just a
death or even a 'reduction' but, quite literally, a 'devolution' in which
Her very flesh is punished for Her presumption. As She passes through
the stages of her unlived life, aging two thousand years in a few
minutes, the 'language strange' of her beauty shreds and flakes away,
Her power wrinkles, Her magic dries up, and the meaning of her
'terrible priority' is revealed as de-generation rather than generation.
More terrible than the transformation of Dr. Jekyll or Dorian Gray, this
'reduction' or 'devolution' of goddess to beast is the final judgment upon
Her pride and ambition.

She is not only a turn-of-the-century bestseller but also, in a number of
dramatic ways, one of the century's literary turning points, a pivot on
which the ideas and anxieties of the Victorians began to swivel into what
has come to be called 'the modern.' If She is a classic *Belle Dame Sans
Merci*, for instance, the stony wasteland that She rules is modern in its air
of sexual and historical extremity. And certainly in England the
ceremonial sexual act that brought about Her 'reduction' or 'devolution'
was followed by a number of similar scenes in turn-of-the-century and
modernist tales, ranging from Wilde's *Salome* (1894), Macdonald's *Lilith*
(1895), and Stoker's *Dracula* (1897), to T. S. Eliot's 'The Love Song of St
Sebastian,' D. H. Lawrence's 'The Woman Who Rode Away,' and
Faulkner's 'A Rose for Emily.' In all these works, a man or a group of
men must achieve or at least bear witness to a ceremonial assertion of
phallic authority that will free all men from the unmanning enslavement
of Her land.

To notice that common anxieties impel these tales toward an
uncommonly ferocious denouement is not, however, to understand the
real psychological, social, and historical anxieties that underlie them.
What, after all, worried Rider Haggard so much that he was driven to
create his extraordinary complex fantasy about Her and Her realm in just

six volcanically energetic weeks? Why did thousands and thousands of Englishmen respond to his dreamlike story of Her with as much fervor as if he had been narrating their own dreams? I believe that the charisma of this novel arose from the fact that the work itself explored and exploited three intimately interrelated contemporary phenomena: the nineteenth-century interest in Egypt, the nineteenth-century fascination with spiritualism, and the nineteenth-century obsession with the so-called New Woman.

It is significant that the wisdom of other cultures, and specifically the wisdom of ancient Egypt was gradually emerging in the nineteenth century through the work of spiritualist 'adepts' like Madame Blavatsky, for spiritualism, with its different but equally serious emphasis on a realm of otherness, was the second contemporary phenomenon that Haggard's novel exploited. The novelist himself had actually been a spiritualist in his youth, attending séances presided over by women, which dramatized yet again the fragility of the control the rational western mind had achieved over a world of things and people that might at any moment assert a dangerously alien autonomy. Where both materialist science and traditional Christian theology declared that there was nothing (for the dead were, if anywhere, elsewhere), spiritualism seemed to prove that there was something. When theosophy, fostered by spiritualist ideas, summarized a set of radical hermeticist propositions about reality, reminding readers that, as Madame Blavatsky argued, such mysticism had always flowed like an underground river below western thought, patriarchal rationalism was even more seriously shaken. Finally, the appearance of Madame Blavatsky's notorious *Isis Unveiled* (1877) must have not only cemented the connections between the 'adepts' of Egypt and such challenges to a commonly agreed-upon 'reality,' but also emphasized the link between – on the one hand – the alternative intellectual possibilities propounded by theosophy and – on the other hand – the possibilities of female rule, or misrule.

The figure of the New Woman, with its evocation of such unruly females as the Egyptian Cleopatra and the pseudo-Egyptologist Madame Blavatsky, vividly suggested an ultimate triumph of otherness. Feminist thinkers had long understood this point, quite consciously identifying their work for women's rights with such related challenges to patriarchal authority as spiritualism, abolitionism, and the Home Rule movement in Ireland. But even without overt articulations of the links between feminism and other antipatriarchal movements, the very idea of the New Woman was so threatening that her aspirations tended to evoke all the other subversive aspirations that were suddenly, or so it seemed, being voiced throughout the Empire, with some even being conveyed from the invisible world of the dead.

It is notable, too, that Haggard's adult reading as well as his childhood listening was at least at one point focused on the work of a female imagination: Olive Schreiner's *The Story of an African Farm* (1883), the first bestselling novel ever written about Africa, which was after all, a book by a woman, and a feminist one at that. Like Englishmen from Gladstone to Rhodes, Haggard read the book with fascination and excitement. At his first opportunity, he sought out its author to express his admiration, and his charismatically fierce Ayesha may even have been half-consciously modeled on Schreiner's fierce but equally charismatic Lyndall. At the same time, moreover, *She* may also have been half-consciously patterned on yet another work *about* the problem of feminist assertiveness. Tennyson's 1847 *The Princess*, in which, as in *She, three* bewildered men penetrate a female stronghold and explore the perils of role reversal.

It is no coincidence, therefore, that within a decade of *She's* publication two of Haggard's most sophisticated contemporaries recorded dreams and recounted adventures that drew upon the elaborate configuration of anxieties that *She* enacted. First, Sigmund Freud had a dream that, as his self-analysis revealed, depended heavily on details borrowed from *She*. In this dream, Freud wrote, he had been given a strange task that

> related to a dissection of the lower part of my own body, my pelvis and legs, which I saw before me as though in the dissecting-room. . . . Finally I was making a journey through a changing landscape with an Alpine guide who carried me [part of the way]. The ground was boggy; we went round the edge; . . . Before this I had been making my own way forward over the slippery ground with a constant feeling of surprise that I was able to do so well after the dissection. At last we reached a small wooden house at the end of which was an open window. There the guide set me down and laid two wooden boards, . . . so as to bridge the chasm which had to be crossed over from the window. At that point I really became frightened about my legs, [and] awoke in a mental fright.

As Freud himself rather dryly remarks, 'a full analysis of this dream' would take up quite a number of pages, but he does undertake a partial explanation, which, significantly, emphasizes the influence of imagery drawn from *She*, a work he calls 'A strange book . . . full of hidden meaning. . . . The eternal feminine, the immortality of our emotions . . .' and which, as one critic has recently argued, may have helped him conceptualize the psychic geography that was to be so crucial to his theory of 'layered personality.' What are we to make, though, of the fact that Freud's Haggardesque adventure begins with a pelvic dissection that implies a desexing and that his journey ends in feelings of impotence and terror? Like Leo and Holly, who have to be carried on litters into the womb/tomb that is Her land, Freud seems to have been castrated and infantilized early in this dream, so that when he is borne inward over slippery, boggy ground, it is hard, given his own hermeneutics, to avoid seeing his journey not as a classic trip into the self but as a voyage into the other, and specifically into an other who is horrifyingly female. His final despairing vision of 'the chasm which had to be crossed' would inevitably, then, lead to a sense of failure and 'mental fright,' not because (as he suggests) he wonders how much longer his legs will carry him toward the end of his self-analysis, but because he fears that he will reach an end that must inevitably include an impotent confrontation of – even an engulfment in – the otherness of the female, whose power is shrouded in a darkness that lies at the heart of his own culture.

It is significant, however, that Freud's dream broods so insistently on 'the chasm that had to be crossed' by means of narrow planks, for this frightening image derives, we should remember, from what is essentially the turning point of Haggard's tale. Holly, Leo, and Job can only bridge the gulf they must cross in order to reach the 'place of Life' when, 'like a great sword of flame, a beam from the setting sun [pierces] the . . . heart of the darkness' and they are given a symbolic preview of the fate in store for Ayesha. It is possible, therefore, that in his dream allusion to this moment, Freud was not only enacting crucial male anxieties but also offering himself a paradigmatically patriarchal hope, the hope of renewal through a reiteration of the Law of the Father.

Interestingly, the most important *fin de siècle* work that we can associate with *She* also pays tribute to this crucial moment. In his *Heart of Darkness* (1899), written not long after Freud dreamed this dream, Conrad designs for Marlow a pilgrimage whose guides and goal are as eerily female as those Holly and Leo must confront and conquer. Just as Leo and Holly must ritually pass through the matriarchal territory of the Amahaggar in order to reach Her deadly land of Kôr, for instance, Marlow must pass through an antechamber ruled by two 'uncanny and fateful' women who are 'guarding the door of Darkness.' When he reaches a key way station on his African journey, moreover, he is 'arrested' by 'a small sketch in oils' done by the mysterious Kurtz, a totemic-seeming image of 'a woman, draped and blindfolded, carrying a lighted torch.' Vaguely evoking an image of justice, the picture disturbingly suggests the contradictions between power (the torch) and powerlessness (the blindfold) and thus it introduces the idea of the other who has been excluded and dispossessed but who, despite such subordination, exercises a kind of indomitable torchlike power.

Whether or not it is justified, the sense of the imminent danger She represents was shared not only by anxious romancers like Keats and Swinburne, Macdonald and Wilde, but also by such disparate figures as Joseph Conrad, Rider Haggard, and Sigmund Freud. There *is*, after all, to quote Conrad, 'something ominous and stately in her deliberate progress' through the nineteenth century.

4 The Decadent and the New Woman in the 1890s*

LINDA DOWLING

Linda Dowling is the author of a much cited book, *Language and Decadence in the Victorian Fin de Siècle* (see Further Reading), in which she argued that Decadence was, among other things, a counterpoetics and critique which emerged from a late nineteenth-century crisis in attitudes to language precipitated by the new comparative philology imported from Germany. In the essay reprinted here (which predates *Language and Decadence*) Dowling focuses on the broader cultural meanings of the Decadent, whom she links to the New Woman as both cultural demon and force for change. Dowling rethinks the Decadent and the New woman as both cultural symbols and progressive forces, and attempts to locate them (in both guises) in a revised genealogy of modernism (see Introduction, p. 8).

In 1888 Ernest Dowson decided to join two Oxford friends in annotating a copy of Olive Schreiner's famous novel, *The Story of an African Farm* (1882). Six years after its publication, Schreiner's book had come to be recognized as one of those that cast, as one reviewer put it, 'an electric light' upon women's psychology, a topic that was increasingly absorbing the attention of late-Victorian novelists, journalists, critics, and general reading public. Victor Plarr and Frank Walton, the two young men who thought up the satiric annotation scheme, wanted to adopt the heavily pedantic manner of German commentators on the classics. Dowson, choosing instead the persona of 'Anatole de Montmartre,' threw himself into the work with enthusiasm. In the Dowson–Schreiner connection, modern literary historians are likely to see another of those striking contrasts – like the histrionic oppositions of luxury and squalor languor and activism, asceticism and sensuality, art and life – often found

*Reprinted from *Nineteenth Century Fiction*, 33 (1979), pp. 434–53

characteristic of the Victorian *fin de siècle*. In particular, the conjunction of feminist author and Rhymers' Club poet brings to mind another pair of apparent opposites: the 'decadent dandy' and the 'New Woman.' These two creatures, by now fully enrolled in the *fin de siècle* bestiary as the sphinx, the androgyne, or the ballet girl, have been portrayed by modern scholars, not simply as antithetical figures in a deeply self-divided decade, but as antagonistic principles intent on each other's destruction.[1]

Contemporary Victorian observers of the decadent and the New Woman, however, took quite another view. For the most part antagonistic both to literary decadence and New Woman fiction, literary critics and reviewers persistently identified the New Woman with the decadent, perceiving in the ambitions of both a profound threat to established culture. And the conservative late-Victorian critics who identified the New Woman with the decadent wrote, despite their prejudices and exaggerations, from a perception of real coherence within contemporary avant-gardism that has for the most part been obscure to later students of *fin de siècle* literature. The sense of similar artistic concerns shared by New Woman fiction and literary decadence eludes us if, for example, we apply the 'New Woman versus decadent dandy' model to the case of Schreiner and Dowson.

Although Dowson annotated as 'Anatole de Montmartre,' there was little satire, little of the dandiacal *boulevardier* in what he wrote.[2] Dowson, who had first read the novel at Oxford the summer before, admired Schreiner's work profoundly. Its pessimism, its portrayal of isolated consciousness and desire quenched in futility, and most of all, its narrative method – what Schreiner had called the 'method of the life we all live'[3] – all earned Dowson's praise. In a vehement marginal aside he wrote:

> The time for romance, for novels written in the stage method is gone. In a worldly decaying civilization, in an age of nostalgia like the present – what is the meaning of Mr Rider Haggard? He is an anachronism. It is to books like *Madame Bovary* & de Maupassant's *Une Vie* to books like these one must go to find the true significance of the XIXth Century.

And a few lines on, when Schreiner, disdaining the pleas of critics like Andrew Lang for wild African adventures, insisted that the modern writer must 'squeeze the colour from his brush, and dip it into the grey pigments around him,' Dowson, who would soon become the most skillful English singer of Verlaine's *chanson grise*, paused to underscore 'grey pigments' (*Letters*, 10).

Dowson's admiration of Schreiner, had his annotations been published in his own time, would not have surprised his contemporaries. To most late Victorians the decadent was new and the New Woman decadent.

The origins, tendencies, even the appearance of the New Woman and the decadent – as portrayed in the popular press and periodicals – confirmed their near, their unhealthily near relationship. Both inspired reactions ranging from hilarity to disgust and outrage, and both raised as well profound fears for the future of sex, class, and race. To Dowson's apprehensive contemporaries, the figures of the New Woman and the decadent, like the artists who created them and the works in which they appeared, seemed to be dangerous avatars of the 'New,' and were widely felt to oppose not each other but the values considered essential to the survival of established culture.

From a modernist or 'post-modernist' point of view, of course, New Woman fiction and literary decadence may seem like the most pallid of artistic insurgencies. Here, as always, the characteristic impulse of modernism to repudiate its own past obscures an essential truth. Even if critics and observers exaggerated the power to transform contemporary culture that the *fin de siècle* avant-garde possessed, they rightly estimated its hostile intentions. Though the apocalypse of Victorian civilization they feared was delayed considerably beyond the end of the century, it was to arrive. And late Victorians had correctly identified as its harbingers the decadent and the New Woman, whose quarrel with established culture, however quaintly *'fin de siècle'* it may now appear, was the first rebellious expression of that disenchantment of culture with culture that Lionel Trilling has taught us to recognize as 'modernism.'

The commentators who identified the New Woman with the decadent were seldom content merely to denounce the sexual expressiveness in literature espoused both by 'decadent' writers (those who imitated or were interested in Continental avant-garde experiments) and by the New Woman novelists (a group which included both men and women). Reviewers felt compelled instead to warn their readers of the evolutionary and worse, the revolutionary dangers to Victorian civilization embodied in the new avant-gardism. When they described their lurid vision of cultural apocalypse, critics of the 'New' inevitably adopted what had become a familiar journalistic vocabulary of crisis. Invoking the analogy of the French Revolution, for instance, had by the 1890s become an almost reflexive rhetorical gesture among journalistic writers, one merely signaling a writer's urgent dismay or his sense of inevitable, inevitably disastrous consequences. Thus we hear the Reverend W. F. Barry comparing the New Woman's revolt against sexual authority to the 'Insurrection of Women' of October 1789 and arguing that the typical heroine of the 'New' fiction was no more than Rousseau's savage.[4] So, too, Elizabeth Chapman, reaching a bit farther back for her historical comparison, attacks the heroine of Mona Caird's *The Daughters of Danaus* (1894) as 'a *frondeuse,* in full rebellion not merely against institutions which she disapproves and dislikes, but as it would seem, against law *quâ* law, against authority *quâ* authority.'[5]

Though few heroines of New Woman fiction actually dabbled in revolutionary politics, such alarmed commentators as Barry and Chapman persistently looked beyond specific episodes to read in the New Woman's insistence on sexual equality and self-development a manifesto of contemporary anarchism. If we smile at the repeated warnings of apocalypse made by critics of the New Woman and the decadent, we nonetheless recognize in their apocalyptic vocabulary a genuinely anguished expression of cultural anxiety, a sense that the 'New' might betoken cultural changes even less comprehensible than those which the constantly recurring images of decline, decay, and end were meant to control. To compare the avant-gardist revolt to the French Revolution or to contemporary political anarchism was, to be sure, merely to substitute analogy for explanation. Such analogies at least allowed critics of the 'New' to posit order, however threatened, as the essential context for disorder even as the analogy of anarchism itself registered some of their deepest cultural fears.

This is the context, for instance, in which Hugh E. M. Stutfield could warn that 'the aesthetic sensualist and the communist are, in a sense, nearly related. Both have . . . a common parentage in exaggerated emotionalism. . . . In these days the unbridled licentiousness of your literary decadent has its counterpart in the violence of the political anarchist.'[6] In *The New Antigone*, his anti-New Woman romance of 1887, W. F. Barry dramatized the contemporary view by portraying his anarchists simply as decadent aesthetes, as men who are 'gentle almost to effeminacy,' whose 'out-of-the-way learning contrasted singularly with the mincing, tender tones in which they gave utterance to it' and who 'satirised everything that was not sensuous feeling, that did not feed delightful moments.'[7] Though we may today wonder how these Bunthornes and Postlethwaites of revolutionary change could have seriously alarmed anyone, the loosening of sexual controls apparently encouraged by literary decadence and New Woman fiction was almost universally believed by late-Victorian critics to threaten the vital bonds of state and culture. This is also the context in which we hear *Punch* calling Grant Allen, the social reformer and author of *The Woman Who Did* (1895), a 'sans-culotte' and find the writer and advocate of 'free love,' Richard Le Gallienne, compared by *Punch* to Proudhon.

Even Madame Sarah Grand, whose vast book *The Heavenly Twins* (1893) became one of the most widely read of the New Woman novels, portrayed her heroine as a woman with a potential for anarchic violence. Angelica, who by masquerading as her own twin brother has enjoyed the sexually disinterested friendship of a handsome young musician, justifies her actions after she is found out by saying,

'I had the ability to be something more than a young lady, fiddling away her time on useless trifles, but I was not allowed to apply it systematically, and ability is like steam – a great power when properly applied, a great danger otherwise. . . . This is the explosion,' – glancing round the disordered room, and then looking down at her masculine attire.[8]

In fact, Angelica's experiment has fatal consequences, sending her young man into a long decline from which he never recovers; he dies, like Sue Bridehead's unnamed undergraduate in *Jude the Obscure* (1895), a victim of the curiosity and fey experimentalism of the New Woman. Similarly, the heroine of Emma Frances Brooke's *A Superfluous Woman* (1894) yearns for the destruction of society itself. Caught up in her sexual passion for a young peasant, Jessamine Halliday tells herself fiercely that if she could, merely by thrusting out her little finger, 'topple down the whole hateful fabric of London society,' she would do so in an instant.[9]

In the same way, many late-Victorian critics of the avant-garde used the vocabulary of apocalypse to express their urgent sense of cultural crisis, their fear of imminent besiegement, betrayal, and collapse. Convinced that both literary decadence and New Woman fiction sanctioned and incited an unrestrained egoism, critics repeatedly warned of the threat posed to the macrocosm of Victorian civilization if such dangerously volatile literary tendencies should enter into combination with other forces agitating for radical social and political change. In 1889 the *Westminster Review* predicted that the ego of woman

> will yet roll over the world in fructifying waves, causing incalculable upheaval and destruction. The stirrings and rumblings now perceivable in the social and industrial worlds, the 'Bitter Cries' of the disinherited classes, the 'Social Wreckage' which is becoming able to make itself unpleasantly prominent, the 'Problems of Great Cities,' the spread of Socialism and Nihilism, are all intimately connected with the ascent of [this] Ego.[10]

Five years later the *Speaker* would identify George Egerton as a 'moral anarchist' and hear in her *Discords* (1894) the 'voice from a class growing larger and ever most insistent.'[11] The same voice, the reviewer noted, spoke from John Davidson's ballads; it was heard as well, as we now recognize, in the poems of Rudyard Kipling, John Barlas, and Francis Adams, and in the fiction of George Gissing, Arthur Morrison, and Thomas Hardy.

To explain why late-Victorian critics proceeded so unhesitatingly from individual literary texts to rather cosmic conclusions about the collapse of their culture, we need only recall the deeply held Victorian conviction that woman was the inspiration and guardian of civilization, that upon the 'acquiescent feminine smile,' as the heroine of *The Story of a Modern Woman* (1894) bitterly reminds herself, 'the whole fabric of civilisation rested.'[12] As the controversy over the New Woman grew, so did the number of apostrophes to this animating and preserving ideal. Here, for example, is *Punch*'s address to 'A Fair Unknown':

> The Militant Daughters, of Key and Club,
> Whose Crown is swagger, whose wit a snub,
> They wilt like ghosts at the eye of day
> In the simple charm of your sweet array.
> And yours is the soul that makes men fight
> For the cause that is yours – for the cause of right.
> And the decadent herd may moan and rave,
> And leave the temple to dig the grave,
> But life will blossom, while maids like you
> Will keep men noble and straight and true[13]

The New Woman, on the other hand, was perceived to have ranged herself perversely with the forces of cultural anarchism and decay precisely she wanted to reinterpret the sexual relationship. Like the decadent, the heroine of New Woman fiction expressed her quarrel with Victorian culture chiefly through sexual means – by heightening sexual consciousness, candor, and expressiveness. It was this fundamental kinship that suggested all the other similarities so frequently described by late-Victorian critics of literary decadence and New Woman fiction.

Critics were convinced, for example, that literary decadence and New Woman fiction both traced their 'neuropathic' or 'erotomaniac' tendencies to the influence, the lubricious and morbidly analytical influence, of contemporary French literature. W. F. Barry discovered in Mrs Humphrey Ward's *Marcella* (1894) 'the French combination of action and sentiment, the sensuous introspection, the careful Epicurean tasting of life's flavours, and the doctrine of 'thrill,' which . . . are not only decadent in their origin, they bring the taint into the book which describes them.' 'Has the New Woman,' asked Barry, 'a lesson to learn from that school?' ('Strike,' 307–8). Other critics warned that, from wherever the literary decadent and the New Woman might have derived their inspiration, both had a pernicious effect on contemporary literature. Thus Mrs Oliphant protested the disposition of New Woman novelists 'to place what is called the Sex-question above all others as the theme of fiction,'[14] and Thomas Bradfield wondered, was this dominant note of sexuality 'a sign that English fiction has entered upon a stage of decadence.'?[15]

Certainly such an emphasis on sex rudely violated the polite norms of Victorian realism. The 'fiction of sexuality,' argued James Ashcroft Noble, distorted the true proportions of life in the same way a convex mirror distorted the human face – 'the colossal nose which dominates the face being represented by one colossal appetite which dominates life.' To present men and women as merely or mainly conduits of sexual emotion was, in Noble's eyes, 'as ludicrously inartistic as it is to paint a face as a flat, featureless plain, from which the nose rises as a lonely eminence.'[16] What Noble saw as an attack upon 'artistic' proportion, as a subordination of whole to part, is, of course, precisely what more advanced critics like Richard Le Gallienne and Havelock Ellis defined as literary decadence. Writing in much the same Shandyan vein, Le Gallienne noted that it was typical of French decadents like J. K. Huysmans to be more interested in the colors of a tippler's nose than in the state of his soul: 'the real core of decadence is to be found in its isolated interests.[17]

If the insistent sexual emphasis of the avant-garde seemed to be making an anarchic chaos of conventions of literary form, its critics believed just as strongly that it would dangerously confuse established assumptions about class. They deplored the sympathy for unsavory topics on the part of 'decadent essayists and "yellow" lady novelists,' protesting the tendency to introduce into 'New' literary works 'unfortunates' and other members of the unsavory lower classes. Though some heroines of New Woman fiction consorted with 'unfortunates' because, impelled by revolutionary or socialist principles, they actively sought to right social wrongs, they were, like the decadents, also deeply attracted by what seemed to be the mysterious otherness of the lower classes. Even as Mrs Ward's Marcella busily concocts straw-plaiting schemes for her cottagers, for example, she is drawn to 'their peasant lives, which were so full of enigma and attraction to her, mainly because of their very defectiveness, their closeness to an animal simplicity, never to be reached by any one of her sort.'[18]

Nor was the New Woman unmoved by the sexual allure of the lower-class male. She did not, it is true, embrace *déclassé* amours with the same abandon shown by some of Arthur Symons's poetic speakers; but within rather carefully limited fictional circumstances some heroines of New Woman fiction did experience the *frisson* that would later more completely overpower Forster's Helen Schlegel and Lawrence's Lady Chatterley. Thus we find Jessamine Halliday recalling with delight her rescue by the stolid young peasant Colin Macgillvray. Lying in bed, 'as bare to feeling as any pagan girl,' she imagines that 'his rude forceful pressure returned again upon her slender figure with an alluring yet terrifying sweetness.' Soon the girl who had once deliberately chosen 'dejected aesthetic hues' of pale primrose, wan yellow, and cream to complement her 'melancholic Burne-Jones droop of lips and chin' is dashing off like a village maid to buy cherry-colored ribbons (*A Superfluous Woman*, I, 143, 189, 85).

Picturesque enough when set in a romanticized Scottish glen, the New Woman's experience of lower-class life seldom brought about any change more significant than new ribbons. Typically, the fictional heroine's descent into the world of 'unfortunates' was a brief and usually abortive passage in her hegira towards a more fully realized selfhood – that is to say, in most novels at least, marriage. Jessamine returns to London to reinfatuate the biggest catch in Europe, Marcella marries an earl, and W. F. Barry's Hippolyta takes the veil. Nonetheless, the New Woman had compromised both her sex and her class by her experiments, and she was accused of setting a dangerous and hypocritical example. The lower classes could scarcely be expected to demonstrate her own calm passion and sense of responsibility and could never hope to escape, as the New Woman generally did, the heavy sanctions of affronted respectability.

It was even more usual for her critics to portray the New Woman as herself belonging to the lower classes. Indeed, many of the heroines found in George Egerton's extraordinarily successful collections of short stories, *Keynotes* (1893) and *Discords*, did inhabit the indeterminate netherworld of the poorer classes. Yet it was the New Woman's demands for education, for equality, for meaningful work that led critics to identify the feminist agitation of these fictional heroines with the unrest of the poor and disenfranchised. The New Woman's eagerness for education, in particular, seemed to align her and her authors, whose 'robust ungrammaticality' was frequently sneered at, with the lamentable products of the Board Schools and working-man's institutes, with all those who labored to 'improve' themselves.

Despite the upper-class backgrounds of most New Woman heroines and despite the aristocratic sympathies of decadent writers, we thus find the ambitions of both the New Woman and the decadent meeting accusations of 'Cockney impudence' – the customary charge, since Keats, brought against artistic innovation in the realm of sensuous experience. Critics of the avant-garde were convinced that this 'Cockney' emphasis on sensation and cheap self-culture they perceived in both literary decadence and New Woman fiction would not only sap the moral sense of the individual but would undermine the distinctions of class. In an age of sciolism, of 'smattering and chattering,' they agreed, half knowledge would clearly prove more dangerous to persons of limited education than to those of wider culture; but the danger ultimately threatened culture itself. Thus many late Victorians felt that women readers, particularly young women, were especially vulnerable to the unwholesome influences found equally in New Woman fiction and literary decadence. At best only half educated, women would undoubtedly pursue the literary fashion for 'chirurgical realism' or 'redundant sexuality' with the same heedless self-indulgence with which an earlier generation had followed Parisian bonnets. 'I do not wish to say anything unfair,' wrote Hugh Stutfield, 'but I think it cannot be denied that women are chiefly responsible for the "booming" of books that are "close to life" – life, that is to say, as viewed through sex-maniacal glasses.' It was, continued Stutfield, the duty of women to stem the morbid hysteria fed by the 'new' art and literature by refusing to buy such books ('Tommyrotics,' 843–4). Six months later, Mrs Oliphant, aghast at the success of Grant Allen's *The Woman Who Did*, pleaded with the public to restrain itself – the novel, not yet out a year, was in its twentieth impression and 'the conversation of the drawing-room is already most sensibly affected. Things are discussed freely and easily which it would a few years ago have been a shame to mention or to think of' ('Anti-Marriage,' 149).

Yet critics of the avant-garde saw an even more dangerous threat in the twin programs and attitudes of the decadent and the New Woman: they jeopardized the very survival of the race. Max Beerbohm had cheerfully pointed out that the amalgamation of the sexes was 'one of the chief planks in the decadent platform,'[19] but if this were true, *Punch* wondered, how would the race perpetuate itself? *Punch*'s 'Angry Old Buffer' complained that

> a new fear my bosom vexes;
> Tomorrow there may be *no* sexes!
> Unless, as end to all pother,
> Each one in fact becomes the other.
> E'en *then* perhaps they'll start amain
> A-trying to change back again!
> Woman *was* woman, man *was* man,
> When Adam delved and Eve span,
> Now he can't dig and she won't spin,
> Unless 'tis tales all slang the sin!
>
> (27 April 1895, p. 203)

Punch devoted a good deal of space to the eugenic dangers raised by contemporary male effeminacy and female mannishness; the New Woman 'made further development in generations to come quite impossible' (21 July 1894, p. 27), while the 'New Man' was, in a word, 'Woman' (24 Nov. 1894, p. 249). In a poem entitled 'Misoneogyny,' 'A. Bachelor' argues that the New Woman is a decadent monster of

> no lasting vitality,
> Only existing in fancy and print;
> It is just an unlovely abstract personality,
> Coin from the end-of-the-century mint.
>
> (20 July 1895, p. 35)

And this, of course, was exactly how both the New Woman and the decadent chose to view themselves – as asynchronous creatures, prematurely old or precociously modern, but in either case irretrievably out of phase with their own time. The eponymous heroine of Ménie Muriel Dowie's *Gallia* (1895), for example, admits that you 'cannot make yourself the old style of woman; you cannot interfere with the clock of evolution that is wound up and goes on in each of us' only to be told by the man to whom she has unsuccessfully proposed that she is 'the perfectly hapless kind of modern woman. There is no place in all the world for you. You are not wanted, because you are for no use.'[20]

Though, as we have seen, critics loathed the preoccupation with sex and sexual expressiveness characteristic of literary decadence and New Woman fiction, other commentators, encountering the Baudelairean misogyny of a Des Esseintes or the pathological sexual aversion of a Sue Bridehead, nonetheless became alarmed by what they feared was a profound rejection of procreative sex in the 'New' literature. Elizabeth Chapman, discovering that Hadria, the heroine of Mona Caird's *The Daughters of Danaus*, despised 'mother earth' for being pliantly submissive to the dictatorship of men, was moved to exclaim, 'What a paradox is here! What a strange inversion of the natural order! How the intellect must have been warped, and the heart embittered, of a woman who could couple such a word as "uninspired" with such an idea as motherhood!' (*Marriage Questions*, 29).

Inevitably, the revolt of the New Woman and the decadent against what was 'natural,' their 'warped' and 'morbid' intellects, their extreme self-consciousness, seemed to their late-Victorian critics to isolate them both in a chilly realm of sterility, ascesis, or cerebral lechery, cut off from the springs of instinctive reproductive life. And yet, though Gwen Waring, the heroine of Iota's *A Yellow Aster* (1894), voids herself of all maternal emotion and exclaims shudderingly, 'This one-flesh business, this is a horrid thing,'[21] not every New Woman shrank from procreative sex; indeed many heroines embraced motherhood as the eugenic solution to their quarrel with society. We find the disappointed Gallia, for instance, conquering her unconventional passion in favor of a matter-of-factly procreative union with Mark Gurdon, a fine physical specimen she describes as 'keen and gamey and lifey' (*Gallia*, 215). We know, on the other hand, that Jessamine Halliday, in finally preferring the diseased and debauched Lord Heriot to her sturdy Highland peasant, has made a terrible eugenic decision; after bearing Heriot two children, Jessamine lives, albeit just barely, to see her idiot daughter murder her deformed son – an episode that anticipates Hardy's treatment of racial exhaustion and the deadly struggle between old and 'New' in *Jude the Obscure*. For New Women like Gallia and Jessamine, bearing children becomes an existentially redeeming act; for George Egerton's heroines, motherhood is a passion as intense as sex itself.

Even so, critics feared that the New Woman, in her hypermodernity, her ambitious attempt to transcend established notions of sexual consciousness and behavior, would irreversibly unfit herself for her essential role as wife and mother – that, in short, she would follow the decadent down the road to personal and, ultimately, racial extinction. Max Nordau's *Degeneration* (1895) is merely the most famous of the attacks on the new avant-gardism that warned that real dangers were posed to culture and the continuance of the race by specimens as mentally and physically defective as the 'decadent aesthete.' Fifteen years earlier, Olive Schreiner's heroine, Lyndall, had mocked the conventional argument this way: 'Go on; but when you have made women what you wish, and her children inherit her culture, you will defeat yourself. Man will gradually become extinct from excess of intellect, the passions which replenish the race will die' (*African Farm*, 194). Other late Victorians worried about more immediate problems: the voluntary sterility of 'glorified spinsterhood' and, since they assumed that the New Woman could achieve sexual equality only by controlling her fertility, the unavoidable resort to abortion or infanticide. And they had grounds: Frau Irma von Troll-Borostyani, for one, doubted that the New Woman's free love unions would produce any considerable increase in illegitimate children, but if they did, recommended chloroform.[22] Thus Laura Marholm Hansson, viewing the New Woman and her ambitions from a contemporary Continental perspective, expressed the feelings of many late Victorians when she concluded that

> the many honest people who think they hear in the Woman
> Movement the memento mori of a race, and the gnawing of the
> death-worm, are not so far wrong. As it manifests itself outwardly it
> is a sign of decay and corruption, and where it has produced
> conditions – or more accurately has grown out of conditions – as in
> the lauded lands of woman's emancipation, the decline of a race is
> clearly shown.[23]

Critics of the *fin de siècle* avant-garde thus understood a truth that has now grown obscure: in a cultural context of radical anxiety, the decadent and the New Woman were twin apostles of social apocalypse. And they were so not least because they saw themselves that way. This is the truth contained in the central metaphor employed by enemies of the avant-garde to express their urgent dismay: late-Victorian England, as involved in problems of Empire as Imperial Rome in its decline, had entered its Silver Age – English culture, on the analogy with Rome, was threatened from without, betrayed from within.[24] And though – or perhaps because – they were attempting to overthrow the cultural assumptions of their critics, the decadent and the New Woman both assented to the truth of this metaphor. English decadents had long since learned to say with

French avant-garde writers like Verlaine, 'Je suis l'Empire à la fin de la décadence,' and to portray themselves as languidly awaiting immolation at the hands of huge white barbarians. And in the same way, we find such loyal advocates of the new avant-gardism as Havelock Ellis arguing that the New Woman would herald 'a reinvigoration as complete as any brought by barbarians to an effete and degenerating civilization.'[25]

An anxious survey of contemporary artistic developments thus convinced late-Victorian critics that the New Woman and the decadent embodied forces at once passively degenerate and actively destructive and, unexpectedly, the partisans of the 'New' agreed. The avant-garde and its enemies confronted each other over an abyss of cultural anxiety, and both understood that the New Woman and the decadent, in turning against the established culture that might have cherished them as its latest and most nearly perfect creations, were determined to subvert high culture by asserting the claims of the 'low,' the 'unnatural,' and the 'unfortunate.' Anxiety brings with it confusion, and in their anxious confusion of New Woman with decadent, decadent with barbarian, we discover why enemies of the avant-garde – like the avant-gardists themselves – were able to portray the decadent and the New Woman as at once the corrupt defenders on the walls and as the vulgar encircling hordes below.

As Renato Poggioli has shown,[26] this paradoxical identification of decadent with barbarism, of defender with attacker, grew out of a determination within *fin de siècle* avant-gardism to save culture by destroying it. Even if the renovation of the old can only be realized through apocalypse, the decadent spirit, for all its fierce nostalgia for a defunct and greater past, will not hesitate to embrace the 'New': 'The craving for novelty and notoriety,' wrote Hugh Stutfield scathingly, '. . . and a feverish desire to be abreast of the times may be reckoned among the first-fruits of decadentism' ('Tommyrotics,' 844). This is the context in which decadence, in the extremity of its reactionary nostalgia, meets the futurist impatience of avant-gardism in a shared hope for a new primitivism. Though the activist program of the avant-gardist may seem to contrast sharply with the morbid passivity of the decadent, the anticipation of renewal through apocalypse is essentially the same.

This is why, as Poggioli reminds us, the decadent at once hoards the choicest fragments of a dying culture and conspires with the hordes without to lay waste to the imperial city; and why, too, critics viewed the embrace of decadent and barbarian, scholar and Cockney, as an apocalyptic embrace. By aligning themselves with the vulgar, the ugly, the forbidden, the outré, the writers of the *fin de siècle* avant-garde were intent on breaching the constrictive and defensive walls of Victorian aesthetic decorum and building anew. Here we encounter an important paradox: the new world they wished to realize would, they thought, restore nature – an idea of nature enriched by urban tension and complexity, made vibrant by sexual expressiveness, made strange by irony, slang, and archaism.

This is precisely the sense in which the pastoralism of so much Edwardian and Georgian literature is not so much a repudiation as a belated fulfillment of the new primitivism of the *fin de siècle* avant-garde. For when what we mean by pastoral is less a matter of shepherdesses and sheep than a mode by which the civilized imagination exempts itself from the claims of its own culture, pastoral – from the conventional form we find in the work of Norman Gale or the early Yeats to the 'urban pastoral' we meet in the London poems of Wilde, Henley, Symons, Dowson, Le Gallienne, Wratislaw, and Horne – is the characteristic mode of *fin de siècle* avant-gardism. Pastoral, easily lending itself to the short forms and small effects, the elegance and diminutive grace that so interested 'decadent' writers of the period, accommodated equally the exploration of innocence and corruption – especially the corruption of age – that we find in Dowson's poems, in *Dorian Gray*, and in the bitter conviction of so many New Woman heroines that they stood on the brink of irrevocable sexual obsolescence. Unlike romance, with its extended narrative and its 'stage method' coincidences and conclusions, pastoral meant to avant-garde writers image, impression, mood, and vision, and it offered them, with its essentially static mode, a paradoxical means of expressing their obsession with flux and insubstantiality. Thus the note of despair in the voice of Schreiner's Lyndall: 'We are sparks, we are shadows, we are pollen, which the next wind will carry away. We are dying already; it is all a dream' (*African Farm*, 217) or the conviction of Dixon's Mary Erle that 'Nature – insolent, triumphant Nature – cares nothing for the individual. . . . Summer and winter, seed-time and harvest, will come and go in the ages to come, but I – *I shall not be here*' (*Modern Woman*, 314).

From Theocritus and Virgil to the present, pastoral has been recognized as a highly conventional mode. This was precisely the source of its attraction for avant-garde writers: as pastoral celebrated a highly artificial view of nature, it could be used to express their own ambition to live and create *à rebours*. This is why, for instance, the New Woman was recognized as a full participant in the *fin de siècle* revolt against nature. A yellow aster was, after all, nothing more (or less) than the New Woman's green carnation. Whether the irritable dismissal of Nature's inventive power was pronounced by a J. A. M. Whistler or a Hadria, whether the self-consciously experimental life was led by a Dorian Gray or a Gwen Waring, avant-garde writers were seeking to violate established notions of nature and the 'natural' in order to recover and legitimize for art precisely that realm of private, self-ironic, and visceral experience which the bawdy of Joyce, the phallic consciousness of

Lawrence, and the confessionalism of Lowell and Plath would so fully explore in the next century.

As the *fin de siècle* revolt against nature was thus at another level a revolt against established culture, this rejection of culture by culture – by the fastidious scholars of literary decadence and by the boldly learned ladies of New Woman fiction – expressed the fundamental desire of the *fin de siècle* avant-garde: the dream of living beyond culture, the dream of pastoral. Though we may perhaps be surprised to find the decadent, that lingering, overbred flower of culture, rejecting culture, Poggioli reminds us that the decadent characteristically believes he can overthrow civilization or acquiesce in its overthrow because he himself is all the culture he needs. This *fin de siècle* ideal of a shapely and fully expressive self-sufficiency is what we encounter in the deep admiration of Whitman and Thoreau voiced by writers like Wilde, Johnson, Symonds, Ellis, and Yeats, and we discover it as well in the powerful appeal that Rimbaud possessed for Dowson: 'le grand déclassé,' as Dowson called him, 'so consistent in his social hatred that he threw away his identity & dropped finally into the crowd just when he was at the zenith of his success' (*Letters*, 144). The words, we now recognize, would come to apply to Wilde as well.

The desire to throw identity away and live beyond culture lies at the center and is the explanation of such obscure longings as are felt in the many utopian novels of the nineties and after, and in the Romany worship of George Borrow and Augustus John. It is at the center, as well, of New Woman fiction, as when it makes Lyndall, finally acceding to her lover's passion, say to him, 'I will not go down country . . . I will not go to Europe. You must take me to the Transvaal. That is out of the world' (*African Farm*, 239). It prompts Hippolyta's suburban idyll of anonymity as 'Mrs. Malcolm.' It makes Gwen Waring say, 'Sir Humphrey, I wish quite intensely, we were both of us in another position, in quite a low, unknown one, then we need not marry' (*Aster*, II, 56). It is heard when Jessamine, musing upon her peasant's ignorance of her true social position, says to herself, 'I am in a sort his creation. I am just what I would be if he were Adam and I Eve. All the rest seems to fall away' (*A Superfluous Woman*, II, 95). It is the voice from Yeats's little house 'of clay and wattles made' and the voice from Johnson's 'Morfydd.'

In light of the antagonistic relation of the avant-garde to late-Victorian culture, the New Woman's prominence in this catalog is scarcely surprising. Her fierce insistence on a renovation of the sexual relationship becomes, in this context, the very epitome of the *fin de siècle* desire to live beyond culture. This is why, for instance, Whitman and 'Whitmania,' though they are scarcely mentioned in New Woman fiction, were so persistently invoked by *Punch* to explain the New Woman phenomenon: not only had the poet of 'barbaric yawp' hymned the new primitivism sought by the decadent spirit, he had promised simultaneously that sex – whether it was the 'amativeness' of men and women or the 'adhesiveness' of men and men – would be the means by which conventional culture would be transcended.

Among 'decadent' writers, the issue was made more complicated by a typical and powerful impulse to self-parody. We are dealing with mockery of the notion that a newly expressive sexual impulse would allow the 'decadent' to live and create beyond culture when, for instance, Aubrey Beardsley in his pornographic travesty, *The Story of Venus and Tannhäuser*, introduces into an Arcadian valley Sporion and his debauched crew, 'hoping to experience a new frisson in the destruction of some shepherd's or some satyr's naiveté,' only to have the sophisticates themselves corrupted by the newly instructed peasants who, 'full of the new tricks they had learnt that morning . . . played them passionately and roughly, making havoc of the cultured flesh.'[27] In the same spirit, Dowson satirized a new artistic colony proposed by some friends, predicting it would be 'à la Thoreau, of "Hobby Horse" people & a few elect outsiders each with a "belovèd" – (please mind the accent) where there will be leisure only for art & unrestrained sexual intercourse' (*Letters*, 46).

The typically 'decadent' posture of self-parody, however, cannot at such moments obscure the essential seriousness of the attempt to transcend established culture through sex. Even though Dowson, who at this time was trying to recruit a purely 'spiritual mistress taken from one of the classes outside Society' (*Letters*, 45), doubted the efficacy of unrestrained intercourse in achieving this end, he firmly agreed that 'no "belovèd" is admissible who has breathed the poisonous atmosphere of a drawing-room' (*Letters*, 46). And this desire to transcend established culture by turning to lovers – spiritual or otherwise – from the classes outside accepted society would, of course, intensify in the next century, coloring the imaginations of such figures as Ford's Tietjens, Forster's Maurice, Eliot's Prufrock, Joyce's Stephen as well as most of the characters of Lawrence.

No less did the heroines of New Woman fiction understand the power of the sexual impulse to alter, or if need be, overthrow conventional culture. Lyndall yearns for a world freed from the hateful constriction of sexual identity, a world where she may say, 'When I am with you, I never know that I am a woman and you are a man; I only know that we are both things that think' (*African Farm*, 210). Grant Allen's Herminia, in *The Woman Who Did*, immolates the present upon the pyre of the future, fervently believing that if she can sacrifice her own 'respectability,' her daughters and granddaughters will live free. And for a brief, abandoned moment, Jessamine sweeps everything – even the future – away, crying, 'I care for nothing! I care for nothing! There is no meaning anywhere –

save *this*. What was I born for if this is wrong?' (*A Superfluous Woman*, II, 190). Jessamine, oblivious to everything but the urgency of her passion, is unaware that behind her there is 'an old world in collapse, with faint thunders of falling cities.'

An old world in collapse, with faint thunders of falling cities – this is the vision of social apocalypse that impelled the enemies of the avant-garde to identify, with a clairvoyance born of deep cultural anxiety, the New Woman and the decadent as twin avatars of the 'New.' And it was the vision that animated the New Woman and the decadent as well: thrust by the antinomian claims of their experimental energies into the breach between the apocalyptic ruins of the old and the barely imaginable world of the 'New,' they saw themselves as the very emblems of the *fin de siècle* avant-garde. If their repudiation of late-Victorian culture, their embrace of the vulgar, the ugly, and the unnatural, finally failed to bring about the new primitivism they so fervently sought, they were not mistaken about the apocalypse they prophesied. Only now, gazing backwards at the *fin de siècle* from a point well beyond the modernist moment, do we glimpse them as apostles of a world they could only imagine.

Notes

1. See ELLEN MOERS, *The Dandy: Brummel to Beerbohm* (New York: Viking, 1960); and JOSEPH STEIN, 'The New Woman and the Decadent Dandy,' *Dalhousie Review*, 55 (1975), 54–62. For an informative account of New Woman fiction, see A. R. CUNNINGHAM, 'The "New Woman Fiction" of the 1890's,' *Victorian Studies*, 17 (1973), 177–86. CUNNINGHAM's *The New Woman and the Victorian Novel* (New York: Barnes and Noble, 1978) will include chapters on New Woman popular fiction, on Hardy, and on Meredith and Gissing, Lloyd Fernando's *'New Women' in the Late Victorian Novel* (University Park: Pennsylvania State Univ. Press, 1977) treats New Woman themes and characters in the works of George Eliot, Meredith, Moore, Gissing, and Hardy. ELAINE SHOWALTER, in *A Literature of Their Own: British Women Novelists from Brontë to Lessing* (Princeton: Princeton Univ. Press, 1977), considers Olive Schreiner, Sarah Grand, and George Egerton as feminist authors who 'had but one story to tell, and exhausted themselves in its narration' (ch. 7). It will be useful to remember that not all New Woman novels were written by feminists. A number of novels discussed in the following pages were meant by their authors to portray the New Woman's dangerous limitations or self-delusion. Such hostile or qualified characterizations of the New Woman, however, are nonetheless significant expressions of the pervasive cultural anxiety which this essay takes as its subject.
2. Dowson's annotations were preserved by VICTOR PLARR and published in his *Ernest Dowson 1888–1897: Reminiscences, Unpublished Letters and Marginalia* (London: Elkin Matthews, 1914). See also *The Letters of Ernest Dowson*, ed. DESMOND POWER and HENRY MAAS (Rutherford, N.J.: Fairleigh Dickinson Univ. Press, 1967), p. 10, hereafter cited as *Letters* in my text.

3. 'Preface to the Second Edition,' *The Story of an African Farm* (Harmondsworth: Penguin, 1971), p. 27.

4. 'The Strike of a Sex,' *Quarterly Review*, 179 (1894), 289–318.

5. *Marriage Questions in Modern Fiction, and Other Essays on Kindred Subjects* (London and New York: John Lane, 1897), p. 28. CHAPMAN's book was one of three published in a feminist 'Eve's Library' series by the *tendenz* publisher John Lane.

6. 'Tommyrotics,' *Blackwood's Edinburgh Magazine*, June 1895, p. 841.

7. *The New Antigone: A Romance*, 3 vols (London and New York: Macmillan, 1887), III, pp. 183, 184.

8. *The Heavenly Twins* (New York: Cassell, 1893), p. 450. 'Sarah Grand' was the pseudonym of FRANCES ELIZABETH MCFALL.

9. *A Superfluous Woman*, 3 vols (London: Heinemann, 1894), II, p. 89.

10. 'The Apple and the Ego of Woman,' *Westminster Review*, 131 (1889), 377.

11. 'Socio-Literary Portents,' *Speaker*, 22 Dec. 1894, p. 684.

12. ELLA HEPWORTH DIXON, *The Story of a Modern Woman* (New York: Cassell, 1894), p. 166.

13. *Punch, or the London Charivari*, 2 June 1894, p. 256. ELIZABETH CHAPMAN, in *Marriage Questions*, protested the persistent disparagement of women in *Punch*: 'in an organ which takes thought for the poor; which champions the down-trodden . . . [woman] sees herself mirrored as harsh and sour and prudish and physically repulsive – a gaunt, ill-dressed, sexless monster *pour rire*' (p. 85).

14. 'The Anti-Marriage League,' *Blackwood's Edinburgh Magazine*, Jan. 1896, pp. 136–7.

15. 'A Dominant Note of some Recent Fiction,' *Westminster Review*, 142 (1894), 543.

16. 'The Fiction of Sexuality,' *Contemporary Review*, April 1895, pp. 493–4.

17. *Retrospective Reviews: A Literary Log*, 2 vols (London: John Lane, 1896), I, p. 231.

18. *Marcella*, 2 vols (New York and London: Macmillan, 1894), I, p. 145.

19. 'A Defense of Cosmetics,' *Yellow Book*, I (1894), 78.

20. *Gallia* (London: Methuen, 1895), p. 214.

21. *A Yellow Aster*, 3 vols (London: Hutchinson, 1894), II, 87. 'Iota' was the pseudonym of KATHLEEN MANNINGTON CAFFYN.

22. TROLL-BOROSTYANI's *Die Gleichstellung der Geschlechter* (1888) and *Das Recht der Frau, Vermächtniss einer Unglücklichen* (1885) were published in Zurich and reviewed by W. F. Barry in 'The Strike of a Sex.'

23. *Studies in the Psychology of Woman*, trans. Georgia A. Etchinson (Chicago and New York: Herbert S. Stone, 1899), p. 301.

24. See RAYMOND F. BETTS, 'The Allusion to Rome in British Imperialist Thought of the Late Nineteenth and Early Twentieth Centuries,' *Victorian Studies*, 15 (1971), 149–59. For an optimistic contemporary view of the analogy, see C. DALE, 'The Women of Imperial Rome and English Women of To-day,' *Westminster Review*, 141 (1894), 490–502.

25. *The New Spirit* (London: George Bell, 1890), p. 9.

26. *The Theory of the Avant-Garde*, trans. GERALD FITZGERALD (Cambridge, Mass.: Harvard Univ. Press, 1968) and 'Qualis Artifex Pereo! or Barbarism and Decadence,' *Harvard University Library Bulletin*, 13 (1959), 135–59.

27. *The Story of Venus and Tannhäuser* (London: Leonard Smithers, 1907), pp. 50, 53.

5 Psychopathia Sexualis: Stevenson's *Strange Case**

STEPHEN HEATH

Stephen Heath is a Fellow of Jesus College, Cambridge and has been influential in disseminating the ideas and methodologies of the French structuralist critic Roland Barthes, both through his translation of Barthes' work, and through his own critical practice. He has had a long association with the British journal of film theory, *Screen*, and with its left-leaning, psychoanalytic semiotics. He has written extensively on literary representation as part of a discourse on sexuality (see, for example, *The Sexual Fix*, London: Macmillan, 1982). In the essay reproduced below Heath examines the narrative structure and the narrative exclusions or silences of Stevenson's well-known tale, which he reads as symptomatic of both a crisis in cultural values (particularly in relation to the conceptualisation of the civilised) and a crisis in the representation of masculinity and sexuality (see Introduction, pp. 9–10).

> There is something almost impertinent in the way . . . in which Mr Stevenson achieves his best effects without the aid of the ladies, and 'Dr Jekyll' is a capital example of his heartless independence.
>
> Henry James[1]

The first incident that is reported to us in Stevenson's *Strange Case of Dr Jekyll and Mr Hyde* (1886) as an indication of Hyde's 'furious propensity to ill' (p. 90)[2] concerns 'a girl of maybe eight or ten' who collides with him in the street one night: 'the two ran into one another naturally enough at the corner; and then came the horrible part of the thing; for the man trampled calmly over the child's body and left her screaming on the ground' (p. 31). A number of contemporary readers were dissatisfied with this: 'the first incident which is meant to show the diabolical character of Mr Hyde is inadequate', commented the anonymous reviewer in *The Athenaeum*.[3] On

*Reprinted from *Critical Quarterly*, 28 (1986), pp. 93–108

the face of it there is no reason why such an attack on a child would not qualify as 'diabolical', but it is indeed clear that inadequacy was felt, and in the text itself whose difficulties of *vraisemblance* are immediately symptomatic: what exactly was the little girl doing running through the streets at 'about three o'clock of a black winter morning' with 'all the folks asleep' (p. 37)? Enfield, who gives the report quoted above, is himself uneasy about its effect: 'It sounds nothing to hear, but it was hellish to see' (p. 31). On the face of it, again, it would sound something to hear; the report in the text, however, has no confidence and so it can end up sounding nothing, prompting Enfield's unease. A similar problem arises with the only other such reported incident, the Carew murder, another trampling in the street. The violence is more marked, now we *are* to hear and see something ('the bones were audibly shattered and the body jumped upon the roadway', p. 47), but the figure of the victim, 'an aged and beautiful gentleman with white hair' (p. 46), is also somehow unlikely, still not quite right (the same difficulties of *vraisemblance*: he too is only doubtfully found late at night near the river, unsure of his way). There is a suggestion of anachronism – 'such an innocent and old-world kindness of disposition' (p. 46), as though one of the Cheeryble brothers has lived on into the wrong book and is being punished for his pains.

A girl of eight or ten, and then an aged and beautiful gentleman . . . With the former in mind, Hopkins wrote to Bridges: 'the trampling scene is perhaps a convention: he [Stevenson] was thinking of something unsuitable for fiction'.[4] Random violence, in other words, has replaced a sexual drive which it thus serves to express; the nocturnal settings, the not-quite-rightness, the feeling of some inadequacy are so many signs of this (the little girl and the gentleman really should not be where they are in the text). Stevenson would no doubt have protested to Hopkins as he protested elsewhere: 'people are so filled full of folly and inverted lust, that they can think of nothing but sexuality'; for him, 'the beast Hyde' who is let out 'is no more sensual than another, but . . . is the essence of cruelty and malice, and selfishness and cowardice: and these are the diabolic in man'.[5] The protest has a kind of self-defeating truth: if people are so filled full of folly and inverted lust, this must be central for what Hyde represents, all those 'lower elements' (p. 83); and when Jekyll first tries his experiment, he is indeed conscious before all else of 'a current of disordered sensual images running like a mill race in [his] fancy' (p. 83). The violence itself is a convention, as Hopkins says, but this means too that it is significant, precisely a representation; it fits sexuality for the story, reflects the terms of understanding and argument, the very *case* that is made (so the violence is *conventionally* random: equally, the little girl and the gentleman really should be where they are in the text).

The little girl is one of the very few female references in a story that does, in James's words, 'without the aid of the ladies'. These references themselves moreover remain brief, keeping women very much in the story's margins: a group of women 'wild as harpies' after Hyde had attacked the girl (p. 32); 'a maid-servant living alone' who witnesses the Carew murder (p. 46); women in the streets of Soho and the woman who keeps Hyde's lodgings there (pp. 48–9); Jekyll's housemaid who breaks into 'hysterical whimpering' (pp. 63–4); and finally a woman street-vendor whom, we learn in a passing sentence at the end of the book, Hyde strikes when she offers him her wares ('He smote her in the face, and she fled', p. 94). All these women are simply found in the streets or are glimpsed as servants of one kind or another; the brevity of their appearance goes along with their lowness of class which itself in turn runs into their marginalisation in the given middle-class male story-world. James was more than right: there are indeed no *ladies*, no women who could enter the story, play a part. The female is shut out, a thing of the streets which then take on this femaleness. On their weekly Sunday ramble, Enfield and Utterson see streets as women: 'the shop fronts stood along that thoroughfare with an air of invitation, like rows of smiling saleswomen. Even on Sunday, when it veiled its more florid charms and lay comparatively empty of passage, the street shone out in contrast to its dingy neighbourhood, like a fire in a forest' (p. 30). The last image has the presence of one of the dream symbols Freud was to analyse a few years later – in Dora's second dream, for example – and the phrase 'lay comparatively empty of passage', after the smiling saleswomen and the veiling of the more florid charms, brings a certain suggestive ambiguity, itself comes 'with an air of invitation': the male passenger's – or reader's – eye is 'instantly caught' (p. 30).

The maleness of the story's world is evident: Jekyll and Hyde, of course, and also 'Mr Utterson the lawyer' whose portrait opens the first chapter and 'Mr Richard Enfield, his distant kinsman, the well-known man about town' (p. 29), and also Utterson and Jekyll's friend 'the great Dr Lanyon' (p. 36); these are the principals, the story's narrators and actors – two doctors, a lawyer, a man about town, and then Hyde, 'the fiend' (p. 85). None of them in the story has anything to do with women and there are no equal women: Jekyll has had 'pleasures' and been guilty of 'irregularities' (p. 81) but has no wife; Hyde has lodgings in Soho but we know only the incidents already mentioned; Utterson lives in 'his bachelor house' (p. 35) and Enfield and Lanyon too are apparently celibate. The world here is that of Jekyll's 'pleasant dinners [given] to some five or six old cronies, all intelligent reputable men, and all judges of good wine' (p. 43). The main – the only – affection is the 'bond' between Enfield and Utterson (p. 29) who count their silent Sunday walks as 'the chief jewel of each week' (p. 30). In this context the dedication of the story makes every sense. Stevenson dedicates it to a woman, his cousin Katherine de Mattos (*née* Stevenson), with a snatch of

verse about 'home', 'the north countrie', and 'the bands that God decreed
to bind' and that it is 'ill to loose', a wish to be still as of old – 'Still will
we be the children of the heather and the wind' (p. 28). The story is sent
to Katherine 'by the one that loves you – Jekyll, and not Hyde'[6] but the
story sent is then Hyde, and not Jekyll: not heather and wind and the
broom 'blowing bonnie' (p. 28) but streets and doors and locked rooms;
not children, not the Katherine of Louis's childhood, but the immediate
assault on the child, the little girl left screaming in the opening pages.
The only woman is outside the story, lost, a dedication and its memory.

Getting to the story, having it told, is complicated, far from easy. First
the title, *Strange Case of Dr Jekyll and Mr Hyde*, then the dedication. 'To
Katherine de Mattos', with its accompanying verse, then the opening
chapter, 'Story of the door', with which story the story begins. Nothing
that follows, however, goes quite so simply and the reader is surely
struck by the extent to which the story is overrun by its narration, the
latter strangely present as what the story is about. The basic narrative is
one of discovery, that of the double identity Jekyll–Hyde, repeating
something of Jekyll's own initial recognition of 'the thorough and
primitive duality of man' (p. 82), and the organising image for this
narrative is the breaking down of doors, learning the secret behind them;
thus we move from the 'Story of the door' that Enfield recounts to
Utterson as they stand before the door in question, the sinister
back-entrance to Jekyll's house, 'equipped with neither bell nor knocker'
(p. 30), to the final assault on Jekyll's laboratory, 'the wreck of the door
fell inwards' (p. 69). At the same time, the narration is an entanglement
of wills, letters, accounts, a whole series of precautions in telling, so
many 'enclosures' in and round the story, adapting a word that appears
both when Utterson opens the envelope from the now dead Lanyon
('Within there was another enclosure . . .', p. 58) and when he unseals the
packet that is found with Hyde's body after the breaking down of the
laboratory door ('several enclosures fell to the floor', p. 72). Before
Utterson can read 'Henry Jekyll's full statement of the case', which he
has in his hand, he must first return home to read 'Dr Lanyon's
narrative', and when he had the latter in his hand, he was unable to read
it until Jekyll's death . . .

For the story these precautions are justified: doors are broken down
but everything must be enclosed, discovering and telling the secret are
perilous. Utterson seeks knowledge from the great Dr Lanyon: ' "If any
one knows, it will be Lanyon," he had thought' (p. 36); but when Lanyon
– the any one – knows, he dies: ' "I have had a shock," he said, "and I
shall never recover" . . . in something less than a fortnight he was dead'
(pp. 57–8). Jekyll himself dies of the story, racing to finish his statement,
getting it over quickly, bringing it and the story and himself and the
reader to an end: 'Nor must I delay too long to bring my writing to an

end; for if my narrative has hitherto escaped destruction, it has been by a combination of great prudence and great good luck . . . Here, then, as I lay down the pen, and proceed to seal up my confession, I bring the life of that unhappy Henry Jekyll to an end' (pp. 96–7). Safety lies in silence, the virtue of Enfield and Utterson's bond ('they said nothing', p. 30). Writing is a risk but necessary, the vehicle of a knowledge that needs enclosures, something that must be told but must also have protections in the telling.

So what is at stake in this strange-case story? Stevenson, in a subsequent essay on dreams, described clearly his aim to express 'that strong sense of man's double being which must at times come in upon and overwhelm the mind of every thinking creature', referring directly to his own experience when a student, to the feeling he then had from his dreams of leading 'a double life – one of the day, one of the night'.[7] Exactly in these terms, Jekyll-and-Hyde has become a stock reference for the idea of 'a profound duplicity' in every individual human being (p. 81), that 'thorough and primitive duality in man'. 'My devil had been long caged,' says Jekyll, 'he came out roaring' (p. 90): Hyde is Jekyll's reverse identity, the same man but with a different side ascendant; just as his handwriting is identical with Jekyll's but differently sloped, 'a rather singular resemblance' (p. 55). The names are significant enough, with their letters too in mirror image like the handwriting, *e y* / *y e*: *Jekyll*, the I, the *je*, that kills represses *Hyde*, the hidden, the inner he – 'He, I say – I cannot say, I' (p. 94) – that destroys the unity and the identity of the I, of me; Freud's *Es* or id as his English translators will say and as *Hyde* already suggests, giving the *yd* in the middle of the *he*. I cannot say *I* because I am split, am a unity only in the imaginary, as in the decent healthy representations of Utterson, Enfield, Lanyon, the enclosures that can no longer hold, that the story ends. And Stevenson gestures towards Freud, towards the work going on and to come, perfectly envisageable as he writes his story: 'Others will follow, others will outstrip me on the same lines; and I hazard the guess that man will be ultimately known for a mere polity of multifarious, incongruous and independent denizens . . .' (p. 82).[8] Hyde, moreover, is explicitly described in his undermining of Jekyll's identity in terms of a transgression of the law of the father: 'Jekyll had more than a father's interest; Hyde had more than a son's indifference' (p. 89). As the story runs out, Jekyll recounts Hyde's final attacks: 'scrawling in my own hand blasphemies on the pages of my books, burning the letters and destroying the portrait of my father' (p. 96). No more portrait, no more of the father's word; only the mirror in which Jekyll sees in himself the appearance of Hyde, 'that ugly idol in the glass' (p. 84), only the text and what, for all the enclosures, it reveals.

So far so good. This *Strange Case of Dr Jekyll and Mr Hyde* can stand as one of those works in which the unconscious is glimpsed but not heard, an example of the challenge to 'the very fortress of identity' (p. 83) in the latter part of the nineteenth century, contemporary with von Hartmann, Nietzsche and so on whose ideas could be made to provide parallels with Stevenson's version of the human duality. Jekyll's I is overwhelmed by what lies beneath it, by its inner fissures and depths, but this underconsciousness is then only representable as darkness and animality, 'the beast Hyde' with all his 'ape-like' tricks (pp. 47, 96, 97). The reader, 'every thinking creature', can then recognise himself in this telling of 'man's double being', finds his own Hyde (we need to keep to the text's conventional male generalisations here); thus Hopkins: 'You are certainly wrong about Hyde being overdrawn: my Hyde is worse'.[9] As for what this recognition might involve, Stevenson, as we have seen, plays down sexuality, the problem is hypocrisy: 'The harm was in Jekyll, because he was a hypocrite . . . The hypocrite let out the beast Hyde'.[10] But not just in Jekyll, rather in Jekyll in society: it is the desire 'to carry [his] head high' and to stand with grave countenance 'before the public' that leads him to 'a profound duplicity of life' (p. 81). Or as Freud will put it some twenty years later: 'Experience teaches us that for most people there is a limit beyond which their constitution cannot comply with the demands of civilization. All who wish to be more noble-minded than their constitution allows fall victims to neurosis; they would have been more healthy if it could have been possible for them to be less good'.[11] Indeed, Stevenson's world in the *Strange Case of Dr Jekyll and Mr Hyde* is very much that of Freud's ' "Civilized" sexual morality and modern nervous illness' (1908), the essay from which that previous quotation was drawn, and of all the other discussions of sexual–social standards that are rife in the last decades of the nineteenth century. The argument for Stevenson too is about harm, the harm done by a false morality and *its* ideas of harm: there is 'none – no harm whatever – in what prurient fools calls "immorality" ', nothing 'diabolic' in 'this poor wish to have a woman, that they make such a cry about'.[12] Later, in his dying years, Stevenson returned to the question: 'If I had to begin again . . . I believe I should try to honour Sex more religiously. The worst of our education is that Christianity does not recognize and hallow Sex. It looks askance at it, over its shoulder, oppressed as it is by reminiscences of hermits and Asiatic self-tortures.'[13] The sexual, in other words, is not a problem, the problem is everything else – social attitudes, morality, hypocrisy.

The negation here, exactly what the story is telling, is male sexuality, taken for granted and repressed in the one operation, simply 'this poor wish to have a woman'. But then a woman is also just what is excluded from the story, making it strange (and prompting James's comment); all we have is the childhood cousin in the wings of the dedication, plus a few supernumeraries, the servants and the harpies in the street. The negation of male sexuality goes along with the exclusion of a woman. In the overall system of sexuality that is tightened to perfection in the nineteenth century, male sexuality is repetition, unquestioned; female sexuality is query, riddle, enigma. Or, to put it another way, increased awareness of and attention to matters of identity and sexual identity, including direct challenges to the fixed terms and assumptions of 'man' and 'woman' (by developing women's movements, for example), gives a problem of representation the working out of which is done by shifting the problem on to the woman ('What does woman want?', to use Freud's famous question from within the perspective of this shift) and thus safeguarding the man (men are men and there is little else to say). Difference must be maintained and dealt with on *her*, not brought back onto him; 'the two sexes' are clear and simultaneously all the difficulty is with the woman, male sexuality then figuring as the truly unspeakable at the same time that it represents itself – covers itself – in the continual refurbishment of those terms and assumptions of 'man' and 'woman'. In *Jude the Obscure* (1895), Hardy looks at Sue, 'the new woman' of the period (this appellation is already a containing response to feminist refusals of conventions of female identification), as an alienation of womanhood, the womanhood of the contrasting Arabella: where the latter is 'a complete and substantial female animal', the former is 'ethereal', 'boyish', 'not a woman', having all the symptoms of hysteria, the modern nervous illness of the confusion of sexual identity.[14] No marriage laws could have solved Sue's problems since she is the problem, her identity as a woman, her sexuality. Thus Edmund Gosse, himself a friend and collaborator of Stevenson's, could write, catching up the contemporary concern with sexuality and its terms: 'Arabella is the excess of vulgar normality; every public bar and village fair knows Arabella, but Sue is a strange and unwelcome product of exhaustion. The *vita sexualis* of Sue is the central concern of the book, and enough is told about it to fill the specimen tables of a German specialist.'[15] As against which, Jude, though sharing his cousin Sue's 'sensitiveness', is normally male (the male *is* normal), subject, of course, to 'animal passion for a woman' (Stevenson's 'poor wish'),[16] this being a natural, if possibly regrettable, fact of man's being. Jude's problems are thus social, to do with class and education, and female, to do with Arabella who seduces him, mediating 'the unvoiced call of woman to man', and with Sue, the 'conundrum' of sexual identity he cannot solve.[17] None of this fundamentally touches Jude and male sexuality which is guaranteed by fixing Sue as the problem and which can be simply recorded, the usual repetition of terms, as basic 'instinct', however much Jude, bent on a life of the mind, may feel such an instinct to involve 'degradation' and bemoan his 'erotolepsy'.[18] It is not Jude but Sue who is the case for the German medical–sexological specialist and has the *vita sexualis*; and the difference of Stevenson's text, its strange case, is that it gives up any Sue and is about sexuality nevertheless, male sexuality – unquestionable, unrepresentable, but glimpsed all the same as a question of representation in this Jekyll-and-Hyde story.

'All who wish to be more noble-minded than their constitution allows fall victims to neurosis', wrote Freud, as we saw above, discussing civilised sexual morality and modern nervous illness; and Jekyll indeed wished 'to carry [his] head high'. The *Strange Case of Dr Jekyll and Mr Hyde*, however, refuses the image of neurosis and uses rather that of perversion: Jekyll's potion undoes that 'suppression of the perverse instincts' that takes place 'under the influence of education and social demands'.[19] For Freud perversion and neurosis stand in the relation of positive to negative, neurotics being a class of people who, faced with cultural requirements, have only succeeded in an apparent and increasingly unsuccessful suppression of their instincts: 'I have described the neuroses as the "negative" of the perversions because in the neuroses the perverse impulses, after being repressed, manifest themselves from the unconscious part of the mind – because the neuroses contain the same tendencies, though in a state of "repression", as do the positive perversions.'[20] Crucially, this positive/negative relation is immediately taken over by Freud into an observation of sexual difference:

> The discovery that perversions and neuroses stand in the relation of positive and negative is often unmistakeably confirmed by observations made on the members of one generation of a family. Quite frequently a brother is a sexual pervert, while his sister, who, being a woman, possesses a weaker sexual instinct, is a neurotic whose symptoms express the same inclinations as the perversions of her sexually more active brother. And correspondingly, in many families the men are healthy, but from a social point of view immoral to an undesirable degree, while the women are high-minded and over-refined, but severely neurotic.[21]

Which we can restate in the terms of the system of representation, the sexuality that Freud here knows as his social reality, as the complementary contrast of Sue Bridehead and Henry Jekyll as Edward Hyde. Excluding women, Stevenson loses the key to the stable representation of men (she is ill, not him). The generically enclosed world of the adventure story can make up for this (the Stevenson of *Treasure Island*, significantly then a story for *boys*, published in *Young Folks*) but the result is also the fascination with the double, men as unstable, something else; a fascination of which the *Strange Case of Dr Jekyll and Mr Hyde* is evidently the prime example.

The book takes its precautions, sets its enclosures: catching at a difficult recognition of male sexuality as problematic and not just untroublingly given, it continually goes back over the terms of the given system of representation, works with its problems. Mention was made earlier of the inadequacy of the incidents designed to characterise Hyde's behaviour and mark the nature of his monstrosity but their representational adequacy must now also be noted. Hyde tramples over a little girl and does the same to a benign old gentleman whom he clubs to death: the first is a central Victorian male investment in and fixation of the female (the female without the woman, a *ruly* body, without trouble for men); the second a central Victorian celebration of the patriarch, the benevolent paternalism of the male (the male without the man, an authoritative image of order, the serenity of social and family good): Little Nell and Mr Cheeryble both . . . The two are beaten out of the story as it turns to the other side of the man Jekyll, as though they no longer have a place but with nothing to put in their place, so that there they are anyway in the story's path, all it can say, and yet they not saying – the felt inadequacy – what it is implicating itself in saying.

For what can Stevenson say in his story of male sexuality? The answer is Hyde, the hidden of Jekyll, the he under I. And of Hyde Stevenson can only say that it is a matter of hypocrisy, Hyde as creation of civilised sexual morality, which is to forget the stress on 'man's double being', on that as essential. Hyde is beyond neurosis, the civilised sexual representation crucially developed round women; though Jekyll in Hyde (or Hyde before he gains his irreversible domination) is heard 'Weeping like a woman or a lost soul' (p. 69) and seen 'wrestling against the approaches of the hysteria' (p. 78), as if traces of that known representation, its morality, could still redeem the situation. What he has, what comes out, is the 'furious propensity to ill', which is all that Stevenson in the story can finally say: the idea of the hidden, this 'hyding', is also the hidden as representation. Breaking down the doors, entering the secret room, leads only to all those precautionary writings of which this story is the chief. Unsurprisingly, the *Strange Case of Dr Jekyll and Mr Hyde* has its own precautionary history, is itself a substitute or replacement writing: the version we have is the rewrite of one written on waking from a dream – 'a hectic fever following a hemorrhage of the lungs, culminated in the dream of Jekyll and Hyde' – and cast into the fire after comments from Stevenson's wife Fanny;[22] and it is also the second attempt at a story on 'man's double being', coming after one entitled *The Travelling Companion* which was 'returned by an editor on the plea that it was a work of genius and indecent' and which was again burned by Stevenson.[23]

The secret behind the door is a dead secret, Jekyll and Hyde are gone and Utterson is left with his enclosures: Lanyon's terror at 'the moral turpitude that man unveiled to me' ('What he told me . . . I cannot bring my mind to set on paper', p. 80), Jekyll's abbreviated statement and confession ('It is useless . . . to prolong this description', p. 96). What

Jekyll states and confesses are some common themes from late nineteenth-century thinking that Freud will share too: the overvaluation of consciousness, the ego as façade, the conflict of instinct and civilisation, the force of aggressive drives. In its very imagery Freud's account of the super-ego and conscience has much to connect with Stevenson's story's terms: 'Civilization . . . obtains mastery over the individual's dangerous desire for aggression by weakening and disarming it and by setting up an agency within him to watch over it, like a garrison in a conquered city' (compare Stevenson on Jekyll's potion as attacking 'the very fortress of identity').[24] The relation of the super-ego to the father and the attribution to it of the father's power and image is matched by the interaction of Jekyll and Hyde as father and son, as well as by Jekyll's use of his own father as his point of conscience (in an aptly odd turn of phrase, Jekyll looks back to the days of childhood 'when I had walked with my father's hand', p. 91); the potion produces Hyde by annihilating the super-ego and Hyde then vents his fury on its figures – the portrait of Jekyll's father, the patriarch in the street. Sketched out in this way, however, such themes remain only general, just themes, undifferentiated, another mode of hiding.

Undifferentiation is the mode of Stevenson's formulations: 'The prim obliterated polite face of life, and the broad, bawdy, and orgiastic – or maenadic – foundations, form a spectacle to which no habit reconciles me'.[25] Yet that spectacle is forced by women, woman, procreation: the immediately preceding comment in the letter from which that statement is taken is 'as for Fanny and her brood, it is insane to think of'. The letter is written some eight years later than the *Strange Case of Dr Jekyll and Mr Hyde*, in 1894, a few weeks before Stevenson's death. But the spectacle and the reaction, the exclusion of women from the world of his writings, are always there, part of his work. To Marcel Schwob, his French translator, he writes in 1890: '*Vous ne détestez pas alors mes bonnes femmes? moi je les déteste.* I have never pleased myself with any women of mine . . .'[26] Women are a sign of something in men that it would be better not to have to think about, that erupts in the *Strange Case*, hopefully once and for all: '*Jekyll* is a dreadful thing, I own; but the only thing I feel dreadful about is that damned old business of the war in the members. This time it came out; I hope it will stay in, in future.'[27] Ironically enough, the recipient of that hope was J. A. Symonds, a homosexual suffering from the social denial of his real sexual nature, later to collaborate with Havelock Ellis for the first volume, on 'inversion', of the latter's *Studies in the Psychology of Sex* (1897). The 'strange sense of man's double being which must at times come in upon and overwhelm the mind of every thinking creature' gives us the *Strange Case of Dr Jekyll and Mr Hyde* and its posing and eliding of the issue of man, sliding as it does between male and human, between a sexual–instinctual problematic of masculinity and an undifferentiating psychological recognition of the beyond of consciousness, of ego *and* id. The story *starts* from the exclusion of the woman which is the *condition* of a questioning of the man and also its *limitation*, the specifics of difference are pulled back into general themes. The title, in fact, is misleading or, to put it another way, is itself one of the precautions and a symptom of the problem of representation: nothing about the story is really strange other than that it should be thought strange, the strange case of male sexuality is precisely unstrange by being made into this strange case which comes out of, works with the assumptions of, the given system of representation. Male sexuality is neither the foregone conclusion of an animal passion nor the horror of an unspeakable darkness but once it is envisaged within this system that is all that can be said, all that is allowed.

It is significant in this context that doctors and medical science are so important in the story, that it is indeed a *case*. Doctors, their science, guarantee order and identity in nineteenth-century representation of the personal: they know, speak and order the sexual (which has its discursive existence, is officially representable, in this medicalisation); they deal with it in women, specify the woman, contain her excess, her difference, her protest – as hysteria, for example, moving from her history to his diagnosis. Freud's radical contribution here is to unmedicalise the sexual, to produce a theory of sexuality that will implicate women and men back into their history, the human individual as a precarious construction of sexual identity. His cases then come out like stories, which is strange to him from his orthodox medical training ('it still strikes me myself as strange that the case histories I write should read like short stories');[28] but Stevenson's story can only come out like a case, mixed up with doctors and labelled strange since its question – about man, not woman – has no representation available from them. And it is thus perfectly right that in the figure of Jekyll it is, literally, the doctor who cracks up.

What can we see in all this is Stevenson's closeness to his age. It is at the end of the nineteenth century that is begun and developed the scientific study of the human sexual. Stevenson's time is the time of the pioneer sexologists: *Strange Case of Dr Jekyll and Mr Hyde* is published in the same year as Krafft-Ebing's *Psychopathia Sexualis* whose initial recognition of 'the incompleteness of our knowledge concerning the pathology of the sexual life' might be taken as an insight into the difficulty Stevenson has in his story.[29] Much of the debate in the new sexology turned on the question of the inherited (congenitalism) or acquired (environmentalism) nature of sexual perversions and this debate was quickly recast in its terms by the emergence of a biological-developmental conception of sex derived from the theory of evolution.

Thus the vision of life, in Krafft-Ebing's work, as 'a never-ceasing duel between the animal instinct and morality', can be given a specific force: 'It is well known that under pathological circumstances, relations obliterated in higher development and absent in health, return and simulate conditions found in lower and even in primitive forms.'[30] 'Obliterated', interestingly, is Stevenson's word too, 'the prim obliterated polite face of life': the development of the human species forgets, but what is forgotten is also the foundation, underlies the development and, pathologically, can come back against it; 'the animal in man springs to the surface',[31] or 'the beast Hyde', *'ape-like'* (Stevenson's evolutionary reference-word). Everyone comments on the uncannily suggestive deformity of Hyde's appearance ('something seizing, surprising and revolting', p. 78) and his grotesque littleness ('particularly small', p. 48), his gentleman's clothes flapping off him as though foreign to his body ('this ludicrous accoutrement was far from moving me to laughter', p. 78). The depiction of Hyde in this way is Stevenson's image of the higher and the lower, of the animal that the human contains hidden, the primitive stage of the later achievement.

The new sexology begins with and from *perversions*. What it studies is the *pathology* of the sexual, and a significant area of attention is then the *criminal*–sexual. The animal in man comes in extreme to the surface in what Krafft-Ebing calls the 'Lust-Murder',[32] sexual murder in which killing replaces the sexual act, and which the sexologists will describe in Jekyll-and-Hyde terms: 'the sexual murderer does not know the sinister, bestial drive to kill that lies dormant within him, to come to life at the first unfortunate opportunity'.[33] The inadequacy of the Hyde incidents might in this light be read as their contemporary strength. These incidents are symbolically right: the little girl and the old gentleman are central representative figures as mentioned above; and they are contextually right: Stevenson moves onto the same terrain as the sexologists, finds perversions and the lust-murder – finds them as much as can be expected within the public story as opposed to the professionally enclosed scientific paper or the academic monograph with its prudent Latin. But the problem is then exactly this recourse to the pathological: the difficulty of representation is simply solved by pathology, turned into the strange case, Hyde.

Hyde is not just the hidden but also the hide of the beast that he is. The 'animal', indeed, is Stevenson's cover, what he hides in to write his story: we all have the animal in us (the phylogenetic paradigm) but the animal is a representation of the male sexual which is pathological (perversions, lust-murder). Stevenson, who does without the ladies, will thus claim gynaecocracy as ideal: 'My ideal would be the Female Clan'.[34] Of course, the only female clan of his story is the gathering of 'wild harpies' bent on tearing Hyde limb from limb, 'a circle of such hateful faces' (p. 32). Stevenson can settle nothing: the male when finally confronted is animal violence, pathological, but the female is a dream of past (Katherine) or future (the Female Clan ideal), with her presence insignificant (the supernumerary servants), heavily sensual (like the inviting streets) or more violent still (those 'hateful faces'). All that can hold our faith, just about, is the shaken but healthy identity of Utterson, Enfield, the bond of men – a kind of professional moral celibacy, being men like that. Sexology too has something of this in its beginnings, its initial representations of sexuality: as long as it remained with pathology and kept normal sexual development out of its picture, a certain stability of identity could be assured, for all the deviations. The evolutionary conception challenges this, giving the normality of the achieved civilisation a history that includes the integration and limitation of a whole number of component impulses that are themselves, therefore, perfectly normal; *and* it also allows its defence, civilisation versus the animal, the higher versus the lower.

Strange Case of Dr Jekyll and Mr Hyde has the challenge and the defence; that is its historical moment. What it cannot then have in either its story or its writing is any history, in the sense in which Freud introduces a history of the individual, of sexual identity; instead, it has in the one a mere device, the potion, and in the other an enclosing label, the 'animal'. Hysteria had served in the nineteenth century as the representation of women and of sexuality, the latter dealt with in the former. It is a male representation, men's story, but it is also women's narrative, at once because it names something *from* them and because it becomes a construction within which women speak and speak against. Juliet Mitchell talks of 'the hysteric's voice' as '*the woman's masculine language*': 'both simultaneously the woman novelist's refusal of the woman's world . . . and her construction from within a masculine world of that woman's world'.[35] Now at the end of the century Stevenson provides a text – perhaps *the* text – for the representation of men and sexuality, excluding women and so the sexual and so hysteria and then finding the only language it can for what is, therefore, the emergence of the hidden male: the animal, the criminal, *perversion*. Perversion is men's narrative and their story. When the masks of hysteria are down and the system of representation it keeps going wavers, that is what they say. Not that perversion *is* the word on male sexuality, simply there is no other representation, and this one, at least, offers a reconstruction from within a masculine world of that masculine world: perversion replaces and complements hysteria, positive to negative, maintaining male and female, man and woman, at whatever cost, as the terms of identity. A *psychopathia sexualis* is no psychoanalysis.

Two brief points – two suggestions – as a coda. First, Freud in *Civilization and its Discontents* (1930), his greatest statement on civilised sexual morality and modern nervous illness, goes over many of the themes described above, extending his own theories towards possible acceptance of 'aggressive instincts' independent of the libido: 'men are . . . creatures among whose instinctual endowments is to be reckoned a powerful share of aggressiveness'.[36] In the course of the book, man and men are the reference; women are excluded, to make only one significant return when Freud comes to consideration of love. Women stand for love, the beginning of civilisation and the menace of its disruption; the work of civilisation, 'the business of men', demands instinctual sublimations 'of which women are very little capable': 'women soon come into opposition to civilization and display their retarding and restraining influence – those very women who, in the beginning, laid the foundations of civilization by the claims of their love'.[37] What to do with women, between the ennobling Katherine and the orgiastic Fanny and her brood, that damned old business of the war in the members? From Stevenson to Freud and back, that question gives us civilisation and its discontents, a reflection on men and society, on man, a whole darkening vision of the human as male.

Second, towards the end of 1881 Stevenson began to plan a collaboration with Edmund Gosse on a series of murder papers for *The Century Magazine*, 'a retelling, in choice literary form, of the most picturesque murder cases of the last hundred years'.[38] Nothing came of the project which was abandoned some time in the following year. In 1885 Stevenson wrote *Strange Case of Dr Jekyll and Mr Hyde* with its crimes 'of singular ferocity' (p. 46) but nevertheless inadequate, not quite the truth. Three years later saw the Whitechapel murders (Whitechapel indeed 'some place at the end of the world' for an Enfield or an Utterson, p. 31): night-time lust-murders (Krafft-Ebing will discuss them as such).[39] Those murders are the real edge of Stevenson's story and they in turn will rejoin its fiction, lead back into the given representation. During their investigations, the police were conducted by a well-known medium, R. J. Lees, to what his powers told him was the murderer's home: 'Lees came to a halt in front of an impressive mansion . . . The chief inspector was crestfallen. The house they were facing was the home of a fashionable and highly respected physician.'[40] The physician's wife admitted to unexplained absences of her husband who himself admitted to losses of memory and the discovery of inexplicable blood stains on his clothing. This physician is generally identified as Sir William Gull, doctor to the Royal Family, whose daughter has confirmed the police visit and the admissions.[41] From the start the Whitechapel murders will thus include the doctor and 'double being' in their story, but the point here is that Stevenson in *his* fiction, whatever the inadequacy felt, gets it right – the imbrication of the male sexual, the criminal, the medical, the terror at night in the London streets, as an available reality for the contemporary imagination. The world of men is the higher world of stability and value, of civilisation indeed, but the male in men is darkness and so pathology and so a lower form; the world of women is love and ideal, but the female in women is Sex unhallowed, the fact of sexuality and its challenge to stability and value: in that tourniquet of doubt and vengefulness, exclusion and horror, Stevenson fashions his story. The success of the book was assured: it became the stock reference it had to be.

Notes

1. HENRY JAMES, 'Robert Louis Stevenson', *The Century Magazine* vol. XXXV, no. 6 (April 1888), p. 878.
2. ROBERT LOUIS STEVENSON, *The Strange Case of Dr Jekyll and Mr Hyde and Other Stories* ed. Jenni Calder (Harmondsworth: Penguin English Library, 1979). All quotations are from this edition and page references are given in brackets in the text. The title of the first edition was *Strange Case of Dr Jekyll and Mr Hyde* (i.e. without an initial definite article) and that title is here used throughout.
3. 'Our library table', *The Athenaeum* no. 3038 (16 January 1886), p. 100.
4. G.M. HOPKINS, letter to Bridges, 28 October 1886, *The Letters of Gerard Manley Hopkins to Robert Bridges* ed. C.C. Abbot (London: Oxford University Press, 1935), p. 238.
5. STEVENSON, letter to John Paul Bocock, November 1887, *Robert Louis Stevenson The Critical Heritage* ed. Paul Maixner (London: Routledge & Kegan Paul, 1981), p. 231.
6. STEVENSON, letter to Katherine de Mattos, 1 January 1886, *The Works of Robert Louis Stevenson: The Skerryvore Edition* (London: William Heinemann, 1924), vol. 28, p. 303. This letter, which accompanied a presentation copy of the story, gives an additional stanza and a title, 'Ave!', to the dedicatory poem. Two more poems to Katherine were published a year later in Stevenson's volume *Underwoods* (London: Chatto & Windus, 1887): numbers IX, pp. 17–18 ('A lover of the moorland bare'), and XIX, p. 41 ('We see you as we see a face'); much the same terms of figuration and address are to be found in these.
7. STEVENSON, 'A chapter on dreams' (1888), *Across the Plains* (London: Chatto & Windus, 1892), pp. 249, 234.
8. Stevenson seems to have had at least some direct acquaintance with contemporary psychological work. His wife records in connection with *Strange Case* that her husband 'was deeply impressed by a paper he read in a French scientific journal on sub-consciousness'; Mrs R.L. STEVENSON, 'Note', *Skerryvore Edition* vol. 4, pp. xviix–viii.
9. HOPKINS, letter to Bridges, 28 October 1886, p. 238.
10. STEVENSON, letter to John Paul Bocock, November 1887, p. 231.
11. SIGMUND FREUD, ' "Civilized" sexual morality and modern nervous illness', *The Standard Edition of the Complete Psychological Works of Sigmund Freud* (London: Hogarth Press, 1953–74), vol. IX, p. 191.
12. STEVENSON, letter to John Paul Bocock, November 1887, p. 231.
13. STEVENSON, letter to R.A.M. (Bob) Stevenson, September 1894, *Skerryvore Edition*, vol. 30, p. 353.

14. THOMAS HARDY, *Jude the Obscure*, ed. C.H. Sisson (Harmondsworth: Penguin English Library, 1983), pp. 81, 281, 208, 429.
15. EDMUND GOSSE, 'Mr Hardy's new novel', *Cosmopolis*, vol. 1 no. 1 (January 1896), p. 67.
16. HARDY, *Jude the Obscure*, p. 139.
17. Ibid., pp. 83, 189.
18. Ibid., pp. 244, 146.
19. FREUD, ' "Civilized" sexual morality and modern nervous illness', p. 190.
20. Ibid., p. 191.
21. Ibid., pp. 191–2.
22. Mrs R.L. STEVENSON, 'Note', pp. xviii, xix-xx.
23. STEVENSON, 'A chapter on dreams', p. 250.
24. FREUD, *Civilization and its Discontents* (1930), *Standard Edition*, vol. XXI, pp. 123–4.
25. STEVENSON, letter to R.A.M. Stevenson, September 1894, p. 349.
26. STEVENSON, letter to Marcel Schwob, 19 August 1890, *Skerryvore Edition*, vol. 29, p. 198.
27. STEVENSON, letter to J.A. Symonds, spring 1886, *Skerryvore Edition*, vol. 28, p. 323.
28. FREUD, *Studies on Hysteria*, *Standard Edition*, vol. 11, p. 160.
29. R. VON KRAFFT-EBING, *Psychopathia Sexualis*, fifth edition, trans. C.G. Chaddock (Philadelphia & London: F.A. Davis, 1892), p. iv.
30. EDWARD CHARLES SPITZKA, 'Note in regard to "primitive desires" ' (1881), cit. FRANK J. SULLOWAY, *Freud, Biologist of the Mind* (London: Burnett Books, 1979), p. 292.
31. JAMES G. KIERNAN, 'Sexual perversion, and the Whitechapel murders' (1888), cit. ibid., p. 293.
32. '*Lustmord*'; KRAFFT-EBING, *Psychopathia Sexualis*, pp. 62–7.
33. MAGNUS HIRSCHFELD (1868–1935), *Sexual Anomalies and Perversions: a Summary of the Works of the Late Professor Dr Magnus Hirschfeld*, ed. Norman Haire (London: Encyclopaedic Press, 1952), p. 457; cf. HIRSCHFELD, *Geschlechtskunde* (Stuttgart: Julius Püttmann, 1930), vol. III, pp. 553f.
34. Stevenson, letter to R.A.M. Stevenson, September 1894, p. 350.
35. JULIET MITCHELL, 'Femininity, narrative and psychoanalysis', *Women: the Longest Revolution* (London: Virago, 1984), p. 290.
36. Freud, *Civilization and its Discontents*, p. 111.
37. Ibid., p. 103.
38. EDMUND GOSSE, 'Personal memories of Robert Louis Stevenson', *The Century Magazine*, vol. L, no. 3 (July 1895), p. 452, cf. STEVENSON, letters to Gosse, 26 December 1881 and 23 March 1882, *Skerryvore Edition*, vol. 28, pp. 73 and 86–7.
39. KRAFFT-EBING, *Psychopathia Sexualis*, p. 64.
40. FRED ARCHER, *Ghost Detectives: Crime and the Psychic World* (London: W.H. Allen, 1970), p. 16.
41. See THOMAS E.A. STOWELL, ' "Jack the Ripper" – a solution?', *The Criminologist*, vol. 5, no. 18 (November 1970), pp. 49–50. Stowell, in fact, argues for Gull as an accomplice rather than as the actual murderer. For the fullest account of Gull as 'Jack the Ripper', see STEPHEN KNIGHT, *Jack the Ripper: the Final Solution* (London: George G. Harrap, 1976) esp. pp. 180–210; and for the contrary view, DONALD RUMBELOW, *The Complete Jack the Ripper* (London: W.H. Allen, 1976), pp. 150–5.

6 Homosexual Scandal and Compulsory Heterosexuality in the 1890s*

RICHARD DELLAMORA

Richard Dellamora is professor of English and Cultural Studies at Trent University, Ontario. The extract reproduced below is the final chapter of his important study of sexual–aesthetic discourses in nineteenth-century England. In his book Dellamora attempts to supplement the wide-ranging accounts of nineteenth-century homosexuality provided by socio-historic gay studies (such as the work of Jeffrey Weeks), with a study of what he calls 'micropractices' which show how 'individual subjects respond at the very moments when codes of sexuality are being induced and/or imposed'.† He also aims to build on and refine Foucault's arguments on the construction of homosexuality during the nineteenth century. Like Eve Kosofsky Sedgwick (see Further Reading) Dellamora investigates desire between men, but he aims to move beyond what he sees as her female-centred view in which male–male desire is always mediated through a woman. Beginning with Tennyson and proceeding via Hopkins and Swinburne to the novels of Oscar Wilde and Thomas Hardy, Dellamora examines efforts by male writers to refashion masculine gender norms (see Introduction, pp. 10–11).

I

The phrase 'compulsory heterosexuality' is most familiar from its use in Adrienne Rich's essay, 'Compulsory Heterosexuality and Lesbian Existence,' in which she argues that feminists have often analyzed the malaise of contemporary gender roles without addressing problems inherent in the enforced induction of women into heterosexuality, an

*Reprinted from Richard Dellamora, *Masculine Desire: The Sexual Politics of Victorian Aestheticism* (Chapel Hill and London: University of North Carolina Press, 1990), pp. 193–217
†DELLAMORA, op.cit., p. 1

induction that imposes, for most, a secondary status. Rich maintains to the contrary that women need to analyze 'the institution of heterosexuality itself as a beach-head of male dominance.' In addition to this first sort of blindness, she sees a second, namely blindness to a spectrum of bonds between women. Writing from a lesbian point of view, she proposes that feminists adopt two new terms, '*lesbian existence*' and the '*lesbian continuum*.' '*Lesbian existence* suggests both the fact of the historical presence of lesbians and our continuing creation of the meaning of that existence. I mean the term *lesbian continuum* to include a range – through each woman's life and throughout history – of woman-identified experience.'[1]

Although Rich's arguments may seem remote from the sexual politics of the 1890s, they are not: first, because the advent of the science of sexology in the 1890s implements a medical discourse that gained a pervasive influence in the construction of gender relations later, and second, because both of her leading ideas have analogues in the public contest over the meaning of masculinity that takes place in the press and courts during the decade. Journalistic reviewing and reporting as well as sensational trials enabled (male) hegemonic culture to subordinate the new self-consciousness of men who desire other men. Yet these efforts, successful though they were, throw into relief by contrast a varied homosexual renaissance during the decade. To name this phenomenon, Rich's argument prompts the phrase, '[male] homosexual existence.' Similarly, one may speak of a 'homosocial continuum' or, better, of 'a male homosocial continuum.' The phrase, however, already familiar to readers of this volume, reminds gay-identified men not of the sort of shared self-recognition that Rich seeks to encourage among female readers, but rather of the processes, immanent and explicit, that stand in the way of homosexual awareness and self-identification among males. Scandal is only one, though a highly visible, process among these.

The present chapter touches on a number of scandals of the closing years of the nineteenth century: the scandals attending passage of the 1885 Act, under which Oscar Wilde was charged; the Cleveland Street scandal and the literary scandal following publication of *The Picture of Dorian Gray*; the Wilde trials themselves; and finally, the scandal associated with the appearance of Thomas Hardy's *Jude the Obscure* in book form, in November 1895, six months after the trials. During the decade, scandals provide a point at which gender roles are publicly, even spectacularly, encoded and enforced. Moreover, in the 1890s crises of gender have important connections with other institutional and ideological difficulties. In this chapter, for example, a link becomes evident between the sacrifice of homosexuals, contradictory elements within the myth of the gentleman, and the impasse in which Liberals found themselves after Gladstone's resignation in 1894. The plight of homosexuals vis-à-vis the Radical press and Liberal parliamentarians has analogues in the fate of other marginal groups that looked to the Liberals for support. Moreover, their share in the growing tendency to identify and to exclude homosexuals from male elites signals a problem posed especially for them by the ambiguous and overdetermined relation between being a Liberal and being a 'gentleman.'

Heretofore, political historians, by which I mean male political historians, have been blind to the significance of homosexual scandal in the 1890s. For example, despite the notoriety of the Wilde trials, his name is not indexed in major studies by D. A. Hamer and Peter Stansky. Yet these trials touched the very center of the establishment. A less defensive approach by historians would acknowledge the crisis of masculinity at the time. And a less pure history, which permitted itself to be contaminated by literary scandal and gossip, would recognize how anxiety about gender roles inflects a wide range of interactions. Not incidentally, and if I may adapt another phrase from Rich, revisionary history of this sort would enable historians 'to deal with' male homosexual 'existence as a reality, and as a source of knowledge and power.'[2] Again, the growth of knowledge and power attendant on public speech about male–male desire helped precipitate the reaction of 1895.

Social historians have focused on the 1890s as a time when scientists began to reinscribe natural definitions of gender differences. Sheila Jeffreys, for instance, points out that an emergent group of celibate women found its members labeled as deviant by Havelock Ellis before the end of the decade.[3] Ellis threatened to stigmatize such women as 'lesbians' by defining the word not in terms of sexual preference but in terms of gender inversion; in other words women became 'lesbians' by invading public (male) space, by living with each other and apart from men, and by working and earning in new ways. Ellis's definition countered women's struggle for emotional, professional, and economic autonomy by defining being-in-the-place-of-a-man as sexually perverse. Similarly, Jeffrey Weeks has pointed out that, despite sexologists' efforts to decriminalize homosexual behavior, their naturalizing definitions insisted on the permanent character of real manliness and womanliness while in effect bringing homosexuals under control of medical regulation.[4] These two different phenomena bring into contact the concurrent struggles of women and self-identified male homosexuals, since the same antithetical categorization that labels homosexuals 'abnormal' also entails the subordination of women in strongly differentiated roles within the family. As Weeks says, 'the concept of heterosexuality was invented (*after* the former [i.e., *after* homosexuality]) to describe, apparently, what we now call bisexuality, and then "normality."'[5] The fourth scandal treated here, which deals with publication of *Jude*, touches on new Women and lesbianism, since Hardy is aware that the characterization of Sue Bridehead implicitly raises the question of inversion. Sue's remarriage to Phillotson at the end of the novel returns her to a peculiarly perverse normalcy while her aspirations to autonomy are made to connote deviance. Hence *Jude* itself, despite Hardy's anger at the defeat of Jude and Sue, may be regarded as a virtual instance of the precipitation of the categories of 'homosexual' and 'heterosexual' at century's end. As my discussion shows, however, the scandal itself has less to do with the struggles of New Women than it has to do with stresses within male homosocial institutions.

II

Late in the century, masculine privilege was sustained by male friendships within institutions like the public schools, the older universities, the clubs, and the professions. Because, however, the continuing dominance of bourgeois males also required that they marry and produce offspring, the intensity and sufficiency of male bonding needed to be strictly controlled by homophobic mechanisms. The resulting situation was a double bind in which 'the most intimate male bonding' was prescribed at the same time that 'the remarkably cognate' homosexuality was proscribed.[6] Hardy's novel offended by touching a nerve of homophobia within London's literary clubmen. During the decade, the clubs provided a semipublic space in which 'gentlemen' might be discriminated from *Somdomites*, to use the Marquess of Queensberry's spelling. After the publication of *The Picture of Dorian Gray*, for instance, Wilde was publicly humiliated at the Crabbet Club by George Curzon, an acquaintance of his Oxford years.[7]

In the mid-Victorian period, it was not necessary to have attended public school or university in order to become a gentleman – as long as one had 'by some means ... acquired higher education or professional status.' After '1870–1 when entry to public service by privilege, purchase of army commissions and the religious tests [at university] were finally abolished,' it seemed that access to the status of gentleman was now open, at least in theory, to any bright, hardworking young man.[8] The ascendancy of bourgeois values implicit in the reforms, however, was quickly accompanied by attempts to entrench privilege within a new upper-middle-class elite. Entry into this group was henceforth to be controlled by admission to a public school. After 1880, the all-male public school reached its full development as the *open sesame* to the professions – and to Empire. Parallel with this social formation, one also finds a literature of masculine crisis in works like Robert Louis Stevenson's *The Strange Case of Dr Jekyll and Mr Hyde* (1886), Oscar Wilde's *The Picture of Dorian Gray* (1890), and Henry James's "The Beast in the Jungle" (1903).[9]

The connection between the two phenomena lies in the fact that the male homosocial structure that Sedgwick describes was inherently unstable, and this instability issued in acute crisis once 'homosexual existence' became both visible and vocal during the 1890s. In the closing years of the century, some graduates refused to relinquish the homosexual bonding (and, at times, practices) that they had encountered earlier at school. This refusal, regressive in late-Victorian terms, put in question the masculinity so carefully groomed within the schools as the visible sign of and prerequisite for the exercise of power. Fissures in masculinity also undercut male privileges within the family, privileges already under stress as a result of changing roles for women, of feminist agitation, and, in the 1890s, so-called 'New Woman' fiction.[10] In reaction to the crisis, Jeffrey Weeks notes a succession of well-orchestrated moral panics – in the 1860s, in the 1880s, and again at the time of the Wilde trials.[11] In this situation, the sexual continuum functions differently among men than among women. When Rich speaks of a 'lesbian continuum,' she means a range of woman-centered experience that bonds women across time and space, whether or not they perceive signs of deviance in that experience. Likewise the idea of a male homosocial continuum is crucial to Sedgwick's model, but in her use the attraction/repulsion of sodomy is to the fore; and even a hint of self-recognition drives 'straight' men to ostracize and oppress their self-identified male homosexual fellows.[12]

At the time of the Wilde trials, homosexual activity became a matter of concern in the highest political circles, and expedience required that Wilde be sacrificed as a substitute for more highly placed quarry in the Liberal government and the aristocracy. As I have shown in preceding chapters, there were special connections between Liberalism and self-awareness on the part of men who enjoyed sexual and emotional relations with other men. For one, there was the subterranean tradition of Utilitarian polemic on behalf of decriminalizing sexual activity between males. Originating in Bentham's unpublished writings, the tendency surfaces in the pornographic *Don Leon* at the time of the first reform bill and later in subdued fashion in Mill's *On Liberty*. In terms of personal relations, I have pointed out that at Oxford in the 1860s Old Mortality included men who were to shape both Liberal and homosexual consciousness. And I have adduced the interweaving of members of both groups at Oxford in the mid-1870s.

Apart from particular personalities, moreover, there was special reason for Liberal sensitivity to allegations of deviance. As already indicated, in the nineteenth century the idea of the 'gentleman' became an important part of bourgeois ideology. The term could be used in validating the seizure of power from the aristocracy while cloaking the ambitions of a class in the rhetoric of a moral, even seemingly democratic ideal – since anyone, regardless of initial rank, might theoretically aspire to become a gentleman. The ideal of the gentleman should be regarded as one of two myths basic to bourgeois ideology, the other being that of the Angel in the House, the ideal woman removed from the struggles of the workplace and sequestered at home.[13] Robin Gilmour sees the special value of the term 'gentleman' in the fact that it combined elements of an older social hierarchy, one of 'rank' or 'degree,' with those of the emerging order of class. The category was permeable to seepage from below, hence could accommodate the demands of a new class to be included in the distribution of power and privilege. As a traditional rank, moreover, the term implied deference from inferiors, an acquiescence essential if the bourgeoisie were to be free to subsume the demands and interests of workers within a politics directed primarily toward securing middle-class interests.[14] In the period after 1867, however, workers began to challenge this prerogative in ways that gentlemen found threatening.

The rank of gentleman was based historically in the values of the landed gentry. In the sixteenth century, a man could aspire to become a gentleman if he were engaged in one of a limited range of occupations 'which reinforced the stability of a social hierarchy based on the ownership of land.' Requisite to the rank was to be able to 'live without manual labour.'[15] This requirement, however, introduced a contradiction into the role as experienced in nineteenth-century terms. The emphasis on leisure, explicit in earlier formulations, persisted in the nineteenth century – but potentially at the expense of the middle-class husband's commitment to work. The two demands, for leisure *and* production, were at odds, a contradiction that becomes evident in a number of 1890s scandals.

Gilmour argues that Victorians attempted to resolve the conflict between the two norms precisely

> by broadening the basis of gentility in the public schools. By the last quarter of the nineteenth century it was almost universally accepted that a traditional liberal education at a reputable public school should qualify a man as a gentleman, whatever his father's origins or occupation. This had the effect of removing some of the ambiguities, but at the cost of standardising the product.[16]

The public schools inculcated 'Christian manliness,' an approach to masculinity closely associated with the Broad Church movement. In a book-length study, Norman Vance has shown how Victorian churchmen attempted to form a clerisy whose plan of action combined a belief in divine telos with a program of Liberal political reform. The line of development in the group devolves from Coleridge to the Rev. F. D. Maurice, to Thomas Arnold, headmaster at Rugby, and to Benjamin Jowett. Later, proponents of Christian manliness like Thomas Hughes and Charles Kingsley 'tried to make manliness an up-to-date practical ethic for everyman, supplanting the old aristocratic ideal of chivalry but retaining something of its glamour and moral grandeur.' Their religious awareness 'crystallized ... into a vigorously combative Christianity involving urgent ethical and spiritual imperatives.'[17] When their Liberal counterparts in Parliament went to the polls to seek voters' support, they did so in part as 'real' men combining glamor, pugnacity, and a sense of disinterested mission.

Yet this pugnacity, again contradictorily, was to be defensive, not exuberant or aggressive in character. In his book, *The Lights of Liberalism*, Christopher Harvie has argued that the cohesive group of Liberal intellectuals that existed at Oxford from the 1860s to 1886 formed a novel sort of intelligentsia, which gained influence by advocating the entry of marginal groups, especially male workers, into the political mainstream but in ways that recognized 'the importance in British politics of institutional loyalties and initiatives, subordinate to national politics but still checking and directing them.'[18] This middling position, though vulnerable to potentially disabling pressures from both above and below on the class scale, indicates an approach to politics in which not positive action but rather responsiveness to the demands and needs of those on the margin and deference to constituted authorities combine.

In another recent study, Regenia Gagnier has argued that the literary scandal attending publication of *The Picture of Dorian Gray* was one in which journalists who identified themselves with middle-class gentlemen attacked Wilde's dandyism, a term which Gagnier associates with the aristocracy or what she refers to as 'high Society.' Gagnier, however, misplaces the dandy. Although some aristocrats were dandies, the 'dandy' as a popular phenomenon is middle-class – as she herself has shown in her account of the history of the dandy, few of whom were aristocrats. Dandyism was associated with middle-class uppityism, so that we find, for instance, Bulwer-Lytton, a genuinely aristocratic dandy of the 1830s, attacking Tennyson's poems of 1833 for their 'effeminacies,' for 'a want of all manliness in love, ... an eunuch strain.'[19] In the nineteenth century, 'effeminacy' as a term of personal abuse often connotes male–male desire, a threat of deviance that seems to haunt gentlemen should they become too gentle, refined, or glamorous.[20]

As Gilmour points out, dandyism also reflects a loss of balance between the dual imperatives of leisure and work incumbent upon Victorian gentlemen. The dandy is too relaxed, too visible, consumes to excess while producing little or nothing. Since the ideal of the gentleman also implies a divide within the middle-class managerial elite between those in service professions and those in industry and commerce, the dandy reflects negatively on gentlemanliness itself. As Gilmour comments:

On the debit side there is the historical alienation of the educated elite from trade and technical knowledge, with consequences that were perceived by Matthew Arnold as early as 1868, when he reported for the Schools Enquiry Commission on upper- and middle-class education on the Continent: 'we have amongst us the spectacle of a middle class cut in two in a way unexampled anywhere else,' he wrote of English education, with 'a professional class' which identified with the aristocracy 'but without the idea of science,' and an 'immense business class ... cut off from the aristocracy, and the professions, and without governing qualities.[21]

In the 1890s it was becoming evident that the loss of British preeminence in trade and industry signaled a decline in national power. In this context, the gentleman himself might appear effete and ineffectual. Populist hostility to dandies might reflect back onto gentlemen and even onto the Liberal party.

III

A number of specific circumstances contributed to create a situation in the 1890s in which both personal and literary scandals were to be expected: one was the male homosocial basis of leading institutions; another was the progress and increasing visibility of marginal groups, of laboring men, of male homosexuals, and especially of women. Even when women were not heeded, still they were heard; and the addition of voices of another gender unsettled male leaders. As one parliamentarian said to Josephine Butler: 'We know how to manage any other opposition in the House or in the country, but this is very awkward for us – this revolt of women. It is quite a new thing: what are we to do with such an opposition as this?'[22] The emergence of women like Butler as effective campaigners and public speakers reminded male politicians that public voices are gendered, a realization that directed their attention subsequently to the masculine character of their own bearing and utterance. In the last years of the century, both in literacy discussion and in politics proper, those men who write from a hegemonic point of view increasingly seek to delimit the appropriate bonds of masculine expression.

Other factors, however, were also crucial in establishing the climate of scandal. In the 1890s, a sensationalizing, populist press provided the textual space in which scandals might be generated. The press and magazines made possible the marketing of Wilde's persona upon which he based his career. Wilde was better and earlier known as a celebrity than as an author. His visibility made his extravagance much more of an affront than would otherwise have been the case. And, after his fall, celebrity made him a better example of the wages of difference.

After 1867, as well, some workers had the vote, and the tendency of gentlemen to affiliate themselves with the upper classes became a political drawback. In the ensuing decades, differences between middle-class Liberals or Radicals and Whig aristocrats on issues like Home Rule for Ireland resulted in the defection of the latter group. 'By 1893 there were only 41 peers who were prepared to vote for Gladstone's second Home Rule Bill. 419 voted against it.'[23] As Liberals lost support among their former aristocratic allies, workers also became more politically independent. Moreover, Liberals found themselves outflanked on the right by Tory legislation favorable to unionized workers. In 1875 the Tory government of Disraeli had passed legislation undoing the Criminal Law Amendment Act of 1871, a bill effectively outlawing picketing during industrial disputes and passed, ironically enough, during Gladstone's reform administration. Action by labor unions climaxed in the London dock strike of 1889. By 1891 strikes had also occurred 'at the Cardiff and Limerick docks, Leeds gas works, Bradford cotton mills, the Plymouth Colliery, and [among] . . . railway employees in Ireland and Scotland.'[24] Additionally, some workers and their leaders in the 1880s asserted an alternative political ideology in socialism.[25] At times women's agitation joined hands with socialist politics as in the case of Margaret McMillan and her sister Rachel. Startled into political consciousness by Stead's pamphlet, *The Maiden Tribute of Modern Babylon*, Margaret moved to London and took part in the 1889 strike.[26] These changes in the body politic did not spell the end of alliance between Liberals and members of the working class, but there was need to rethink liberalism and the politics of gentlemen more generally.[27]

The first homosexual scandal of the new decade, the Cleveland Street scandal of 1889–90, crosses lines of class, embracing aristocrats and 'gentlemen' on one side, telegraph boys and members of the Household Cavalry on the other. Without a muckraking London weekly, the *North London Press*, and a Radical editor named Ernest Parke, the case that triggered the sensation would have gone unnoticed. The police, the courts, even parliamentarians including Labouchère, were involved in contradictory ways both to inflame and to suppress the matter. The scandal began quietly enough when 'a fifteen-year-old messenger boy called Charles Swinscow' was noticed to have an unusual amount of spending money.[28] Luke Hanks, the Post Office constable who interviewed him, discovered that the money came not from thefts of small sums at the Post Office but from earnings that Swinscow made selling sexual services to gentlemen in a house at 19 Cleveland Street. In the ensuing series of events, the Prince of Wales and the Prime Minister, Lord Salisbury, intervened so as to enable one of the clients, an equerry to the Prince named Lord Arthur Somerset, to escape prior to issue of an arrest warrant. Salisbury and the Prince were motivated by a need to protect the Heir Apparent, Prince Albert Victor, from being implicated in male–male sexual activities.[29]

After Parke broke word of the entanglement of aristocrats in the scandal, journalists portrayed the young men involved as working-class youths seduced by decadent aristocrats. Yet the case makes more sense when viewed in terms of efforts to quell members of the working classes. Since a great deal of business was conducted by means of postal money orders, financial security was a serious concern. But the origin of the scandal suggests resentment of young males who had access to more money than they could obtain by regular work. As with gambling, another focus of current agitation, male prostitution in part offended because 'the desire to take unearned gains' was regarded as immoral.[30] Walkowitz has argued that the 1885 act enabled police to separate the 'decent' poor from their at times delinquent sisters. Weeks argues that in late Victorian legislation male homosexuals were placed in the same category as prostitutes: '*All* male homosexual activities were illegal between 1885 and 1967'; and 'in terms of social obloquy, all homosexual males as a class were equated with female prostitutes.'[31] A scandal like that of Cleveland Street helped police to discourage young workers from enhancing their earnings through casual sex or other unconventional means. These men were induced instead to play their necessary roles in the army and at home. Unfortunately for clients, these efforts, epitomized in the Labouchère amendment, also encouraged males in the sex trade to become extortionists and blackmailers.[32]

The publication of *The Picture of Dorian Gray* in an American journal in 1890, on the heels of the scandal, accentuated the deviant connotations of Wilde's text. Male reviewers took advantage of the opportunity for conserving the authority of male privilege under pressure. Most critics disliked the novel – and for good reason. In it, Wilde eschews the portrayal of middle-class life. The *déclassé* milieu of the actress Sybil Vane, with whom Dorian is briefly infatuated, provides a mirror, at once both distorting and revealing, of dominant values. Sybil's family is a reservoir of intense and unresolved ambitions, including sexual ones. Her histrionic mother sees Sybil as the means of fulfilling her ambitions for herself and her son, James, whom she plans to send to Australia to make his fortune. (Like Arabella in Hardy's novel, *Jude the Obscure*, James subsequently returns from Down Under without money.) For his part, Sybil's brother has an incestuous regard for his sister, and he threatens with violence the 'gentleman' who has taken her up. (Sybil never does learn his name.) On the other hand, the callousness of the upper-class milieus in which Dorian circulates might well prompt one to embrace the antiaristocratic politics of a Labouchère. Yet in choosing these two worlds for his protagonist, Wilde tacitly reveals his personal preference of these environments over his genteel home and charming family in Tite Street.

Although Wilde often alludes to details, situations, and events that connote homosexuality, Dorian lives not in a homosexual subculture but rather in what Sedgwick might term a male homosocial environment. Still the intersection of Sybil's world with Dorian's is the site of scandal, a fact that reviewers at once recognized. A former friend of Wilde, W. E. Henley, linked the novel and its author with the Cleveland Street scandal, which as I have mentioned included aristocrats and telegraph boys among others:

> The story – which deals with matters only fitted for the Criminal investigation Department or a hearing *in camera* – is discreditable alike to author and editor. Mr Wilde has brains, and art, and style; but if he can write for none but outlawed noblemen and perverted telegraph-boys, the sooner he takes to tailoring (or some other decent trade) the better for his own reputation and the public morals.[33]

Gagnier attributes the hostile reception of the novel to a conflict between reviewers who identified with the 'gentleman' produced by the public schools and a writer who associated himself with aristocrats in his social life, his writing, and his dandyish pose.[34] Wilde's friends, however, were drawn primarily from the middle class; and I have already argued above that in Britain the dandy was most significant in relation to contradictory elements within the myth of the gentleman. For most of his career Wilde had managed to balance hard work with an affectation of leisurely indifference. What did him in was his increasing association with 'homosexual existence'. Wilde-as-dandy provided something of an early warning signal that the combined prescription and proscription of intense male bonding at public school and the older universities was vulnerable to changes in masculine self-identification. As male homosexuality became visible in public and in texts during the 1890s, 'the emphasis on gender construction of the British male' that characterized the schools began to be perceived as problematic.[35] Hence the need to separate the gentlemen from the dandies, to retrench, to generate scandals, and to expel embarrassments like Wilde.

Ed Cohen has remarked the extent to which the trials were a male spectacle: 'Court attendance was exclusively male. The defendant, the prosecution, all the court officials, as well as the audience and press, were also male; hence all that transpired and all that was reported occurred within an entirely male-defined social space for the benefit of a male public.'[36] What he does not mention, however, is the intricate web weaving Wilde and his activities together with others. Ellmann points out that those in court were not only males but likewise hypocrites – not simply because, except for one, the witnesses against Wilde were all known prostitutes or blackmailers nor only because both defense and prosecution excluded the name of the aristocrat, Alfred Douglas, from the proceedings but also because homosexual behavior was 'common in the English public schools which most of the legal personages present had attended.' Edward Carson, who defended Queensberry in the libel suit, was 'a fellow-student of Wilde's from Trinity College, Dublin'; one of the prosecutors, Charles Gill, was also a graduate of Trinity.[37] Sir Frank Lockwood, the Solicitor-General, who prosecuted Wilde at the second trial, was the uncle of Maurice Schwabe, who had introduced Wilde to Alfred Taylor, the man whose trial on charges of indecency was linked with Wilde's. Schwabe fled the country after Wilde's arrest. Lockwood's relentless pursuit of Wilde reflects in part the fact that barbs aimed at him fell close to home.

Most graduates of the public schools did the expected thing, grew up, married, and entered the professions or civil service. Nonetheless, and although the facts themselves are well known, it is still easy to underestimate the efflorescence of culture, positive about male–male desire, just before the Wilde trials. In 1894, Edward Carpenter gave a public lecture at Manchester on the topic of homogenic love.[38] Writers like Symonds and Carpenter and others like Douglas used written language quietly to campaign on behalf of decriminalizing male homosexual behavior.[39] Brian Reade points out that 1894 marks the high-water mark of publications that valorized male homosexual feeling within the general ambit of 'culture,' whether of contemporary painting, of poetry, or of High Anglican religious sentiment. In these years appeared, according to Reade, the first fictional work in England 'published for ordinary and unlimited distribution which involved romantic pederasty.'[40] The work in question was Wilde's 'The Portrait of Mr. W. H.,' published in *Blackwood's Edinburgh Magazine* in 1889. A second such story, 'The Priest and the Acolyte,' was published anonymously in December 1894, in the *Chameleon*, a short-lived undergraduate publication at Oxford. Wilde's prosecutors in 1895 alleged that he had written the story.

Pornography was another area in which homosexuals protested public intolerance. Cohen, for instance, has pointed out that the author(s) of the pornographic novel, *Teleny*, assert the pleasurableness of their sexuality, then base a claim for tolerance on the naturalness of 'joy'; the protagonist argues:

> Had I committed a crime against nature when my own nature found peace and happiness thereby? If I was thus, surely it was the fault of my blood, not myself. Who had planted nettles in my garden? Not I. They had grown there unawares from my very childhood. I began to feel their carnal sting long before I could understand what conclusion

they imported. When I had tried to bridle my lust, was it my fault if the scale of reason was far too light to balance that of sensuality? Was I to blame if I could not argue down my raging motion? Fate, Iago-like, had clearly shewed me that if I would damn myself, I could do so in a more delicate way than drowning. I yielded to my destiny and encompassed my joy.[41]

Significant areas of cultural production were becoming the property, so to speak, of makers who were either not male or not 'straight.' Elaine Showalter has described the struggle to turn back female dominance of the novel after George Eliot's death, a struggle climaxing in the 1890s' battle over 'New Woman' fiction.[42] In the theater, Wilde was triumphant – even if, on occasion, censored. And in the arts and crafts movement, he was promoting the sexually ambiguous art of Aubrey Beardsley and creating opportunities for two homosexuals, Charles Ricketts and C. H. Shannon, the former of whom Wilde referred to as the model of Basil Hallward in *The Picture of Dorian Gray*.'[43] In 1894, Ricketts and Shannon led the world in the production of a new genre, the art-book.[44] And when Alfred Douglas in 1896 attacked Lord Rosebery and other prominent Liberals for having conspired against Wilde, Douglas did so in the pages of *La Revue Blanche*, the avant-garde journal that also published the lithographs of Pierre Bonnard.[45] Artistic modernity and an enlightened approach to morals legislation were, if briefly, aligned.

All three sorts of discourse – scientific, aesthetic, and pornographic – comprise aspects of homosexual existence at the time of Wilde's downfall. Each discourse implies a network of practitioners and places of meeting. The networks overlapped; there is, for instance, an oral tradition that *Teleny* was a composite work, written in rotation by a number of Wilde's acquaintances, then edited by Wilde himself.[46] And there were other networks and meeting places as well, for instance in the Anglican church, as David Hilliard has pointed out, and in less reputable places like the Crown and the Windsor Castle pubs, in hotels like the Savoy, in public spaces such as Leicester Square, and in male brothels like the Hundred Guineas Club. The efflorescence of homosexual existence, however, was about to end.

A political crisis in the Liberal party in 1894–95 further determined the moment of Wilde's trials as ripe for a public demonstration of homophobic solidarity. When Gladstone finally retired as leader of the party in 1894, Liberals faced a choice between Lord Rosebery and Sir W. V. Harcourt. The latter was the darling of the Temperance wing of the party, a group whose loyalty to the Liberals depended on perennially deferred pledges to reform the administration of liquor licensing.[42] Once prime minister, Rosebery tried to unite the party around the issue of reform of the House of Lords. Despite the appeal of the issue, however, he was unable to move it forward because he and the party were in basic disagreement as to the character of reform. He himself inclined to a limit on the power of veto. Reform in this vein would, however, result in increased legitimacy for the upper chamber and would thereby retrench what many saw as an anachronistic institution. Radicals like Labouchère favored not reform but outright abolition. When Rosebery became prime minister in 1894, Labouchère, a supporter of Harcourt, successfully proposed in the House of Commons 'a strong anti-Lords resolution.'[48] If Gagnier is correct, as she appears to be, in identifying Rosebery as a homosexual, in his person outmoded privilege was closely aligned with sexual nonconformity.[49] Labouchère's anger in 1894 corroborates the suggestion made earlier that the 1885 amendment was precisely aimed – as does the attack in *Truth* on Alfred Douglas in June 1895. According to Labouchère's paper, Douglas deserved 'an opportunity to meditate . . . in the seclusion of Pentonville Prison.'[50]

Douglas attempted to use the occasion of the trials to expose the hypocrisy of the establishment. He responded to Labouchère's attack with a private communication in which he asserted

> that he knew forty or fifty men in the best society, hundreds of undergraduates at Oxford, not to mention 'a slight sprinkling of dons,' who were homosexual. Lots of boys around Piccadilly lived on prostitution. He was sending a pamphlet by Krafft-Ebing, which he was now having translated, asking for the repeal of an Austrian law against homosexuals.

And on June 28, in a letter that Douglas wrote to Stead, now editor of the *Review of Reviews*,

> he dealt directly with homosexuality, pointed out that the laws were very different in France, that lesbianism was tolerated in England, that dealing with male prostitutes was no worse than dealing with female ones, and that his father practiced fornication and adultery, advocated free love, and maltreated both his first and second wives. Stead refused to publish this, and so did Labouchère.

Writing a year later in *La Revue Blanche*, Douglas proposed a conspiracy theory to account for anomalies in the process and the vigor of the prosecution: 'Oscar Wilde's conviction was one of the last acts of the discredited Liberal Party, which is now reduced [i.e., after the defeat of 1895] to an exceptional minority in the House of Commons.'[51] More Adey gave a similar account to a French writer in June 1895.[52] Nonetheless, in comparison with the Cleveland Street scandal, what distinguishes the Wilde trials may perhaps be an *absence* of conspiracy. From above fell silence – hence the Solicitor-General and police were free to pursue a conviction with zeal. Wilde was sacrificed to protect the establishment, namely to protect Douglas most directly, but Rosebery also.

Rosebery's name connects with the trials at two points. Douglas's brother Francis, Viscount Drumlanrig, had been a 'private secretary,' to Rosebery. In 1893, Rosebery had become involved in a major row with Douglas *père* after arranging for Francis to receive the seat in the Lords that his father had renounced. A year later, Francis was dead, probably a suicide 'to avoid a scandal in which his and Rosebery's homosexual affair would become public.'[53] Queensberry took his resolve publicly to attack Wilde after he decided that his eldest son had died in the aftermath of a homosexual affair. Queensberry's son died on October 18, 1894; on November 1, in a letter in which he refers to 'the Snob Queers like Roseberry [*sic*],' Queensberry remarks to the father of his first wife:

> I smell a Tragedy behind all this and have already *got Wind* of a more *startling one*. If it was what I am led *to believe*, I of all people could and would have helped him, had he come to me with a confidence, but that was all stopped by you people – we had not met or spoken frankly for more than a year and a half. I am on the right track to find out what happened. *Cherchez la femme*, when these things happen. I have already heard something that quite accounts *for it all*.

Later, during the first trial, Wilde's counsel, Sir Edward Clarke, made the mistake of reading a number of Queensberry's letters into the record, including one of July 6, in which Queensberry refers to 'the Rosebery–Gladstone–Royal insult that came to me through my other son.' Even though this particular reference is to the title and not to sexual matters, introduction of Rosebery's name effectively tied the hands of those, including Rosebery himself, at a level above that of Sir Frank Lockwood, the Solicitor-General. Otherwise, intervention *might* have been possible after the second trial ended in a hung jury. Lockwood, however, was quick to point out that 'the abominable rumors against Rosebery' made a third trial necessary. Ellmann reports that according to gossip Rosebery 'had considered doing something to help Wilde until Balfour told him, "If you do, you will lose the election." (In the event, he lost the election anyway.)'[54]

IV

The tightening constraints did not affect only male homosexuals and those involved with them. Sexually conventional men, lesbians, and New Women also were vulnerable. In 1895, likewise, literary scandal attended publication in book form of Thomas Hardy's *Jude the Obscure*. Hardy's writing, like that of Wilde and contemporary feminists, subverted male privilege in marriage. That arbiter of public decency, the *Pall Mall Gazette*, in a review of November 12 called the novel 'Jude the Obscene'; and the London *World* ran its review 'under the title "Hardy the Degenerate." ' Mrs Oliphant reviewed the book as a polemic against marriage. Most spectacularly, Bishop William Walsham How of Wakefield burned the book – then added injury to insult by instigating 'the withdrawal of the novel from W. H. Smith's huge circulating library.'[55]

Hardy's novel was, however, offensive in other ways as well. *Jude the Obscure* is notable for the weakness within it of same-sex bonding – at least for its protagonists, Jude and Sue. Jude has no male friends; he has no entry into the male homosocial enclaves to which he is so strongly drawn, especially Oxford. And he repeatedly fails in attempts to achieve a mentor-protégé relationship. His one relationship of the kind, with a village schoolteacher named Phillotson, proves to be disastrous for both men. And Hardy is mordant about the putative solidarity that exists among working-class males. In focusing on a man whose life is characterized by exclusion from male homosocial ties, Hardy implicitly condemns institutions like Oxford, where a cherished sense of belonging was purchased at the price of a snobbish exclusivity. Hardy might also be seen as demythologizing the figure of the gentleman, since in humble, diffuse ways Jude seeks entry into an occupation that would make him a simulacrum of a gentleman. Hardy points out the cruelty to which Jude's naive pursuit of this substitute ambition exposes him. Again not surprisingly, gentlemanly reviewers reacted against the novel. In his life of Hardy, Michael Millgate points out that Hardy was especially aggrieved at 'fellow members of the Savile Club' who wrote 'hostile reviews' in the 1890s. Millgate remarks that Hardy's dismay 'reflected his sense, ingrained from childhood, that friendship was inseparable from loyalty, and also his bitter realization that his years of investment in clubbability and *bonhomie* were not, after all, standing him in good stead.'[56] *Jude* repudiates such affiliations; instead, the novel reaffirms Hardy's awareness of himself as an outsider and asserts his fellowship with someone as estranged as Jude Fawley.

Hardy was especially upset by his friend Edmund Gosse's ambivalent review of the novel on November 8.[57] And though Gosse gave as his reason the bleakness of the book, other causes of concern lay close to hand. Like Hardy, Gosse was a clubman; like Hardy, he also felt a need to belong to a number of male elites: to a circle of eminent writers, to another of journalists, and to the social world of the aristocracy.[58] Yet like Hardy himself, Gosse, though a man of letters, was not a university man. And despite the fact that he had advanced far, receiving offers of professorships from Yale, Harvard, and Johns Hopkins universities and winning appointment to the Clark Lectureship at Cambridge University in 1884, he fell victim to attack by a former friend, John Churton Collins, in the *Quarterly Review*.[59] Gosse's penchant for hasty and erroneous research made him vulnerable, and even though establishment support carried him through, 'as a serious scholar he was now irrevocably handicapped.'[60] Gosse had good reason to be troubled by a novel that traces the decline and fall of a book-loving young man unable to enter the university world.

Especially only six months after the Wilde trials, Gosse had further reason for discomfort, reason divined by Hardy himself, in the nonconformity of Sue Bridehead, the novel's heroine. Gosse, who was an acquaintance of Wilde and a heterosexual by choice rather than by inclination, panicked at the time of the trial and wrote a letter asking his and Wilde's mutual friend, Robert Ross, to stay away from the Gosse household.[61] Gosse's long and ardent friendship with the sculptor Hamo Thornycroft depended for its stability on the conscious suppression of desire on Gosse's part.[62] As it turns out, the Thornycrofts were visitors to Hardy at Max Gate in September 1895. Writing to Gosse shortly after publication of the review, Hardy specifically raises the question of sexual inversion – but in such a way as to allay, if possible, Gosse's anxiety. There is, Hardy writes, 'nothing perverted or depraved in Sue's nature. The abnormalism consists in disproportion; not in inversion.'[63]

In a well-known passage from the postscript to the 1912 edition of *Jude the Obscure*, Hardy suggests that Sue may reasonably be regarded as a type of 'the woman of the feminist movement – the slight pale "bachelor" girl – the intellectualized, emancipated bundle of nerves that modern conditions were producing, mainly in cities as yet.'[64] Feminist critics, however, are not so sure that Sue is a feminist. Penny Boumelha for one suggests that if Sue is a type, she resembles not so much the turn-of-the-century feminist as the phenomenon of the New Woman, a figure drawn from contemporary life but also prominent in the popular press and in a number of novels that have been described as New Woman fiction. While neither the type nor the fiction are uniform, the New Woman is self-consciously critical of marriage; and her novel is often 'dominated' by the ideal of 'free union,' a monogamous relationship 'based on the notion of substituting the sanction of personal feeling for the degrading economic [and, one might add, sexual] basis of legal marriage.'[65] Hardy and Sue are at one in resisting marriage as a license 'to be loved on the premises.'[66]

In truth, Sue's ideal, frustrated in the novel, affiliates her with both the New Woman and with feminism as well as with the critique of marriage in writers like Symonds and Kains-Jackson. Earlier feminists like Harriet Taylor and John Stuart Mill had attacked the idea, still prevalent in the 1890s, of the conjugal rights of husbands.[67] And contemporary feminists like Elizabeth Wolstenholme Elmy and Francis Swiney emphasize

'woman's right to physical integrity and self-determination.'[68] These
writers resisted male control of women's bodies – whether as the object
of sexual advances or as bearers of children. Male homosexual
polemicists, New Women, and feminists in their different ways all posed
a challenge to male prerogatives and to the appropriation of women's
bodies for purposes of social production.

One of the significant questions of contemporary women's history is
how it came about that feminism, prominent in the 1890s, had by 1930
given way to reconfirmed ideals of the biological basis of women's roles
and to a militant conviction that women's destiny lay in monogamous
marriage.[69] One element lies in the professional development of sexology,
for despite the fact that turn-of-the-century sexologists regarded
themselves as intellectually and socially liberal and although in many
respects they were – for instance, in supporting 'the removal of penal
laws against homosexuality' – in other respects their work was all too
evidently reactive. In particular, they tended to confirm conventional
gender roles on the ground that the bourgeois construction of gender
was 'natural,' i.e., that it is biologically and not socially based. Weeks
comments: 'Their achievement has been to *naturalise* sexual patterns and
identities and thus obscure their historical genealogy.'[70] Taking this tack,
sexologists labeled individuals who resisted conventional gender
expectations – individuals like New Women or feminists or fictional
characters like Sue Bridehead – as abnormal, neurotic, or even perverse.
When Hardy in 1912 refers to Sue as the ' "bachelor" girl of modern
urban experience,' he reflects the bias of contemporary sexology, a field
with which his earlier use of the word 'inversion' in relation to Sue
indicates his familiarity. Since, unlike the actual 'bachelor' girls of the
turn of the century, Sue is unable to compete with men for suitable work
or to find a flat for herself in a large city, she seems an unsuitable object
for Hardy's epithet.

As well, Hardy's attraction to a free-love relationship and his revulsion
from marriage do not comprise a repudiation of compulsory
heterosexuality. Instead his comment on Sue's 'disproportion' implies a
principle of indwelling proportion in gender. In the novel he enforces
upon her what Rich sees as one prime element of compulsory
heterosexuality, namely 'the socialization of women to feel that male
sexual "drive" amounts to a right.'[71] There is a glaring contrast between
Hardy's ability to empathize with Jude's point of view and his inability
at times to enter imaginatively into Sue's. And this observation holds
even though Sue faces choices in some ways like Jude's. In the late
Victorian period, professional achievement for women usually meant a
celibate life shared in a community of women.[72] But for Sue, Hardy
sketches only alternatives: disabling normalcy or degrees of deviance.
His position foreshadows the formulation of the lesbian type two years

later by Havelock Ellis. Signs of gender inversion in Sue's behavior and later criticism of her as 'frigid' make her a fictional occasion of scandal.[73] The more authentic base of scandal, however, exists in the fact that for as long as she can, she speaks intellectually and that she aspires to be a different sort of woman – even if neither she nor Hardy can say what feminine difference means.

By century's end, she and her real-life analogues were represented as scandalous examples of what-not-to-be. The description of female inversion that Havelock Ellis proffers in 1897 in his classic text, *Sexual Inversion*, provides a good terminus for a discussion of the structure and motivation of homosexual scandal in the 1890s. Ellis distinguishes lesbian behavior not on the basis of sexual inversion but on the basis of gender inversion.[74] Today, the definition of lesbian depends on the choice of sexual object – not so for Ellis. For him what matters is an inappropriate mode of self-presentation. He writes of lesbians as follows:

> When they still retain female garments, these usually show some traits of masculine simplicity, and there is nearly always a disdain for the petty feminine artifices of the toilet. Even when this is not obvious, there are all sorts of instinctive gestures and habits which may suggest to female acquaintances the remark that such a person 'ought to have been a man.' The brusque energetic movements, the attitude of the arms, the direct speech, the inflexions of the voice, the masculine straightforwardness and sense of honour, and especially the attitude towards men, free from any suggestion either of shyness or audacity, will often suggest the underlying psychic abnormality to a keen observer.
>
> In the habits not only is there frequently a pronounced taste for smoking cigarettes, often found in quite feminine women, but also a decided taste and toleration for cigars. There is also a dislike and sometimes incapacity for needlework and other domestic occupations, while there is some capacity for athletics.[75]

In six case studies, Ellis includes women who had no genital contact with other women but who did engage in 'passionate friendships,' relationships of a sort that were widely practiced and accepted among middle-class women throughout the Victorian period.[76]

By labeling as perverse what once had been accepted as normal, sexologists helped induce the process whereby women by the late 1920s were faced with an either/or choice: either heterosexual marriage or social ostracism as lesbians.[77] The development of this antithetical categorization narrowed drastically the range of possibilities for women – though in the present context the main point is that Sue's worry about loss of moral and bodily autonomy was not out of place in the 1890s nor eccentric nor a sign of frigidity nor lesbianism. Sheila Jeffrey's chronicle of the decline of the single woman in the first quarter of the twentieth century reminds one of how difficult it was for women to achieve the independence that Sue seeks.

As well, one sees how the pattern of scandal in the 1890s, both literary and personal, followed a course that in retrospect appears nearly predictable: social change, instability and agitation for reform, open expressions of difference, produced reaction in both ugly and enlightened guises. Scandal issued in the reaffirmation of the naturalness of gender norms, of manly men and womanly women, of marriage, of the return of middle-class women to the home, and of the primacy of mothering. Neither Wilde's 'effeminacy' nor Sue's 'bachelor' ways were to be tolerated. Yet insofar as scandalous tests and behavior in the 1890s contradicted the universality of these norms, they continued to imply the possibility and need for other responses to the crises of sexual identity and male privilege in the 1890s.

Notes

1. ADRIENNE RICH, 'Compulsory Heterosexuality and Lesbian Existence', *Signs* 5 (1980), 631–60.
2. Ibid., 633.
3. SHEILA JEFFREYS, *The Spinster and Her Enemies: Feminism and Sexuality, 1880–1930* (London: Pandora, 1985), chap. 6.
4. JEFFREY WEEKS, *Sexuality and its Discontent: Meanings, Myths and Modern Sexualities* (London: Routledge and Kegan Paul, 1985), chap. 4.
5. Ibid., 69.
6. EVE KOSOFSKY SEDGWICK, 'The Beast in the Closet: James and the Writing of Homosexual Panic.' In *Sex, Politics and Science in the Nineteenth Century Novel*, ed. RUTH BERNARD YEAZELL. Selected papers from the English Institute, 1983–84. N.s. 10 (Baltimore: Johns Hopkins University Press, 1986), 152.
7. RICHARD ELLMANN, *Oscar Wilde* (Markham, Ont: Viking, 1987), 302.
8. NOEL ANNAN, 'The Intellectual Aristocracy' in *Studies in Social History: a Tribute to G. M. Trevelyan*, ed. HAROLD PLUMB, 1955 (reprint Freeport, N.Y. Books for Libraries Press, 1969), 248, 247.
9. SEDGWICK, 'The Beast in the Closet'; ELAINE SHOWALTER, 'Syphilis, Sexuality and the Fiction of the Fin de Siècle'. In *Sex, Politics and Science in the Nineteenth Century Novel*, ed. RUTH BERNARD YEAZELL. Selected papers from the English Institute, 1983–84. N.s. 10 (Baltimore: Johns Hopkins University Press, 1986).
10. For statistics on changing occupational notes for single women, see MARTHA VICINUS, *Independent Women: Work and Community for Single Women, 1850–1920* (Chicago: University of Chicago Press, 1985), chap. 1.
11. JEFFREY WEEKS, *Sexuality and Its Discontents*, 49, 44; *Sex, Politics and Society: The Regulation of Sexuality Since 1800* (New York: Longman, 1981), chap. 5; *Coming Out: Homosexual Politics in Britain from the Nineteenth Century to the Present* (London: Quartet Books, 1974), chap. 1.
12. EVE KOSOFSKY SEDGWICK, *Between Men: English Literature and Male Homosocial Desire* (New York: Columbia University Press, 1985), 1–3.

13. Although the British model is inegalitarian in ways that are occluded in American ideology, the two myths are analogous with those that Smith-Rosenberg sees as a key element in the emergence of a bourgeois class in the United States during the 1830s. She refers to these as 'The Myth of the Common Man' and the 'Cult of True Womanhood' ('Writing History,' 34).

14. ROBIN GILMOUR, *The Idea of the Gentleman in the Victorian Novel* (London: George Allen, 1981), 8. Cf. (and contrast) Michael Moon's analysis of the situation in the United States ('Gentle Boy').

15. GILMOUR, *Idea of the Gentleman*, 7, 6.

16. Ibid., 8.

17. NORMAN VANCE, *Sinews of the Spirit: The Ideal of Christian Manliness in Victorian Literature and Religious Thought* (Cambridge: Cambridge University Press, 1985), 9, 3.

18. CHRISTOPHER HARVIE, *Lights of Liberalism: University Liberals and the Challenge of Democracy, 1860–1886* (London: Allen Lane, 1976), 18.

19. REGENIA GAGNIER, *Idylls of the Marketplace: Oscar Wilde and the Victorian Public* (Stanford, Calif: Stanford University Press, 1986). BULWER-LYTTON quoted in R. B. MARTIN, *Tennyson: The Unquiet Heart* (New York: Oxford University Press, 1980), 169.

20. DAVID HILLIARD, 'Unenglish and Unmanly: Anglo-Catholicism and Homosexuality.' *Victorian Studies* 25 (1982), 181–210.

21. GILMOUR, *Idea of the Gentleman*, 98.

22. Quoted in JUDITH WALKOWITZ, 'Male Vice and Female Virtue: Feminism and the Politics of Prostitution in Nineteenth Century Britain.' In *Powers of Desire: The Politics of Sexuality*, ed. ANN SNITOW, CHRISTINE STANSELL, and SHARON THOMPSON (New York: Monthly Review Press, 1983), 421.

23. DAVID ALLEN HAMER, *A Study of Four Ministries, 1868–1892* (Toronto: Heinemann, 1969), 21.

24. LEE M. EDWARDS, 'The Heroic Worker and Hubert von Herkomer's *On Strike.*' *Arts Magazine* 62 (September, 1987), 29–35.

25. STANLEY PIERSON, *Marxism and the Origins of British Socialism: The Struggle for a New Consciousness* (Ithaca, New York: Cornell University Press, 1973), chap. 6.

26. LEWIS CHESTER, DAVID LEITCH, and COLIN SIMPSON, *The Cleveland Street Affair* (London: Weidenfeld and Nicholson, 1976), 161–2.

27. PETER CLARKE, *Liberals and Social Democrats* (Cambridge: Cambridge University Press, 1978).

28. CHESTER, LEITCH, and SIMPSON, *Cleveland Street Affair*, 15.

29. Information in this paragraph is from ibid.

30. DAVID C. ITZKOWITZ, 'The (Other) Great Evil: Gambling, Scandal and the Anti-Gambling League.' (Paper presented at the annual meeting of the Midwest Victorian Studies Association, Chicago, April 1987), 4.

31. JEFFREY WEEKS, 'Inverts, Perverts and Mary-Annes: Male Prostitution and the Regulation of Sexuality in England in the Nineteenth and Early Twentieth Centuries.' *Journal of Homosexuality* 6 (Fall 1980–Winter 1981), 113–34; he sees the equation at work again in the 1898 Vagrancy Act (117).

32. CHESTER, LEITCH, and SIMPSON, *Cleveland Street Affair*, 62.

33. GAGNIER, *Idylls of the Marketplace*, 59.

34. Ibid., chap. 2.

35. Ibid., 94.

36. ED COHEN, 'Writing Gone Wilde: Homoerotic Desire in the Closet of Representation.' *PMLA* 102 (1987) 801–13.

37. ELLMANN, *Oscar Wilde*, 434, 447, 414, 431–2.

38. BRIAN READE, *Sexual Heretics: Male Homosexuality in English Literature from 1850 to 1900* (London: Routledge and Kegan Paul, 1970), 52.

39. GAGNIER, *Idylls of the Marketplace*, 162, 206; JOHN ADDINGTON SYMONDS, *Male Love: A Problem in Greek Ethics* (New York: Pagan Press, 1983), 109–13.

40. READE, *Sexual Heretics*, 28.

41. Cited by COHEN, *Writing Gone Wilde*, 805. Although a number of writers have pointed out the difficulties, conceptual and political, in the argument that homosexual desire is 'natural,' the contention has a longstanding place in eighteenth- and nineteenth-century homosexual apology (WEEKS, *Sexuality and Its Discontents*, chap. 4; CHRISTOPHER CRAFT, ' "Kiss Me with Those Red Lips": Gender and Inversion in Bram Stoker's *Dracula*.' *Representations* 8 (Fall 1984), 107–33; D. A. MILLER, '*Cage aux Folles*: Sensation and Gender in Wilkie Collins's *The Woman in White*.' In *The Making of the Modern Body: Sexuality and Society in the Nineteenth Century*, ed. CATHERINE GALLAGHER and THOMAS LAQUEUR (Berkeley and Los Angeles: University of California Press, 1987); Walt Whitman, Jeremy Bentham, and the anonymous author of *Don Leon* all have recourse to the argument.

42. See ELAINE SHOWALTER, *A Literature of Their Own: British Women Novelists from Bronte to Lessing* (Princeton N.J.: Princeton University Press, 1977), chaps 6–8, and 'Syphilis, Sexuality, and Fiction'.

43. ELLMANN *Oscar Wilde*, 295.

44. COLLEEN DENNEY, 'English Book Designers and the Role of the Modern Book at L'Art Nouveau. Part Two: Relations Between England and the Continent.' *Arts Magazine* 61 (June 1987), 49–57.

45. Ibid., 54.

46. COHEN, 'Writing Gone Wilde,' 803, 811–12 n. 7.

47. DAVID ALLEN HAMER, *Liberal Politics in the Age of Gladstone and Roseberry: A Study in Leadership and Policy* (Oxford: Clarendon Press, 1972), chap. 8. PETER STANSKY, *Ambitions and Strategies: The Struggle for the Leadership of the Liberal Party* (Oxford: Clarendon Press, 1964), chap. 4.

48. HAMER, *Liberal Politics*, 204.

49. GAGNIER, *Idylls of the Marketplace*, 206.

50. ELLMANN, *Oscar Wilde*, 444.

51. Ibid., 445n; Douglas's theory, translated in GAGNIER, *Idylls of the Marketplace*, 206. STANSKY reports that the Liberals 'suffered the greatest defeat of either party since 1832' (*Ambitions and Strategies*, 178).

52. GAGNIER, *Idylls of the Marketplace*, 206.

53. Ibid.

54. Quotations in ELLMANN, *Oscar Wilde*, 402, 423, 437, 434.

55. MICHAEL MILLGATE, *Thomas Hardy: A Biography* (New York: Random House, 1982), 369, 371, 372.

56. Ibid., 373.

57. Ibid., 370.

58. ANN THWAITE, *Edmund Gosse: A Literary Landscape, 1849–1928* (Chicago: University of Chicago Press, 1984).

59. Ibid., chap. 10.

60. Ibid., 295.

61. Ibid., 359–60.

62. Ibid., 320–22.

63. Letter of November 20, 1895, quoted by MILLGATE, *Thomas Hardy*, 354.

64. THOMAS HARDY, *Jude the Obscure* (Toronto: Macmillan, 1969), viii.

65. See PENNY BOUMELHA, *Thomas Hardy and Women: Sexual Ideology and Narrative Form* (Madison: University of Wisconsin Press, 1982), chaps 4, 7; SHOWALTER, *Literature of Their Own*, chap. 7; LLOYD FERNANDO, ' "*New Women' in the Late Victorian Novel*" ' (University Park: Pennsylvania State University Press, 1977); GAIL CUNNINGHAM, *The New Woman and the Victorian Novel* (New York: Barnes and Noble, 1978).

66. HARDY, *Jude the Obscure*, viii, 267.

67. J. S. MILL *The Subjection of Women* (Cambridge, Mass.: MIT Press, 1984), chap. 2.

68. JEFFREYS, *Spinster and Her Enemies*, 30.

69. GEORGE CHAUNCEY, 'From Sexual Inversion to Homosexuality: Medicine and the Changing Conceptualization of Female Deviance.' *Salmagundi*, 58–59 (Fall 1982–Winter 1983), 114–46; JEFFREYS, *Spinster and Her Enemies*; WEEKS, *Sexuality and Its Discontents*.

70. WEEKS, *Sexuality and Its Discontents*, 71, 80, and chap. 4.

71. RICH, 'Compulsory Heterosexuality and Lesbian Existence,' 638.

72. VICINUS, *Independent Women*.

73. SHOWALTER, 'Syphilis, Sexuality, and Fiction.'

74. See GEORGE CHAUNCEY's discussion of the two terms in 'Female Deviance.'

75. Ellis quoted in JEFFREYS, *Spinster and Her Enemies*, 106.

76. Ibid., 107; CAROLL SMITH-ROSENBERG, 'The Female World of Love and Ritual: Relations Between Women in Nineteenth-Century America.' *Signs* 1 (1975), 1–29; LILIAN FADERMAN, *Surpassing the Love of Men: Romantic Friendship and Love Between Women from the Renaissance to the Present* (New York: Morrow, 1981). Though romantic friendships among women could be problematic, nonetheless they are widely tolerated in the nineteenth century. Cf PAULA BENNETT, *My Life a Loaded Gun: Female Creativity and Feminist Poetics* (Boston: Beacon Press, 1986), chap. 2.

77. JEFFREYS, *Spinster and Her Enemies*, chap. 9.

7 Writing Gone Wilde: Homoerotic Desire in the Closet of Representation*

ED COHEN

Ed Cohen is Assistant Professor in English at Rutgers University and has published a number of articles on gay identity. The argument pursued in the essay reproduced here is developed in greater detail in Cohen's Foucauldian study of late nineteenth-century discourses of (homo)sexuality, *Talk on the Wilde Side* (see Further Reading). In the present essay (at points employing a critical language which appears to derive from Jacques Lacan, the French theorist of psychoanalysis) Cohen examines the representational strategies of Wilde's fiction, and the public response to Wilde's writing and to the court trials of 1895 as part of a contest about the discursive production of masculinity and the deployment of the male body (see Introduction, pp. 11–12).

Oh! It is absurd to have a hard and fast rule about what one should read and what one shouldn't. More than half of modern culture depends on what one shouldn't read.

Algy to Jack in The Importance of Being Earnest

. . . every reader of our columns, as he passed his eye over the report of Wilde's apology for his life at the Old Bailey, must have realized, with accumulating significance at each line, the terrible risk involved in certain artistic and literary phrases of the day. Art, we are told, has nothing to do with morality. But even if this doctrine were true it has long ago been perverted, under the treatment of the decadents, into a positive preference on the part of 'Art' for the immoral, the morbid, and the maniacal. It is on this narrower issue that the proceedings of the last few days have thrown so lurid a light. . . . But this terrible case . . . may be the

*Reprinted from *Publications of the Modern Language Association of America*, 102 (1987), pp. 801–13

means of incalculable good if it burns in its lesson upon the literary
and moral conscience of the present generation.

> The *Westminster Gazette* (6 Apr. 1895) assessing the Marquis
> of Queensbury's acquittal on charges of criminal libel.

Prologue: A Trying (Con)text

During the late spring of 1895, the trials of Oscar Wilde erupted from the
pages of every London newspaper. The sex scandal involving one of
London's most renowned popular playwrights as well as one of the most
eccentric members of the British aristocracy titillated popular opinion.
And why not? For it had all the elements of a good drawing-room
comedy – or, in Freudian terms, of a good family romance. The
characters were exact: the neurotic but righteously outraged father (the
Marquis of Queensbury), the prodigal and effeminate young son (Alfred
Douglas), and the degenerate older man who came between them
(Wilde). Wilde was portrayed as the corrupting artist who dragged
young Alfred Douglas away from the realm of paternal solicitude down
into the London underworld, where homosexuality, blackmail, and male
prostitution sucked the lifeblood of morality from his tender body. How
could such a story have failed to engage the public imagination?

Yet the widespread fascination with Wilde's trials should not be
viewed solely as the result of a prurient public interest, nor should it be
seen only as the product of a virulent popular desire to eradicate
'unnatural' sexual practices. Rather, the public response must be
considered in the light of the Victorian bourgeoisie's larger efforts to
legitimate certain limits for the sexual deployment of the male body and,
in Foucault's terms, to define a 'class body.' The middle-aged,
middle-class men who judged Wilde – both in the court and in the press
– saw themselves as attempting not merely to control a 'degenerate'
form of male sexuality but also to ensure standards for the health of their
children and their country.[1] To this end, the court proceedings against
Wilde provided a perfect opportunity to define publicly the authorized
and legal limits within which a man could 'naturally' enjoy the pleasures
of his body with another man. The trials, then, can be thought of as a
spectacle in which the state, through the law and the press, delimited
legitimate male sexual practices (defining them as 'healthy,' 'natural,' or
'true') by proscribing expressions of male experience that transgressed
these limits.[2] The legal proceedings against Wilde were therefore not
anomalous; rather, they crystallized a variety of shifting sexual ideologies
and practices. For what was at issue was not just the prosecution of
homosexual acts per se or the delegitimating of homosexual meanings.

At issue was the discursive production of 'the homosexual' as the antithesis of the 'true' bourgeois male.

In Britain during the late nineteenth century, 'the homosexual' was emerging as a category for organizing male experience alongside other newly recognizable 'types' ('the adolescent,' 'the criminal,' 'the delinquent,' 'the prostitute,' 'the housewife,' etc.).[3] Coined by the Swiss physician Karoly Benkert in 1869 and popularized in the writings of the German sexologists, the word (along with its 'normal' sibling, 'the heterosexual') entered English usage when Krafft-Ebing's *Psychopathia Sexualis* was translated during the 1890s. The shift in the conception of male same-sex eroticism from certain proscribed *acts* (the earlier concepts 'sodomite' and 'bugger' were identified with specific legally punishable practices [see Trumbach; Gilbert]) to certain kinds of *actors* was part of an overall transformation in class and sex-gender ideologies (see Weeks, *Coming Out*, esp. chs. 1–3). If we think of the growth and consolidation of bourgeois hegemony in Victorian Britain as a process whereby diverse sets of material practices ('sex' and 'class' among others) were organized into an effective unity (see Connell), then we can see that 'the homosexual' crystallized as a distinct subset of male experience only in relation to prescribed embodiments of 'manliness.' This new conceptualization reproduced asymmetrical power relations by privileging the enactments of white middle-class, heterosexual men (see Cominos for the classic description of this privilege; see also Thomas).

In *Between Men: English Literature and Male Homosocial Desire*, Eve Kosofsky Sedgwick explores the range of 'maleness' in English literature between the late eighteenth and early twentieth centuries and proposes that the normative structuring of relations between men established other male positionings within the larger sex-gender system.[4] Investigating the strategies whereby literary texts (primarily nineteenth-century novels) constructed a 'continuum of homosocial desire,' she illustrates that these texts articulate male sexuality in ways that also evoke asymmetrical power relations between men and women. Hence, she suggests that we must situate both the production and the consumption of literary representations depicting male interactions (whether overtly sexualized or not) within a larger social formation that circulates ideologies defining differences in power across sex and class.

This suggestion seems particularly applicable to Wilde's texts, which embody an especially contradictory nexus of class and sexual positionings. As the son of a noted Irish physician, Sir William Wilde, and a popular nationalist poet, Lady Jane Wilde (also called 'Speranza'), Wilde was educated in a series of public schools and colleges before attending Oxford. After receiving a double 'first' in 1879, Wilde 'went down' to London, where, owing to his father's death and his family's insolvency, he was forced to earn his own income. From that time until his imprisonment in

1895, Wilde consciously constructed and marketed himself as a liminal figure within British class relations, straddling the lines between nobility, aristocracy, middle class, and – in his sexual encounters – working class. The styles and attitudes that he affected in his writing and his life creatively packaged these multiple positionings; 'I have put all my genius into my life,' Wilde observed in his famous remark to André Gide; 'I have only put my talents into my work.' Typically, literary critics have explained this overdetermined positioning by situating Wilde among the nineteenth-century manifestations of decadence and dandyism, thereby emphasizing that his aesthetic paradoxically signified his dependence on the prevailing bourgeois culture and his detachment from it.[5] Yet his literary and personal practices also embodied a more contradictory relation to sexual and class ideologies.

As Regenia Gagnier demonstrates, these contradictions became evident in the contemporary reviews of *The Picture of Dorian Gray*:

> One is struck by the profusion of such terms [in the reviews of *Dorian Gray*] as 'unclean,' 'effeminate,' 'studied insincerity,' 'theatrical,' 'Wardour Street aestheticism,' 'obtrusively cheap scholarship,' 'vulgarity,' 'unnatural,' 'false,' and 'perverted': an odd mixture of the rumors of Wilde's homosexuality and of more overt criticism of Wilde as a social poseur and self-advertiser. Although the suggestion was couched in terms applying to the text, the reviews seemed to say that Wilde did not know his place, or – amounting to the same thing – that he did know his place and it was not that of a middle-class gentleman.
>
> (p. 59)

In Gagnier's analysis, the immediate critical response to *Dorian Gray* denounced the text's transgression of precisely those class and gender ideologies that sustained the 'middle-class gentleman': the novel was seen as 'decadent' both because of 'its distance from and rejection of middle-class life' and because 'it was not only dandiacal, it was "feminine" ' (p. 65). Thus, the *Athenaeum* would refer to the book as 'unmanly, sickening, vicious (although not exactly what is called "improper"), and tedious and stupid' (Mason p. 200). And the *Scotts Observer* would remark:

> Mr. Wilde has again been writing stuff that were better unwritten and while 'The Picture of Dorian Gray,' which he contributes to *Lippincott's*, is ingenious, interesting, full of cleverness, and plainly the work of a man of letters, it is false art – for its interest is medico-legal; it is false to human nature – for its hero is a devil; it is false to morality – for it is not made sufficiently clear that the

writer does not prefer a course of unnatural iniquity to a life of cleanliness, health and sanity.

(Mason, pp. 75–6)

Emphasizing that Wilde's novel violated the standards of middle-class propriety, these characterizations illustrate the intersection of Victorian class and gender ideologies from which Wilde's status as the paradigmatic 'homosexual' would emerge. For, in contrast to the 'manly' middle-class male, Wilde would come to represent – through his writing and his trials – the 'unmanly' social climber who threatened to upset the certainty of bourgeois categories.

To situate Wilde's emergence as 'a homosexual' in late nineteenth-century literary (con)texts and thereby explore the ways that sex-gender ideologies shape specific literary works, I focus first on *Teleny*, a novel widely attributed to Wilde and one of the earliest examples of male homoerotic pornography, whose encoding of sexual practices between men moves athwart those ideologies that sought to 'naturalize' male heterosexuality. Then by analyzing the better-known and yet manifestly 'straight' text *The Picture of Dorian Gray*, I illustrate that even in the absence of explicit homosexual terminology or activity, a text can subvert the normative standards of male same-sex behavior. In considering how these works challenge the hegemonic representations of male homoerotic experience in late Victorian Britain, I suggest how textual depictions of male same-sex experience both reproduce and resist the dominant heterosexual ideologies and practices.

Through the Revolving Door: The Pornographic Representation of the Homoerotic in *Teleny*

In *The Other Victorians*, Steven Marcus states:

The view of human sexuality as it was represented in the [late Victorian] subculture of pornography and the view of sexuality held by the official culture were reversals, mirror images, negative analogies of each other. ... In both the same set of anxieties are at work; in both the same obsessive ideas can be made out; and in both sexuality is conceived of at precisely the same degree of consciousness.

(pp. 283–4)

While Marcus's analysis suggestively projects the 'pornotopia' as the underside of bourgeois society, it fails to consider the ways that Victorian pornography not only reflected but refracted – or perhaps, more specifically, *interrupted* – the assumptions and practices of the dominant culture.[6] In other words, since Marcus relates the production of the pornographic only to institutionally legitimated forms of the sexual and the literary, he obscures the degree to which such an unsanctioned (and hence uncanonized) genre could provide positive articulations of marginalized sexual practices and desires.

One such textual affirmation can be found in *Teleny: Or, The Reverse of the Medal: A Physiological Romance*. Written in 1890 (the same year 'The Picture of Dorian Gray' appeared in *Lippincott's Monthly Magazine*), *Teleny* is reputed to be the serial work of several of Wilde's friends (who circulated the manuscript among themselves), with Wilde serving as general editor and coordinator.[7] Even if this genealogy proves apocryphal, the unevenness of its prose styles suggests that the novel was the collaboration of several authors and possibly a set of self-representations evolving out of the homosexual subculture in late Victorian London.

Chronicling the ill-fated love between two late nineteenth-century men, *Teleny* unfolds as a retrospective narrative told by the dying Camile Des Grieux to an unnamed interlocutor. Prompted by his questioner, Des Grieux unfolds a tale of seductions, sex (homo- and hetero-, oral and anal), orgies, incest, blackmail, rape, suicide, death, and love. Aroused by his passion for the beautiful – and well-endowed – young pianist René Teleny, Des Grieux opens himself to the varied possibilities of male sexual expression only to find himself drawn back again and again to a single object of desire: the male body of his beloved Teleny. Thus, Des Grieux's narrative represents an explicit set of strategies through which the male body is ensnared in the passions and excesses of homoerotic desire.

Introducing the image of its fatal conclusion, the novel's opening sentence directs us immediately to the body on which the narrative is inscribed: 'A few days after my arrival in Nice, last winter, I encountered several times on the Promenade a young man, of dark complexion, thin, a little stooped, of pallid color, with eyes – beautiful blue eyes – ringed in black, of delicate features, but aged and emaciated by a profound ailment, which appeared to be both physical and moral' (p. 21). The novel's conclusion can be initially 'read off' from Des Grieux's degenerate condition only because his body serves as the 'recording surface' for the story.[8] The narrator underscores this relation between body and narrative: 'The account that follows is not, then, a novel. It is rather a true story: the dramatic adventures of two young and handsome human beings of refined temperament, high-strung, whose brief existence was cut short by death after flights of passion which will doubtless be misunderstood by the generality of men' (p. 22). Here the generic 'human beings' distinguishes the protagonists from the 'generality of men' who will doubtlessly misunderstand them, introducing a fundamental opposition 'fleshed out' in the text: by juxtaposing male same-sex passion with a cultural concept of 'manliness' that seeks to exclude it, the novel deconstructs those definitions of human nature that deny the homoerotic as unnatural. Thus, even before its pornographic plot begins, the text attaches itself to the male body as the surface on which its markings will become legible and simultaneously undertakes to use this legibility to validate same-sex desire.

Within the novel's narrative logic, this validation derives from the irrationality of the attraction uniting Des Grieux and Teleny, in spite of their manifestly masculine (and hence ideologically rational) positioning. In the first chapter, positing their almost mystical affinity, Des Grieux recalls their 'predestined' meeting at a London charity concert. On stage, Teleny, the pianist, senses the presence of a 'sympathetic listener,' who inspires him to incredible heights of virtuosity. In the audience, Des Grieux responds to Teleny's performance by visualizing a set of extravagant and exotic scenes – portraying classical European images of non-European sexualized otherness – which, we soon learn, are the same visions that Teleny conjures as he plays. Indeed, these images are so distinct that Des Grieux experiences them physically: 'a heavy hand [that] seemed to be laid on my lap, something was hent and clasped and grasped, which made me faint with lust' (p. 27). In the midst of this masturbatory incantation, Des Grieux succumbs to the novel's first stirrings of priapic ecstasy. Thus, when the young men meet and their first touch (a properly masculine handshake) 'reawakens Priapus,' Des Grieux feels that he has been 'taken possession of' (p. 29). The ensuing conversation leads the men to recognize their affinity and, at the same time, foregrounds the irrationality underlying their erotic connection. Describing the music that has brought them together as the product of a 'madman,' Teleny hints at 'insanity' and 'possession,' enmeshing the two in a web of superstition and 'unreason.' By violating the dominant Victorian associations of masculinity with science and reason, the first encounter between the lovers casts their attraction as an implicit challenge to the normative ideologies for male behavior.

Following this initial highly charged meeting, the next four chapters elaborate the deferral of its sexual consummation, recounting Des Grieux's emotional turmoil as he comes to recognize, accept, and ultimately enjoy his physical desire for Teleny. The sexual content of this portion of the novel depicts primarily illicit – if not taboo – heterosexual practices. All these manifestly straight incidents, however, portray the heterosexual as a displacement of the true affection of one man for another; they juxtapose the universal acceptability and 'naturalness' of heterosexual passion (even if accompanied by incest or violence) to the execration and 'unnaturalness' of homoerotic desire.

As Des Grieux begins to make sense of his obsession with Teleny, he realizes that this natural–unnatural distinction is itself learned (i.e., cultural): '. . . I had been inculcated with all kinds of wrong ideas, so when I understood what my *natural* feelings for Teleny were I was staggered, horrified . . .' (p. 63; my emphasis). This inverted use of the word *natural* deconstructs the mask of ideological neutrality and underscores the moral implications it attempts to conceal. Once he accepts that he 'was born a sodomite,' Des Grieux can remark that 'I read all I could find about the love of one man for another, that loathsome crime against nature, taught to us not only by the very gods themselves, but by all of the greatest men of olden times. . . .' Thus the text mocks the culture's pretension in defining as a 'crime against nature' that which *his* nature demands and which the 'very gods themselves' and the 'greatest men of olden times' have practiced. By subverting the claims to 'natural' (read 'ideological') superiority by 'honorable [heterosexual] men,' the narrative's logic opens the possibility for a counterhegemonic representation of homoerotic desire.

The first sexual encounter between Des Grieux and Teleny inaugurates this new representation of same-sex desire by reviving the 'fatedness' of the relationship. As Des Grieux, convinced of the hopelessness of his passion for a man, stands on a bridge over the Thames and contemplates 'the forgetfulness of those Stygian waters,' he is grabbed from behind by the strong arms of his beloved Teleny, who is drawn to the spot by supernatural premonition (explained by Teleny's 'gypsy blood'). This charmed meeting culminates in a scene of extravagant and abandoned lovemaking through which the two men form an inseparable bond that sustain them for many climaxes and an unforgettable orgy. The charm is broken, however, when Teleny – through a combination of boredom, irrepressible lust, and economic necessity – is led into an affair with Des Grieux's mother. The shock of discovering that his mother has usurped his place in Teleny's bed sends Des Grieux into a decline from which he never recovers, and the shock of being found out causes Teleny to take his own life.

This summary can only hint at the profusion of sexual representation the novel engenders. Despite its tragic ending, its depiction of male homoerotic desire and practice insists on not only the possibility but the naturalness of same-sex eroticism. Thus, in reflecting on the story of his first night with Teleny, Des Grieux offers one of the most articulate defenses of same-sex love to be found in late Victorian fiction. Responding to his interlocutor's question, 'Still, I had thought, on the morrow – the intoxication passed – you would have shuddered at the thought of having a man for a lover?' Des Grieux asks:

> Why? Had I committed a crime against nature when my own nature found peace and happiness thereby? If I was thus, surely it was the fault of my blood, not myself. Who had planted nettles in my garden?

Not I. They had grown there unawares from my very childhood. I began to feel their carnal sting long before I could understand what conclusion they imported. When I had tried to bridle my lust, was it my fault if the scale of reason was far too light to balance that of sensuality? Was I to blame if I could not argue down my raging motion? Fate, Iago-like, had clearly shewed me that if I would damn myself, I could do so in a more delicate way than drowning. I yielded to my destiny and encompassed my joy.

(p. 119)

By juxtaposing his homoerotic 'nature' to a Victorian definition that criminalized it, Des Grieux's statement foregrounds the moral-ideological concerns implied in this naturalizing terminology. In so doing, he articulates a theory of 'innate difference' similar to the third-sex theories first proposed by the late nineteenth-century apologists for same-sex desire (Edward Carpenter, J. A. Symonds, and Havelock Ellis).[9] Since these formulations assume the opposition between intellect and passion – or between male and female – found elsewhere in late Victorian discourse, they necessarily encode the implicit bias on which these dichotomies depend. Here, however, the polarities are resolved through an alternative outlet, physical and moral: joy. In affirming the naturalness of Des Grieux's homoerotic experience, this new joyous possibility undermines the monovocalizing strategies the bourgeois heterosexual cultural used to ensure the reproduction of its dominance and thus opens up the possibility of representing a plurality of male sexualities.

Behind the Closet Door: The Representation of Homoerotic Desire in *The Picture of Dorian Gray*

What if someone wrote a novel about homosexuality and no body came? To what extent is *The Picture of Dorian Gray* this book? And what does it mean to say that a text is 'about' homosexuality anyway?

While *The Picture of Dorian Gray* has generated much speculation and innuendo concerning its author's sexual preferences, the aftermath of Wilde's trials has left no doubt in the critical mind that the 'immorality' of Wilde's text paralleled that of his life. Yet this critical reflection has never directly addressed the question of how Wilde's 'obviously' homoerotic text signifies its 'deviant' concerns while never explicitly violating the dominant norms for heterosexuality. That Wilde's novel encodes traces of male homoerotic desire seems to be ubiquitously, though tacitly, affirmed. Why this general affirmation exists has never been addressed. To understand how 'everyone knows' what lurks behind Wilde's manifestly straight language (i.e., without descending to a crude biographical explanation), we must examine the ways that Wilde's novel moves both with and athwart the late Victorian ideological practices that naturalized male heterosexuality.[10]

The Picture of Dorian Gray narrates the development of male identity within a milieu that actively subverts the traditional bourgeois representations of appropriate male behavior. While it portrays a sphere of art and leisure in which male friendships assume primary emotional importance and in which traditional male values (industry, earnestness, morality) are abjured in favor of the aesthetic, it makes no explicit disjunction between these two models of masculinity; rather, it formally opposes an aesthetic representation of the male body and the material, emotional, sexual male body itself. In other words, *The Picture of Dorian Gray* juxtaposes an aesthetic ideology that foregrounds representation with an eroticized milieu that inscribes the male body within circuits of male desire. To understand how this opposition operates, we must first consider the components of the male friendships in the novel.

The text of *Dorian Gray* develops around a constellation of three characters – Lord Henry Wotten, Basil Hallward, and Dorian Gray – who challenge the Victorian standards of 'true male' identity. Freed from the activities and responsibilities that typically consumed the energies of middle-class men, they circulate freely within an aestheticized social space that they collectively define. As inhabitants of a subculture, however, they still use a public language that has no explicit forms to represent (either to themselves or to one another) their involvements; hence, they must produce new discursive strategies to express concerns unvoiced within the dominant culture. In producing these strategies, the novel posits its moral and aesthetic interests. By projecting the revelation, growth, and demise of Dorian's 'personality' onto an aesthetic consideration of artistic creation, Wilde demonstrates how the psychosexual development of an individual gives rise to the 'double consciousness' of a marginalized group.[11] Dorian Gray is to some extent born of the conjunction between Basil's visual embodiment of his erotic desire for Dorian and Lord Henry's verbal sublimation of such desire. From this nexus of competing representational modes, Dorian Gray constitutes his own representations of identity. But who then is Dorian Gray?

Within the narrative structure, Dorian is an image – a space for the constitution of male desire. From the time he enters the novel as the subject of Basil's portrait until the moment Wilde has him kill himself into art, Dorian Gray provides the surface on which the characters project their self-representations. His is the body on which Basil's and Lord Henry's desires are inscribed. Beginning with an interview between these two characters, the novel constructs Dorian as a template of desire by thematizing the relation between the inspiration derived from

Dorian's 'personality' and the resulting aesthetic products. For Basil, Dorian appears as an 'ideal,' as the motivation for 'an entirely new manner in art, an entirely new mode of style.' Dorian's mere 'visible presence' enables Basil to represent emotions and feelings that he found inexpressible through traditional methods and themes: 'I see things differently now. I think of them differently. I can recreate life in a way that was hidden from me before' (p. 150).

But what gives Basil's relation to Dorian this transformative power? In describing his friendship with Dorian to Lord Harry, Basil narrates the story of their meeting:

> I turned halfway round, and saw Dorian Gray for the first time. When our eyes met I felt I was growing pale. A curious sensation of terror came over me. I knew I had come face to face with someone whose mere personality was so fascinating, that if I allowed it to do so it would absorb my whole nature, my very art itself. . . . Something seemed to tell me that I was on the verge of a terrible crisis in my life. I had a strange feeling that fate had in store for me exquisite joys and exquisite sorrows.
>
> (p. 146)

Dorian's 'personality' enchants Basil and throws him back upon himself, evoking a physical response that is then translated into a psychic, verbally encoded interpretation. As an artist, Basil resolves this crisis by experientially and aesthetically transforming his representations of this experience. His fascination with Dorian leads him to foreground their erotic connection ('We were quite close, almost touching. Our eyes met again.' [p. 147]) and at the same time to legitimate it in the sublimated language of aesthetic ideals ('Dorian Gray is to me simply a motive in art.' [p. 151]).

This symbolic displacement of the erotic onto the aesthetic is reiterated by the absent presence of the 'picture' within the novel. While homoerotic desire must be muted in a literary text that overtly conforms to dominant codes for writing – which have historically excluded same-sex desires as unrepresentable – it is nevertheless metonymically suggested by a verbally unrepresentable medium, the painting, whose linguistic incommensurability deconstructs the apparent self-sufficiency of these representational codes. Since the portrait stands outside the text and evokes an eroticized tableau transgressing the limits of verbal representation, it establishes a gap whereby unverbalized meaning can enter the text. In particular, its visual eroticism suffuses the dynamic between Dorian and Basil, thereby foregrounding the male body as the source of both aesthetic and erotic pleasure. The portrait provides the space within which, in contemporary psychoanalytic terminology, the phallic activity of 'the gaze' encroaches on the dominant linguistic unrepresentability of male same-sex eroticism.[12] Thus, the picture's absent presence (which motivates the narrative development) interrupts the novel's overt representational limits by introducing a visual, extraverbal component of male same-sex desire.

Since Wilde defines painting as an active expression of personal meanings, Basil's 'secret' infuses Dorian's picture with a vitality and passion that fundamentally change its 'mode of style.' Yet this secret does not lie in the work of art itself but rather grows out of Basil's emotional and erotic involvement with Dorian Gray, thereby establishing a new relation between the artist and his subject. As Basil eventually explains to Dorian:

> . . . from the moment I met you, your personality had the most extraordinary influence over me. I was dominated soul, brain, and power by you. You became to me the visible incarnation of that unseen ideal whose memory haunts us artists like an exquisite dream. I worshipped you. I grew jealous of everyone to whom you spoke. I wanted to have you all to myself. I was only happy when I was with you. When you were away from me you were still present in my art. . .
>
> (pp. 267–8)

The emotional intensity with which Wilde describes Basil's passion for Dorian belies the Platonic invocation of 'the visible incarnation of that unseen ideal,' since this verbal interpretation merely echoes the available public forms of expression. That Wilde displaces Basil's physical domination onto a dream (albeit exquisite) indicates that there is no publicly validated visible reality to express male homoerotic desire. But because painting can only occur in the nonlinear, and hence extralinguistic, space where Basil synthesizes the visual elements of his emotional and aesthetic inspiration, this visual expression and its verbal analogue are necessarily disjunct. Thus, although Basil's painting is entirely exterior to the text, it provides the reference point for a mode of representation that admits the visible, erotic presence of the male body.

Nowhere is this disjunction made more obvious than in Wilde's distinction between Basil's visual and physical involvement with Dorian and Lord Henry's detached, ironic, and self-conscious verbal stance. In contrast to Basil, who has surrendered his 'whole nature,' his 'whole soul,' his 'very heart itself,' to the immediacy of Dorian Gray, Lord Henry first becomes interested in Dorian through the story of Basil's passion. As a consummate aesthete, Lord Henry derives his passions not from direct engagement with his object but through mediated representations. By separating 'one's own soul' from the 'passions of one's friends' (p. 153), Wilde opposes Lord Henry's self-objectifying archness to Basil's passionate engagement with his inspiration's embodiment. To the extent that Basil, as a painter, seeks to create a spatialized frame that synthetically mirrors his emotional and erotic reality, Lord Henry, as a conversationalist, segments this aesthetic space into the paradoxes and conundrums that characterize his linguistic style. Basil himself exposes the logic behind this verbal analytics when he says to Lord Henry: 'You are an extraordinary fellow. You never say a moral thing and you never do a wrong thing. Your cynicism is simply a pose' (p. 144). It is precisely this cynical posture that distinguishes the two modes of representation the characters engender. For while Basil registers his passion in expressive forms, Lord Henry maintains an autonomous 'pose' by detaching himself from his own passions. He never does a wrong thing because he distances himself from the material world of activity by representing reality, both to himself and to others, as an ongoing conversation in which he never says a moral thing. This discursive maneuver, which collapses the physical plenitude of bodily reality into abstract conceptualization, interrupts the visual inscription of Basil's picture and thereby opens the space from which 'Dorian Gray' emerges.[13]

Chronologically, this emergence coincides with Basil and Lord Harry's rivalry for Dorian's attention. In recounting his story to Lord Harry, Basil initially hesitates to introduce Dorian's name for fear of violating his 'secret'. He pleads with Lord Henry not to 'take away from me the one person who gives my art whatever charm it possesses,' yet his plea merely confirms their competition for the same 'wonderfully handsome young man.' Though the motives behind this competition are left unspoken, it unfolds during Dorian's final sitting for his portrait. Here, in Basil's studio, the conflict plays itself out as a seduction: Lord Henry woos Dorian away from the adoring gaze of the painter to awaken him to a new, symbolic order of desire – an order at the very heart of the narrative.

Responding to Dorian's complaint that Basil never speaks while painting, Basil allows Lord Henry to stay and entertain Dorian. While Basil puts the finishing touches on the canvas, Lord Henry charms Dorian with a discussion of morality:

> The aim of life is self-development. To realize one's nature perfectly – that is what each of us is here for. People are afraid of themselves nowadays. They have forgotten the highest of all duties is the duty that one owes to oneself. Of course they are charitable. They feed the hungry and clothe the beggar. But their souls starve and are naked. Courage has gone out of our race. Perhaps we never really had it. The terror of society, which is the basis of morals, and the terror of God, which is the secret of religion – these are the two things that govern us.
>
> (p. 158)

As Lord Henry's words provide Dorian with new vistas on the moral prejudices of their era, his 'low musical voice' seduces the younger man, who becomes transfigured: '. . . a look came into the lad's face . . . never seen there before.' Simultaneously, Basil inscribes this 'look' – the object of both his artistic and erotic gaze – onto the canvas, thus doubly imbuing his aesthetic image with the representations of male homoerotic desire.

By dialectically transforming Lord Henry's verbal and Basil's visual representations, Dorian enters into the circuits of male desire through which these characters play out their sexual identities. He inspires both Basil and Lord Henry to new heights of expression, but only by internalizing and modifying images through which the older men would have themselves seen. Thus, the development of Dorian's 'perfect nature' underscores the disjunction between male homoerotic experience and the historical means of expressing it, so that his strategic mediation between them enables desire to enter the novel explicitly. Lord Henry continues his moral panegyric, once again voicing the problem:

> The body sins once and has done with sin, for action is a mode of purification. Nothing remains then but the recollection of a pleasure, or the luxury of a regret. The only way to get rid of a temptation is to yield to it. Resist it, and your soul grows sick with longing for those things it has forbidden to itself, with desire for what its monstrous laws have made monstrous and unlawful.
>
> (p. 159)

Temptation resisted, Lord Harry suggests, gives rise to the image of a desired yet forbidden object. This overdetermined representation, in turn, mediates between the active body and the reflective mind by forbidding those desires that the soul's monstrous laws proscribe. Thus, these laws – the social representations of self-denial – separate the body as a source of pleasure from the interpretation of that pleasure as sin. By negating pleasure, the natural expression of the body, society (introjected here as 'soul') inhibits the body's sensuous potential and circumscribes feeling within established moral codes.

Responding passionately to Lord Henry's critique of this interdictive morality, Dorian senses 'entirely fresh influences . . . at work within him [that] really seemed to have come from himself.' Since the older man's words counterpose the social to the personal, the desiring associated with self-development to the interdictions of culture, his influence on Dorian emphasizes the sensual as a strategy for resisting society's limitations. 'Nothing can cure the soul but the senses, just as nothing can cure the senses but the soul.' Although Lord Henry speaks only of the body's sensual possibilities, Dorian uses these words to formulate a new self-image: 'The few words that Basil's friend had said to him – words spoken by chance, no doubt, and with willful paradox in them – had touched some secret chord that had never been touched before, but that he felt was now vibrating and throbbing to curious pulses' (p. 160). By defining Dorian's formerly inchoate feelings and sensations, Lord Henry's language creates a new reality for Dorian ('. . . mere words. Was there anything so real as words'), and Basil's canvas records Dorian's changing self-image – but only as expressed through Basil's desire. The rivalry between the two older friends for Dorian's affection vitalizes the surface of Basil's painting by attributing an erotic charge to Dorian's body itself. And as this body becomes the object of male attention and representation, the young man's concept of his own material being is transformed – he is 'revealed to himself.'

Looking on his completed portrait for the first time, Dorian encounters himself as reflected in the 'magical mirror' of Basil's desire. This image organizes the disparate perceptions of his body into an apparently self-contained whole and reorients Dorian in relation both to his own identity and to his social context. He begins to conceive of his beauty as his own, failing to understand it as the product of the images that Basil and Lord Harry dialectically provide for him. Wilde describes this change as a physical response, thereby foregrounding the connection between psychic representation and somatic perception while indicating that this seemingly coherent internal representation synthesizes a complex nexus of social relationships. Hence, Dorian's identification with the painted image constitutes a misrecognition as much as a recognition, leading him to confuse an overdetermined set of representations with the 'truth' of his experience.

Within these (mis)representations Dorian comes to view his body as distinct from his soul and mis-recognizes the certainty of his aging and death. Splitting his self-image into two, Basil's visual representation and Lord Henry's verbal portrait, Dorian internalizes an identity that excites his body only to make it vulnerable to the passage of time. The transitiveness of this new self-recognition manifests itself as physical experience: 'As he thought of it [his body's aging] a sharp pang of pain struck through him like a knife and made each delicate fibre of his nature quiver' (p. 167). To avoid aging, Dorian inverts the imaginary and the real and thus conceptualizes the painful disjunction between the image of his body and his body itself as a form of jealousy:

> How sad it is! I shall grow old, and horrible, and dreadful. But this picture will always remain young. It will never be older than this particular day of June. . . . If it were only the other way! If it were I who was to be always young, and the picture that was to grow old! For that – for that – I would give everything. Yes there is nothing in the world I would not give! I would give my soul for that.
>
> (p. 168)

In voicing this statement, Dorian executes a linguistic schism – dividing the 'I' against itself – which repositions him within the narrative flow. As the 'I' of the speaking character is projected against the visual image of the 'I,' his body is evacuated and thereby removed from the flow of time.

Dorian stakes his soul for the preservation of his physical beauty, of his body image, and Wilde makes the motive for this wager clear: Dorian fears that time will rob him of the youth that makes him the object of male desire: ' "Yes," he continued to Basil], "I am less to you than your ivory Hermes or your silver faun. You will like them always. How long will you like me? Til I have my first wrinkle, I suppose, I know now, that when one loses one's good looks, whatever they may be, one loses everything. Your picture has taught me that" ' (pp. 168–9). In portraying Dorian's self-perception as a function of Basil's erotic and aesthetic appreciation, Wilde fuses the artifacts of homoerotic desire and the representations that Dorian uses to constitute his identity. The classical images of male beauty and eroticism make Dorian jealous because he fails to understand that the body can have simultaneous aesthetic and erotic appeal. His focus on visual and sexual desirability emphasizes the importance that culturally produced representations have in the construction of male identity.

In describing Dorian's identity as a product of aesthetic and erotic images, Wilde locates 'the problem' of male homoerotic desire on the terrain of representation itself. Since his characters encounter one another at the limits of heterosexual forms, they produce multiple positionings for articulating different desires, evoking possibilities for male same-sex eroticism without explicitly voicing them. Instead, Wilde posits many uncovered secrets (Basil's 'secret,' Dorian's 'secrets,' Lord Henry's continual revelation of the 'secrets of life,' even the absent portrait itself), thereby creating a logic of displacement that culminates in Dorian's prayer for eternal youth. Standing outside the text and yet initiating all further narrative development, the prayer is marked only by a caesura that transforms the relation between representation and desire. In a moment of textual silence, Dorian – misperceiving the true object of Basil's feeling – defends his idealized self-image by invoking the magical aspects of utterance. To maintain his identity as the object of another man's desire, he prays to exchange the temporality of his existence for the stasis of an erotically charged visual representation. Inasmuch as Basil's secret – his 'worship with far more romance than a man usually gives a friend' (in the 1890 edition) – radiates from the canvas reflecting its subject's beauty, Dorian's profession, 'I am in love with it, Basil. It is part of myself. I feel that,' underscores the degree to which his male self-image reverberates with the passion of same-sex desire. And this passionate attachment inspires the supplication that makes his portrait perhaps the most well-known nonexistent painting in Western culture.

Not coincidentally, then, the famous reversal between the character and his portrait first appears to stem from the failure of the novel's only explicitly heterosexual element. By introducing the feminine into a world that systematically denies it, Dorian's attraction to the young actress Sibyl Vane (a vain portent?) seems to violate the male-identified world in which Basil and Lord Henry have 'revealed [Dorian] to himself.' Yet, Sibyl's presence can never actually disturb the novel's male logic, for her appearance merely shows how much an overtly heterosexual discourse depends on male-defined representations of female experience. For Dorian, Sibyl exists only in the drama. Offstage, he imbues her with an aesthetic excess, so that her reality never pierces his fantasy. His remarks to Lord Henry demonstrate that Dorian's passion is the passion of the voyeur, whose desiring gaze distances the viewer from the possibility (necessity?) of physical consummation: '

> 'Tonight she is Imogen.' [Dorian] answered, 'and tomorrow she will be Juliet.'
>> 'When is she Sibyl Vane?'
>> 'Never.'

(p. 200)

When Dorian impassions Sibyl with a single kiss (the only physical [sexual?] expression that evades his aesthetic voyeurism), her own real passion renders her incapable of making a male-defined representation of female passion 'real.' Thus she fails to achieve the aesthetic standard he expects of her in the role of Juliet, and Dorian – unable to sustain his heterosexual fantasy – abandons her.[14]

This abandonment leads Sibyl to suicide and introduces the disjunction between Dorian and his portrait. Returning home after his final scene with her, Dorian finds the picture changed, marked by 'lines of cruelty around his mouth as clearly as if he had been looking into a mirror after he had done some dreadful thing' (p. 240). He senses anew that this representation 'held the secret of his life, and told *his story*' (p. 242; my emphasis). Where once the painting had been confined to the atemporality of the aesthetic moment, it now becomes the surface that records the narrative of his life, not only serving as a static reflection of the interiority of his soul but also telling his soul's story. A 'magical mirror,' it turns Dorian into a 'spectator of [his] own life,' thus creating a divided consciousness that initiates the remaining action in the novel.

As Dorian realizes the separation between self-representation and self-image, his behavior becomes ominous and degenerate. He enters into a world of self-abuse and destruction, through which he effects the downfall of many innocent men and women, and yet his body shows no sign of these activities. Only the picture – now locked away in an inaccessible room – reveals the depths to which he has descended. For, as the portrait tells his story, it graphically reveals the details of all he does. In time, the portrait's increasing grotesqueness begins to haunt Dorian. His awareness of the terrifying gap between the man whom others see and the representation that only he may view serves as the limit against which he conceives of his existence. He immerses himself in the life of the senses to test the absoluteness of this limit but finds that he cannot break through it. So long as he remains inscribed within the network of representations – both verbal and visual – that the painting constructs, he can only embody the agonizing dichotomy that it engenders.

Ultimately, seeking to free himself from the images that have ensnared and 'destroyed' him, Dorian kills the man who 'authored' the 'fatal portrait.' This murder removes the one person to whom Dorian could impute responsibility for the portrait. The picture, which now also depicts the horror of Basil's death, remains only to remind Dorian of the monstrosity of his life. In the final pages of the novel, Dorian resolves to destroy the image. Standing before it, he faces both the material representation of his existence and the distance between that representation and himself. As he plunges the knife into the canvas that reveals his secret, he rends this disjunction, finally breaking free of its absolute limit. Yet, since the price of this freedom is the destruction of the complex configuration of images that motivate both the character and the narrative, the act that concludes the novel does so only by killing Dorian into art.

As his death brings the interplay between representation and the body full circle, the images that Dorian had reflected through his entry into the male-defined world presented by Basil Hallward and Lord Henry Wotten are once again inscribed on his body. And so, in the end, Dorian's corpse becomes the surface that records his narrative, liberating Dorian in death from the consciousness divided between experience and representation that had marked his life.

Coda: Out of the Theoretical Closet

To the extent that Wilde and contemporaries like him were beginning to articulate strategies to communicate – both to themselves and to others – the experience of homoerotic desire, their texts enact and virtually embody this desire. But since these men were also writing within a larger culture that not only denied but actively prosecuted such embodiments, they were forced to devise ways to mediate their expressions of passion. While in certain uncanonized genres, like pornography and to some extent poetry (e.g., the 'Uranian' poets), relatively explicit statements of same-sex eroticism were possible, these statements were still posed in relation to the social norms that enjoined them. Thus, although *Teleny* explicitly represents sexual practices between men for an audience who either enjoyed or at least sympathized with such practices, it still reinscribes these representations within the (hetero)sexual symbolic order that it sought to interrupt. In a more canonized work, such as *The Picture of Dorian Gray*, the mediations are necessarily more complex. Wilde's text doubly displaces male homoerotic desire, thematizing it through the aesthetic production of a medium that the novel cannot represent. Basil's portrait of Dorian can embody his desire for the eponymous character, and yet male homoerotic passion remains, in the dominant representational codes of the period, *peccatum illude horribile non nominandum inter christianos* – or, in a bad paraphrase of Lord Alfred Douglas, a love whose name the text dare not speak. In *The Picture of Dorian Gray*, Wilde problematizes representation per se to move athwart the historical limitations that define male homosexuality as 'unnameable,' thereby creating one of the most lasting icons of male homoerotic desire.

By approaching *Teleny* and *The Picture of Dorian Gray* as complex cultural artifacts, we recognize them not just as texts but as contexts. For, as Raymond Williams says, 'If art is a part of the society, there is no solid whole, outside it, to which by the form of our question, we concede priority' (p. 45). Instead of seeing these literary works as ideological reflections of an already existing reality, we must consider them elements in the production of this reality. In analyzing the textual strategies through which these two novels put male desire for other men into discourse, we begin to understand some of the historical forms that such relations between men took and thereby begin to suggest others that they can take.[15]

Notes

1. Press reports of the trials note that court attendance was exclusively male. The defendant, the prosecution, all the court officials, as well as the audience and press, were also male; hence all that transpired and all that was reported occurred within an entirely male-defined social space for the benefit of a male public.

2. For the theoretical underpinnings of this argument see Michel Foucault's *History of Sexuality*. Here Foucault counters the post-Freudian notion that Victorian practice repressed natural sexuality and, instead, considers the positive strategies that enveloped the body within particular historical discursive apparatuses. He suggests that the bourgeoisie's concern with regulating its own sexual practices stemmed not from an interdictive moral ideology but rather from an attempt to define its materiality – its body – as a class:

   The emphasis on the body should undoubtedly be linked to the process of growth and establishment of bourgeois hegemony: not, however, because of the market value assumed by labor capacity, but because of what the 'cultivation' of its own body could represent politically, economically, and historically for the present and the future of the bourgeoisie. . . .

(pp. 125–6)

3. That 'homosexuality' stood in a negative relation to 'heterosexuality' is metaphorically indicated by the term *invert*, which historically preceded *homosexual* and often served as a synonym (see Chauncey for a more precise explanation of these two terms). Since this essay attempts to explore two particular textual negotiations of the emerging heterosexual–homosexual opposition, the use of both these terms here seems anachronistic. Thus, I use them advisedly and often quarantine them between quotation marks to indicate that I am quoting from the larger cultural (con)text in which they have become commonplace. In a recent article Tim Calligan, Bob Connell, and John Lee note the enduring effects of this opposition (p. 587). For details of the development of 'the adolescent,' see ARIÈS; GILLIS, *Youth*; GORHAM: and DONZELOT. On 'the criminal,' see LOMBROSO'S *Criminal Man and The Female Offender*. JUDITH WALKOWITZ details the emergence of 'the prostitute.' For 'the delinquent' see FOUCAULT, *Discipline*, and GILLIS, "Evolution." On 'the homosexual' see WEEKS, *Coming Out*; PLUMMER; FADERMAN; KATZ; and CHAUNCEY.

4. The term belongs to GAYLE RUBIN, who initially defined it as 'the set of arrangements by which a society transforms biological sexuality into products of human activity and in which these transformed sexual needs are satisfied' (p. 159).

5. For a comprehensive survey of the critical appraisal of Wilde as 'decadent' and 'dandy,' see GAGNIER, especially ch. 2, 'Dandies and Gentlemen.'

6. I take the concept 'interruption' from DAVID SILVERMAN and BRIAN TORODE who define it as a practice that 'seeks not to impose a language of its own but to enter critically into existing linguistic configurations, and to re-open the closed structures into which they have ossified' (p. 6). This notion of interruption as a critical refiguring of ossified linguistic structures – itself a wonderful metaphor for ideological attempts to petrify historically constructed, hegemonically organized semiotic equivalences into timeless, natural usages – provides an excellent analytical tool for examining subcultural discourses that challenge a dominant culture's monovocalizing practices. I apply it to resistant or counterhegemonic textual strategies that reopen the polyvalence of linguistic practices – here specifically the homoerotic challenge to the conception of heterosexuality as natural.

7. This account is paraphrased from WINSTON LEYLAND'S introduction to the Gay Sunshine reprint of *Teleny*. Leyland takes most of his information from H. M. Hyde's introduction to the 1966 British edition, which Hyde derives in part from the introduction of a 1934 French translation written by Leonard Hirsch, the London bookseller whose shop was supposedly the transfer point for the various authors.

8. This terminology, which is implicit throughout my essay, derives from Gilles Deleuze and Félix Guattari. They develop the metaphors of 'marking the body' and 'recording surfaces of desire' to elaborate the mechanisms through which desire invests somatic experience as well as to consider the ways in which the socius 'codes' the body. See especially their part 3. 'Savages, Barbarians, Civilized Men.'

9. For a discussion of these initial apologies for homoerotic behavior see JEFFREY WEEKS, *Coming Out* and *Sexuality and Its Discontents*. On the body-mind dichotomy in nineteenth-century discourse, see ROSALIND COWARD.

10. For a selection of articles showing how the contemporary press responded to *Dorian Gray*, along with Wilde's replies to these criticisms, see STUART MASON. Later explanations of the relation between Wilde's personal and textual sexuality include G. WILSON KNIGHT's "Christ and Wilde," which attributes Wilde's 'perverse pleasures' (p. 138, quoting Wilde's *De Profundis*) to his 'mother fixation,' to his mother's having 'dressed him as a girl until he was nine,' and to his 'love of flowers and of male and female dress.' Knight reads *Dorian Gray* as the 'subtlest critique of the Platonic Eros ever penned' (p. 143) – without stooping to textual exegesis – and then justifies Wilde's 'homosexual engagements' as 'a martyrdom, a crucifixion, a self-exhibition in agony and shame' deriving from both 'the instinct . . . to plunge low when disparity between near-integrated self and the community becomes unbearable' and 'a genuine liking for the lower orders of society' (144–5). RICHARD ELLMANN informs us that Wilde changes the date of Dorian's murder of Basil Hallward from 'the eve of his own thirty-second birthday' in the original Lippincott's version to 'the eve of his own thirty-eighth birthday' in the bound edition to mask the reference to his first sexual experience with Robbie Ross, which – according to a mathematical extrapolation from Ross's memoirs – must have occurred during Wilde's thirty-second year (p. 11). Other critical works that acknowledge Wilde's homosexuality without analyzing the 'homotextual problematic' include those by PHILIP COHEN, JEFFREY MEYERS, and CHRISTOPHER NASSAAR. Meyers is especially interesting, given his explicit project of examining the homosexual 'in' literature, but unfortunately his eclectic methodology quickly descends into the biographical and associational strategies that characterize most criticism on *Dorian Gray*.

11. My use of 'double consciousness' derives largely from JACK WINKLER's article relating the work of Sappho as a lesbian poet to the public discourse of the Greek polis. Winkler develops a concept reminiscent of W. E. B. Du Bois's notion of the 'twoness' of the Afro-American experience (16–17) to refer to the overdetermined conditions of Sappho's representations. Because of her 'double consciousness,' Winkler suggests, the marginalized poet can speak and write in the dominant discourse but subvert its monolithic truth claims by recasting them in the light of personal, subcultural experience: 'This amounts to a reinterpretation of the kinds of meaning previous claims had, rather than a mere contest of claimants; for supremacy in a category whose meaning is agreed upon' (p. 73). Applying this theory of 'reinterpretation.' I conclude that Wilde repeatedly deals with heterosexual morality to deconstruct its social force through wit and witticism.

12. On the connection between the construction of male sexual identity, visual eroticism, and desire see JANE GALLOP's discussion of French feminist theory. Also see TORIL MOI's suggestion, in her discussion of the readings of Freud in the texts of Luce Irigaray, that 'the gaze [is] a phallic activity linked to anal desire for the sadistic mastery of the object' (p. 134).

13. GALLOP connects 'phallic suppression' and the evacuation of the body (p. 67).

14. Many of Sibyl's roles involve her cross-dressing as a boy, which further complicates the problematic construction of heterosexual desire within the novel. For example, playing Rosalind dressed as a boy, she stirs the desire

of Orlando, who is saved from the 'horror' of this same-sex passion by the underlying premise that the boy is indeed a girl. (Of course, in Shakespearean theater, where boys played the female characters, the complexities were redoubled.) Dorian's remark on Sibyl's 'perfection' in boy's clothes and *Portrait of Mr W. H.* which argues for the homoerotic inspiration of Shakespeare's sonnets, would both indicate that Wilde intended this resonance.

15. I wish to express my gratitude to all those who have commented on the numerous successive versions of this article. I especially wish to thank Regenia Gagnier, whose enthusiasm and support have encouraged me to persevere; Mary Pratt, who has taught me by her example that care and concern are the most essential elements of good scholarship; and Mark Frankel, at whose desk in Lytton basement this essay was first begun and to whom it is dedicated.

Works Cited

ARIÈS, P. *Centuries of Childhood.* Trans. Robert Baldick (London: Cape, 1962).

CALLIGAN, TIM, BOB CONNELL, and JOHN LEE. 'Towards a New Sociology of Masculinity.' *Theory and Society* 14.5 (1985): 551–604.

CHAUNCEY, GEORGE, 'From Sexual Inversion to Homosexuality.' *Salmagundi* 58–9 (1982–83): 114–46.

COHEN, PHILIP, *The Moral Vision of Oscar Wilde* (London: Fairleigh Dickinson, UP, 1978).

COMINOS, P. 'Late Victorian Sexual Respectability and the Social System.' *International Review of Social History* 8 (1963): 18–48, 216–50.

CONNELL, R. W. 'Class, Patriarchy and Sartre's Theory of Practice.' *Theory and Society* 11 (1982): 305–20.

COWARD, ROSALIND. *Patriarchal Precedents* (London: Routledge, 1983).

DELEUZE, GILLES, and FÉLIX GUATTARI. *Anti-Oedipus: Capitalism and Schizophrenia,* trans. Robert Hurley, Mark Seem, and Helen R. Lane (New York: Viking, 1977).

DONZELOT, JACQUES. *The Policing of Families.* Trans. Robert Hurley (New York: Pantheon, 1979).

DU BOIS, W. E. B. *The Soul of Black Folks* (Greenwich: Fawcett, 1961).

ELLMANN, RICHARD. 'The Critic as Artist as Wilde.' *Wilde and the Nineties.* Ed. Charles Ryskamp (Princeton: Princeton University Library, 1966), p. 1–20.

FADERMAN, LILLIAN. *Surpassing the Love of Men* (New York: Morrow, 1981).

FOUCAULT, MICHEL, *Discipline and Punish,* trans. Alan Sheridan (New York: Vintage, 1979).

–––. *The History of Sexuality.* Vol. 1 (New York: Vintage, 1980).

GAGNIER, REGENIA. *Idylls of the Marketplace: Oscar Wilde and the Victorian Public* (Stanford: Stanford University Press, 1986).

GALLOP, JANE. *The Daughter's Seduction: Feminism and Psychoanalysis* (Ithaca: Cornell University Press, 1982).

GILBERT, ARTHUR, 'Buggery and the British Navy, 1700–1861.' *Journal of Social History* 10.1 (1976): 72–97.

GILLIS, JOHN. 'The Evolution of Delinquency, 1890–1914.' *Past and Present* 67 (1975): 96–126.

–––. *Youth and History* (New York: Academic, 1974).

GORHAM, DEBORAH. *The Victorian Girl and the Feminine Ideal* (Bloomington: Indiana University Press, 1982).

HYDE, H. MONTGOMERY. *The Trials of Oscar Wilde.* (London: Hodge, 1948).

KATZ, JONATHAN. *Gay/Lesbian Almanac* (New York: Harper, 1983).

KNIGHT, G. WILSON. 'Christ and Wilde.' *Oscar Wilde: A Collection of Critical Essays.* Ed. Richard Ellmann (Englewood Cliffs: Prentice, 1969) pp. 38–50.

LEYLAND WINSTON. Introduction. Wilde, *Teleny* 5–19.

LOMBROSO CAESAR. *Criminal Man* (London, 1875).

–––. *The Female Offender* (New York, 1897).

MARCUS, STEVEN. *The Other Victorians* (New York: Basic, 1964).

MASON, STUART, *Oscar Wilde: Art and Morality* (New York: Haskell, 1971).

MEYERS, JEFFREY, *Homosexuality and Literature* (London: Athlone, 1977).

MOI, TORIL. *Sexual/Textual Politics: Feminist Literary Theory* (New York: Methuen, 1985).

NASSAAR, CHRISTOPHER. *Into the Demon University* (New Haven: Yale University Press, 1974).

PLUMMER, KENNETH, ed. *The Making of the Modern Homosexual* (London: Hutchinson, 1981).

RUBIN, GAYLE. 'The Traffic in Women.' *Towards an Anthropology of Women*, ed. Rayna Reiten (New York: Monthly Review, 1975), pp. 157–210.

SEDGWICK, EVE KOSOFSKY. *Between Men: English Literature and Male Homosocial Desire* (New York: Columbia University Press, 1985).

SILVERMAN, DAVID and BRIAN TORODE. *The Material World* (London: Routledge, 1980).

THOMAS, KEITH. 'The Double Standard.' *Journal of the History of Ideas* 20.2 (1959): 195–216.

TRUMBACH, RANDOLPH. 'London's Sodomites: Homosexual Behavior and Western Culture in the 18th Century.' *Journal of Social History* 11.1 (1977): 1–33.

WALKOWITZ, JUDITH. *Prostitution and Victorian Society* (New York: Cambridge University Press, 1980).

WEEKS, JEFFREY. *Coming Out: Homosexual Politics in Britain from the Nineteenth Century to the Present* (New York: Quartet, 1977).

–––. *Sexuality and Its Discontents* (London: Routledge, 1985).

WILDE, OSCAR. 'The Picture of Dorian Gray.' *Lippincott's Monthly Magazine* July 1890: 3–100.

–––. *The Picture of Dorian Gray. The Portable Oscar Wilde*, ed. R. Aldington and S. Weintraub (New York: Viking, 1974).

---. *Teleny* (San Francisco: Gay Sunshine, 1984).

WILLIAMS, RAYMOND. *The Long Revolution* (London: Chatto, 1961).

WINKLER, JACK. 'Garden of Nymphs: Public and Private in Sappho's Lyrics.' *Women's Studies* 8 (1981): 65–91.

8 Different Desires: Subjectivity and Transgression in Wilde and Gide*

JONATHAN DOLLIMORE

Jonathan Dollimore is Reader in the School of English and American Studies at the University of Sussex. The essay reprinted here was later incorporated into his book *Sexual Dissidence: Augustine to Wilde, Freud to Foucault* (Oxford: Oxford University Press, 1991), a wide-ranging examination of the social marginality and symbolic centrality of homosexuality from the early modern period to the present. Like several other essays reprinted in this volume this one very self-consciously re-reads the nineteenth-century *fin de siècle* from and for the end of the twentieth century. Dollimore co-opts Wilde for current debates in literary theory, gender studies and queer theory. He also assigns Wilde a role in the perpetual crisis in English Studies when he represents him as attacking those wholesome, manly, simple ideals that came to form the ethical base of 'English' (see Introduction, pp. 12–13).

In Blidah, Algeria, in January 1895 André Gide is in the hall of a hotel, about to leave. His glance falls on the slate which announces the names of new guests: 'suddenly my heart gave a leap; the two last names . . . were those of Oscar Wilde and Lord Alfred Douglas.'[1] Acting on his first impulse, Gide 'erases' his own name from the slate and leaves for the station. Twice thereafter Gide writes about the incident, unsure why he left so abruptly; first in his *Oscar Wilde* (1901), then in *Si le grain ne meurt* (*If It Die*, 1920, 1926). It may, he reflects, have been a feeling of *mauvaise honte* or of embarrassment: Wilde was becoming notorious and his company compromising. But also he was severely depressed, and at such times 'I feel ashamed of myself, disown, repudiate myself'.[2] Whatever

*Reprinted from *Textual Practice*, 1 (1987), pp. 48–67

the case, on his way to the station he decides that his leaving was cowardly and so returns. The consequent meeting with Wilde was to precipitate a transformation in Gide's life and subsequent writing.

Gide's reluctance to meet Wilde certainly had something to do with previous meetings in Paris four years earlier in 1891; they had seen a great deal of each other across several occasions, and biographers agree that this was one of the most important events in Gide's life. But these meetings had left Gide feeling ambivalent towards the older man, and it is interesting that not only does Gide say nothing in *If It Die* about Wilde's obvious and deep influence upon him in Paris in 1891, but, according to Jean Delay, in the manuscript of Gide's journal the pages corresponding to that period – November–December 1891 – are torn out.[3]

Undoubtedly Gide was deeply disturbed by Wilde, and not surprisingly, since Gide's remarks in his letters of that time suggest that Wilde was intent on undermining the younger man's self-identity, rooted as it was in a Protestant ethic and high bourgeois moral rigour and repression that generated a kind of conformity to which Wilde was, notoriously, opposed. Wilde wanted to encourage Gide to transgress. It may be that he wanted to re-enact in Gide the creative liberation – which included strong criminal identification – which his own exploration of transgressive desire had produced nine years earlier. (Wilde's major writing, including that which constitutes his transgressive aesthetic, dates from 1886 when, according to Robert Ross, he first practised homosexuality.[4]) But first Wilde had to undermine that law-full sense of self which kept Gide transfixed within the law. So Wilde tried to decentre or demoralize Gide – 'demoralize' in the sense of liberate from moral constraint rather than to dispirit; or, rather, to dispirit precisely in the sense of to liberate from a morality anchored in the very notion of spirit. ('Demoralize' was a term Gide remembers Wilde using in just this sense, one which, for Gide, recalled Flaubert.) Hence, perhaps, those most revealing of remarks by Gide to Valéry at this time (4 December 1891):

> Wilde is religiously contriving to kill what remains of my soul, because he says that in order to know an essence, one must eliminate it: he wants me to miss my soul. The measure of a thing is the effort made to destroy it. Each thing is made up only of its emptiness.

And in another letter of the same month: 'Please forgive my silence: since Wilde, I hardly exist anymore.'[5] And in unpublished notes for this time he declares that Wilde was 'always trying to instil into you *a sanction for evil*'.[6] So, despite his intentions to the contrary, Wilde at that time seems indeed to have dispirited Gide in the conventional sense. Yet perhaps the contrary intention was partly successful; on 1 January 1892 Gide writes: 'Wilde, I think, did me nothing but harm. In his company I had lost the habit of thinking, I had more varied emotions, but had forgotten how to bring order into them.'[7] In fact, Gide reacted, says Delay, in accordance with his Protestant instincts, reaffirming a moral conviction inseparable from an essentialist conception of self (cf. *Journal*, 29 December 1891: 'O Lord keep me from evil. May my soul again be proud'). Even so, this meeting with Wilde is to be counted as one of the most important events in Gide's life: 'for the first time he found himself confronted with a man who was able to bring about, within him, a transmutation of all values – in other words, a revolution.'[8] Richard Ellmann concurs with this judgement, and suggests further that Wilde's attempt to 'authorize evil' in Gide supplies much of the subject of *The Immoralist* and *The Counterfeiters*, the former work containing a character, Ménalque, who is based upon Wilde.[9]

It is against the background and the importance of that earlier meeting, together with the ambivalence towards Wilde which it generated in Gide, that we return to that further encounter in Algeria four years later. If anything, the ambivalence seems even stronger; in a letter to his mother Gide describes Wilde as a terrifying man, a 'most dangerous product of modern civilization' who had already depraved Douglas *'right down to the marrow'*.[10] A few days later Gide meets them again in Algiers, a city which Wilde declares his intention to demoralize.[11] It is here that there occurs the event which was to change Gide's life and radically influence his subsequent work, an event for which the entire narrative of *If It Die* seems to have been preparing. He is taken by Wilde to a café. It is there that 'in the half-open doorway, there suddenly appeared a marvellous youth. He stood there for a time, leaning with his raised elbow against the door-jamb, and outlined on the dark background of the night.' The youth joins them; his name is Mohammed; he is a musician; he plays the flute. Listening to that music, 'you forgot the time and place, and who you were'.[12] This is not the first time Gide has experienced this sensation of forgetting. Africa increasingly attracts him in this respect;[13] there he feels liberated and the burden of an oppressive sense of self is dissolved: 'I laid aside anxieties, constraints, solicitudes, and as my will evaporated, I felt myself becoming porous as a beehive.'[14] Now, as they leave the café, Wilde turns to Gide and asks him if he desires the musician. Gide writes: 'how dark the alley was! I thought my heart would fail me; and what a dreadful effort of courage it needed to answer: "yes", and with what a choking voice!' (Delay points out that the word 'courage' is here transvalued by Gide; earlier he had felt courage was needed for self-discipline, whereas now it is the strength to transgress.[15])

Wilde arranges something with their guide, rejoins Gide and then begins laughing: 'a resounding laugh, more of triumph than of pleasure, an interminable, uncontrollable, insolent laugh . . . it was the amusement of a child and a devil'. Gide spends the night with Mohammed: 'my joy was unbounded, and I cannot imagine it greater, even if love had been added.' Though not his first homosexual experience, it confirmed his (homo)sexual 'nature', what, he says, was 'normal' for him. Even more defiantly Gide declares that, although he had achieved 'the summit of pleasure five times' with Mohammed, 'I revived my ecstasy many more times, and back in my hotel room I relived its echoes until morning'[16] (this passage was one of those omitted from some English editions). At this suitably climactic moment we postpone further consideration of Gide and turn to the anti-essentialist, transgressive aesthetic which Wilde was advocating and which played so important a part in Gide's liberation or corruption, depending on one's point of view. And I want to begin with an indispensable dimension of that aesthetic: one for which Wilde is yet hardly remembered – or, for some of his admirers, one which is actively forgotten – namely, his advocacy of socialism.

Wilde begins his *The Soul of Man under Socialism* (1891) by asserting that a socialism based on sympathy alone is useless; what is needed is to *'try and reconstruct society on such a basis that poverty will be impossible'*. It is precisely because Christ made no attempt to reconstruct society that he had to resort to pain and suffering as the exemplary mode of self-realization. The alternative is the socialist commitment to transforming the material conditions which create and perpetuate suffering. One might add that, if the notion of redemption through suffering has been a familiar theme within English studies, this only goes to remind us of the extent to which, in the twentieth century, criticism has worked in effect as a displaced theology or as a vehicle for an acquiescent quasi-religious humanism. So Wilde's terse assertion in 1891 that 'Pain is not the ultimate mode of perfection. It is merely provisional and a protest'[17] may still be an appropriate response to those who fetishize suffering in the name, not of Christ, but of the tragic vision and the human condition (sainthood without God, as Camus once put it).

Wilde also dismisses the related pieties, that humankind learns wisdom through suffering, and that suffering humanizes. On the contrary, 'misery and poverty are so absolutely degrading, and exercise such a paralysing effect over the nature of men, that no class is ever really conscious of its suffering. They have to be told of it by other people, and they often entirely disbelieve them.' Against those who were beginning to talk of the dignity of manual labour, Wilde insists that most of that too is absolutely degrading. Each of these repudiations suggests that Wilde was fully aware of how exploitation is crucially a question of ideological mystification as well as of outright coercion: 'to the thinker, the most tragic fact in the whole of the French Revolution is not that Marié Antoinette was killed for being a queen, but that the starved peasant of the Vendée voluntarily went out to die for the hideous cause of feudalism.' Ideology reaches into experience and identity, re-emerging as 'voluntary' self-oppression. But it is also the ruling ideology which prevents the rulers themselves from seeing that it is not sin that produces crime but starvation, and that the punishment of the criminal escalates rather than diminishes crime and also brutalizes the society which administers it even more than the criminal who receives it.[18]

There is much more in this essay, but I have summarized enough to show that it exemplifies a tough materialism; in modern parlance one might call it anti-humanist, not least because for Wilde a radical socialist programme is inseparable from a critique of those ideologies of subjectivity which seek redemption in and through the individual. A case in point would be Dickens's treatment of Stephen Blackpool in *Hard Times* (Wilde made a point of disliking Dickens); another might be Arnold's assertion in *Culture and Anarchy*: 'Religion says: "*The Kingdom of God is within you*"; and culture, in like manner, places human perfection in an *internal* condition, in the growth and predominance of our humanity proper.'[19] But isn't a category like anti-humanism entirely inappropriate, given Wilde's celebration of individualism? The term itself, anti-humanism, is not worth fighting over; I have introduced it only as a preliminary indication of just how different is Wilde's concept of the individual from that which has prevailed in idealist culture generally and English studies in particular. It is this difference which the next section considers.

Individualism

In Wilde's writing, individualism is less to do with a human essence, Arnold's inner condition, than a dynamic social potential, one which implies a radical possibility of freedom 'latent and potential in mankind generally'. Thus individualism as Wilde conceives it generates a 'disobedience [which] in the eyes of anyone who has read history, is man's original virtue. It is through disobedience that progress has been made, through disobedience and through rebellion.'[20] Under certain conditions there comes to be a close relationship between crime and individualism, the one generating the other.[21] Already, then, Wilde's notion of individualism is inseparable from transgressive desire and a transgressive aesthetic. Hence, of course, his attack on public opinion, mediocrity and conventional morality, all of which forbid both the desire and the aesthetic.[22]

The public which Wilde scorns is that which seeks to police culture; which is against cultural difference; which reacts to the aesthetically unconventional by charging it with being either grossly unintelligible or grossly immoral. Far from reflecting or prescribing for the true nature or essence of man, individualism will generate the cultural difference and diversity which conventional morality, orthodox opinion and essentialist ideology disavow. Wilde affirms the principle of differentiation to which all life grows and insists that selfishness is not living as one wishes to live, but asking others to live as one wishes to live, trying to create 'an absolute uniformity of type'. And unselfishness not only recognizes cultural diversity and difference but enjoys them. Individualism as an affirmation of cultural as well as personal difference is therefore fundamentally opposed to that 'immoral ideal of uniformity of type and conformity to rule which is so prevalent everywhere, and is perhaps most obnoxious in England'.[23]

Uniformity of type and conformity to rule: Wilde despises these imperatives not only in individuals but as attributes of class and ruling ideologies. Wilde's Irish identity is a crucial factor in his oppositional stances, and it is instructive to consider in this connection a piece written two years earlier, in 1889, where he addresses England's exploitation and repression of Ireland. 'Mr Froude's Blue Book' is a review of J. A. Froude's novel, *The Two Chiefs of Dunboy*. In the eighteenth century, says Wilde, England tried to rule Ireland 'with an insolence that was intensified by race-hatred and religious prejudice'; in the nineteenth, with 'a stupidity . . . aggravated by good intentions'. Froude's picture of Ireland belongs to the earlier period, and yet to read Wilde's review now makes one wonder what if anything has changed in Tory 'thinking' except that possibly now the one vision holds for both Ireland and the mainland:

> Resolute government, that shallow shibboleth of those who do not understand how complex a thing the art of government is, is [Froude's] posthumous panacea for past evils. His hero, Colonel Goring, has the words Law and Order ever on his lips, meaning by the one the enforcement of unjust legislation, and implying by the other the suppression of every fine natural aspiration. That the government should enforce iniquity, and the governed submit to it, seems to be to Mr Froude, as it certainly is to many others, the true ideal of political science. . . . Colonel Goring . . . Mr Froude's cure for Ireland . . . is a '*Police* at any price' man.[24]

Individualism joins with socialism to abolish other kinds of conformity, including, says Wilde, family life and marriage, each being unacceptable because rooted in and perpetuating the ideology of property.[25] Individualism is both desire for a radical personal freedom and a desire for society itself to be radically different, the first being inseparable from the second. So Wilde's concept of the individual is crucially different from that sense of the concept which signifies the private, experientially self-sufficient, autonomous, bourgeois subject; indeed, for Wilde, 'Personal experience is a most vicious and limited circle' and 'to know anything about oneself one must know all about others'.[26] Typically, within idealist culture, the experience of an essential subjectivity is inseparable from knowledge of that notorious transhistorical category, human nature. This is Wilde on human nature: 'the only thing that one really knows about human nature is that it changes. Change is the one quality we can predicate of it.'[27] To those who then say that socialism is incompatible with human nature and therefore impractical, Wilde replies by rejecting practicality itself as presupposing and endorsing both the existing social conditions and the concept of human nature as fixed, each of which suppositions socialism would contest: 'it is exactly the existing conditions that one objects to . . . [they] will be done away with, and human nature will change.'[28] Elsewhere Wilde accepts that there is *something* like human nature, but, far from being the source of our most profound being, it is actually ordinary and boring, the least interesting thing about us. It is where we differ from each other that is of definitive value.[29]

Art Versus Life

The key concepts in Wilde's aesthetic are protean and shifting, not least because they are paradoxically and facetiously deployed. When, for example, he speaks of life – 'poor, probable, uninteresting human life'[30] – or reality as that to which art is opposed, he means different things at different times. One of the most interesting and significant referents of concepts like life and reality, as Wilde uses them, is the prevailing social order. Even nature, conceived as the opposite of culture and art, retains a social dimension,[31] especially when it signifies ideological mystification of the social. That is why Wilde calls being natural a 'pose', and an objectionable one at that, precisely because it seeks to mystify the social as natural.[32]

Nature and reality signify a prevailing order which art ignores and which the critic negates, subverts and transgresses. Thus, for example, the person of culture is concerned to give 'an accurate description of what has never occurred', while the critic sees 'the object as in itself it really is not'[33] (Wilde is here inverting the proposition which opens Arnold's famous essay 'The function of criticism at the present time'). Not surprisingly, then, criticism and art are aligned with individualism against a prevailing social order; a passage which indicates this is also important in indicating the basis of Wilde's aesthetic of transgressive desire: 'Art is Individualism and Individualism is *a disturbing and disintegrating force*. Therein lies its immense value. For what it seeks to disturb is monotony of type, slavery of custom, tyranny of habit.'[34] Art is also self-conscious and critical; in fact, 'self-consciousness and the critical spirit are one'.[35] And art, like individualism, is oriented towards the realm of transgressive desire: 'What is abnormal in Life stands in normal relations to Art. It is the only thing in Life that stands in normal relations to Art.'[36] One who inhabits that realm, 'the cultured and fascinating liar', is both an object and source of desire.[37] The liar is important because s/he contradicts not just conventional morality but its sustaining origin, 'truth'. So art runs to meet the liar, kissing his 'false beautiful lips, knowing that he alone is in possession of the great secret of all her manifestations, the secret that Truth is entirely and absolutely a matter of style'. Truth, the epistemological legitimation of the real, is rhetorically subordinated to its antitheses – appearance, style, the lie – and thereby simultaneously both appropriated and devalued. Reality, also necessarily devalued and demystified by the loss of truth, must imitate art, while life must meekly follow the liar.[38]

Further, life is at best an energy which can only find expression through the forms that art offers it. But form is another slippery and protean category in Wilde's aesthetic. In one sense Wilde is a proto-structuralist: 'Form is the beginning of things. . . . The Creeds are believed, not because they are rational, but because they are repeated. . . . Form is everything . . . Do you wish to love? Use Love's Litany, and the words will create the yearning from which the world fancies that they spring.'[39] Here form is virtually synonymous with culture. Moreover, it is a passage in which Wilde recognizes the priority of the social and the cultural in determining meaning, even in determining desire. So for Wilde, although desire is deeply at odds with society in its existing forms, it does not exist as a pre-social authenticity; it is within and in-formed by the very culture which it also transgresses.

Transgression and the Sense of Self

Returning now to Gide, we are in a position to contrast his essentialism with Wilde's anti-essentialism, a contrast which epitomizes one of the most important differences within the modern history of transgression. In a way that perhaps corresponds to his ambivalence towards Wilde, Gide had both submitted to and resisted the latter's attempts to undermine his sense of self. Both the submission and the resistance are crucial for Gide's subsequent development as a writer and, through Gide's influence, for modern literature. The submission is apparent enough in the confirmation of his homosexual desire and the way this alters his life and work. In 1924 he published *Corydon*, a courageous defence of homosexuality which he later declared to be his most important book

(*Journal*, 19 October 1942). In *Corydon* he did not just demand tolerance for homosexuality but also insisted that it was not contrary to nature but intrinsically natural; that heterosexuality prevails merely because of convention; that historically homosexuality is associated with great artistic and intellectual achievement, while heterosexuality is indicative of decadence. About these provocative and suspect claims I have only the space to observe that the fury they generated in the majority of commentators is as significant as Gide's reasons for making them in the first place. Two years later Gide published the equally controversial commercial edition of *If It die*, which, as already indicated, contained, for that time, astonishingly explicit accounts of his homosexuality, and for which, predictably, Gide was savagely castigated. Much later still, Gide was to write to Ramon Fernandez, confirming that 'sexual non-conformity is the first key to my works'; the experience of his own deviant desire leads him first to attack sexual conformity and then 'all other sphinxes of conformity', suspecting them to be 'the brothers and cousins of the first'.[40]

But Gide – having with Wilde both allowed and encouraged the subversion of an identity which had hitherto successfully, albeit precariously, repressed desire – does not then substitute for it the decentred subjectivity which animates Wilde's aesthetic; on the contrary, he reconstitutes himself as an essentially new self. Michel in *The Immoralist* (1902) corresponds in some measure to Gide in Algiers (while, as earlier remarked, another character in that novel, Ménalque, is probably based on Wilde). For Michel, as for Gide, transgression does not lead to a relinquishing of self but to a totally new sense of self. Michel throws off the culture and learning which up to that point had been his whole life, in order to find himself: that 'authentic creature that had lain hidden beneath ... whom the Gospel had repudiated, whom everything about me – books, masters, parents, and I myself had begun by attempting to suppress. ... Thenceforward I despised the secondary creature, the creature who was due to teaching, whom education had painted on the surface.' He composes a new series of lectures in which he shows 'Culture, born of life, as the destroyer of life'. The true value of life is bound up with individual uniqueness: 'the part in each of us that we feel is different from other people is the part that is rare, the part that makes our special value.'[41]

Whereas for Wilde transgressive desire leads to a relinquishing of the essential self, for Gide it leads to a discovery of the authentic self. As he writes in *If It Die*, it was at that time in Algiers that 'I was beginning to discover myself – and in myself the tables of a new law'.[42] And he writes to his mother on 2 February 1895: 'I'm unable to write a line or a sentence so long as I'm not in *complete possession* (that is, WITH FULL KNOWLEDGE) of myself. I should like very submissively to follow nature – the unconscious, which is within myself and must be *true*.'[43] Here again there is the indirect yet passionate insistence on the naturalness, the authenticity of his deviant desire. With that wilful integrity – itself a kind of perversity? – rooted in Protestantism, Gide not only appropriates dominant concepts (the normal, the natural) to legitimate his own deviation, but goes so far as to claim a sanction for deviation in the teachings of Christ.[44] (In his journal for 1893 (detached pages) he wrote: 'Christ's saying is just as true in art: "Whoever will save his life (his personality) shall lose it".' He later declared, after reading Nietzsche's *Thus Spake Zarathustra*, that it was to this that Protestantism led, 'to the greatest liberation'.[45]) Delay contends, plausibly, that some of the great Gidean themes, especially those entailing transgression, can be found in the rebellious letters that he wrote to his mother in March 1895, letters inspired by his self-affirmation as a homosexual.[46]

It would be difficult to overestimate the importance, in the recent history of Western culture, of transgression in the name of an essential self which is the origin and arbiter of the true, the real and the moral – that is, the three main domains of knowledge in Western culture: the epistemological, the ontological and the ethical. Its importance within the domain of sexuality and within discourses which intersect with sexuality is becoming increasingly apparent, but it has been central also in liberation movements which have not primarily been identified with either of these. This, finally, is Gide in 1921:

> The borrowed truths are the ones to which one clings most tenaciously, and all the more so since they remain foreign to our intimate self. It takes much more precaution to deliver one's own message, much more boldness and prudence, than to sign up with and add one's voice to an already existing party. . . . I believed that it is above all to oneself that it is important to remain faithful.[47]

Paradox and Perversity

The contrast between Gide and Wilde is striking: not only are Wilde's conceptions of subjectivity and desire anti-essentialist but so too – and consequently – is his advocacy of transgression. Deviant desire reacts against, disrupts and displaces from within; rather than seeking to escape the repressive ordering of sexuality, Wilde reinscribes himself within and relentlessly inverts the binaries upon which that ordering depends. Inversion, rather than Gide's escape into a pre- or trans-social reality, defines Wilde's transgressive aesthetic. In Gide, transgression is in the name of a desire and identity rooted in the natural, the sincere and the authentic; Wilde's transgressive aesthetic is the reverse: *in*sincerity, *in*authenticity and *un*naturalness become the liberating attributes of decentred identity and desire, and inversion becomes central to Wilde's expression of this aesthetic, as can be seen from a selection of his *Phrases and Philosophies for the Use of the Young* (1894): I

> If one tells the truth, one is sure, sooner or later, to be found out.
> Only the shallow know themselves.
> To be premature is to be perfect.
> It is only the superficial qualities that last. Man's deeper nature is
> soon found out.
> To love oneself is the beginning of a lifelong romance.[48]

In Wilde's writings a non-centred or dispersed desire is both the impetus for a subversive inversion *and* what is released by it. Perhaps the most general inversion operating in his work reverses that most dominating of binaries, nature/culture; more specifically, the attributes on the left are substituted for those on the right:

X	for	Y
surface		depth
lying		truth
change		statis
difference		essence
persona/role		essential self
abnormal		normal
insincerity		sincerity
style/artifice		authenticity
facetious		serious
narcissism		maturity

For Michel in *The Immoralist* and to an extent for Gide himself, desire may be proscribed, but this does not affect its authenticity; if anything, it confirms it. In a sense, then, deviant desire is legitimated in terms of culture's opposite, nature, or, in a different but related move, in terms of something which is pre-cultural or *always more than* cultural. Gide shares with the dominant culture an investment in the Y column above; he appropriates its categories *from* the dominant *for* the subordinate. In contrast, for Wilde transgressive desire is both rooted in culture and the impetus for affirming different/alternative kinds of culture. So what in Gide's conception of transgression might seem a limitation or even a confusion – namely, that the desire which culture outlaws is itself thoroughly cultural – in fact facilitates one of the most disturbing of all forms of transgression: the outlaw turns up as inlaw; more specifically, that which society forbids Wilde reinstates through and within some of its most cherished and central cultural categories – art, the aesthetic, art criticism, individualism. At the same time as he appropriates those categories he also transvalues them through inversion, thus making them now signify those binary exclusions (the X column) by which the dominant culture knows itself (thus abnormality is not just the opposite, but *the necessarily always present* antithesis of normality). It is an uncompromising inversion, this being the (perversely) appropriate strategy for a transgressive desire which is of its 'nature', according to this culture, an inversion.

But inversion has a specific as well as a general target: as can be seen from the *Phrases and Philosophies* just quoted, Wilde seeks to subvert those dominant categories which signify *subjective depth* Such categories (the Y column) are precisely those which ideologically identify (interpellate?) the mature adult individual, which confer or ideologically coerce identity. And they too operate in terms of binary contrast: the individual knows what he – I choose the masculine pronoun deliberately[49] – is in contrast to what he definitely is not or should not be. In Wilde's inversions, the excluded inferior term returns as the *now superior* term of a related series of binaries. Some further examples of Wilde's subversion of subjective depth are:

A little sincerity is a dangerous thing, and a great deal is absolutely fatal.[50]

All bad poetry springs from genuine feeling.[51]

In matters of grave importance, style, not sincerity, is the *vital* thing.[52]

Only shallow people . . . do not judge by appearances.[53]

Insincerity . . . is merely a method by which we can multiply our personalities. Such . . . was Dorian Gray's opinion. He used to wonder at the shallow psychology of those who conceived the Ego in man as a thing simple, permanent, reliable, and of one essence. To him man was a being with myriad lives and myriad sensations, a complex, multiform creature.[54]

At work here is a transgressive desire which makes its opposition felt as a disruptive reaction upon, and inversion of, the categories of subjective depth which hold in place the dominant order which proscribes that desire.

The Decentred Subject and the Question of the Postmodern

Wilde's transgressive aesthetic relates to at least three aspects of contemporary theoretical debates: first, the dispute about whether the inversion of binary opposites subverts or, on the contrary, reinforces the order which those binaries uphold; second, the political importance – or irrelevance – of decentring the subject; third, postmodernism and one of its more controversial criteria: the so-called disappearance of the depth model, especially the model of a deep human subjectivity. Since the three issues closely relate to each other, I shall take them together.

It might be said that Wildean inversion disturbed nothing; by merely reversing the terms of the binary, inversion remains within its limiting framework: the world turned upside down can only be righted, not changed. Moreover, the argument might continue, Wilde's paradoxes are superficial in the pejorative sense of being inconsequential, of making no difference. But we should remember that in the first of the three trials involving Wilde in 1895 he was cross-examined on his *Phrases and Philosophies*, the implication of opposing counsel being that they, along with *Dorian Gray*, were 'calculated to subvert morality and encourage unnatural vice'.[55] There is a sense in which evidence cannot get more material than this, and it remains so whatever our retrospective judgement about the crassness of the thinking behind such a view.

One of the many reasons why people thought as they did was to do with the perceived connections between Wilde's aesthetic transgression and his sexual transgression. It is not only that at this time the word 'inversion' was being used for the first time to define a specific kind of deviant sexuality and deviant person (the two things now being indissociable), but also that, in producing the homosexual as a species of being rather than, as before, seeing sodomy as an aberration of behaviour,[56] society now regarded homosexuality as rooted in a person's identity; this sin might pervade all aspects of an individual's being, and its expression might become correspondingly the more insidious and subversive. Hence in part the animosity and hysteria directed at Wilde during and after his trial.

After he had been found guilty of homosexual offences and sentenced to two years' imprisonment with hard labour, the editorial of the London *Evening News* subjected him to a vicious and revealing homophobic attack. He had, it claimed, tried to subvert the 'wholesome, manly, simple ideals of English life'; moreover, his 'abominable vices . . . were the natural outcome of his diseased intellectual condition'. The editorial also saw Wilde as the leader of a likeminded but younger subculture in London.[57] The view expressed here was, and indeed remains, for some, a commonplace: sexual deviation is symptomatic of a much wider cultural deterioration and/or subversion. There is an important sense in which Wilde confirmed and exploited this connection between discursive and sexual perversion: 'What the paradox was to me in the sphere of thought, perversity became to me in the sphere of passion.'[58] This feared crossover between discursive and sexual perversion has sanctioned terrible brutalities against homosexuals, at the same time, at least in this period, it was also becoming the medium for what Foucault calls a reverse or counter-discourse,[59] giving rise to what is being explored here in relation to Wilde – what might be called the politics of inversion/perversion (again crossing over and between the different senses of these words). Derrida has argued persuasively for binary inversion as a politically indispensable stage towards the eventual displacement of the binary itself.[60] The case of Wilde indicates, I think, that in actual historical instances of inversion – that is, inversion as a strategy of cultural struggle – it already constitutes a displacement, if not of the binary itself, then certainly of the moral and political norms which cluster dependently around its dominant pole.

We begin to see, then, why Wilde was hated with such an intensity, even though he rarely advocated in his published writings any explicitly immoral practice. What held those 'wholesome, manly, simple ideals of English life' in place were traditional and conservative ideas of what constituted human nature and human subjectivity, and it was *these* that Wilde attacked: not so much conventional morality itself as the ideological anchor points for that morality, namely notions of identity as subjective depth, whose criteria appear in the Y column above. And so it might be said that here, generally, as he did with Gide more specifically, Wilde subverts the dominant categories of subjectivity which keep desire in subjection, and subverts the essentialist categories of identity which keep morality in place. Even though there may now be a temptation to patronize and indeed dismiss both the Victorians' 'wholesome, manly, simple ideals of English life' and Wilde's inversion of them, the fact remains that, in successively reconstituted forms, those ideals, *together with* the subject positions which instantiate them, come to form the moral and ethical base of English studies in our own century, and, indeed, remain culturally central today.

I am thinking here not just of the organicist ideology so characteristic of an earlier phase of English studies, one that led, for example, to the celebration of Shakespeare's alleged 'national culture, rooted in the soil and appealing to a multi-class audience', but more specifically and importantly of what Chris Baldick in his excellent study goes on to call its 'subjective correlative', namely, the '*maintenance of the doctrine of psychic wholeness in and through literature as an analogue for a projected harmony and order in society*'.[61] For I. A. Richards, all human problems (continues Baldick) become problems of mental health, with art as the cure, and literary criticism becomes 'a question of attaining the right state of mind to judge other minds, according to their degree of immaturity, inhibition, or perversion'. As Richards himself puts it, sincerity 'is the quality we most insistently require in poetry. It is also the quality we most need as critics.'[62] As a conception of both art and criticism, this is the reverse of Wilde's. Similarly with the Leavises,

whose imperative concept was the related one of 'maturity', one
unhappy consequence of which was their promotion of the 'fecund'
D. H. Lawrence against the perverse W. H. Auden. As Baldick goes on
to observe, 'this line of critics is not only judicial in tone but positively
inquisitorial, indulging in a kind of perversion-hunting' which is itself
rooted in 'a simple model of [pre- or anti-Freudian] normality and
mental consistency'.[63]

This tradition has, of course, been subjected to devastating critiques in
recent years; in particular, its notions of subjective integration and psychic
wholeness have been attacked by virtually all the major movements within
contemporary critical theory including Marxism, structuralism,
post-structuralism and psychoanalysis. Yet Wilde's subversion of these
notions is still excluded from consideration, even though we now think we
have passed beyond that heady and in many ways justified moment when
it seemed that only Continental theory had the necessary force to displace
the complacencies of our own tradition. The irony, of course, is that while
looking to the Continent we failed to notice that Wilde has been and
remains a very significant figure there. (And not only there: while the
Spectator (February 1891) thought *The Soul of Man under Socialism* was a
joke in bad taste, the essay soon became extremely successful in Russia,
appearing in many successive editions across the next twenty years.)
Perhaps, then, there exists or has existed a kind of 'muscular theory', which
shares with the critical movements it has displaced a significant blindness
with regard to Wilde and what he represented. This almost certainly has
something to do with the persistence of an earlier attempt to rid English
studies of a perceived 'feminized' identity.[64]

Recent critics of postmodernism, including Fredric Jameson, Ihab
Hassan, Dan Latimer and Terry Eagleton,[65] have written intriguingly on
one of its defining criteria: the disappearance of the depth model. In a
recent essay, Eagleton offers an important and provocative critique of
post-modernism: 'confidently post-metaphysical [it] has outlived all that
fantasy of interiority, that pathological itch to scratch surfaces for
concealed depths.' With the postmodern there is no longer any subject to
be alienated and nothing to be alienated from, 'authenticity having been
less rejected than merely forgotten'. The subject of postmodernist culture
is 'a dispersed, decentred network of libidinal attachments, emptied of
ethical substance and psychical interiority, the ephemeral function of this
or that act of consumption, media experience, sexual relationship, trend
or fashion'. Modernism, by contrast, is (or was) still preoccupied with the
experience of alienation, with metaphysical depth and/or the psychic
fragmentation and social wretchedness consequent upon the realization
that there is no metaphysical depth or (this being its spiritual
instantiation) authentic unified subject. As such, modernism is
'embarrassingly enmortgaged to the very bourgeois humanism it

141

otherwise seeks to subvert'; it is 'a deviation still enthralled to a norm, parasitic on what it sets out to deconstruct'. But, concludes Eagleton, the subject of late capitalism is actually neither the 'self-regulating synthetic agent posited by classical humanist ideology, nor merely a decentred network of desire [as posited by postmodernism], but a contradictory amalgam of the two'. If in one respect the decentred, dispersed subject of postmodernism is suspiciously convenient to our own phase of late capitalism, it follows that those post-structuralist theorists who stake all on the assumption that the unified subject is still integral to contemporary bourgeois ideology, and that it is always a politically radical act to decentre and deconstruct that subject, need to think again.[66]

Eagleton's argument can be endorsed with yet further important distinctions. First, even though the unified subject was indeed an integral part of an earlier phase of bourgeois ideology, the instance of Gide and the tradition he represents must indicate that it was never even then exclusively in the service of dominant ideologies. Indeed, to the extent that Gide's essentialist legitimation of homosexual desire was primarily an affirmation of his own nature as pederast or paedophile, some critics might usefully rethink their own assumption that essentialism is fundamentally and always a conservative philosophy. In Gide we find essentialism in the service of a radical sexual nonconformity which was and remains incompatible with conventional and dominant sexual ideologies, bourgeois and otherwise. Even a glance at the complex and often contradictory histories of sexual liberation movements in our own time shows that they have, as does Eagleton's contradictory subject of late capitalism, sometimes and necessarily embraced a radical essentialism with regard to their own identity, while simultaneously offering an equally radical anti-essentialist critique of the essentializing sexual ideologies responsible for their oppression.

This is important: the implication of Eagleton's argument is not just that we need to make our theories of subjectivity a little more sophisticated, but rather that we need to be more historical in our practice of theory. Only then can we see the dialectical complexities of social process and social struggle. We may see, for example, how the very centrality of an essentialist concept to the dominant ideology has made its appropriation by a subordinate culture seem indispensable in that culture's struggle for legitimacy; roughly speaking, this corresponds to Gide's position as I am representing it here. The kind of challenge represented by Gide – liberation in the name of authenticity – has been more or less central to many progressive cultural struggles since, though it has not, of course, guaranteed their success.[67] Conversely, we may also see how other subordinate cultures and voices seek not to appropriate dominant concepts and values so much as to sabotage and displace them. This is something we can observe in Wilde.

Whether the decentred subject of contemporary post-structuralism and postmodernism is subversive of, alternative to, or actually produced by late capitalism, there is no doubt that Wilde's exploration of decentred desire and identity scandalized bourgeois culture in the 1890s and in a sense cost him his life. The case of Wilde might lead us to rethink the antecedents of postmodernism and, indeed, of modernism as they figure in the current debate which Eagleton addresses. Wilde prefigures elements of each, while remaining importantly different from – and not just obviously prior to – both. If his transgressive aesthetic anticipates postmodernism to the extent that it suggests a culture of the surface and of difference, it also anticipated modernism in being not just hostile to but intently concerned with its opposite, the culture of depth and exclusive integration. Yet Wilde's transgressive aesthetic differs from some versions of the postmodern in that it includes an acute political awareness and often an uncompromising political commitment; and his critique of the depth model differs from the modernist in that it is accompanied not by *Angst* but by something utterly different, something reminiscent of Barthes's *jouissance*, or what Borges has perceptively called Wilde's 'negligent glee ... the fundamental spirit of his work [being] joy'.[68]

An anti-essentialist theory of subjectivity can in no way guarantee, *a priori*, any effect, radical or otherwise; nor, more generally, can any transgressive practice carry such a guarantee. But there is much to be learned retrospectively both from the effects of anti-essentialism and the practice of transgression, especially in the light of the currently felt need to develop new strategies and conceptions of resistance. Orthodox accounts of resistance have proved wanting, not least essentialist ideas of resistance in the name of the authentic self, and – in some ways the opposite – resistance in terms of and on behalf of mass movements working from outside and against the dominant powers. And so we have become acutely aware of the unavoidability of working from within the institutions that exist, adopting different strategies depending on where and who we are, or, in the case of the same individual, which subject positions s/he is occupying. But is this the new radicalism, or incorporation by another name?

It is in just these respects, and in relation to such pressing questions, that, far from finding them irrelevant – the one a *passé* wit and the other a passé moralist/essentialist – I remain intrigued with Wilde and Gide. In different ways their work explores what we are now beginning to attend to again: the complexities, the potential and the dangers of what it is to transgress, invert and displace *from within*;[69] the paradox of a marginality which is always interior to, or at least intimate with, the centre.

I began with their encounter in Algiers in 1895. Gide, dispirited in the sense of being depressed and unsure of himself, sees the names of Wilde and Douglas and erases his own name as a result, pre-empting perhaps the threat to his own identity, social and psychic, posed by Wilde's determination to demystify the normative ideologies regulating subjectivity, desire and the aesthetic. Nevertheless the meeting does occur, and Gide does indeed suffer an erasure of self, a decentring which is also the precondition for admitting transgressive desire, a depersonalization which is therefore also a liberation. Yet, for Gide, transgression is embraced with that same stubborn integrity which was to become the basis of his transgressive aesthetic, an aesthetic obviously indebted, yet also formed in reaction to, Wilde's own. Thus liberation from the self into desire is also to realize a new and deeper self, belief in which supports an oppositional stand not just on the question of deviant sexual desire, but on a whole range of other issues as well, cultural and political. Integrity here becomes an ethical sense inextricably bound up with and also binding up the (integral) unified self.[70] So the very categories of identity which, through transgression, Wilde subjects to inversion and displacement are reconstituted by Gide for a different transgressive aesthetic, or, as it might now more suitably be called in contradistinction to Wilde, a transgressive ethic: one which becomes central to the unorthodoxy which characterizes his life's work. In 1952, the year after his death, his entire works were entered in the Roman Catholic Index of Forbidden Books; six years earlier he had been awarded the Nobel Prize for Literature.

Wilde's fate was very different. Within weeks of returning from Algiers to London he was embroiled in the litigation against Queensberry which was to lead to his own imprisonment. He died in Paris in 1900, three years after his release. So, whereas Gide lived for fifty-seven years after that 1895 encounter, Wilde survived for only six. And yet it was also Wilde's fate to become a legend. Like many legendary figures, he needs to be rescued from most of his admirers and radically rethought by some, at least, of his critics.

Notes

Thanks to Joseph Bristow for his comments on an earlier draft of this paper.

1. André Gide, *If It Die* (1920; private edn 1926), trans. Dorothy Bussy (Harmondsworth: Penguin, 1977), p. 271.
2. Ibid., pp. 271, 273.
3. Jean Delay, *The Youth of André Gide*, abridged and trans. J. Guicharnaud (Chicago and London: University of Chicago Press, 1956–57), p. 290.
4. Richard Ellmann (ed.), *The Artist as Critic: Critical Writings of Oscar Wilde* (1968; London: W. H. Allen, 1970), p. xviii. Those aspects of Wilde's transgressive

aesthetic which concern me here derive mainly from work published across a relatively short period of time, the years 1889–91. My reading of Wilde is avowedly partial. There is, of course, more – much more – to be said; about these works, about different works not discussed here, about Wilde himself, especially about other of his ideas which intersect with and contradict the perspective explored here. My concern, though, is to address aspects of his work which have been largely ignored. What Richard Ellmann said of Wilde nearly twenty years ago is still true today: he 'laid the basis for many critical positions which are still debated in much the same terms, and which we like to attribute to more ponderous names' (ibid., p. x). Thomas Mann compared Wilde with Nietzsche; Ellmann in 1968 added the name of Roland Barthes. In 1987 we could add several more; more constructive, though, will be the renewed interest in Wilde that is sure to be generated by the expected publication this year of Ellmann's major biography [RICHARD ELLMANN, *Oscar Wilde* (Markham, Ontario: Viking 1987; Harmondsworth: Penguin, 1988)].

 5.   J. Guicharnaud (trans.), *Correspondence 1890–1942, André Gide – Paul Valéry* (1955), cited here from the abridged version, *Self-Portraits: The Gidel Valéry Letters* (Chicago and London: University of Chicago Press, 1966), pp. 90, 92.

 6.   DELAY, op. cit., p. 291.

 7.   ANDRÉ GIDE, *Journals*, 4 vols (New York: Alfred A. Knopf, 1947–51).

 8.   DELAY, op. cit., pp. 289, 90, 291, 295.

 9.   RICHARD ELLMANN (ed.), *Oscar Wilde: A Collection of Critical Essays* (Englewood Cliffs, NJ: Prentice-Hall, 1969), p. 4.

10.   Quoted from DELAY, op. cit., p. 391 (my italics).

11.   ANDRÉ GIDE, *Oscar Wilde*, trans. Bernard Frechtman (New York: Philosophical Library, 1949).

12.   GIDE, *If It Die*, pp. 280, 281.

13.   Ibid., pp. 236–7, 247–9, 251, 252, 255, 258–9.

14.   Ibid., p. 264.

15.   DELAY, op. cit., p. 394.

16.   GIDE, *If It Die*, pp. 282, 284–5.

17.   OSCAR WILDE, *The Soul of Man under Socialism* (1891), reprinted in Ellmann (ed.), *The Artist as Critic*, pp. 256 (his italics), 286–8, 288.

18.   Ibid., pp. 259, 268, 260, 267.

19.   MATTHEW ARNOLD, *Culture and Anarchy* (1869; London: Smith Elder, 1891), p. 8.

20.   WILDE, *The Soul of Man under Socialism*, pp. 261, 258.

21.   Wilde reiterates this elsewhere: see OSCAR WILDE, 'Pen, pencil and poison' (1889), in ELLMANN (ed.), *The Artist as Critic*, p. 338; 'The critic as artist' (1890), in ELLMANN (ed.), *The Artist as Critic*, p. 360. Cf. Ellmann's formulation of Wilde's position: 'since the established social structure confines the individual, the artist must of necessity ally himself with the criminal classes' (ELLMANN (ed.), *Oscar Wilde*, p. 3).

22.   See also WILDE, 'The critic as artist', p. 341; WILDE, *The Soul of Man under Socialism*, pp. 271–4.

23.   WILDE, *The Soul of Man under Socialism*, pp. 273, 284–5, 286.

24.   OSCAR WILDE, 'Mr Froude's Blue Book' (1889), in ELLMANN (ed.), *The Artist as Critic*, pp. 136–7.

25.   WILDE, *The Soul of Man under Socialism*, p. 265.

26.   OSCAR WILDE, 'The decay of lying' (1889), in ELLMANN (ed.), *The Artist as Critic*, p. 310, and 'The critic as artist', p. 382.

27. WILDE, *The Soul of Man under Socialism*, p. 284.
28. Ibid., p. 284.
29. WILDE, 'The decay of lying', p. 297.
30. Ibid., p. 305.
31. For example, WILDE, 'The critic as artist', pp. 394, 399.
32. OSCAR WILDE, *The Picture of Dorian Gray* (1890–1; Harmondsworth: Penguin, 1949), p. 10.
33. WILDE, 'The critic as artist', pp. 343, 368.
34. WILDE, *The Soul of Man under Socialism*, p. 272 (my italics).
35. WILDE, 'The critic as artist', p. 356.
36. OSCAR WILDE, 'A few maxims for the instruction of the overeducated', *The Complete Works*, with introduction by Vyvyan Holland (London and Glasgow: Collins, 1948), p. 1203.
37. WILDE, 'The decay of lying', pp. 292 and 305.
38. Ibid., p. 305.
39. WILDE, 'The critic as artist', p. 399.
40. DELAY, op. cit., p. 438.
41. ANDRÉ GIDE, *the Immoralist* (1902; Harmondsworth: Penguin, 1960), pp. 51, 90, 100.
42. GIDE, *If It Die*, p. 298.
43. DELAY, op. cit., p. 396.
44. GIDE, *If It Die*, p. 299.
45. DELAY, op. cit., p. 467.
46. Ibid., p. 407.
47. GIDE, *Journals*, p. 338. Cf. ibid., pp. 371–6.
48. OSCAR WILDE, *Phrases and Philosophies for the Use of the Young* (1894), in ELLMANN (ed.), *The Artist as Critic*, pp. 433–4.
49. The attacks on Wilde after his trial frequently reveal that it is masculinity which felt most under threat from him, and which demanded revenge.
50. WILDE, 'The critic as artist', p. 393.
51. Ibid., p. 398.
52. OSCAR WILDE, *The Importance of Being Earnest* (1894–9), ed. R. Jackson (London: Ernest Benn, 1980), p. 83 (my italics).
53. WILDE, *The Picture of Dorian Gray*, p. 29.
54. Ibid., pp. 158–9.
55. H. M. HYDE, *Oscar Wilde: A Biography* (1976; London: Methuen, 1982), p. 271.
56. MICHEL FOUCAULT, *The History of Sexuality*, vol. 1: *An Introduction* (1978; New York: Vintage Books, 1980), p. 43.
57. H. M. HYDE, *The Trials of Oscar Wilde* (London: William Hodge, 1948), p. 12.
58. OSCAR WILDE, *De Profundis* (1897), in *The Letters of Oscar Wilde* (London: Rupert Hart-Davis, 1962); cited from the abridged edition, *Selected Letters* (London: Oxford University Press, 1979), p. 194. In certain important respects, *De Profundis* is a conscious renunciation by Wilde of his transgressive aesthetic. This is a work which registers many things, not least Wilde's courage and his despair during imprisonment. It also shows how he endured the intolerable by investing suffering with meaning, and this within a confessional narrative whose aim is a deepened self-awareness: 'I could not bear [my sufferings] to be without meaning. Now I find hidden somewhere away in my nature something that tells me that nothing in the whole world is meaningless ... that something ... is Humility.' Such knowledge and such humility, for Wilde

(and still, for us now), is bought at the cost of fundamentally – deeply – renouncing difference and transgression and the challenge they present. In effect, Wilde repositions himself as the authentic, sincere subject which before he had subverted: 'The supreme vice is shallowness,' he says in this work, and he says it more than once. And later: 'The moment of repentance is the moment of initiation' (ibid., pp. 195, 154, 215). This may be seen as that suffering into truth, that redemptive knowledge which points beyond the social to the transcendent realization of self, so cherished within idealist culture; those who see *De Profundis* as Wilde's most mature work often interpret it thus. I see it differently – as tragic, certainly, but tragic in the materialist sense of the word: a defeat of the marginal and the oppositional of a kind which only ideological domination can effect; a renunciation which is experienced as voluntary and self-confirming but which is in truth a self-defeat and a self-denial massively coerced through the imposition, by the dominant, of incarceration and suffering and their 'natural' medium, confession. What Wilde says here of the law is true also of the dominant ideologies he transgressed: 'I . . . found myself constrained to appeal to the very things against which I had always protested' (ibid., p. 221).

59. FOUCAULT, op. cit., p. 101.
60. JACQUES DERRIDA, *Positions* (London: 1981), pp. 41–2.
61. C. BALDICK, *The Social Mission of English Criticism 1848–1932* (Oxford: Clarendon, 1983), pp. 213–18 (my italics).
62. I. A. RICHARDS, quoted in ibid., p. 215.
63. Ibid., p. 217.
64. B. DOYLE, 'The hidden history of English studies', in PETER WIDDOWSON (ed.), *Re-reading English* (London: Methuen, 1982); TERRY EAGLETON, *Literary Theory: An Introduction* (Oxford: Blackwell, 1983); BALDICK, op. cit. On Wilde in Germany see MANFRED PFISTER (ed), Oscar Wilde, *The Picture of Dorian Gray* (München: Wilhelm Fink, 1986).
65. FREDRIC JAMESON, 'Postmodernism and consumer society', in H. FOSTER (ed.), *The Anti-Aesthetic: Essays on Postmodern Culture* (Washington, DC: Bay Press, 1983); FREDRIC JAMESON, 'Postmodernism, or the cultural logic of late capitalism', *New Left Review*, 146 (1984); IHAB HASSAN, 'Pluralism in postmodern perspective', *Critical Inquiry*, 12, 3 (1986), pp. 503–20; DAN LATIMER, 'Jameson and postmodernism', *New Left Review*, 148 (1984), pp. 116–28; TERRY EAGLETON, 'Capitalism, modernism and postmodernism', in *Against the Grain* (London: Verso, 1986), pp. 131–47.
66. EAGLETON, 'Capitalism, modernism and postmodernism', pp. 143, 132, 145, 143–5.
67. M. BERMAN, *The Politics of Authenticity: Radical Individualism and the Emergence of Modern Society* (London: Allen & Unwin, 1971).
68. ELLMANN (ed.), *Oscar Wilde*, p. 174.
69. See JACQUES DERRIDA, *Of Grammatology* (1967), trans. Gayatri Spivak (Baltimore, Md, and London: Johns Hopkins University Press, 1976), pp. lxxvi–lxxviii; DERRIDA, *Positions*, pp. 41–2; R. TERDIMAN, *Discourse/Counter Discourse: Theory and Practice of Symbolic Resistance in Nineteenth-Century France* (Ithaca, NY: Cornell University Press, 1985), esp. Introduction. Some of the most informative work addressing inversion and transgression is historically grounded; I have in mind especially recent work on early modern England. See, for example, D. KUNZLE, 'World turned upside down: the iconography of a

European broadsheet type', in Barbara Babcock (ed.), *The Reversible World: Symbolic Inversion in Art and Society* (Ithaca, NY, and London: Cornell University Press, 1978); Christopher Hill, *The World Turned Upside Down: Radical Ideas during the English Revolution* (Harmondsworth: Penguin, 1975); P. Stallybrass and A. White, *The Politics and Poetics of Transgression* (London: Methuen, 1986); S. Clark, 'Inversion, misrule and the meaning of witchcraft', *Past and Present*, 87 (1980), pp. 98–127. Kunzle, discussing the iconography of the world turned upside-down broadsheets, offers a conclusion which registers the complex potential of inversion and is, quite incidentally, nicely suggestive for understanding Wilde: 'Revolution appears disarmed by playfulness, the playful bears the seed of revolution. "Pure" formal fantasy and subversive desire, far from being mutually exclusive, are two sides of the same coin' (op. cit., p. 89). This is the appropriate point at which to note that the fuller study to which this article is a contribution necessarily addresses other considerations in relation to transgression in Wilde and Gide, most especially those of class race and colonialism. A crucial text for the latter is Gide's *Travels in the Congo* (1927–8), trans. D. Bussy (Harmondsworth: Penguin, 1986). But see also Jean-Paul Sartre, *What is Literature?* (1948; London: Methuen, 1967), esp. pp. 52, 98–9, 133.

70. It is instructive to see in Gide's writing how complex, vital and unconventional the existential and humanist commitment to sincerity of self could be, especially when contrasted with its facile counterpart in English studies, or indeed (a counter-image) the reductive ways in which it is sometimes represented in literary theory. See especially the following entries in Gide's *Journals*: 21 December and detached/recovered pages for 1923; January 1925; 7 October and 25 November 1927; 10 February (especially) and 8 December 1929; 5 August and September 1931; 27 June 1937.

9 'Terrors of the Night': *Dracula* and 'Degeneration' in the Late Nineteenth Century*

DANIEL PICK

Daniel Pick's essay was written when he was a Research Fellow at Christ's College Cambridge. Some of the material in this essay is included in 'Fictions of degeneration', Chapter 6 of Pick's *Faces of Degeneration* (see Further Reading), a wide-ranging cultural history in which he explores the genealogy of the concept of degeneration in France, Italy, and England in the nineteenth century. The present essay links the silences and ambiguities of *Dracula* to the contradictions in the wider cultural discourse of degeneration, and reads Stoker's novel as simultaneously sensationalising the horrors of degeneration and defusing them by constructing a reassuring narrative which depicts their containment (see Introduction, p. 15).

'It is nineteenth century up-to-date with a vengeance.' (*Dracula* p. 36)[1]

This essay seeks to address *Dracula* historically and to suggest some of its crucial discursive contexts. Bram Stoker's text was published in 1897, the very year after the term 'psychoanalysis' is said to have been coined.[2] Nevertheless, *Dracula* inhabits, like many other late nineteenth-century fictions, a world of representation which now seems insistently and tantalisingly pre-Freudian.[3] The adjacent dates – signalling for Stoker as for Freud a critical, albeit relatively late, 'career launch' into fame – mask the enduring separation between their languages on fantasy and demons, as between their respective interpretations of dreams. They were not at all, as one commentator has recently claimed, 'telling the same story'.[4]

Part of the novel's task was to represent, externalise and kill off a distinct constellation of contemporary fears. Corruption and degeneration, the reader discovers, are identifiable, foreign and

*Reprinted from *Critical Quarterly*, 30 (1988), pp. 71–87

superable; but the text also recognises a certain sense of failure – an element of horror is always left over, uncontained by the terms of the story as by the intrepid party who stalked the Count: an English aristocrat, a brave American hunter, two doctors, a lawyer and his devoted, dutiful (but endangered) wife. The vampire is allowed no direct voice or expression, but nor is any other figure given full narrative mastery. The novel refuses to provide a synthesis, proceeding instead through a series of separate diaries, reports and letters. It seeks to deal with a number of contemporary social debates, but reaches in the face of them a kind of paralysis, as though the narrative never came to represent the danger it hints. There are points where the description seems frozen at the threshold between Victorian evolutionism and psychoanalysis:

> ... I saw around us a ring of wolves, with white teeth and lolling red tongues, with long, sinewy limbs and shaggy hair. They were a hundred times more terrible in the grim silence which held them than even when they howled. For myself, I felt a sort of paralysis of fear. It is only when a man feels himself face to face with such horrors that he can understand their true import. (p. 13)

Although Professor Van Helsing is famed for his 'absolutely open mind' (p. 112), the novel chronically reverts to closed, cautionary tale, warning of the perils of a wandering consciousness or body, the potentially fatal risks of entering mysterious new places and knowledges: Trance/Trans/ Transylvania. But the narrative is itself prone to carelessness, wandering off the point or hinting too much. As Montague Summers observed in his early study of the vampire (1928): 'If we review *Dracula* from a purely literary point of approach it must be acknowledged that there is much careless writing....'[5] The text is careless in some respects but painstaking in its insistence on the inadequacy of nineteenth-century materialism and determinism. *Dracula* thirsts to cross the threshold into a new conception of subjectivity and science, say psychoanalytic, towards which, simultaneously, it seems to be remarkably resistant. We are shown how the doctors in the novel kept coming up against an impasse, rejecting any organic explanation of Lucy Westenra's illness, but reluctant to follow through to any alternative explanation: '... but as there must be a cause somewhere, I have come to the conclusion that it must be something mental' (p. 111); 'I have made careful examination but there is no functional cause' (p. 114).

Stoker and Freud could have known nothing of one another at the time of *Dracula*. Even in 1913 Freud made no mention of this horror story when he discussed vampires in *Totem and Taboo*.[6] By then the tale was something of a *cause célèbre* – nine English editions had already appeared as well as a considerable subsidiary literature.[7] But perhaps Freud's omission is unsurprising. The context of his brief observations on the vampire was strictly anthropological, nothing to do with the popular novel.

Although Freud said nothing about *Dracula*, he did discuss a book published the year after, Rudolf Kleinpaul's *Die Lebendigen und die Toten in Volksglauben, Religion und Sage* (1898), which had included a useful account of the vampire myth. Indeed according to this authority, as recounted by Freud, once upon a time '*all* of the dead were vampires, all of them had a grudge against the living and sought to injure them and rob them of their lives' (p. 59). In the course of history, so the argument continued, the perceived malignity of the dead diminished and narrowed, frequently restricted to those with a particular right to feel resentment, for instance, murdered people, or 'brides who had died with their desires unsatisfied' (ibid). Kleinpaul described various tribes in which the dead were cast as murderously threatening creatures. They lusted to bring the living within their fold: 'The living did not feel safe from the attacks of the dead till there was a sheet of water between them. That is why men liked to bury the dead on islands or on the farther side of rivers; and that, in turn, is the origin of such phrases as 'Here and in the Beyond' (ibid).

In reading the various recent studies on tribal taboos around death, Freud had been struck by the frequency with which the dead were imbued with evil designs and a will to 'infect' the living. 'We know that the dead are powerful rulers; but we may perhaps be surprised when we learn that they are treated as enemies. The taboo upon the dead is – if I may revert to the simile of infection – especially virulent among most primitive peoples (p. 51). In many tribes, for instance in Polynesia, Melanesia and Africa, those who had had a close relationship or intimate dealings with the dead were seen to have been themselves morally touched and contaminated by death. They became anathema for the community. Thus there were villages in the Philippine Islands where:

> a widow may not leave her hut for seven or eight days after the death; and even then she may only go out at an hour when she is not likely to meet anybody, for whoever looks upon her dies a sudden death. To prevent this fatal catastrophe, the widow knocks with a wooden peg on the trees as she goes along, thus warning people of her dangerous proximity; and the very trees on which she knocks soon die. (p. 53)

Evidence from Frazer and others was given to show that widowers too were subject to restrictions of contact with other members of the community; restrictions which were in fact barriers to *temptation*. The taboos operated to prevent the fulfilment of the bereaved's desire to find a substitute partner: 'Substitutive satisfactions of such a kind run counter to the sense of mourning and they would inevitably kindle the ghost's wrath' (p. 54). The wrathful dead themselves were often unnameable: indeed anything which might evoke and hence invoke the dead had to be prevented, '[f] or they [e.g. the Tuaregs of the Sahara] make no disguise of the fact that they are *afraid* of the presence or of the return of the dead person's ghost; and they perform a great number of ceremonies to keep him at a distance or drive him off' (p. 57).

Freud linked such myths and taboos to the guilt, remorse, pain and hate experienced by the bereaved, remarking that these folk tales and taboos had to be reversed. In fact the tale inverted the relation of subject and predicate: it was not the demons that produced guilt, but the other way round. Demons and spirits, Freud argued, were 'only projections of man's own emotional impulses' (p. 92). He noted the unconscious desire to protect the 'innocence' of the mourner, to project the evil wishes on to the dead, as though thereby, despite the impossibility, to free the living of ambivalence. Ghosts, vampires, demons, spirits functioned at once to punish and exonerate the living, threatening and reprieving at the same moment. The trouble with the dead, it seemed, was that they would not stay dead and buried, least of all in the memories of the living. Like blood-sucking vampires, they haunted the memory of the bereaved and drained them of their vitality.

Freud's own concern here was at the juncture of psychoanalysis and anthropology, not social history. The aim, after all, was not specifically the analysis of recent culture, but the pursuit of the 'primitive' as royal road to the understanding of the origin of more widely shared terrors, totems and projections. In *Totem and Taboo* there is no exploration of the significance of the *renewed* late nineteenth-century interest in the uncanny, the immaterial, the supernatural and the beyond; yet that interest was to be found repeatedly and variedly in fiction, anthropology, psychology and criminology, as well as at the Society for Psychical Research of which Freud became a corresponding member.[8] The Society was founded in 1882 with a commitment to the 'open-minded' investigation of the occult, ghosts, haunted houses, possession and trances. It connected with a much wider European intellectual reappraisal of positivism and naturalism which crystallised in the 1890s. Van Helsing would no doubt have been an ideal member; after all he constantly doubted his senses and questioned his rationalist assumptions, always striving to see beyond 'our scientific, sceptical matter-of-fact nineteenth century' (*Dracula*, p. 238).

To try to read *Dracula* historically, rather than anthropologically or trans-historically, involves, initially, a certain capacity of resistance on the part of the reader. For it is tempting to 'fall prey' to the mythological, folkloristic connotations of the vampire story and declare the novel merely a new twist to an old tale, the reiteration of antique taboos on death. The cinema often contributes to this collapse of history, be eliding the differences between *Dracula* and *Frankenstein,* placing them together in much the same castle, the same period, as if there were one undifferentiated 'gothic' nineteenth century, homogenous from beginning to end. To say that Stoker's best-seller was very much a Victorian, or indeed more specifically a late nineteenth-century text may even appear perverse. It was, after all, only the latest in a long history of literary representations of the vampire which itself ran back into a vast range of myths. In 1819 Polidori's *The Vampyre* had appeared (under the name of Byron) and made just this point; the 'superstition', we are told, was very general in the East and had spread into Europe through Hungary, Poland, Austria and Lorraine.'[9] Or as a subsequent account put it: 'Assyria knew the vampire long ago and he lurked amid the primaeval forests of Mexico before Cortes came.'[10]

Any specific representation of the vampire, it could then be argued, fades into a longer history which in turn dissolves into timeless myth. Some things, we are reminded in *Dracula,* are historically recalcitrant, unamenable to 'modern' transformation:' . . . the old centuries had, and have powers of their own which mere "modernity" cannot kill' (p.36). Perhaps one could seek in Proppian fashion to pare away the idiosyncrasies of Stoker's tale in order to locate across the centuries the basic shared form of vampire narratives, the essential morphological elements into which, apparently, any tale might be decomposed.[11] Thus a recent study of the vampire from the nineteenth century through to contemporary cinema has insisted that despite the 'unique achievement' of each classic of the genre, '[a] close extended look . . . will allow us to see the shape and the particular significance of the entire series . . .'.[12] What is offered in that particular approach to the vampire is certainly a useful compendium of examples, but *Dracula* as such is largely displaced from the later nineteenth century; there is indeed only the briefest consideration of any of the wider historical questions and debates at the time of its writing.

Dracula, however, has many contemporary references and resonances not even to be found in one of its most immediate 'sources', Le Fanu's *Carmilla* (1872).[13] Above all, whilst Le Fanu's tale had been securely located in Styria, Stoker's novel brings Dracula to London, articulating a vision of the bio-medical degeneration of the race in general and the metropolitan population in particular. Although versions of such a theory had found expression in specialist journals and treatises since the 1850s, it had only become a major issue of social debate and political speculation in the 1880s and 1890s.[14] The network of *Dracula's* images and terrors can be read in the context of a multitude of other contemporary representations: from government inquiries to popular pamphlets, statistical surveys, laboratory experiments, political programmes and philosophical investigations. The ambiguities of representation in the novel were in part bound up with contradictions in that wider discourse of degeneration throughout the period: the process of pathological decay, it seemed, was at once precisely contained (there were certain identifiable degenerate categories of being who eventually became sterile) and ubiquitous, affecting whole populations. The reassuring function of the novel – displacing perceived social and political dangers onto the horror story of a foreign Count finally staked through the heart – was undermined by the simultaneous suggestion of an invisible and remorseless morbid accumulation within, distorting the name and the body of the West (Lucy Westenra), transmitting unknown poisons from blood to blood.

The novel, excruciatingly, says nothing of the sexual fantasies and fears it articulates so graphically as vampire attack and blood pollution. The text resists the 'temptation' of spelling out any notion of sexuality, for which, indeed, it lacks any developed terms of description: resistance, frustration, failure of insight are crucial 'themes' in Stoker's story, and it is as if the narrative itself takes a certain delight in resistance, deafness to the very words on the page, despite its own admonition: '[Van Helsing to Seward] You do not let your eyes see nor your ears hear . . .' (p. 191). Harker proposes to his future wife a union of ignorance: 'Are you willing, Wilhelmina, to share my ignorance? Here is the book. Take it and keep it, read it if you will, but never let me know . . .' (p. 104). Yet denial provides no defence against Dracula. To be asleep or merely careless is to risk the vampire's bite and the fall into hypnotic fascination.

Orthodox medicine itself is shown to be in much the state of a sleep-walker, semi-consciously stumbling along well-worn routes, unable to cross conceptual frontiers and understand the condition of its patients: Dr Seward [of his patient Renfield] '. . . I do not follow his thought'; 'I wish I could get some clue to the cause'; 'I wish I could fathom his mind' (pp. 107, 116). Renfield constantly escapes the doctor's grasp: he slips all too easily out of his cell and of any existing psychiatric schema. Seward never does get to the 'heart' of the 'mystery', never succeeds in becoming 'master of the facts of his hallucination' (p. 60), persisting too single-mindedly in his materialist research on the brain. Only very slowly does he come to sense that his patient's condition is bound up with Dracula and some wider contemporary perversion of the evolutionary 'struggle for survival' which has blurred the question of 'fitness' and 'unfitness': 'My homicidal maniac is of a peculiar kind. I shall have to invent a new classification for him, and call him a zoophagous (life-eating) maniac; what he desires is to absorb as many lives as he can, and has laid himself out to achieve it in a cumulative way' (pp. 70–1). Seward's 'obtuse' reluctance to make any unconventional diagnosis about Lucy Westernra finally exasperates even his mentor, Van Helsing: 'Do you mean to tell me, friend John, that you have no suspicion as to what poor Lucy died of; not after all the hints given, not only by events, but by me?' (p. 191).

The subjects of hysteria and hypnotism, which for a long time in the nineteenth century had been pushed out to the fringes and beyond of orthodoxy and respectability, had lately been returned to the medical centre-stage, at least in Paris, and could no longer be dismissed as mere occult practice or superstition by the modern doctor: '[Van Helsing] I suppose now that you do not believe in corporeal transference. No? Nor in materialisation. No? Nor in astral bodies. No? Nor in the reading of thought. No? Nor in hypnotism? —' '[Seward] Yes' I said. 'Charcot has proved that pretty well' (p. 191).

But the medical audience 'lured' from abroad by Charcot's famous Tuesday demonstrations at the Salpêtrière was frequently appalled to learn of the presence of another theatre of hysteria where quacks, charlatans and music-hall actors entertained large crowds. The individual could, supposedly, be seduced or induced to commit terrible crimes. Crowds and mobs could be whipped up into anarchic frenzies by the hypnotic potential of 'morbid, excitable leaders'.[15] This is the period indeed that sees the reappearance of great hypnotists: Charcot *and* Donato, stage-name of a former Belgian naval officer, D'Hont, who causes sensation and scandal as he tours the European theatres, provoking furious debate on the very legality of the public spectacle of magnetism and hypnotism.[16] The 'hypnotic menace' becomes a matter of forensic investigation and grave public concern — famous cases and trials underscore the possibility of subliminal manipulation, of innocent women induced to commit hideous crimes, even 'murder under hypnosis'[17] — at the same time that it is a terrain of new artistic and medical exploration towards the unconscious.

Of how much Stoker, a man of the theatre who was later to express a particular interest in the question of imposture (and Donato was unmasked on stage for his tricks).[18] knew of this directly we cannot be sure, but echoes of the criminal trials, public performances and dubious private consultations will have reached him. Certainly Dracula too is cast as a form of hypnotist on the stage of Europe, part fake, part genius: '[Harker] I felt myself struggling to awake some call of my instincts . . . I was becoming hypnotised' (p. 44). '[Mina Murray] I was bewildered, and strangely enough, I did not want to hinder him' (p. 287). The novel sets up a contest of hypnotic powers: the good scientist and the evil vampire compete for the loyalty of the wavering hysterical women, for whom there is always only one step from 'horrid flirt' (p. 58) to the 'nightmare' of a demonic possessed sexuality: 'She seemed like a nightmare of Lucy as she lay there; the pointed teeth, the bloodstained voluptuous mouth — which it made one shudder to see — the whole carnal and unspiritual appearance, seeming like a devilish mockery of Lucy's sweet purity' (p. 214).

Everyone, it appears in the novel, is obliged to doubt not only their own descent but their own health and mental order or else to fall into mere self-delusion. Thus Mina Murray is forced to 'suppose I was hysterical . . .' (p. 184). Lord Godalming 'grew quite hysterical' (p. 230); even Van Helsing, the seemingly secure centre of reason and wisdom – 'one of the most advanced scientists of the day', 'both in theory and in practice' (p. 112) – enigmatically collapses at one point into a 'disturbed' and disturbing condition. Seward records how in the face of Lucy's death, Van Helsing became hysterical: '. . . he gave way to a regular fit of hysterics . . . He laughed till he cried and I had to draw the blinds lest anyone should see us and misjudge . . .' (p.174). Strange perturbations are repeatedly described, and not simply in relation to the external figure of Dracula, casting doubt on whether anyone can be, as Lucy Westenra considers Seward, 'absolutely imperturbable' (p. 55). Indeed, thwarted in love, the doctor is forced to rely on drugs to put him to sleep (p. 101). It is increasingly unclear what could constitute a protection from illness and vice in the novel; whether for instance 'good breeding' means anything; for who could be better bred than Count Dracula himself? Amidst the 'whirlpool of races' (p. 28) which made up European history, the Count was descended from a noble line of 'survivors': 'for in our veins flows the blood of many brave races who fought as the lion fights, for lordship' (p. 28).

The novel is in one sense committed to the contradistinction of vice and virtue, purity and corruption, human and vampire; but it tacitly questions the possibility of such sharp separations, in this like so many medical-psychiatrists of the period convinced that no complete dividing line lay between sanity and insanity but rather a vast and shadowy border-land: '[Van Helsing] For it is not the least of its terrors that this evil thing is rooted deep in all good . . .' (p. 241), Darwin too, it should be remembered, had already dealt his 'blow' to 'human narcissism' (as Freud was later to view it) by warning that there was no absolute evolutionary separation from the world of the animals, no escape from the stigma of that descent. Behind even the most imperiously 'contemptuous' human smile, one usually caught the glint of a set of once ferocious teeth:

> He who rejects with scorn the belief that his own canines, and their occasional great development in other men, are due to our early progenitors having been provided with these formidable weapons, will probably reveal by sneering the line of his descent. For though he no longer intends, nor has the power, to use these teeth as weapons, he will unconsciously retract his 'snarling muscles' . . . – so as to expose them ready for action, like a dog prepared to fight.[19]

Stoker's text was paralysed at a threshold of uncertainty, at the turning point between a psychiatric positivism (which the novel derided) and the glimpsed possibility of a new exploration of the unconscious. The rejection of conventional science in the novel was conceived to involve not so much a leap into the future as a return to an earlier knowledge: Van Helsing stoically accepts and manipulates folklore, amalgamating it with the latest evidence from the laboratory and the clinic. He is repeatedly forced to point out the power of the irrational and the inexplicable, the fact that there were more wonders in heaven and earth than were dreamt of in nineteenth-century naturalist philosophy. Nevertheless he finally explains to the other protagonists that the fearful enigma of the vampire has to be approached not through a popular physiognomy but through the insights of a craniometry currently being developed in modern criminal anthropology:

> The criminal always works at one crime – that is the true criminal who seems predestinate to crime, and who will of none other. This criminal has not full man-brain. He is clever and cunning and resourceful; but he be not of man-stature as to brain. He be of child-brain in much. Now this criminal of ours is predestinate to crime also; he too have child-brain ... The Count is a criminal and of criminal type. Nordau and Lombroso would so classify him, and *qua* criminal he is of imperfectly formed mind. (pp. 341–2)

Stoker's novel refers to Max Nordau and Cesare Lombroso, to a whole realm of investigation into degeneration and atavism, which itself wavered between a taxonomy of visible stigmata and the horror of invisible maladies, between the desired image of a specific, identifiable criminal type (marked out by ancestry) and the wider representation of a society in crisis, threatened by waves of degenerate blood and moral contagion.[20] Like Lombroso and the earlier important French theorist of degeneration, Bénédict-Augustin Morel,[21] Jonathan Harker journeys from specific images of deformity (goitre in particular: 'Here and there we passed Cszeks [sic] and Slovaks, all in picturesque attire, but I noticed that goitre was painfully prevalent' (p. 7), towards the citadel of full-blown degeneracy. From early work on cretinism and goitre, a medico-psychiatric theory had emerged in which the degenerate was cast as a kind of social vampire who corrupted the nation and desired, in Lombroso's words, 'not only to extinguish life in the victim, but to mutilate the corpse, tear its flesh and drink its blood'.[22]

The possible identification of the delinquent and the degenerate through physiognomy were part of the problematic of many late nineteenth-century novels as of criminal anthropology itself in the period. The idea that different categories of delinquent possessed specific traits and that a new science might chart precisely the features of the 'born criminal' aroused vast interest and enthusiasm, but also growing criticism and ridicule. By the 1890s, the cruder versions of Lombrosian and other degenerationist schema (the simian eyebrows, handle-shaped ears and so on) were being challenged and even satirised by dissenting experts in medical lecture courses and at international congresses of criminal anthropology.[23] New biological determinist arguments emerged, concentrating not on the face of the criminal, but on the supposedly obscure anomalies of the blood, internal organs, nervous system and brain.

Dracula is full of aspiring physiognomists, seeking to probe demeanours, features and expressions: '[Harker] Doctor, you don't know what it is to doubt everything, even yourself. No you don't; you couldn't with eyebrows like yours.' '[Van Helsing] seemed pleased, and laughed as he said: "So! You are a physiognomist" ' (p. 188). Lucy points out to Mina how Seward 'tries to read your thoughts', and then asks '[d]o you ever try to read your own face? *I do*, and I can tell you it is not a bad study . . .' (p. 55). Good and evil are sometimes written in the features, sometimes erased by them. Distance and perspective alter the nature of what is seen. Thus the 'women looked pretty, except when you got near them . . .' (p.3). Physiognomy is seen to be an enigmatic and potentially counter-productive study; the face is at once a camouflage and a symptom. Dracula after all can change his form at will, and even when in human shape his appearance seems to mislead. Thus the Count's hands, for instance look initially to be 'rather white and fine', but on closer inspection, 'they were rather coarse – broad with squat fingers . . . [and] hairs in the centre of the palm' (p. 18). 'The marked physiognomy' of his face is described in meticulous detail:

> . . . high bridge of the thin nose and peculiarly arched nostrils, with lofty domed forehead, and hair growing scantily round temples, but profusely elsewhere. His eyebrows were very massive, almost meeting over the nose, and with bushy hair that seemed to curl in its own profusion. The mouth, so far as I could see it under the heavy moustache, was fixed and rather cruel-looking, with peculiarly sharp white teeth; these protruded over the lips, whose remarkable ruddiness showed astonishing vitality in a man of his years. For the rest, his ears were pale and at the tops extremely pointed; the chin was broad and strong, and the cheeks firm though thin. The general effect was one of extraordinary pallor. (pp. 17–18)

Dracula picked up a wider debate on the physiognomy of the 'born criminal' and the nature of the recidivist (a figure who had increasingly dominated European debate on law and order in the last quarter of the century);[24] it might even be said to be *parasitic*, like its own villain, feeding off a social moral panic about the reproduction of degeneration, the poisoning of good bodies and races by bad blood, the vitiation of healthy procreation. The novel provided a metaphor for current political and sexual political discourses on morality and society, representing the price of selfish pursuits and criminal depravity. The family and the nation, it seemed to many, were beleagured by syphilitics, alcoholics, cretins, the insane, the feeble-minded, prostitutes and a perceived 'alien invasion' of Jews from the East who, in the view of many alarmists, were feeding off and 'poisoning' the blood of the Londoner.[25] Significantly, it was an unscrupulous Jew who aided and abetted Dracula's flight from his hunters: 'We found Hildescheim in his office, a Hebrew of rather the Adelphi type, with a nose like a sheep, and a fez. His arguments were pointed with specie – we doing the punctuation – and with a little bargaining he told us what he knew' (p. 349).

The parasite might be called a key-word of the period; it cropped up at decisive moments in a multitude of social and political discussions. In 'The science of the future: a forecast', in *Civilization: Its Cause and Cure* (1889), for instance, Edward Carpenter had argued that primitive tribes might be more barbarous than the civilised but they were healthier and biologically stronger. Their society was 'not divided into classes which prey upon each other; nor is it consumed by parasites. There is more true social unity'.[26] Or take the American Eugene Talbot's *Degeneracy. Its Signs, Causes and Results* (1898) which summed up advances in current European criminological research with the view that the essence of crime was to be found in 'parasitology':

> the essential factor of crime is its parasitic nature. Parasites, in a general way, may be divided into those which live on their host, without any tendency to injure his well-being (like the dermodex in the skin follicles); those which live more or less at his expense, but do not tend to destroy him; and finally those which are destructive of the well-being of man and lack proper recognition of individual rights which constitute the essential foundation of society.[27]

The image of the parasite and the blood-sucker informed late nineteenth-century eugenics and the biological theory of degeneration. The parasite argued Edwin Ray Lankester, famous zoologist and curator at the British Museum, in his important 'revisionist' work, *Degeneration, a Chapter in Darwinism* (1880) demonstrated the possibility of a successful evolutionary adaptation to the environment which constituted nevertheless degeneration, the return from the heterogeneous to the homogeneous, the complex to the simple.[28] Darwin it seemed to many had been too optimistic, had suggested, despite his relative caution in extrapolating from the biological to the political, that evolution and progress were tied together. He had thought too little about who and what might best survive in an arguably noxious and degenerate environment – late nineteenth-century London, for instance.[29]

Dracula descended on that London, thus descending in a sense into the much wider social debate of the 1880s and 1890s about the morbidity and degeneracy of the average inhabitant of the metropolis. The city dweller, it seemed, had become a monstrous physical travesty. One of the vexed questions of the debate in degenerationist medical psychiatry was whether such stunted creatures tended eventually towards sterility and self-extinction or, on the contrary, towards a dreadful fecundity, which defied death, spawning offspring to infinity; like the undead in *Dracula* who 'cannot die, but must go on age after age adding new victims and multiplying the evils of the world' (p. 214). As the evil Count gloats, the bad blood he disseminates will spread ever further, constantly finding new carriers: 'My revenge is just begun! I spread it over centuries, and time is on my side' (p. 306). Early in the novel, Dracula amazes Harker by his perfect command of the English language and his familiarity with the layout of London. The Count explains that he had mastered this knowledge because he longed to 'go through the crowded streets of your mighty London, to be in the midst of the whirl and rush of humanity, to share its life, its change, its death . . .' (p. 20). As he warns his guest/risoner, 'you dwellers of the city cannot enter into the feelings of the hunter' (p. 18). When Harker finally realises what 'sharing' London's life and death actually means, he is utterly appalled by the vision of a future vampire-ridden city, '. . . perhaps for centuries to come, he might amongst its teeming millions, satiate his lust for blood, and create a new and ever widening circle of semi-demons to batten on the helpless' (p. 51).

The theory of degeneration seemed to raise difficult moral questions about the relation between the victim and the agent. The degenerates had inherited an affliction, which they then risked visiting upon the next generation. The potential carriers had a duty to protect themselves (for the good of society) from a process of morbidity which, like Dracula, had many forms and disguises. As a French expert, Dr Legrain, was to put it in 1889: 'Le dégénéré apparaît alors comme une vaste synthèse, un conglomérat d'états morbides différents, au milieu desquels il est obligé de se frayer une voie, en conservant très difficilement son équilibre. Ses délires sont multiples, polymorphes, protéiformes'.[30]

Stoker's story continually hinted at a whole set of questions about 'polymorphous perversity', fantasy, desire and will, which could only be characterised very obliquely as the 'strange and uncanny' (p. 14) or the 'living ring of terror' (p. 13). Incarcerated in the castle, Harker declares: '. . . I am either being deceived, like a baby, by my own fears, or else I am in desperate straits . . .' (p. 27). But Harker in fact is shown to succumb to sexual fantasies without being bitten; it is seemingly his own thoughts which place him in desperate danger. Whilst kept prisoner, he wanders beyond the bounds of his permitted space, unable to heed

Dracula's warning: 'Let me advise you, my dear young friend – nay, let me warn you with all seriousness, that should you leave these rooms you will not by any chance go to sleep in any other part of the castle. It is old, and has many memories, and there are bad dreams for those who sleep unwisely' (p. 33).

It is with good reason that the novel's characters fear sleep: '[Lucy] I tried to go to sleep, but could not. Then there came to me the old fear of sleep, and I determined to keep awake' (p. 142). When Harker falls asleep in the wrong room, he awakes 'uneasily' to find three young women before him, a prisoner to his own wicked, burning desire' (p. 37), captivated by a 'thrilling' and 'repulsive' scene:

> I was afraid to raise my eyelids, but looked out and saw perfectly under the lashes. The fair girl went on her knees and bent over me, fairly gloating. There was a deliberate voluptuousness which was both thrilling and repulsive, and as she arched her neck she actually licked her lips like an animal, till I could see in the moonlight the moisture shining on the scarlet lips and on the red tongue as it lapped the white sharp teeth. Lower and lower went her head as the lips went below the range of my mouth and chin and seemed about to fasten on my throat . . . I could feel the soft, shivering touch of the lips on the super-sensitive skin of my throat, and the hard dents of two sharp teeth, just touching and pausing there. I closed my eyes in a languorous ecstasy and waited – waited with beating heart. (p. 38)

At this decisive moment, the Count reappears with a fury beyond 'the demons of the pit . . .' (p. 38), to reclaim the young man as his own: 'This man belongs to me!': '[y]es I too can love . . .' (p. 39). Dracula protected Harker from himself. As the young lawyer had earlier admitted, 'of all the foul things that lurk in this hateful place the Count is the least dreadful to me . . .' (p. 36).

Stoker's novel, for all its 'mythological' and folkloristic insistence, must be read in relation to a whole set of late nineteenth- and early twentieth-century concerns, images and problems. The novel in part explored and was in part imprisoned by its own situation: that powerful felt moment of interim ('this dreadful thrall of night and gloom and fear', p. 45), on the verge of the new century, in a kind of corridor between different forms of knowledge and understanding. The novel at once sensationalised the horrors of degeneration and charted reassuringly the process of their confinement and containment. The terrors and the contradictions were never quite banished, despite the deeply consoling, conservative representation of cheerful beer-swilling, cap-doffing London labourers, Jonathan Harker's dramatic upward social mobility (he rises 'from clerk to master in a few years', p. 158), and Mina Harker's restoration as subservient, faithful wife and mother.

By 1905, something had changed in Stoker's work; the vision of paralysis had shifted, as though he could now represent the nineteenth century as a long period of dark superstition which had given way to twentieth-century clarity and enlightenment. Perhaps the new tone owed something to certain recent events. In the immediately preceding years the theory of the degeneration of the Londoner in particular and the race in general had been used to explain the reverses of the Boer War, but had been subjected to serious cross-examination and some devastating criticism in the much publicised inter-departmental government report of 1904.[31] The wilder claims of the existence of a huge, stunted degenerate urban population had been discounted: the process of 'deterioration', the inquiry concluded, was confined to certain slum areas. Moreover something, it seemed, was being done about alien immigration – the Royal Commission had been completed in 1903 and a new Act was passed in 1905.[32]

Where *Dracula* had turned on the vision of degeneration and corruption, Stoker's new novel, entitled *The Man* (1905),[33] was a kind of 'positive eugenic' homily, the saga of the struggle to get good stock together, in order to achieve female beauty, pride and self-reliance (p. 3) and male strength, intelligence, bravery and determination (p. 4). Although petrified in an interminable, hackneyed romance, the text uttered prosaically and routinely the words 'sex' and 'sexuality', for as we are reminded, 'sex is sex all through. It is not, like whiskers or a wedding-ring, a garnishment of maturity' (p. 19). The very perception of sex and childhood had changed, it was suggested, from an ill-informed past where the infant was treated by adults as a kind of neuter object without feelings – 'the baby was "it" to a man' (p. 18) – and, one might add, the representation of fear, desire and subjectivity had shifted in Stoker's own writing from the earlier novel where the vampire had constituted an ambiguous, threatening third person: 'I saw It – Him'; 'He – It!' (*Dracula*, p. 85); 'It – like a man' (p. 84).

The coincidence of timing was again striking: 1905 was the year of Freud's *Three Essays on the Theory of Sexuality*.[34] Stoker no doubt knew little or nothing of this, but he too charted masculinity, feminity and their discontents, through the destiny of the daughter of Stephen Norman, who has been brought up as a 'tom boy' and indeed christened Stephen herself, at the instigation of her dying mother ('let her be indeed our son! Call her by the name we both love!', p. 16), in order to console the father for his bitter disappointment at the gender of his child.

In *The Man* women are still shown to be constantly in danger not only from 'a certain [male] resentment' (p. 20) but also from themselves. Stephen's very physiognomy, we are told, suggests the prospect of 'some trouble which might shadow her whole after life' (p. 3); moreover her description is strangely reminiscent of the female vampires in the earlier text; she too has a trace of Eastern blood and a seductive mouth 'the voluptuous curves of the full, crimson lips' (p. 3), albeit no sharp, deadly teeth. The total effect is declared to be 'admirable', emblematic of a fine lineage: 'In her the various elements of her race seemed to have cropped out' (p. 3). She has a 'wide, fine forehead', 'black eyes', 'raven eyebrows', 'acquiline nose', a face which 'marked the high descent from Saxon through Norman'. The dangers are all internal, there are no monsters: the only 'wolf' in the story is not 'the wicked wolf that for half a day had paralysed London' (*Dracula*, p. 140), but in fact her saviour: Harold An Wolf. The crisis stems from Stephen's wilfulness and forwardness: she comes close to disaster in usurping the male role and proposing marriage to a worthless man only to be rejected and humiliated.

A hint of the new story had certainly been there in *Dracula* when Mina Murray speaks scathingly of the 'New Woman' writers who 'will some day start an idea that men and women should be allowed to see each other asleep before proposing or accepting' and even speculates that 'the New Woman won't condescend in future to accept; she will do the proposing herself' (p. 89), but in *The Man*, a certain style of indirectness and displacement has gone, as though the author is insisting that the veil of the vampire can now be seen through, leaving in place of the Count's castle and its surrounding wolves, only the occasional necessary sexual euphemism where total frankness still remained out of the question. We are presented with knock-about adventure, patriotism, long descriptions of the true qualities of fine men and women amongst the superior races, and various 'matter of fact' comments on the distance still to be traversed to dispel all remaining sexual mystery: 'Perhaps some day, when Science has grappled successfully with the unseen, the mysteries of sex will be open to men . . .' (p. 103). Through hundreds of pages, the protagonists battle with those enduring mysteries of sexuality, caught up in a drama of profound misunderstanding, a personal 'trial' culminating in shipwreck and temporary blindness. Before their final union, the hero and the heroine are to be overwhelmed by emotional frustration, remorse and the most painful confusions of identity.

Thus in 1905 *Dracula* was banished and replaced with a melodrama of psychological suffering, neurosis, cruelty and redemption, full of 'longings and outpourings of heart and soul and mind' (p. 104). Of course, vampires have returned in innumerable guises in cinema, theatre and writing since then. But at that moment for Stoker, there were no psychotic, 'undead' blood-sucking creatures needed. For the lovely, impetuous Stephen and the lovesick Harold there were only long and lonely private mental torments – 'the tortures and terrors of the night' (p. 104).

Notes

1. BRAM STOKER, *Dracula, A Tale* [1897]. The World's Classics (Oxford: Oxford University Press, 1983).
2. See PETER GAY, *Freud, A Life for our Time* (London, J.M. Dent & Sons), p. 103.
3. For a related discussion on this point which has already appeared in *Critical Quarterly*, see STEPHEN HEATH, 'Psychopathia sexualis: Stevenson's *Strange Case*', XXVIII (spring–summer 1986), 93–108.
4. GREGORY A. WALLER, *The Living and the Undead. From Stoker's Dracula to Romero's Dawn of the Dead* (Urbana and Chicago: University of Illinois Press, 1986), p. 66.
5. MONTAGUE SUMMERS, *The Vampire: His Kith and Kin* (London: Kegan Paul, 1928), p. 334.
6. SIGMUND FREUD, *Totem and Taboo* (1913), *The Standard Edition of the Complete Psychological Works of Sigmund Freud* (London: Hogarth, 1955), 24 vols, vol. XIII. Note that ERNEST JONES followed Freud in his disregard of *Dracula*. There is no mention of Stoker's novel in Jones's chapter on 'The Vampire' in *On the Nightmare* (London: Hogarth, 1931).
7. The ninth edition was published in London in 1912; cf. SUMMERS, op. cit., ch. 5, pp. 271–340, 'The Vampire in Literature'.
8. See the list of members, *Proceedings of the Society for Psychical Research*, XXV (1911).
9. 'The vampyre: a tale by Lord Byron', *The New Monthly Magazine and Universal Register*, II (January–June 1819), pp. 195–206, p. 195.
10. SUMMERS, op. cit., p. ix.
11. See V. Propp, *Morphology of the Folktale* [1928] (Austin and London: University of Texas Press, 1968), p. 96.
12. WALLER, op. cit., p. 6.
13. J. SHERIDAN LE FANU, *Carmilla, In a Glass Darkly* (London: R. Bentley & Son, 1872), 3 vols, vol. III.
14. See GARETH STEDMAN JONES, *Outcast London: A Study in the Relationship Between Classes* [1971] (Harmondsworth: Penguin, 1984).
15. See for instance GUSTAVE LE BON, *The Crowd. A Study of the Popular Mind*, trans. from the French (London: T. F. Unwin, 1896). For a general survey, see ROBERT A. NYE, *The Origins of Crowd Psychology. Gustave Le Bon and the Crisis of Mass Democracy in the Third Republic* (London and Beverley Hills: Sage, 1975); and SUSANNA BARROWS, *Distorting Mirrors. Visions of the Crowd in Late Nineteenth-Century France* (New Haven and London: Yale University Press, 1981).
16. See for instance CLARA GALLINI, *La sonnambula meravigliosa. Magnetismo e ipnotismo nell'ottocento italiano* (Milan: Feltrinelli, 1983).
17. See RUTH HARRIS, 'Murder under hypnosis in the case of Gabrielle Bompard: psychiatry in the courtroom in belle époque Paris', in *The Anatomy of Madness, Essays in the History of Psychiatry*, ed. W. Bynum, R. Porter and M. Shepherd (London: Tavistock, 1985), vol. II, ch. 10.
18. BRAM STOKER, *Famous Imposters* (London: Sidgwick & Jackson, 1910).
19. CHARLES DARWIN, *The Descent of Man and Selection in relation to Sex* (London: John Murray, 1871), 2 vols, vol. I, p. 127.
20. See for instance CESARE LOMBROSO, *L'uomo delinquente* (Milan: Hoepli, 1876); MAX NORDAU, *Degeneration* [1892], translated from the 2nd German edition (London: W. Heinemann, 1895); for various general discussions, cf. SANDER GILMAN and J.

CHAMBERLIN eds, *Degeneration, The Dark Side of Progress* (New York: Columbia University Press, 1985). With regard to Lombroso, I have tried to analyse this contradiction or at least double connotation further, in an essay in *History Workshop Journal*, Issue 21 (spring 1986), 60–86.

21. See BÉNÉDICT-AUGUSTIN Morel, *Traité des dégénérescences physiques, intellectuelles et morales de l'espèce humaine* (Paris: J. B. Baillière, 1857).

22. CESARE LOMBROSO, *Criminal Man According to the Classification of Cesare Lombroso Briefly Summarised by his Daughter, Gina Lombroso Ferrero* (New York and London: G. P. Putnam, 1911), p. xv.

23. See the heated exchanges on the work of Lombroso at the first, second and third congresses of criminal anthropology; *Actes du Premier Congrès International d'anthropologie criminelle*, Turin, 1886; *Actes du Deuxième Congrès . . .*, Paris 1889; *Actes du Troisième Congrès . . .*, Brussels, 1893; note the highly critical appendix on 'degeneration', BENJAMIN BALL, *Leçons sur les Maladies Mentales*, 2nd edn (Paris: Asselin & Houzeau, 1890).

24. See ROBERT NYE, *Crime, Madness and Politics in Modern France. The Medical Concept of National Decline* (Princeton: Princeton University Press, 1984); and L. RADZINOWICZ and R. HOOD, 'Incapacitating the habitual criminal, the English experience', *Michigan Law Review*, LXXVIII (1980), pp. 1305–89.

25. See for example the testimony of Arnold White to the *Royal Commission on Alien Immigration. Minutes of Royal Commission on Alien Immigration* [vol. II of the report] (1903), pp. 15–16; cf. DAVID FELDMAN, 'The importance of being English: social policy, patriotism and politics in response to Jewish immigration, 1885–1906', in *Between Neighbourhood and Nation: Essays in the History of London*, ed. Feldman and Stedman Jones (London: Routledge, in press).

26. EDWARD CARPENTER, *Civilization: its Cause and Cure and Other Essays* (London: Swan Sonnenschein, 1889), pp. 8–9.

27. EUGENE S. TALBOT, *Degeneracy: its Causes, Signs and Results* (London: Walter Scott, 1898), p. 318; cf. Francis Galton's observation that there was an absolute 'contrariety of ideals between the beasts that prey and those they prey upon, between those of the animals that have to work hard for their food and the sedentary parasites that cling to their bodies and suck their blood' *Essays in Eugenics* (London: The Eugenics Education Society, 1909), p. 36.

28. EDWIN RAY LANKESTER, *Degeneration. A Chapter in Darwinism* (London: Macmillan, 1880).

29. Cf. 'Degeneration amongst Londoners', *The Lancet*, I (February 1885), p. 265.

30. M. LEGRAIN, *Hérédité et alcoolisme. Étude psychologique et clinique sur les dégénérés buveurs et les familles d'ivrognes* (Paris: O. Doin, 1889), p. 6.

31. *The Report of the Inter-Departmental Committee on Physical Deterioration* (1904), *Reports from Commissioners, Inspectors and Other Series*, vol. XXXII.

32. *Report of the Royal Commission on Alien Immigration* (1903); *Aliens Act* (1905).

33. BRAM STOKER, *The Man* (London: W. Heinemann, 1905).

34. SIGMUND FREUD, *Three Essays on the Theory of Sexuality* [1905], *The Standard Edition of the Complete Psychological Works of Sigmund Freud* (London: Hogarth, 1953), 24 vols., vol. VII.

10 Syphilis, Sexuality, and the Fiction of the *Fin de Siècle**

Elaine Showalter

Elaine Showalter is professor of English at Princeton University and the author of numerous books and essays dealing with gender issues and the representation of gender and sexuality in a wide range of cultural forms. The essay reprinted here revisits territory that Showalter investigated from a somewhat different perspective in her chapter on late nineteenth-century women novelists (the so-called feminist phase) in *A Literature of Their Own* (London: Virago, 1978). In its reading of *fin de siècle* novels (by men and women) alongside medical and scientific texts and advertisements, and also in relation to contemporary debates about degeneration and sexuality it also anticipates her later book *Sexual Anarchy* (see Further Reading). Showalter ingeniously links together an 'iconography' of degenerative sexual disease, the *fin de siècle* preoccupation with the fantastic mode in literature, and a pervasive gender crisis (see Introduction, pp. 15–16).

If, as Susan Sontag has maintained in *Illness as Metaphor*, tuberculosis and cancer became the symbolic diseases of the nineteenth and twentieth centuries, syphilis was surely the symbolic disease of the *fin de siècle*. Suggesting the dread of sexual contamination during a period of gender crisis, the iconography of syphilis pervades English fiction at the turn of the century. While syphilis and syphilitic insanity constituted the repressed historical referents for the fantastic mode that dominates so much of late Victorian writing, male and female fantasies were very different. For *fin de siècle* women writers, lust was the most unforgivable of the sins of the fathers, and sexual disease was its punishment, a

*Reprinted from *Sex, Politics, and Science in the Nineteenth Century Novel*, ed. Ruth Bernard Yeazell (Baltimore: Johns Hopkins University Press, 1986)

punishment unjustly shared by innocent women and children. By the 1890s the syphilitic male had become an arch-villain of feminist protest fiction, a carrier of contamination and madness, and a threat to the spiritual evolution of the human race. In men's writing of the period, however, women are the enemies, whether as the *femmes fatales* who lure men into sexual temptation only to destroy them, the frigid wives who drive them to the brothels, or the puritanical women novelists, readers, and reviewers who would emasculate their art. By the end of the century, the imaginative worlds of male and female writers had become radically separate, and the sexual struggle between men and women had a counterpart in a literary struggle over the future of fiction.

Why should syphilis have played so central a symbolic role in the fiction of the 1890s? Susan Sontag relates the efflorescence of metaphors of illness to moments when the disease in question is coming under some medical control, but remains frightening and mysterious.[1] Although syphilis was incurable until the twentieth century, the rates of the disease were actually beginning to decline in the 1890s, probably because of improved hygiene, after a period in which alarm over the high incidence of syphilis among soldiers and sailors had led to control of prostitution by the English government in the controversial Contagious Diseases Acts of 1864–86.[2] Culturally, moreover, the discourse on syphilis was part of what Foucault sees as the post-Darwinian theory of degenerescence, part of the new technologies of sex that opened up the domain of social control. In the late nineteenth century, Foucault explains in *The History of Sexuality*, 'the analysis of heredity was placing sex (sexual relations, venereal diseases, matrimonial alliances, perversions) in a position of "biological responsibility" with regard to the species: not only could sex be affected by its own diseases, it could also, if it was not controlled, transmit diseases or create others, that would afflict future generations.'[3] Whereas in the Renaissance syphilis functioned as a religious symbol of the disease in the spirit, and during the Restoration became a political metaphor for the disease in the state, *fin de siècle* English culture treats it as a symbol of the disease in the family.[4]

In the 1890s too, research in medical science and cellular pathology proved what had long been suspected: general paralysis of the insane, a form of madness that affected up to 70 per cent of male asylum patients, was actually the terminal form of syphilis. This understanding of general paralysis – otherwise known as GPI, syphilitic insanity, syphilis of the brain, dementia paralytica, or cerebral syphilis – was the perfect confirmation of late Victorian psychiatry's belief in heredity and visible vice. Among special predisposing causes of insanity, wrote Sir George Savage, 'heredity stands first in importance. . . . The torch of civilization is handed from father to son, and as with idiosyncracies of mind, so the very body itself exhibits well-defined marks of its parentage.'[5] Medical psychiatrists believed that based on the model of dementia paralytica, other forms of insanity could also be traced to indisputable organic cause, and that the physical basis of all mental disease would soon be firmly established. Indeed, Dr C. F. Marshall, who had been the house surgeon for the London Lock Hospital, attributed hereditary insanity in general to the effects of syphilis: 'We often read of vague references to a "hereditary predisposition to nervous disease," a "hereditary tendency to insanity," etc. It would be far more rational to regard these "hereditary tendencies" as nothing more or less than a predisposition to nervous and mental disease due to hereditary syphilis.' Marshall ominously concluded, 'Considering the predilection of syphilis for the nervous system, it is remarkable that insanity is not more widespread than it is.'[6]

In its association with prostitution, adultery, perversity, and violence, furthermore, the characteristics of syphilitic insanity seemed to violate and subvert all of the society's most potent moral norms, to break all the bourgeois rules of sexual and social conduct. The popular image of the male paralytic was established by medical texts, quack advertisements, and sensational literature.

English attitudes must be understood in the historical and social contexts that were defined for women and for men. Victorian men and Victorian women grew up with different kinds of knowledge about syphilis, and consequently different ideas about its symbolic relationship to their own psyches. The hideous ravages of syphilis, from an enormous and Miltonic list of skin disorders – macules, papules, tubercules, pustules, blebs, tumors, lesions, scales, crusts, ulcers, chancres, gummas, fissures, and scars – to cardiovascular disturbances, locomotor ataxia, tabes, blindness, and dementia, made the disease a powerful deterrent in the theological and moral reform campaigns to control male sexuality.

In the Victorian home, handbooks of popular medicine made images of the syphilitic wages of premarital and extramarital sin available for the instruction of the young boy. 'Walter,' the author of *My Secret Life*, recalled being terrified as a child by a book about venereal disease shown to him by his godfather: 'The illustrations in the book, of faces covered with scabs, blotches, and eruptions, took such hold of my mind that for twenty years afterwards the fear was not quite eradicated.'[7] Boys and men were also made constantly aware of the dangers of venereal infection by newspaper advertisements for an exotic catalogue of patent antisyphilis medicines, injections, and ointments: Curtis's Manhood, Sir Samuel Hannay's Specific, Dr Brodum's Botanical Syrup, Dr Morse's Invigorating Cordial, Naples Soap, Armenian Pills, Bumstead's Gleet Cure, Red Drops, The Unfortunate's Friend, and Davy's Lac-Elephantis, a popular nostrum that claimed to be the medicated milk of elephants.[8]

As a result of this publicity, and because anxieties about syphilis were so intense. Victorian nerve specialists complained of rampant syphilophobia among their male patients. Dr William Acton explained that like hysteria, syphilophobia

> will assume every form of venereal disease found or described in books ... every trifling ailment will be exaggerated until the medical man is unable to distinguish what his patient really feels and what he supposes he feels. Did isolated cases only now and then occur, perhaps they might not deserve attention, but so numerous are they in a large capital like London, so anxious are the sufferers to obtain relief by consulting every man who can be supposed to offer them any means of relief, that they spend fortunes in travelling about and visiting every quack.[9]

Although the prostitute had become the official scapegoat for the sexual anxieties of the male community, the male syphilophobic fantasy drew on the guilty acknowledgement of a monstrous sexual self. The disease was the eruption of a repressed desire, the surfacing of a secret life. As Basil Hallward warns Dorian Gray in Wilde's novel, 'People talk of secret vices. There are no such things. If a wretched man has a vice, it shows itself in the lines of his mouth, the droop of his eyelids, and moulding of his hands even.'[10]

Women's attitudes, however, were based on a different moral ideology. For respectable women, syphilis had nothing to do with marital transgression, secret vices, or monstrous desires; it was more likely the wages of ignorance than the wages of sin. In most cases, it occurred as the result of marital intercourse with promiscuous husbands, who communicated the disease to their wives with 'almost unfailing regularity.'[11] Although prostitutes constituted the largest category of female syphilitics and general paralytics, the plight of the diseased wife also generated a potent mythology. One popular manual of venereology gave instructions to the doctor on breaking the bad news to a syphilitic wife. Although Victorian boys were lectured and warned, bright girls, the girls likely to become New Women, learned about syphilis in reading forbidden medical books like the manual just mentioned or the frightening book 'Walter's godfather displayed to him. Cecily Hamilton made the discovery very young: 'By the idle opening of a book ... I remember the thought which flashed into my mind – we are told we have got to be married, but we are never told *that*! It was my first revolt against the compulsory nature of the trade of marriage.'[12] For these feminists, syphilitic insanity was the product of man's viciousness and represented innocent woman's entrapment and victimization. The prolonged feminist campaign against the Contagious Diseases Acts educated women to understand that prostitutes were hapless victims of male lust and that the laws gave sanction to 'a vast male conspiracy to degrade women.'[13] Perverted men, feminists argued, spread syphilis through homosexual acts and then infected the prostitute.

'Among men,' Josephine Butler wrote in a private communication, 'the disease is almost universal at one time or another.'[14] The imagined male conspiracy of doctors, legislators, and libertines coalesced in the rumor that Jack the Ripper was a mad doctor avenging himself on prostitutes for a case of syphilis.[15]

Most important, feminists viewed syphilis as scientific evidence that the sins of the fathers were visited upon the children. It was well known that the worst physical as well as mental effects of syphilis were hereditary. Congenital syphilis, which the Victorians called 'syphilis of the innocents,' is even more devastating than the acquired form of the disease, because it has already entered the secondary phase and begun to attack the nervous system. During the nineteenth century, the infant mortality rate for children of syphilitics was exceptionally high; from 60 per cent to 90 per cent died in their first year. Often deformed or retarded, the syphilitic infant was a pitiful sight, described by one doctor as a 'small, wizened, atrophied, weakly, sickly creature,' resembling a 'monkey or a little old man.'[16] Suffering, apish, shriveled, and prematurely aged, these syphilitic children appeared to feminists as living symbols of the devolutionary force of male vice.

Women's fantasies about syphilis thus centered on the fear of marital penetration and contamination, and on anxieties about hereditary transmission of the disease to children. The seminal fluid might be a deadly injection, and some extreme feminists, like Frances Swiney, believed that sperm itself was a virulent poison and that conjugal intercourse should be restricted to annual occasions.[17]

Freud's case study of the hysterical girl he called Dora shows how completely even the most advanced psychiatrists of the *fin de siècle* accepted the theory of biological responsibility and the sins of the fathers. Dora had been brought for analysis by her father, whom Freud had treated for syphilis before his marriage. In the course of describing a dream, she revealed, to Freud's astonishment, that she knew what her father's illness had been, and that 'she assumed that he had handed on his bad health to her by heredity.' Freud, too, believed this to be the case. Noting that 'a *strikingly high* percentage' of the hysterical women he had treated psychoanalytically had fathers suffering from 'tabes or general paralysis,' Freud had concluded that 'syphilis in the male parent is a very relevant factor in the aetiology of the neuropathic constitution of children.' Yet when Dora made her statement, Freud 'was careful not to tell her' that he agreed.[18] In this specific instance, as well as in his general indifference to Dora's social situation, Freud both protected Dora's father and deprived her of vital reassurance that her 'fantasies' of paternal infection might be legitimate.

Dora's famous second dream, in which on the day of her father's funeral she 'went calmly to her room and began reading a big book that lay on her writing-table,' takes on renewed significance in the contexts of late Victorian medical beliefs. When the contaminating and discrediting father is dead, Dora, like Olive Schreiner and Cecily Hamilton, can read calmly about sexuality and venereal disease in the big book that Freud interpreted as a medical encyclopedia. The sexual anxieties associated with syphilis are thus connected to intellectual and imaginative constraint. 'If her father was dead,' Freud observes, 'she could read or love as she pleased.'[19] To this we might add, noting where the book lay, that she could also *write* as she pleased. Dora's dream suggests that the syphilitic father was an image of creative as well as sexual censorship for women of the *fin de siècle,* an obstacle in the path of erotic and literary freedom.

In fact, *fin de siècle* feminist writers applied the new terminology of Darwinian science to the study of male sexuality and discovered biological sins that could lead to general retrogression. 'Man in any age or country is liable to revert to a state of savagery,' wrote Mona Caird in a series on marriage in the *Westminster Review.*[20] Taking to heart Darwinian arguments about women's self-sacrifice for the good of the species, and sustained by the Victorian belief in women's passionlessness, English radical feminists envisioned themselves as chaste yet maternal heralds of a higher race. In their stories, sexuality is purged, projected, or transcended; sexual disease is male and has nothing to do with the female self.

Rather than protest against evolutionary theories of femininity, moreover, feminists appropriated them. In what seems like a defiant response to the jeremiads of Darwinian psychiatrists against unsexed intellectual women, women who were withering and drying up, 'Ellis Ethelmer' celebrated the gradual disappearance of the 'menstrual habit' among the Newest Women of the age: 'Let it be remembered that menstruation is not an indispensable requisite of either health or maternity,' Ethelmer wrote in 1895; 'with the healthier living and physical training of women in the present day, there is no doubt that the obnoxious phenomenon is already distinctly diminishing in force and prevalence.'[21]

And some feminists fantasized the ultimate biological transcendence and the ultimate evolutionary goal of virgin birth. 'If one could only have a child ... without a husband or the disgrace,' yearns a woman in George Egerton's *Keynotes* (894); 'Ugh, the disgusting men.'[22] In the many feminist utopias written by English and American women of the *fin de siècle,* we can see numerous expressions of the wish for motherhood without the need for dangerous exposure to intercourse and/or disease. Works like Charlotte Perkins Gilman's *Herland* (1915) depict women evolved beyond mere physical reproduction. These inhabitants of a female society bear daughters through parthenogenesis;

sexuality has been so thoroughly eliminated that *Herland* is also free of lesbianism. Their Amazon society has no men, no sexual desire, no syphilis, and no insanity.

In the protest fiction of Sarah Grand, Olive Schreiner, Elizabeth Robins and Ménie Dowie, themes that had been covertly and marginally broached by Victorian women novelists (such as George Eliot in *The Mill on the Floss*, where Wakem's illegitimate son, Jetsome, or his crippled legitimate son, Philip, may be paying for the sins of the father), were given full narrative attention. Sarah Grand's bestseller *The Heavenly Twins* (1893) pioneered the feminist attack on the syphilitic father, offering two heroines who make the right and the wrong choices about marrying syphilitic men. Edith marries a syphilitic naval officer, blind to the clues that he has a venereal disease, although he has 'small, peery' eyes, has deserted the mother of his sickly illegitimate son, and has a head that 'shelved backwards like an ape's.' Edith hopes to reform him by her love, but within a year she is tottering under the 'shadow of an awful form of insanity,' and her syphilitic infant son is 'old, old already, and exhaused with suffering.' Edith quickly sinks into dementia, shrieking 'I want to kill – I want to kill *him*. I want to kill that monstrous child!' The horrified women watching around her bed listen to her raving against 'the arrangement of society which has made it possible for me and my child to be sacrificed in this way,' and Grand warns the reader that 'the same thing may happen now to any mother – to any daughter – and will happen so long as we refuse to know and resist.'[23]

For male writers of the *fin de siècle*, however, the literary uses and meaning of syphilitic insanity were very different. In late Victorian male fantasy fiction, feminist ideology comes under attack, and syphilophobic anxieties appear in the form of fear of female sexuality and intensified misogyny. Bram Stoker's *Dracula* (1897), for example, is often described by feminist critics as a thinly veiled fantasy of contaminating female sexuality, a novel whose central anxiety is 'the fear of the devouring woman.'[24] This rapacious figure is also connected to the New Woman and her insistence on sexual information; as Stoker's Mina observes. 'Some of the "New Women" writers will someday start an idea that men and women should be allowed to see each other asleep before proposing or accepting.' Women seem empowered in the novel. Dracula himself is outnumbered by the sisterhood of seductive female vampires who are part of his incestuous harem and who arouse feelings both of thrilling sensuality and of horrified disgust in the men they offer to kiss. Dracula's daughters are sexually aggressive while men are chaste and passive. Ecstatically waiting to be attacked by one vampire, Jonathan Harker observes that she 'licked her lips like an animal, till I could see in the moonlight the moisture shining on the scarlet lips and on the red tongue as it lapped the white sharp teeth.' The sexual act is represented as contact with a wet red mouth filled with sharp teeth, a *vagina dentata* that is also infected and unclean. The physical and moral transformations suffered by the innocent victims of Dracula in the novel suggest the dangers of syphilis, but here women undergo the worst effects, and the men must 'save' them by such violent medical interventions as decapitation and phallic stakes through the heart.[25]

Lucy Westenra, the first of Dracula's victims, is temporarily protected from his embrace by wreaths of garlic draped around her by Dr Van Helsing. In her white nightdress, as she herself notes in her diary, she is 'like Ophelia in the play, with "virgin crants and maiden strewments"' ' – but a sinister *fin de siècle* Ophelia, who will later rise from the grave in a white shroud to become a vampire who kills children on Hampstead Heath: 'Lucy Westenra, but yet how changed. The sweetness was turned to adamantine, heartless cruelty, and the purity to voluptuous wantonness.'[26] While Dracula, with his peculiar physiognomy and unnatural habits, resembles the syphilitic men who prey on the heroines of feminist novels, the mad and infected Lucy, like Sarah Grand's Edith, turns her aggression first against children.

Lucy's dual nature, her susceptibility to mesmeric trance, and her somnambulistic habits mark her as a nervous heroine of the *fin de siècle*, a sister to Dora and other female hysterics.[27] But Stoker's dark fantasy seems most closely connected with Zola's horrifying description of the syphilitic death of the prostitute Nana, a potent counterpart to feminist allegories of the diseased male. At the end of Zola's novel, the dying Nana is abandoned by her lover; regarding her corpse, her maids are struck by a horror as great as that of Stoker's heroes before Lucy the vampire: 'She's changed, she's changed!'[28]

Zola's deathbed description of Nana, in a novel widely read by the Victorian male avant-garde, must have made an indelible impression:

> She was the fruit of the charnel house . . . a shovelful of corrupted flesh thrown down on the pillow. The pustules had invaded the whole of the face . . . and on that formless pulp, where the features had ceased to be traceable, they already resembled some decaying damp from the grave. One eye . . . had completely foundered among bubbling purulence, and the other, which remained half open, looked like a deep, black, ruinous hole. The nose was still suppurating. Quite a reddish crust was peeling from one of the cheeks and invading the mouth, which it distorted into a horrible grin. And over this loathsome and grotesque mask of death the hair, the beautiful hair, still blazed like sunlight and flowed downward in rippling gold. Venus was rotting.[29]

Like the suppurating Nana, Lucy becomes a 'foul thing,' emblem of a certain kind of *fin de siècle* feminine ending immortalized by the male imagination. H. Rider Haggard's queenly Ayesha, the sex goddess of *She*, also has her final metamorphosis in dissolution; her beautiful hair falls out as she shrivels into an apelike monster.

Yet some male writers were able to make the first break from the moral strangleholds of Victorian sexual anxiety. In the work of Ibsen, Wilde, Stevenson, Hardy, Wells, and Joyce, syphilophobia is not invariably represented as female monstrosity or a rotting Venus; and the sins of the fathers are not lust and vice, but ignorance, guilt, shame, and fear. For this literary avant-garde, syphilis provides the iconography for stories of the mask, the double, and the shadow, and for studies of divided selves in a society where repression and hypocrisy are forms of sexual disease.

In Stevenson's *Dr Jekyll and Mr Hyde* (1886), Jekyll is an anti-Darwinian scientist who rejects the positivist beliefs of his generation, and who has been experimenting with ways to release the psyche from its bondage to physical existence. A social as well as intellectual renegade, Jekyll's needs to pursue pleasure and yet to live up to the exacting moral standards of his bleak professional community have committed him to 'a profound duplicity of life,' accompanied by 'an almost morbid sense of shame.' Coming to acknowledge his sexual longings and fantasies, Jekyll longs to separate his mind and his body, his intellect and his desire: 'If each, I told myself, could be housed in separable identities, life would be relieved of all that was unbearable.'[30]

The 'hairy and libidinous' Hyde, embodiment of Jekyll's irregularities and secret appetites, is described in the physical vocabulary of syphilitic deformity and regression: he is 'abnormal,' 'troglodytic,' 'ape-like' and 'dwarfish,' and he generates 'disgust, loathing, and fear' in the men who see him. Jekyll's metamorphosis into Hyde, first drug-induced and then involuntary, suggests the dramatic personality changes of syphilitic dementia catalogued by Darwinian psychiatrists. Hyde's 'complete moral insensibility' and his impulsive violent crimes resemble the 'paralytic furor' described by doctors like Thomas Austin. As Hyde's crimes become known, Jekyll's friends speculate that the doctor is being blackmailed, paying for youthful transgression: 'the ghost of some old sin, the cancer of some concealed disgrace.' Even Jekyll's frenzied search for the antidote recalls the syphilophobe's pursuit of remedies like the Unfortunate's Friend. Jekyll's suicide can be seen as the last act of degeneration and dementia, or as a desperate escape from public disgrace and paralytic decline. The liberation of Jekyll's mad desire shakes 'the very fortress of identity.' Stevenson represents the split not only in the Jekyll–Hyde personalities but also in the doctor's residence, the 'fortress' in which the dual identities are 'housed.' In the front, there is prosperity, 'a great air of wealth and comfort,' and a luxurious vestibule warmed by 'a bright, open fire.' In the rear is the secret windowless laboratory, filled with disgusting 'chemical apparatus,' and bearing 'in every feature the marks of prolonged and sordid negligence.'[31] In discovering a way to separate the upper and nether aspects of his psyche, Jekyll destroys himself, even though the discovery is the pinnacle of his creative and scientific achievement. Divorced from its passionate drives, reason becomes an empty fortress; neglected and released from the union with the intellect, desire becomes syphilitic frenzy.

In Stevenson's fantasy of the diseased and divided self, passion seems to have no female source or object; the meditation on evil is all in terms of the masculine psyche. The story's narrators – the lawyer Utterson, the physician Lanyon, and finally Jekyll himself – are all bachelors, even celibates. Whereas the typical Victorian male reformer (like Gladstone) sublimated his own sexual fantasies by rescuing fallen women, Utterson boasts that he is frequently 'the last good influence in the lives of down-going men.' The reader assumes that in Jekyll's life, 'nine-tenths a life of effort, virtue, and control,' Hyde's irregularities are sexual.[32] But there were no women in the story until the 1920 film version with John Barrymore misrepresented Stevenson's plot by adding a good and a bad woman to correspond to the conflicting demands of society and the self, an emendation that all subsequent film versions have included.

Actually Jekyll seems to be Hyde's parthenogenic father, with 'more than a father's interest,' as Hyde has 'more than a son's indifference.' Feeling Hyde writhing in his flesh, 'struggling to be born,' Jekyll feels the full horror of his sexual sins.[33] And Hyde, in his murder of the elderly Sir Danvers Carew, and his destruction of the letters and portrait of Jekyll's father, seems to be attempting symbolic acts of parricide that release him from patriarchal heredity.

There are no women in Dorian Gray's downfall either (except for the fatuous Sibyl Vane); Dorian is poisoned by his three aesthetic fathers: Basil Hallward, who appropriates his image for art; Lord Henry Wootton, who encourages him to yield to the desire for the things the world's 'monstrous laws have made monstrous and unlawful,' (p. 26) and the French decadent J. K. Huysmans, whose novel *A Rebours* introduces him to the worship of the senses.[34]

Like Stevenson, Oscar Wilde uses the physical imagery of syphilis to embody the madness that possesses Dorian Gray. Dorian's vice is like 'a horrible malady' (p. 208); the changes that take place in the portrait as the 'leprosies of sin' (p. 175) eat it away are like the progressive pathologies of syphilis: 'hideous face' (p. 173), 'warped lips,' 'coarse bloated hands' (p. 143), a red stain that has 'crept like a horrible disease over the wrinkled fingers' (p. 246), 'misshapen body and failing limbs' (p. 143), a general air of the bestial, sodden and unclean. 'Was it to become a monstrous and loathsome thing,' Dorian wonders, 'to be hidden away in a locked room?' (p. 119). the sudden and uncontrollable frenzy in which 'the mad passions of a hunted animal' (p. 176) seize Dorian and he murders Basil Hallward, even his abrupt rejection of Sibyl Vane, suggest the psychology of general paralysis, In this novel, too, suicide is the final stage of the dementia created by giving way to the tyranny of the passions.

Dorian flirts with Darwinism, playing with ideas of biological determinism, and finding solace in the notion that 'the passion for sin' is programmed into the cells of the brain, so that sexual impulses are irresistible. Yet Wilde is also contemptuous of the materialist and 'shallow psychology' (p. 159) of the Darwinians. Like Stevenson, he insists on the complexity of the psyche, its capacity to house myriad identities and desires. Dorian's 'sin' destroys him because the 'harsh uncomely puritanism' (p. 146) of the day, a puritanism supported by women and by the marriage system, has never allowed the inherited multiform lives of male passion to evolve along with those of thought; 'the senses . . . had remained savage and animal merely because the world had sought to starve them into submission . . . instead of aiming at making them elements of a new spirituality, of which a fine instinct for beauty was to be the dominant characteristic' (p. 145). In a more tolerant society, one in which male desire was not confined by female social convention, Wilde hints, sexual desire would evolve away from perversity, violence, and disease, into something like aesthetic appreciation.

H. G. Wells's *The Time Machine* (1895) transposes the separation of body and mind from an aesthetic to a scientific context. Wells imagines the 'savage and animal' senses as they might become in the remote future if they continued to evolve separately from the rest of the psyche, which in its innocent 'spirituality' would follow its own evolutionary path. The simian Morlocks, 'bleached, obscene and nocturnal' creatures of the nether world of appetite and rapine, inhabit a dark underground labyrinth like Jekyll's laboratory or Dorian's foul dens. When the Time Traveller descends, it is as if he has penetrated the mysteries of the body itself. He is surrounded by the 'throb and hum' of machinery, the 'heavy smell' of blood, and especially by the nauseating sense of physical contact, the 'soft palps' and 'filthily cold' invading hands that feel all over his skin. The loathsome Morlocks, so suggestive of syphilitic deformity and its hereditary results, are the final stages of sexual degeneration, male sewer-dwellers who embody both upper-class fears of the working class, and the feminist dread of masculine desire. In one sense, the Eloi, tiny and exquisitely helpless inhabitants of the Upper-World, are a parody of Dorian Gray's decadent aesthetics. But they also represent the evolutionary result of the feminist avant-garde, refined and spiritualized into an infantile nervous perfection that can no longer think or create. In Eloi society, the Time Traveller notes, there is no syphilis:' the ideal preventive medicine was attained . . . I saw no evidence of any contagious diseases during all my stay.'[35] Yet without the Darwinian grindstone of pain, desire, and repression, humanity grows dull and languid, and decays. That the Morlocks feed upon the Eloi is Wells's mordant response to the sexless feminist utopias.

For Stevenson, Wilde, and Wells, sexual disease and syphilitic insanity were the excrescencies of an unhealthy society, one that systematically suppressed desire and that also produced anxious fathers, febrile art, and divided and disfigured sons. In Ibsen's *Ghosts*, the most famous of all nineteenth-century works about sexual disease, the theme of syphilitic insanity was significantly turned back on women, and on social morality. Ibsen's young artist-hero Oswald Alving goes mad in the final stages of cerebral syphilis inherited from his promiscuous father. But Oswald's mother is forced to recognize that her own pious conventionality and frigidity, rather than male viciousness, had driven her husband to prostitutes. The sins in the plays are not those of the father. As Ibsen's still shocking conclusion forces us to see, the devoted mother is the real executioner of the son, and the real enemy of his artistic genius. Ibsen's ghosts are thus not the invisible spirochetes of syphilis, but the internalized and virulent prohibitions of religion and bourgeois morality. These, Mrs Alving declares, constitute the true hereditary taint:

> It is not only what we have inherited from our fathers and mothers that exists again in us, but all sorts of old dead ideas and all kinds of old dead beliefs . . . They are dormant, and we can never be rid of them. Whenever I take up a newspaper and read it, I fancy I see ghosts creeping between the lines. There must be ghosts all over the world. . . . And we are so miserably afraid of the light.[36]

Produced in London in March 1891, the play provoked an outburst of horror, outrage, and disgust unprecedented in the history of English criticism: 'an open drain; a loathsome sore unbandaged; a dirty act done publicly.' The hysteria over *Ghosts* – over five hundred articles about it were published in England during the following year – suggests how threatened conventional readers felt by Ibsen's intimations that the principles of conjugal obligation, feminine purity, and religious inhibition were not the forces of spiritual evolution but of aesthetic and sexual degeneration.[37]

If *Ghosts* is the *locus classicus* of syphilitic insanity, Hardy's *Jude the Obscure* (1895) is indeed the consummate literary text of late Victorian psychiatry, incorporating the degenerate characters of the ambitious and intemperate working man, the neurasthenic and sexually anxious New Woman, and the morbid and blighted child. Although syphilis does not figure centrally in the text, but hovers on its Gothic margins, Hardy's novel follows Ibsen in turning the question of sexual disease back on the woman.

In his postscript to the novel, Hardy described Sue as 'the woman of the feminist movement – the intellectualized, emancipated bundle of nerves that modern conditions were producing, mainly in cities as yet, who does not recognize the necessity for most of her sex to follow marriage as a profession.'[38] In her aversion to sex and her view of marriage as a 'sordid contract' (p. 323), Sue resembles the celibate heroines of Gilman or Grand, and to some utopian feminists of the period, Sue was indeed an exemplary heroine. Jane Hume Clapperton praised her as one whose sexuality evolved from 'the lower reaches of pure sensation' to 'a higher kind of tender sentiment . . . energized from the intellectual plane.' in which 'all the grossness, i.e. the coarser vibrations of primitive love, are transmuted into the finer vibrations of sympathetic, altruistic feeling.'[39] Furthermore, as Hardy explained in a letter to Edmund Gosse, 'though she has children, her intimacies with Jude have never been more than occasional . . . they occupy separate rooms.'[40] Sue's births are nearly virgin ones. But she is also frigid and neurotic, atrophied and vulnerable. When she breaks down in grief over the death of her children, she forces herself into a 'fanatic prostitution' (p. 437) with Phillotson, a sexual immolation that Hardy presents as the masochistic mirror-opposite of her fear of the body and of the male.

Jude too is doomed by the inexorable laws of nature and inheritance. Late Victorian psychiatrists had warned that working-class men who tried to better themselves were risking madness from a kind of intellectual work their heredity had not prepared them to handle. Sir George Savage had seen 'constant examples in Bethlem of young men, who, having left the plough for the desk, have found, after years of struggle, that their path was barred by social or other hindrances, and disappointment, worry, and the solitude of a great city have produced insanity of an incurable type.'[41] Jude is chiefly broken, however, by his sexuality. Here Hardy was deeply ambivalent. The transgressive sexual images of Stevenson and Wilde, of carnivalesque debauchery and misrule, make a dim appearance in Hardy's realistic narrative with Arabella's pigsty, with the brawling itinerant carnival troupe that appears to defend Phillotson's morals, and with the Great Wessex Agricultural Fair. But for Hardy, fairs, like the ones in *The Mayor of Casterbridge* where Henchard sells his wife, were shameful occasions. And if male sexuality leads to drunkenness, fighting, disease, and transgression, female sexuality, as in *Dracula*, threatens the male with castration. Jude thinks he wants Sue to desire him, but at heart he prefers her 'phantasmal, bodiless' (p. 324) sexlessness to the full-bodied hoggish sensuality of Arabella. As in *The Woodlanders* and other Hardy novels, marriage is a biological trap, a man-trap baited by female allure. Jude wonders whether 'the women are to blame ... or is it the artificial system of things under which the normal sex-impulses are turned into devilish domestic gins and springes' (p. 279). When, on their wedding night, Arabella casually removes her false hair, Jude realizes how thoroughly *he* has been undone by the domestic gin that is also a *vagina dentata*, a hairy springe. Like Nana, Ayesha, or Lucy, she too is horribly changed, reverting to the beast. The misogynistic tableau of the lady's dressing room goes back to Swift; but Hardy gives it the frisson of *fin de siècle* morbidity.

The most troubling character in the novel has always been Little Father Time, the offspring of Jude's botched marriage to the porcine Arabella. His entrance into the novel shatters its structure of narrative realism, and many critics have complained that he seems to come from another planet or another book. Little Father Time's murder of his half-brothers and sisters, and his suicide, Havelock Ellis protested, removed the story from 'the large field of common life into the small field of the police court or the lunatic asylum,' and turned it into a case history of 'gross pathological degenerescence.'[42]

Little Father Time, in my view, can best be understood in the contexts of the feminist protest fiction of the period, and of its conventions relating to the prematurely aged and psychologically disturbed syphilitic child. Hardy adapts these conventions to make Father Time a victim of spoiled heredity like his parents before, a 'preternaturally old boy' (p. 347) who pays with his sanity and his life for the intolerance, cruelty, and narrowness of his society. He is the mad child whose breakdown is the signifier of the conflicts, lies, and hypocrisies of the sexual system. He becomes, as Hardy says,

> the whole tale of their situation. On that little shape had converged all the inauspiciousness and shadow which had darkened the first union of Jude, and all the accidents, mistakes, fears, errors, of the last. He was their nodal point, their focus, their expression in a single term. For the rashness of those parents he had groaned, for their ill-assortment he had quaked, and for the misfortunes of these he had died (p. 411).

Like *Ghosts*, *Jude the Obscure* was greeted with outrage, accused of obscenity, Ibsenity, decadence and degeneration, and ritually compared to slime and filth. Although Wells, Swinburne, and later, Lawrence, admired the novel, many of Hardy's female literary contemporaries saw it as a contemptible study of sexual pathology.[43] During this period of conflict between male and female writers over the representation of sexuality, there also begin to be insistent pronouncements by men on the essential relationship of male sexuality and imaginative power, declaring that, as Gerard Manley Hopkins had stated in 1886, 'the begetting of one's thoughts on paper' is 'a kind of male gift.'[44]

Furthermore, these claims to a phallic literary monopoly came at the end of the richest and most influential period of female literary creativity in English history, and they signal a masculine reappropriation of the field. After the death of George Eliot in 1880, male professional jealousies and animosities that had perhaps been suppressed erupted in critical abuse of women's emasculating effect on the English novel. In 1883 Havelock Ellis could praise Hardy by comparing him to George Eliot, for, as Ellis observed, 'it seems now to stand beyond question that the most serious work in modern English fiction . . . has been done by women.'[45] Ten years later, after essays like George Moore's 'Literature at Nurse' and Hardy's 'Candour in English Fiction,' such comparisons were odious. Women novelists were viewed as shriveled prudes whose malign influence enervated a virile male genre. In the 1890s, after a century in which women writers had shaped the traditions of English fiction, male writers at last achieved unquestioned dominance of the novel.[46]

H. Rider Haggard's immensely popular 'adventure' novel. *She* (1887), provides a fascinating demonstration of the battle for paternal supremacy that seems to be waged beneath the surface of much *fin de siècle* male fantasy fiction. *She* tells the story of the Journey to the Dark Continent of Africa by two Cambridge University scholars to find the legendary city of Kôr, ruled by an immortal white goddess. On one Freudian level, the men are penetrating the mysterious darkness of female sexuality, finding in its deepest vaginal cavern the beautiful and seductive queen Ayesha. Yet other details suggest a more historically specific reading. Cambridge is presented as the last stronghold of pure, homosocial, and potentially homosexual, masculinity, during the decade in which women were pressing for admission to the colleges and to university degrees. The older of the men is a bachelor don who has adopted and jealously raised the younger, hiring a manservant rather than a female nurse, because he is 'determined to have no woman to lord it over me about the child and steal his affections from me.' Confronted by the matriarchal society of Ayesha's tribe, the Amahaggar, the Cambridge scholars are appalled by women's sexual assertiveness in a kinship system where 'descent is traced only through the line of the mother, and . . . they never pay attention to, or even acknowledge, any man as their father, even when their male parentage is perfectly well known.' The power of Ayesha is explicitly compared to that of Queen Victoria, and implicitly suggests the literary reign of George Eliot, a troubling female precursor for Haggard and his male contemporaries. Ayesha's destruction reflects not only Haggard's extreme revulsion from female sexuality, and his wish to appropriate the maternal function, but also his fear of an autonomous

and self-defining female literary tradition.[47] Women writers at the turn of
the century, however, were confined by a conservative sexual ideology
that was an aesthetic dead end. While male writers explored the
multiplicity of the self, the myriad fluid lives of men, women were
limited by the revived biological essentialism of post-Darwinian thought.
The unchanging nature of woman as pure spirit made good politics but
bad fiction. Feminist psychology was too monolithic to provide a
mothering-forth in literature, and its celibacy was increasingly sterile.
The last stand of *fin de siècle* feminism against the sins of the fathers was
Christabel Pankhurst's *The Great Scourge and How to End It* (1913).
Declaring that 75 per cent to 80 per cent of English men were infected
with venereal disease. Pankhurst called for an end to the double
standard. Her solution, however, was *not* female sexual liberation –
'Votes for women and Wild Oats for women!' – but male abstinence:
'Votes for women and chastity for men!' Until men became as virtuous as
women, Pankhurst concluded, and as deeply concerned about
'fatherhood, fathercraft, and the duties . . . of paternity,' marriage was too
dangerous to attempt.[48] Not for another decade could feminist writers
acknowledge that sexual dis-ease could be a creative paralysis and that
the great scourge had taken place not only in men's bodies but also in
women's minds.

Notes

1. Susan Sontag, *Illness as Metaphor* (New York: Vintage Books, 1979), pp. 58–9.
2. See Judith Walkowitz, *Prostitution and Victorian Society* (Cambridge: Cambridge University Press, 1982), pp. 48–53.
3. Michael Foucault, *The History of Sexuality*, trans. Robert Hurley, vol. 1 (New York: Vintage Books, 1980), p. 118.
4. I am indebted to Annabel Patterson for this observation.
5. George Savage, *Insanity and Allied Neuroses* (Philadelphia: Henry C. Lea, 1884), p. 37, quoted in Jane Marcus, 'Virginia Woolf and Her Violin: Mothering, Madness, and Music,' in *Virginia Woolf: Centennial Essays*, ed. Elaine Ginsburg and Laura Moss Gottlieb (Troy, N.Y.: Whitston, 1983). I am indebted to Marcus for an advance copy of this essay.
6. C. F. Marshall *Syphilology and Venereal Disease* (New York: Wood, 1906), p. 216. For general histories of syphilology, see R. S. Morton, *Venereal Diseases* Harmondsworth: Penguin Books, 1974); Theodor Rosebury, *Microbes and Morals* (New York: Viking Press, 1971); and William J. Brown *et al.*, *Syphilis and Other Venereal Diseases* (Cambridge, Mass.: Harvard University Press, 1970).
7. 'Walter,' *My Secret Life*, Quoted in Brian Harrison, 'Underneath the Victorians,' *Victorian Studies* 10 (1967): 256. See also Lyndall Gordon, *Eliot's Early Years* (London: Oxford University Press, 1977), p. 27.
8. See Samuel Hynes, *The Edwardian Turn of Mind* (Princeton, N.J.: Princeton

University Press, 1968), p. 256; JOHN S. HALLER and ROBIN M. HALLER, *The Physician and Sexuality in Urban America* (Urbana: University of Illinois Press, 1974), pp. 264–5; *Davy's Lac-Elephantis* (London: J. Callow, 1815).

9. WILLIAM ACTON, *A Practical Treatise on Diseases of the Urinary and Generative Organs (in Both Sexes)* (London: John Churchill, 1851), pp. 602–3.

10. OSCAR WILDE, *The Picture of Dorian Gray* (Harmondsworth: Penguin Books, 1977), pp. 166–7). All subsequent references to this novel are to this edition and are cited parenthetically by page numbers in the text.

11. JAMES N. HYDE and FRANK H. MONTGOMERY, *Manual of Syphilis and the Venereal Diseases* (Philadelphia, 1895), p. 30.

12. CECILY HAMILTON, *Marriage as a Trade* (New York: Moffat, Yard & Co., 1909), p. 73.

13. WALKOWITZ, *Prostitution and Victorian Society*, p. 128.

14. JOSEPHINE BUTLER, quoted in ibid, p. 130.

15. JUDITH WALKOWITZ, 'Jack the Ripper and the Myth of Male Violence,' *Feminist Studies* 8 (1982): 556.

16. MARSHALL, *Syphilology and Venereal Disease*, p. 306.

17. See HYNES, *Edwardian Turn of Mind*, p. 204.

18. SIGMUND FREUD, *Dora: An Analysis of a Case of Hysteria* (New York: Collier Books, 1964), pp. 93, 35–6, 93.

19. FREUD, *Dora*, pp. 120, 121.

20. MONA CAIRD, 'Phases of Human Development,' *Westminster Review* 141 (1894): 38.

21. ELLIS ETHELMER, *The Human Flower: A Simple Statement of the Physiology of Birth and the Relations of the Sexes* (London, 1895), p. 32. 'Ellis Ethelmer' was the pen name of the feminist activist Elizabeth Wollstoneholme Elmy and her common-law husband, Ben Elmy. Letters in the Macmillan Collection at the British Library suggest that he did most of the writing.

22. GEORGE EGERTON, 'The Spell of the White Elf,' *Keynotes* (London: Virago Press, 1983), p. 80.

23. SARAH GRAND, *The Heavenly Twins* (London: Heinemann, 1894), pp. 178, 280. For a more extensive discussion of this literature, see ELAINE SHOWALTER, *A Literature of Their Own: British Women Novelists from Brontë to Lessing* (Princeton, N.J.: Princeton University Press), pp. 182–215.

24. PHYLLIS ROTH, 'Suddenly Sexual Women in Bram Stoker's *Dracula*,' *Literature and Psychology* 27 (1977): 119.

25. BRAM STOKER, *Dracula* (1897); repr., New York: Doubleday, Page & Co., 1921), pp. 91, 39. The sociohistorical contexts of Stoker's novel as a commentary on venereal disease are discussed by CAROL A. SENF, 'Dracula: Stoker's Response to the New Woman,' *Victorian Studies* 26 (1982): 34–49.

26. STOKER, *Dracula*, pp. 211, 134.

27. See NINA AUERBACH'S fascinating discussion of Lucy in *Woman and the Demon* (Cambridge, Mass.: Harvard University Press, 1982), pp. 22–4.

28. EMILE ZOLA, *Nana* (New York: Greystone Press, n.d.), p. 311.

29. Ibid.

30. ROBERT LOUIS STEVENSON, *The Strange Case of Dr Jekyll and Mr Hyde and Other Stories* (Harmondsworth; Penguin Books, 1979), pp. 81, 82.

31. Ibid., pp. 78, 40, 96, 90, 41, 83, 51, 30.

32. Ibid., pp. 29, 84.

33. Ibid., pp. 89, 95.

34. See JOYCE CAROL OATES, 'The Picture of Dorian Gray: Wilde's Parable of the Fall,' *Critical Inquiry* 7 (Winter 1980): 419–28.

35. H. G. WELLS, *The Time Machine* (1895; repr., New York: Berkley Books, 1982), pp. 49, 83.

36. HENRIK IBSEN, *Ghosts*, in *Four Great Plays by Henrik Ibsen*, trans, R. Farquaharson Sharp (New York: Bantam Books, 1959), p. 99.

37. MICHAEL MAYER, *Ibsen: A Biography* (New York: Doubleday & Co., 1971), pp. 657–9. See also MICHAEL EGAN, *Ibsen: The Critical Heritage* (London: Routledge & Kegan Paul, 1972).

38. THOMAS HARDY, *Jude the Obscure* (Harmondsworth: Penguin Books, 1978), p. 42. All subsequent references to this novel are to this edition and are cited parenthetically by page number in the text.

39. JANE H. CLAPPERTON, *A Vision of the Future* (London: Swan Sonnenschein, 1904), pp. 263–4.

40. Letter to Edmund Gosse, Nov. 30, 1895, in *The Collected Letters of Thomas Hardy*, ed. Richard L. Purdy and Michael Millgate (Oxford: Clarendon Press, 1980), 2:99.

41. SAVAGE, *Insanity*, p. 22.

42. HAVELOCK ELLIS, 'Concerning *Jude the Obscure*,' *Savoy Magazine* Oct. 6, 1896, repr. in R. G. COX, *Thomas Hardy: The Critical Heritage* (London: Routledge & Kegan Paul, 1970), p. 307.

43. See, for example, the review of *Jude* by MARGARET OLIPHANT. 'The Anti-Marriage League,' *Blackwood's Magazine* 159 (Jan. 1896): 135–49.

44. Quoted in SANDRA M. GILBERT and SUSAN GUBAR. *The Madwoman in the Attic* (New Haven: Yale University Press, 1979), p. 3.

45. HAVELOCK ELLIS, 'Thomas Hardy's Novels,' *Westminster Review* (Apr. 1883), repr. in COX, *Thomas Hardy*, p. 104.

46. See PATRICIA STUBBS, *Women and Fiction: Feminism and the Novel, 1880–1920* (New York: Barnes & Noble, 1979), p. 120.

47. H. RIDER HAGGARD *She* (1887; repr., New York: Airmont Classics Series, 1967), pp. 28, 76. I am indebted for the development of these ideas about Haggard to the insights and questions of the Princeton University graduate students in my seminar 'Gender and Literary Theory,' Fall 1984, especially those of Wayne Koestenbaum and Carol Barash.

48. CHRISTABEL PANKHURST *The Great Scourge and How to End It* (London: David Nutt, 1913), pp. 133, 124.

11 Imperial Gothic: Atavism and the Occult in the British Adventure Novel, 1880–1914*

PATRICK BRANTLINGER

Patrick Brantlinger is Professor of English at Indiana University and a former editor of *Victorian Studies*. The extract reproduced here is the penultimate chapter of *Rule of Darkness*, a wide-ranging work of cultural history which both exposes and explores the imperialist attitudes at the heart of nineteenth-century British writing. Brantlinger argues that imperialism, which he construes as an evolving set of attitudes towards and ideas about the rest of the world, pervaded British literature from Tennyson to Conrad, and was a particularly important element of the fiction of the *fin de siècle* (see Introduction, pp. 16–17).

> How thinkest thou that I rule this people? . . . It is by terror. My empire is of the imagination.
>
> —AYESHA IN *She*

I

In 'The Little Brass God,' a 1905 story by Bithia Croker, a statue of 'Kali, Goddess of Destruction,' brings misfortune to its unwitting Anglo-Indian possessors. First their pets kill each other or are killed in accidents; next the servants get sick or fall downstairs; then the family's lives are jeopardized. Finally the statue is stolen and dropped down a well, thus ending the curse.[1] This featherweight tale typifies many written between 1880 and 1914. Its central feature, the magic statue, suggests that Western rationality may be subverted by the very

*Reprinted from *Rule of Darkness: British Literature and Imperialism, 1830–1914* (Ithaca and London: Cornell University Press, 1988), pp. 227–53.

superstitions it rejects. The destructive magic of the Orient takes its
revenge; Croker unwittingly expresses a social version of the return of
the repressed characteristic of late Victorian and Edwardian fiction,
including that blend of adventure story with Gothic elements – imperial
Gothic, as I will call it – which flourished from H. Rider Haggard's *King
Solomon's Mines* in 1885 down at least to John Buchan's *Greenmantle* in
1916. Imperial Gothic combines the seemingly scientific, progressive,
often Darwinian ideology of imperialism with an antithetical interest in
the occult. Although the connections between imperialism and other
aspects of late Victorian and Edwardian culture are innumerable, the link
with occultism is especially symptomatic of the anxieties that attended
the climax of the British Empire. No form of cultural expression reveals
more clearly the contradictions within that climax than imperial Gothic.

Impelled by scientific materialism, the search for new sources of faith
led many late Victorians to telepathy, séances, and psychic research. It
also led to the far reaches of the Empire, where strange gods and
'unspeakable rites' still had their millions of devotees. Publication of
Madame Blavatsky's *Isis Unveiled* in 1877 marks the beginning of this
trend, and the stunning success of Edwin Arnold's *The Light of Asia*
(1879) suggests the strength of the desire for alternatives to both religious
orthodoxy and scientific skepticism.[2] For the same reason, A. P. Sinnett's
Esoteric Buddhism (1883) was widely popular, as was his earlier *The Occult
World* (1881).[3] The standard explanation for the flourishing of occultism
in the second half of the nineteenth century is that 'triumphant
positivism sparked an international reaction against its restrictive world
view.' In illustrating this thesis, Jane Oppenheim lists some
manifestations of that reaction:

> In England, it was an age of . . . the Rosicrucian revival, of cabalists,
> Hermeticists, and reincarnationists. In the late 1880s, the Hermetic
> Order of the Golden Dawn first saw the light of day in London, and
> during its stormy history, the Order lured into its arcane activities not
> only W. B. Yeats, but also the self-proclaimed magus Aleister Crowley.
> . . . Palmists and astrologers abounded, while books on magic and the
> occult sold briskly.[4]

Oppenheim's thesis that 'much of the attraction of these and related
subjects depended on the dominant role that science had assumed in
modern culture' (p. 160) is borne out by the testimony of those drawn to
occultism, among them Arthur Conan Doyle, Annie Besant, Arthur J.
Balfour, and Oliver Lodge. At the same time an emphasis on the occult
aspects of experience was often reconciled with 'science' and even with
Darwinism; such a reconciliation characterizes Andrew Lang's interests in
both anthropology and physic research, as well as the various
neo-Hegelian justifications of Empire. Thus in *Origins and Destiny of*

Imperial Britain (1900), J. A. Cramb argues that 'empires are successive incarnations of the Divine ideas,' but also that empires result from the struggle for survival of the fittest among nations and races. The British nation and Anglo-Saxon race, he contends, are the fittest to survive.[5]

Imperialism itself, as an ideology or political faith, functioned as a partial substitute for declining or fallen Christianity and for declining faith in Britain's future. The poet John Davidson, for instance, having rejected other creeds and causes, 'committed himself to a cluster of ideas centering on heroes, hero worship, and heroic vitalism,' according to his biographer, which led him to pen ardent celebrations of the Empire.[6] In 'St. George's Day,' Davidson writes:

> The Sphinx that watches by the Nile
> Has seen great empires pass away:
> The mightiest lasted but a while;
> Yet ours shall not decay –

a claim that by the 1890s obviously required extraordinary faith.[7] The religious quality of late Victorian imperialism is also evident in much of Rudyard Kipling's poetry, as in 'Recessional':

> God of our fathers, known of old,
>   Lord of our far-flung battle-line,
> Beneath whose awful Hand we hold
>   Dominion over palm and pine –
> Lord God of Hosts, be with us yet,
> Lest we forget – lest we forget![8]

In his study of William Ernest Henley, who did much to encourage the expression of imperialism in *fin de siècle* literature, Jerome Buckley remarks that 'by the last decade of the century, the concept of a national or racial absolute inspired a fervor comparable to that engendered by the older evangelical religion.'[9]

Imperialism and occultism both functioned as ersatz religions, but their fusion in imperial Gothic represents something different from a search for new faiths. The patterns of atavism and going native described by imperialist romancers do not offer salvationist answers for seekers after religious truth; they offer instead insistent images of decline and fall or of civilization turning into its opposite just as the Englishman who desecrates a Hindu temple in Kipling's 'Mark of the Beast' turns into a werewolf. Imperial Gothic expresses anxieties about the waning of religious orthodoxy, but even more clearly it expresses anxieties about the ease with which civilization can revert to barbarism or savagery and thus about the weakening of Britain's imperial hegemony. The atavistic descents into the primitive experienced by fictional characters seem often to be allegories of the larger regressive movement of civilization, British progress transformed into British backsliding. So the first section of Richard Jefferies's apocalyptic fantasy *After London* (1885) is entitled 'The Relapse into Barbarism.' Similarly, the narrator of Erskine Childers's spy novel *Riddle of the Sands* (1903) starts his tale in this way: 'I have read of men who, when forced by their calling to live for long periods in utter solitude – save for a few black faces – have made it a rule to dress regularly for dinner in order to . . . prevent a relapse into barbarism.'[10] Much imperialist writing after about 1880 treats the Empire as a barricade against a new barbarian invasion; just as often it treats the Empire as a 'dressing for dinner,' a temporary means of preventing Britain itself from relapsing into barbarism.

After the mid-Victorian years the British found it increasingly difficult to think of themselves as inevitably progressive; they began worrying instead about the degeneration of their institutions, their culture, their racial 'stock.' In *Mark Rutherford's Deliverance* (1885), William Hale White writes that 'our civilization is nothing but a thin film or crust lying over a volcanic pit,' and in *Fabian Essays* (1889), George Bernard Shaw contends that Britain is 'in an advanced state of rottenness.'[11] Much of the literary culture of the period expresses similar views. The aesthetic and decadent movements offer sinister analogies to Roman imperial decline and fall, while realistic novelists – George Gissing and Thomas Hardy, for instance – paint gloomy pictures of contemporary society and 'the ache of modernism' (some of Gissing's pictures are explicitly anti-imperialist). Apocalyptic themes and images are characteristic of imperial Gothic, in which, despite the consciously pro-Empire values of many authors, the feeling emerges that 'we are those upon whom the ends of the world are come.'[12]

The three principal themes of imperial Gothic are individual regression or going native; an invasion of civilization by the forces of barbarism or demonism; and the diminution of opportunities for adventure and heroism in the modern world. In the romances of Stevenson, Haggard, Kipling, Doyle, Bram Stoker, and John Buchan the supernatural or paranormal, usually symptomatic of individual regression, often manifests itself in imperial settings. Noting that Anglo-Indian fiction frequently deals with 'inexplicable curses, demonic possession, and ghostly visitations,' Lewis Wurgaft cites Kipling's 'Phantom Rickshaw' as typical, and countless such tales were set in Burma, Egypt, Nigeria, and other parts of the Empire as well.[13] In Edgar Wallace's *Sanders of the River* (1909), for example, the commissioner of a West African territory out-savages the savages, partly through police brutality but partly also through his knowledge of witchcraft. Says the narrator: 'You can no more explain many happenings which are the merest commonplace in [Africa] than you can explain the miracle of faith or the wonder of telepathy.'[14]

In numerous late Victorian and Edwardian stories, moreover, occult phenomena follow characters from imperial settings home to Britain. In Doyle's 'The Brown Hand' (1899), an Anglo-Indian doctor is haunted after his return to England by the ghost of an Afghan whose hand he had amputated. In 'The Ring of Thoth' (1890) and 'Lot No. 249' (1892), Egyptian mummies come to life in the Louvre and in the rooms of an Oxford student.[15] In all three stories, Western science discovers or triggers supernatural effects associated with the 'mysterious Orient.' My favorite story of this type is H. G. Wells's 'The Truth about Pyecraft,' in which an obese Londoner takes an Indian recipe for 'loss of weight' but instead of slimming down, begins levitating. The problem caused by oriental magic is then solved by Western technology: lead underwear, which allows the balloonlike Mr Pyecraft to live almost normally, feet on the ground.

The causes of the upsurge in romance writing toward the end of the century are numerous, complex, and often the same as those of the upsurge of occultism. Thus the new romanticism in fiction is frequently explained by its advocates – Stevenson, Haggard, Lang, and others – as a reaction against scientific materialism as embodied in 'realistic' or 'naturalistic' narratives. The most enthusiastic defender of the new fashion for romances was Andrew Lang, who thought the realism of George Eliot and Henry James intellectually superior but also that the romances of Stevenson and Haggard tapped universal, deep-rooted, 'primitive' aspects of human nature which the realists could not approach. 'Fiction is a shield with two sides, the silver and the golden: the study of manners and of character, on one hand; on the other, the description of adventure, the delight of romantic narrative.'[16] Although he sees a place for both kinds of fiction, Lang has little patience with, for example, Dostoevsky's gloomy honesty: 'I, for one, admire M. Dostoieffsky so much ... that I pay him the supreme tribute of never reading him at all' (p. 685). Lang prefers literature of a middle-brow sort, on a level with his own critical journalism, or, farther down the scale of cultural value, he prefers adventure stories written for boys: ' "Treasure Island" and "Kidnapped" are boys' books written by an author of whose genius, for narrative, for delineation of character, for style, I hardly care to speak, lest enthusiasm should seem to border on fanaticism' (p. 690). Lang feels that Haggard is by no means so sophisticated a writer as Stevenson, but this is almost an advantage: the less sophisticated or the more boyish, the better.

All the same, Lang believes, realism in fiction should coexist with romanticism just as the rational, conscious side of human nature coexists with the unconscious. Lang can appreciate realistic novels intellectually, but 'the natural man within me, the survival of some blue-painted Briton or of some gipsy,' is 'equally pleased with a *true* Zulu love story' (p. 689).

He therefore declares that 'the advantage of our mixed condition, civilized at top with the old barbarian under our clothes, is just this, that we can enjoy all sorts of things' (p. 690). Romances may be unsophisticated affairs, but because they appeal to the barbarian buried self of the reader, they are more fundamental, more honest, more natural than realism. In Lang's criticism, romances are ' "savage survivals," but so is the whole of the poetic way of regarding Nature' (p. 690).

An anthropologist of sorts, Lang acquired his theory of savage survivals from his mentor Edward Burnett Tylor, who contends that occultism and spiritualism – indeed, all forms of superstition (and therefore, implicitly, of religion) – belong to 'the philosophy of savages.' Modern occultism, according to Tylor, is 'a direct revival from the regions of savage philosophy and peasant folk-lore,' a reversion to 'primitive culture.'[17] At the same time Tylor associates poetry with the mythology of primitive peoples: 'The mental condition of the lower races is the key to poetry, nor is it a small portion of the poetic realm which these definitions cover' (vol, 2, p. 533). Literary activity in general thus appears to be a throwback to prerational states of mind and society. Similarly, Arthur Machen, author of numerous Gothic horror stories from the 1890s onward, defines literature as 'the endeavour of every age to return to the first age, to an age, if you like, of savages.'[18]

Robert Louis Stevenson, who echoes Lang's defenses of romances as against novels, discovered sources of 'primitive' poetic energy in his own psyche, most notably through the nightmare that yielded *Dr Jekyll and Mr Hyde*. Stevenson entertained ambivalent feelings toward the popularity of that 'Gothic gnome' or 'crawler,' in part because *any* popular appeal seemed irrational or vaguely barbaric to him. Although not overtly about imperial matters, *Jekyll and Hyde*, perhaps even more than *Treasure Island* and *Kidnapped*, served as a model for later writers of imperial Gothic fantasies. Because 'within the Gothic we can find a very intense, if displaced, engagement with political and social problems,' it is possible, as David Punter argues, to read *Jekyll and Hyde* as itself an example of imperial Gothic:

> It is strongly suggested [by Stevenson] that Hyde's behaviour is an urban version of 'going native.' The particular difficulties encountered by English imperialism in its decline were conditioned by the nature of the supremacy which had been asserted: not a simple racial supremacy, but one constantly seen as founded on moral superiority. If an empire based on a morality declines, what are the implications . . .? It is precisely Jekyll's 'high views' which produce morbidity in his *alter ego*.[19]

Jekyll's alchemy releases the apelike barbarian – the savage or natural man – who lives beneath the civilized skin. Not only is this the general fantasy of going native in imperial Gothic, but Hyde – murderous, primitive, apelike – fits the Victorian stereotype of the Irish hooligan, and his dastardly murder of Sir Danvers Carew resembles some of the 'Fenian outrages' of the early 1880s.[20]

Imperial Gothic is related to several other forms of romance writing which flourished between 1880 and 1914. Judith Wilt has argued for the existence of subterranean links between late Victorian imperialism, the resurrection of Gothic romance formulas, and the conversion of Gothic into science fiction. 'In or around December, 1897,' she writes, 'Victorian gothic changed – into Victorian science fiction. The occasion was . . . Wells's *War of the Worlds*, which followed by only a few months Bram Stoker's . . . *Dracula*.'[21] A similar connection is evident between imperial Gothic and the romance fictions of the decadent movement, as in Oscar Wilde's *Picture of Dorian Gray*, which traces an atavistic descent into criminal self-indulgence as mirrored by a changing portrait. Both Stoker's and Wells's romances can be read, moreover, as fanciful versions of yet another popular literary form, invasion-scare stories, in which the outward movement of imperialist adventure is reversed, a pattern fore-shadowed by the returned convict theme in Botany Bay eclogues. *Dracula* itself is an individual invasion or demonic possession fantasy with political implications. Not only is Stoker's bloodthirsty Count the 'final aristocrat,' he is also the last of a 'conquering race,' as Dracula explains to Jonathan Harker:

> We Szekelys have a right to be proud, for in our veins flows the blood of many brave races who fought as the lion fights, for lordship. Here, in the whirlpool of European races, the Ugric tribe bore down from Iceland the fighting spirit which Thor and Wodin gave them, which their Berserkers displayed to such fell intent on the seaboards of Europe, aye, and of Asia and Africa, too, till the peoples thought that the were-wolves themselves had come. Here, too, when they came, they found the Huns, whose warlike fury had swept the earth like a living flame, till the dying peoples held that in their veins ran the blood of those old witches, who, expelled from Scythia, had mated with the devils in the desert. Fool, fools! What devil or what witch was ever so great as Attila, whose blood is in these veins? . . . Is it a wonder that we were a conquering race?[22]

The whirlpool of the Count's own ideas, confounding racism with the mixing of races, pride in pure blood with blood-sucking cannibalism, and aristocratic descent with witchcraft and barbarism, reads like a grim parody of the 'conquering race' rhetoric in much imperialist writing, a premonition of fascism. In common with several other Gothic invaders in late Victorian fiction, moreover. Dracula threatens to create a demonic empire of the dead from the living British Empire. 'This was the being I was helping to transfer to London,' says Jonathan Harker, 'where, perhaps for centuries to come, he might, amongst its teeming millions, satiate his lust for blood, and create a new and ever widening circle of semi-demons to batten on the helpless' (p. 67).

A similar demonic invasion is threatened in Haggard's *She*: Ayesha plans to usurp the British throne from Queen Victoria, though fortunately her second dousing in the flames of immortality kills her before she can leave the Caves of Kôr for London.[23] Horace Holly, the principal narrator of Haggard's romance, explains the situation:

> Evidently the terrible *She* had determined to go to England, and it made me shudder to think what would be the result of her arrival. . . . In the end, I had little doubt, she would assume absolute rule over the British dominions, and probably over the whole earth, and, though I was sure that she would speedily make ours the most glorious and prosperous empire that the world has ever seen, it must be at the cost of a terrible sacrifice of life.[24]

Though Haggard resurrects Ayesha in later romances, his archetype of feminine domination grows tamer and never travels to Britain. Several critics have seen in both *She* and *Dracula* the threat of the New Woman to Victorian patriarchy, and Queen Tera, the mummy who comes to life in Stoker's *Jewel of the Seven Stars* (1903), represents the same threat. Norman Etherington calls Ayesha 'a Diana in jack-boots who preaches materialism in philosophy and fascism in politics' (p. 47), while Nina Auerbach notes that Ayesha's dream of eternal love and immortality is fused with the nightmare of universal empire. In Ayesha's case, 'love does not tranquilize womanhood into domestic confinement, but fuels her latent powers into political life.'[25] Although the New Woman is one of the threats underlying the demonism of Ayesha and also of Dracula and his female victims, however, Haggard's and Stoker's apocalyptic fears are comprehensive: the demons who threaten to subvert the Empire and invade Britain are of both sexes and come in many guises.

Often Wells's translations of Gothic conventions into quasi-scientific ones also suggest demonic subversions of the Empire or – what amounts to the same thing in late Victorian and Edwardian writing – of civilization. 'It occurred to me that instead of the usual interview with the devil or a magician, an ingenious use of scientific patter might with advantage be substituted,' Wells writes of his 'scientific romances.' 'I simply brought the fetish stuff up to date, and made it as near actual theory as possible.'[26] *The War of the Worlds* is the classic science fiction, invasion-from-outer-space fantasy, though Wells wrote many related stories – 'The Empire of the Ants,' for example, in which superintelligent, poisonous ants from the Amazon Basin threaten to overwhelm first British Guiana and then the entire world, founding their insect empire upon the ruins of human ones.

Numerous invasion fantasies were written between 1880 and 1914 without Gothic overtones. The ur-text is Sir George Chesney's *The Battle of Dorking*, which first appeared in *Blackwood's Magazine* in 1871. In the bibliography to *Voices Prophesying War*, I. F. Clarke lists dozens of 'imaginary war' novels published between 1871 and 1914, many of them following an invasion-of-Britain pattern. Among them are T. A. Guthrie's *The Seizure of the Channel Tunnel* (1882), H. F. Lester's *The Taking of Dover* (1888), and the anonymous *The Sack of London in the Great French War of 1901* (1901). Several novels also appeared, both in Britain and elsewhere, with titles along the lines of *Decline and Fall of the British Empire*, as well as invasion-of-India stories.[27] Clearly this was not the fiction of a generation of writers confident about the future of Britain or its Empire. The essence of the genre is captured in P. G. Wodehouse's 1909 parody *The Swoop . . . A Tale of the Great Invasion*, in which Britain is overwhelmed by simultaneous onslaughts of Germans, Russians, Chinese, Young Turks, the Swiss Navy, Moroccan brigands, cannibals in war canoes, the Prince of Monaco, and the Mad Mullah, until it is saved by a patriotic Boy Scout named Clarence Chugwater. The only question left to the reader's imagination is why these various forces of barbarism should want to invade so decrepit a country.[28]

Invasion-scare stories often intersect with spy stories. David Stafford gives 1893 as the date of 'the birth of the British spy novel,' with publication of William Le Queux's *The Great War in England in 1897*, and the subgenre includes many stories, among them Childers's *Riddle of the Sands*, that contain elements of imperial Gothic.[29] Spy stories can be as upbeat as Kipling's *Kim*, full of an evident delight in playing the Great Game in Asia, with little to fear from the bungling French and Russian agents whom Kim helps to foil, or as fear-ridden as Buchan's *Thirty-Nine Steps*, characterized by a breathless paranoia as the hero flees his would-be assassins through a British countryside where no one is to be trusted. Even *Kim*, however, fits Stafford's general description of spy fiction: 'The world presented by these novels is a . . . treacherous one in which Britain is the target of the envy, hostility, and malevolence of the other European powers' (497–98).

All of these popular romance formulas – imperial gothic, Wellsian science fiction, invasion fantasies, spy stories – betray anxieties characteristic of late Victorian and Edwardian imperialism both as an ideology and as a phase of political development. In *The Psychology of Jingoism*, J. A. Hobson interprets the ideological success of imperialism as threatening the entire project of civilizing humanity, including British humanity at home. During mob expressions of jingoism, Hobson declares, 'the superstructure which centuries of civilization have imposed upon . . . the individual, gives way before some sudden wave of ancient savage nature roused from its subconscious depths' (p. 19). If such a regression is possible for the individual who joins the mob, then it is also possible for an entire society – even the seemingly most civilized, most progressive society – and for Hobson one name for such a reversion to barbarism is imperialism, 'a depraved choice of national life' transforming democratic civilization into a savage anarchy clamouring for war. 'For the purposes of the present study . . . the hypothesis of reversion to a savage type of nature is distinctly profitable. The [modern] war-spirit . . . is composed of just those qualities which differentiate savage from civilised man' (p. 19).

II

Numerous travel writers from about 1870 onward lament the decline of exploration into mere tourism. In 'Regrets of a Veteran Traveller' (1897), Frederic Harrison declares: 'Railways, telegraphs, and circular tours in twenty days have opened to the million the wonders of foreign parts.' These signs of technological progress, however, conceal losses: 'Have they not sown broadcast disfigurement, vulgarity, stupidity, demoralisation? Europe is changed indeed since the unprogressive forties! Is it all for the better?'[30] The old ideal of opening up the dark places of the world to civilization, commerce, and Christianity fades into the tourist trade: 'Morally, we Britons plant the British flag on every peak and pass; and wherever the Union Jack floats there we place the cardinal British institutions – tea, tubs, sanitary appliances, lawn tennis, and churches; all of them excellent things in season. But the missionary zeal of our people is not always according to knowledge and discretion' (p. 241). Before the ugly American came the ugly Briton, clutching a Baedeker or a Cook's travel guide. Harrison thinks it has all become too easy, too common, too standardized to be heroic or adventuresome – 'We go abroad, but we travel no longer.'

Imperial Gothic frequently expresses anxiety about the waning of opportunities for heroic adventure. With regression and invasion, this is the third of its major themes (ironic today, given Hollywood's frequent regressions to Haggard and Kipling for its adventure tales, as in *Raiders of the Lost Ark*). Early Victorian adventure writers – Marryat, Chamier, Mayne Reid, R. M. Ballantyne – took as self-evident the notion that England was the vanguard nation, leading the world toward the future. As one of the marooned boys in Ballantyne's *Coral Island* (1856) says, 'We'll take possession of [this island] in the name of the King; we'll . . . enter the service of its black inhabitants. Of course we'll rise, naturally, to the top of affairs. White men always do in savage countries.'[31] Upbeat racism and chauvinism continued to characterize boys' adventure fiction well into the twentieth century, but in imperial Gothic white men do not always rise to the top – just as often they sink into savagedom, cowardice, or exotic torpor, as in Tennyson's 'Lotos Eaters.' Conrad's fictions frequently read like botched romances in which adventure turns sour or squalid, undermined by moral frailty, and the same is true also of Stevenson's most realistic stories – *The Beach of Falesá, The Wreckers, Ebb-Tide*. Lord Jim's failure to live up to his heroic self-image has analogues in many imperial Gothic stories that are not ostensibly critical of imperialism.

The fear that adventure may be a thing of the past in the real world led many writers to seek it in the unreal world of romance, dreams, imagination. 'Soon the ancient mystery of Africa will have vanished,' Haggard laments in an 1894 essay appropriately titled ' "Elephant Smashing" and "Lion Shooting," ' Where, he dolefully asks, 'will the romance writers of future generations find a safe and secret place, unknown to the pestilent accuracy of the geographer, in which to lay their plots?'[32] In similar fashion, in both *Heart of Darkness* and his autobiographical essays, Conrad registers his youthful excitement over the blank places on the map of Africa and the disillusionment he felt when he arrived at Stanley Falls in 1890: 'A great melancholy descended on me . . . there was . . . no great haunting memory . . . only the unholy recollection of a prosaic newspaper "stunt" and the distasteful knowledge of the vilest scramble for loot that ever disfigured the history of human conscience and geographical exploration. What an end to the idealized realities of a boy's daydreams! I wondered what I was doing there.'[33] The stunt was Stanley's 1871 trek into Central Africa in search of Livingstone for the *New York Herald*, the scramble for loot that Conrad saw at first hand King Leopold's rapacious private empire in the Congo.

Arguments defending theosophy and spiritualism often sound like Haggard's and Conrad's laments for the waning of geographical adventure: the disappearance of earthly frontiers will be compensated for by the opening of new frontiers in the beyond. Not only were occultists seeking proofs of immortality and of a spiritual realm above or beneath the material one, they were also seeking adventure. The fantasy element in such adventure seeking is its most obvious feature, as it is also in the literary turn away from realism to romanticism. According to Lang:

> As the visible world is measured, mapped, tested, weighed, we seem to hope more and more that a world of invisible romance may not be far from us . . . The ordinary shilling tales of 'hypnotism' and mesmerism are vulgar trash enough, and yet I can believe that an impossible romance, if the right man wrote it in the right mood, might still win us from the newspapers, and the stories of shabby love, and cheap remorses, and commonplace failures.[34]

But even a well-written impossible romance, as Lang well knows, carries with it more than a hint of childish daydreaming.

If imperialist ideology is atavistic, occultism is obviously so, a rejection of individual and social rationality and a movement backward to primitive or infantile modes of perception and belief. 'Ages, empires, civilisations pass, and leave some members even of educated mankind still, in certain points, on the level of the savage who propitiates with gifts, or addresses with prayers, the spirits of the dead' – so Lang writes in *Cock Lane and Common Sense* (1894), intended in part to expose the spurious aspects of spiritualism.[35] Lang believes that much of what goes by that name is fraudulent:

> As to the idea of purposely evoking the dead, it is at least as impious, as absurd, as odious to taste and sentiment, as it is insane in the eyes of reason. This protest the writer feels obliged to make, for while he regards the traditional, historical, and anthropological curiosities here collected as matters of some interest . . . he has nothing but abhorrence and contempt for modern efforts to converse with the manes, and for all the profane impostures of 'spiritualism' (*Cock Lane*, p. 22).

Like many other well-known Victorians, Lang participated in the Society for Psychical Research, founded in 1882, and even served as its president. But his opinions about psychic phenomena always retain a healthy skepticism. Stopping short of supernatural explanations, Lang favors instead explanations in terms of extraordinary, hitherto unidentified mental powers, including the power of 'unconscious cerebration' to create illusions of ghosts or spirits and to perform telepathic feats. If we assume psychic phenomena do occur, then the theory that they emanate from the subconscious is the chief alternative to what Lang calls 'the old savage theory' of 'the agency of the spirits of the dead.'[36]

Just how the subconscious works – how to explain its mechanisms of projection, hallucination, dreams, and forgetting – was a major issue in late nineteenth-century psychology. British psychologists followed paths similar to those that led to psychoanalysis, and their explanations of psychic phenomena, in common with Freud's, tend toward ideas of regression and unconscious cerebration.[37] In *The Future of an Illusion*, Freud writes that the beliefs of the 'spiritualists' are infantile:

> They are convinced of the survival of the individual soul. . . .
> Unfortunately they cannot succeed in refuting the fact that . . . their spirits are merely the products of their own mental activity. They have called up the spirits of the greatest men . . . but all the pronouncements and information which they have received . . . have

been so foolish . . . that one can find nothing credible in them but the capacity of the spirits to adapt themselves to the circle of people who have conjured them up.'[38]

Freud interprets spiritualist beliefs, as he does all of the 'fairy tales of religion,' as backsliding from adult, conscious rationality into the irrational depths of the subconscious.

Such an explanation of superstitions might do for the psychologists and also for Lang, who as an anthropologist was more interested in the products of myth-making and religion than in experiencing the miraculous himself. For many of Lang's colleagues in psychic research, however, the realm of spirit was not reducible to that of the unconscious, even though the latter might contain unknown, potentially miraculous powers. In his *Encyclopedia Britannica* article on psychical research, Lang notes F. W. H. Myers's various studies; regrettably, Myers 'tended more and more to the belief in the "invasion" and "possession" of living human organisms by spirits of the dead.' He points to the same tendency in the work of the physicist and psychic researcher Oliver Lodge, and adds: 'Other students can find, in the evidence cited [by Lodge and Myers], no warrant for this return to the "palaeolithic psychology" of "invasion" and "possession" ' (p. 547).

Other late Victorians and Edwardians moved in the direction Lang held to be retrograde – away from an early skepticism toward increasing and occasionally absolute faith in occult phenomena, including demonic invasions and possessions of reality. Obviously the will-to-believe in such cases was powerful. A. J. Balfour, for example, Conservative prime minister from 1902 to 1905, produced several 'metaphysical' essays – *A Defence of Philosophic Doubt* (1879). *The Foundations of Belief* (1895), and others – that make the case for faith by sharply dividing science and religion. Balfour argues that the two are separate, equally valid realms; the methods and discoveries of science cannot invalidate those of religion. That his sympathies lie with religion is obvious. In his presidential address to the Society for Psychical Research in 1894, Balfour expresses his joy that the society's work demonstrates 'there are things in heaven and earth not hitherto dreamed of in our scientific philosophy.'[39] Small wonder that in 1916, when the former prime minister (aided by several automatic writers, including Kipling's sister Alice Fleming) began to receive spirit communications from the love of his youth, Mary Lyttelton, he came to believe that the messages were genuine. Small wonder, too, given his political career, that among the themes in the three thousand messages directed to him from the beyond is the establishment of a harmonious world order (Oppenheim, p. 133).

Several early modern writers followed roughly similar paths from doubt to faith. In Kipling's case, the faith was perhaps never firm. While lightly tossing off such ghost stories as 'The Phantom Rickshaw' (1888) and 'The Return of Imray' (1891), the young Kipling showed what he actually thought of occultism in 'The Sending of Dana Da' (1888) – and what he thought was skeptical to the point of sarcasm: 'Once upon a time, some people in India made a new Heaven and a new Earth out of broken teacups, a missing brooch or two, and a hair-brush. These were hidden under bushes, or stuffed into holes in the hillside, and an entire Civil Service of subordinate Gods used to find or mend them again; and every one said: "There are more things in Heaven and Earth than are dreamt of in our philosophy." '[40] Kipling's satire, perhaps inspired by recent exposures of Mme Blavatsky's fraudulence, takes aim at all branches of occultism, including theosophy. The new 'Religion,' he says, 'was too elastic for ordinary use. It stretched itself and embraced pieces of everything that the medicine-men of all ages have manufactured,' including 'White, Gray, and Black Magic . . . spiritualism, palmistry, fortune-telling by cards, hot chesnuts, double-kernelled nuts, and tallow droppings.' It would even 'have adopted Voodoo and Oboe had it known anything about them' (p. 308).

In the story that follows this introduction, Dana Da, a magus from Afghanistan or parts unknown, is hired by an unnamed Englishman to produce a psychic sending or visitation to annoy the Englishman's enemy, Lone Sahib. Because Lone Sahib hates cats, the sending takes the form of an invasion of his bungalow by a plague of supposedly spirit kittens. Lone Sahib and his 'co-religionists' see the kittens as materializations from the beyond, write up a report on them 'as every Psychical Observer is bound to do,' and grow ever more convinced that 'spirits . . . squatter up and down their staircases all night' (p. 313). At the story's end the Englishman who has paid for the sending asks Dana Da how he produced it; the alleged magus replies that he gave Lone Sahib's servant 'two-eight a month for cats – little, little cats, I wrote, and he put them about – very clever man' (p. 320).

Just when Kipling put aside skepticism and began to be something of an occultist himself is not clear, though some accounts attribute the change to the death of his daughter Josephine in 1899. Certainly her death inspired Kipling to write the psychic story 'They' (1904), in which the protagonist communicates with ghostly children in a ghostly country-house setting. But by that time Kipling had also written stories dealing with reincarnation – 'The Finest Story in the World' (1891) and 'Wireless' (1902) – a subject of increasing interest also to his friend Haggard, whose views about spiritual matters are easier to trace because he was always less defensively ironic than Kipling. Some critics dismiss the problem, suggesting that Kipling occasionally includes supernatural elements in his stories merely for artistic purposes, but this approach seems no more explanatory than arguing that Dante writes about heaven and hell for artistic purposes. Nor did Kipling drop the supernatural after the early 1900s: several stories in *Debits and Credits* (1926) deal with the supernatural – 'The Gardener,' 'The Madonna of the Trenches,' and 'The Wish House' – and so do other works among his late fiction.[41]

Haggard was interested in occultism from the time when, as a young man in London, he attended séances at the house of Lady Paulet, who gave him his 'entree to the spiritualistic society of the day.'[42] The apparitions that he saw were not exactly spirits, he thought, but rather the products of 'some existent but unknown force' (vol. 1, p. 41). Occultism shows up in his first novel, *Dawn* (1884), which combines realism with, as George Saintsbury put it, the 'elements of occult arts and astral spirits.'[43] Haggard's second novel, *The Witch's Head* (1884), also supposedly realistic, touches upon the theme of reincarnation. After about 1900, according to Norman Etherington, Haggard dwelt with 'increased fervor on the truth of reincarnation. The idea he had first tentatively expressed in *Witch's Head*, that lovers worked out their relationships in successive lives and literally eternal triangles, became a dominant theme in his later novels. He believed he had caught glimpses of his own previous existences in dreams and visions' (p. 17). In *The Days of My Life*, Haggard describes a series of these visions of former lives, which might almost, Etherington says, 'be tableaux from the ethnographic section of a museum,' similar to 'displays on "the ascent of man" from the Stone Age to the Iron Age' (p. 17). In the first reincarnation Haggard is a primitive man, perhaps of the Stone Age; in the second he is black, again primitive, defending his rude home against attackers who kill him; in the third he is an ancient Egyptian, in love with a 'beautiful young woman with violet eyes'; and in the fourth he is probably an early medieval barbarian, living in 'a timber-built hall' in a land of 'boundless snows and great cold,' though again in love with a violet-eyed woman, the same 'as she of the Egyptian picture.' Haggard believes that these 'dream-pictures' can be explained in one of three ways: '(1) Memories of some central incident that occurred in a previous incarnation. (2) *Racial* memories of events that had happened to forefathers. (3) Subconscious imagination and invention' (vol. 2, p. 168). The third explanation is the easiest to accept, he says, but he clearly favors the first or the second.

Kipling and Haggard often discussed telepathy, ghosts, and reincarnation. Although it is likely that Kipling believed – perhaps always with a certain ambivalence or ironic distance – in some version of occultism at least from 1904 onward, Haggard later opined that he converted Kipling to faith in reincarnation in the 1920s. 'He is now convinced,' Haggard wrote in his diary in 1923, 'that the individual human being is not a mere flash in the pan, seen for a moment and lost forever, but an enduring entity that has lived elsewhere and will continue to live, though for a while memory of the past is blotted out' (quoted in Cohen, p. 122). This may have been only wishful thinking on Haggard's part. In any event, it seems likely that the very ambivalence with which Kipling approached any belief in the supernatural made him all the more ardent an imperialist. On political issues Haggard often seems more supple and thoughtful than Kipling, though always also ardently imperialistic.[44] Thus Haggard was not prepared to blame 'all our Russian troubles' on 'the machinations of the Jews.' Puzzled by Kipling's often belligerent antisemitism, Haggard wrote in 1919: 'I do not know, I am sure, but personally I am inclined to think that one can insist too much on the Jew motive, the truth being that there are Jews and Jews. . . . For my own part I should be inclined to read Trade Unions instead of Jews' (quoted in Cohen, pp. 110–11). In contrast, Kipling, ambivalent about so many matters, is often dogmatic about politics: 'Any nation save ourselves, with such a fleet as we have at present, would go out swiftly to trample the guts out of the world,' Kipling declaimed to Haggard in 1897; 'and the fact that we do not seems to show that even if we aren't very civilized, we're about the one power with a glimmering of civilization in us' (quoted in Cohen, p. 33). The only ambivalence here has to do with the meaning of civilization: perhaps it is a weakness, a disease; perhaps the brave if not civilized thing to do would be to 'trample the guts out of the world.'

Haggard's comparative uncertainty about politics is dimly reflected in the romance conventions he employs in most of his fictions. In common with other advocates of the romance as against the novel, Haggard hesitates at defending his tales as truer than realistic fictions or even as somehow true. He agrees with Lang that he is expressing universal, mythic concerns – writing about what Jung would later call archetypes. But he also knows that his landscapes shade into the fantastic and are therefore highly subjective landscapes of the mind. Just as Lang is inclined to attribute psychic phenomena to the unconscious, so Haggard often suggests that his stories refer more to his own – or perhaps to universal – dream states than to outward reality. Haggard shares this emphasis on fantasy with all Gothic romancers, whose stories always veer toward dreams and the subliminal reaches of the mind.

The subjectivism of Gothic romance as a genre thus intersects with the atavistic character of both imperialist ideology and occultist belief. According to Theodor Adorno, 'occultism is a reflex-action to the subjectification of all meaning, the complement of reification.' Adorno contends that 'occultism is a symptom of regression in consciousness,' diagnosing it specifically as a 'regression to magic under late capitalism' whereby 'thought is assimilated to late capitalist forms' (p. 239).

The power of occultism, as of Fascism, to which it is connected by thought-patterns of the ilk of anti-semitism, is not only pathic. Rather it lies in the fact that in the lesser panaceas, as in superimposed pictures, consciousness famished for truth imagines it is grasping a dimly present knowledge diligently denied to it by official progress in all its forms. It is the knowledge that society, by virtually excluding the possibility of spontaneous change, is gravitating towards total catastrophe. The real absurdity is reproduced in the astrological hocus-pocus, which adduces the impenetrable connections of alienated elements – nothing more alien than the stars – as knowledge about the subject.[45]

Adorno's analysis of the interior parallelism between occultism and fascism suggests also the interior significance (the political unconscious) of imperial Gothic fantasy. The subjective nature of the genre is more or less apparent to all of its best practitioners. The motif of the exploration of the Dark Continent or of other blank spaces of external reality whose meaning seems inward – the fabled journey into the unconscious or the heart of darkness of the explorer – is omnipresent in late Victorian and Edwardian literature. Africa, India, and the other dark places of the earth become a terrain upon which the political unconscious of imperialism maps its own desires, its own fantastic longitudes and latitudes.

All of Haggard's romances, from *King Solomon's Mines* onward, can be interpreted as journeys into the dreams of the protagonists and ultimately of Haggard himself. 'I closed my eyes,' says Horace Holly in *She*, 'and imagination, taking up the thread of thought, shot its swift shuttle back across the ages, weaving a picture on their blackness so real and vivid in its detail that I could almost for a moment think that I had triumphed over Time, and that my vision had pierced the mystery of the Past' (p. 141). After describing his fantasy of Ayesha in her youthful power and glory, Holly adds: 'Let him who reads forgive the intrusion of a dream into a history of fact' (p. 141). Or, as Captain John Good says after the battle with the Masai in *Allan Quatermain*, 'the whole thing seemed more as though one had enjoyed a nightmare just before being called, than as a deed done' (p. 485). Over and over Haggard's adventurers liken their experiences to dreams as they leave the actual geography of Africa or Asia for landscapes that obviously have more affinity to the world of fantasy than to the real one. For Haggard, it requires merely a flip-flopping of the equation to claim the reality of reincarnation and the spirit world that dreams appear to shadow forth.

Haggard's fantasy landscapes often refer less to mental processes than to downright visceral ones, as his characters are swallowed up or temporarily emtombed in chasms, tunnels, crypts, and caves: the Place of Death in *King Solomon's Mines*, the underground river down which the explorers plummet to the land of the Zu-Vendis in *Allan Quatermain*, the Caves of Kôr in *She*. As Holly and Leo Vincy escape the midnight storm that shipwrecks them on the coast of Africa, 'we shot out between the teeth-like lines of gnashing waves into the comparatively smooth water of the mouth of the sea' (*She*, p. 43). As Conrad recognized, the basic regression fantasy of imperial Gothic involves a reverse cannibalism: the nightmare of being swallowed by the world's dark places has as its obverse side the solipsistic fantasy of swallowing the world. In *Heart of Darkness*, Marlow describes Kurtz as an eloquent voice, though uttering emptiness, 'the horror, the horror.' The restraint of the African 'cannibals' who serve as Marlow's crew stands in obvious contrast to the fact that 'Mr Kurtz lacked restraint in the gratification of his various lusts.'[46] At one point Marlow describes Kurtz opening 'his mouth wide – it gave him a weirdly voracious aspect, as though he had wanted to swallow all the air, all the earth, all the men before him' (p. 61). George Gissing, too, sensed in late Victorian imperialism a cannibalism in reverse. In *The Whirlpool* (1897), after his friend Carnaby has ironically mentioned 'nigger-hunting' as an excellent modern sport, Harvey Rolfe responds:

> There's more than that to do in South Africa. . . . Who believes for a moment that England will remain satisfied with bits here and there? We have to swallow the whole, of course. We shall go on fighting and annexing until – until the decline and fall of the British Empire. That hasn't begun yet. Some of us are so over-civilized that it makes a reaction of wholesome barbarism in the rest. We shall fight like blazes in the twentieth century.[47]

Gissing here captures the tone of much late Victorian imperialist propaganda. Rolfe's statement, though ironically made, seems almost to echo Cecil Rhodes's grandiose claims about painting the map of Africa red, or his famous assertion that he 'would annex the planets if I could.'[48] The latter assertion, often quoted out of context, seems much less self-assured when read in relation to what precedes it – a near-lament about the closing off of global frontiers, a lament suspiciously close to spiritualist concerns with astral bodies and astrology: 'The world . . . is nearly all parcelled out, and what there is left of it is being divided up, conquered, and colonised. To think of these stars . . . that you see overhead at night, these vast worlds which we can never reach. I would annex the planets if I could; I often think of that. It makes me sad to see them so clear and yet so far' (p. 190). Rhodes made this statement to the journalist W. T. Stead, who quotes it in his hagiographic *Last Will and Testament of Cecil John Rhodes* (1902). About the only criticism Stead has is that Rhodes was a social Darwinist who never crossed the invisible line between secular ideology and spiritualism. Nevertheless, Stead does his best to bring Rhodes into the occultist fold, attributing an imaginary chain of reasoning to Rhodes which couples survival of the fittest with God's will. Assuming that God *does* exist, Stead makes Rhodes speculate, then in a social Darwinian world He would no doubt make it His will that Britain and the British, the fittest nation and race that history has ever known, should annex as much of the globe as possible, if not the stars. 'If there be a God, I think that what He would like me to do is to paint as much of the map of Africa British red as possible, and to do what I can elsewhere to promote the unity and extend the influence of the English-speaking race' (p. 98).

Of all late Victorian and Edwardian occultists, none was more sanguine than Stead about the truth of his convictions. He believed that God had given him a personal mission as a journalist, to defend the Empire and to trumpet the truths of spiritualism through the world. In reporting the news, he made innovative use of interviews with the great and powerful, and when the great were not available – when they happened to be dead, for example – he questioned them anyway through what he called 'automatic interviews.' Thus he was able to publish the opinions of Catherine the Great on the Russian Question and those of Gladstone's ghost on the budget of 1909. the headline on the front page of the *Daily Chronicle* for 1 November 1909 read: 'Amazing Spirit Interview: The Late Mr Gladstone on the Budget.' In her study of spiritualism Ruth Brandon notes that 'Mr Gladstone, as it happened, had not much of interest to say; but the news (to paraphrase Dr Johnson) lay in his saying it at all' (p. 201).

Through the urgings of his dead friend Julia Ames, Stead made plans to open better communications with the spirit world. In his occultist journal *Borderland* and elsewhere, Stead projected a highly original sort of news agency – one that would transmit news of the beyond through spirit mediumship and that would be named Julia's Bureau. 'What is wanted is a bureau of communication between the two sides,' Julia's ghost told Stead. 'Could you not establish some sort of office with one or more trustworthy mediums? If only it were to enable the sorrowing on the earth to know, if only for once, that their so-called dead live nearer them than ever before, it would help to dry many a tear and soothe many a sorrow. I think you could count upon the eager co-operation of all on this side.'[49]

Over the years Julia sent Stead many spirit letters containing news from the borderland, and she often exhorted him to open a bureau of communication. He saw these exhortations as a great opportunity but also, considering the numbers of both dead and living who might want to avail themselves of the bureau's services, as an enormous undertaking. On this score Julia was reassuring. In a communiqué dated 6 October 1908, four years before Stead went down in the *Titanic*, Julia acknowledged that the population of the spirit world was vast – of course far larger than the one and a half billion in the world of the living. But the desire of the dead to communicate with the living tended to wane quickly; therefore 'I should say that the number of the "dead" who wish to communicate with the living are comparatively few.' Julia's ghost then offers what to any imperialist must have seemed an obvious analogy:

> It is with us as with immigrants to my former country [Australia]. When they arrive their hearts are in the old world. The new world is new and strange. They long to hear from the old home; and the post brings them more joy than the sunrise. But after a very little time the pain is dulled, new interests arise, and in a few years . . . they write no more. . . . The receipt of letters and telegrams has taken away the death-like edge of emigration. 'We shall hear from them again.' 'Write soon.' These are the consolations of humanity even on the physical plane. What the Bureau will do is to enable those who have newly lost their dead to write soon, to hear messages. (pp. 175–6)

The emigration analogy suggests once again the complex, unconscious interconnections between imperialist ideology and occultism. To the ardent imperialist, 'away' can never be 'away'; nothing is foreign, not even death; the borderland itself becomes a new frontier to cross, a new realm to conquer. And with the help of friendly spirits like the Australian Julia, how easy the conquest seems! Just at the moment actual frontiers were vanishing, late Victorian and Edwardian occultist literature is filled with metaphors of exploration, emigration, conquest, colonization. Nor is the news agency metaphor of Julia's Bureau unique. An imagery of telegraphy and cablegrams, telephone and radio, permeates the millennial expectations of the spiritualists, as Kipling shows in 'Wireless.' According to the persistent modernist Stead: 'The recent applications of electricity in wireless telegraphy and wireless telephony, while proving nothing in themselves as to the nature or permanence of personality, are valuable as enabling us to illustrate the difficulties as well as the possibilities of proving the existence of life after death' (p. xii). But though hard to prove, the discoveries of the spiritualists are at least as immense as those of Christopher Columbus: 'In order to form a definite idea of the problem which we are about to attack, let us imagine the grave as if it were the Atlantic Ocean' (p. xii). Using similar language in *Phantom Walls*, Lodge writes of his hope 'to be able to survey the ocean of eternity from Darien-like peaks,' while Arthur Conan Doyle often seems willing to don armor and go crusading in order to conquer death or convince doubters of the truths of spiritualism: 'The greater the difficulty in breaking down the wall of apathy, ignorance, and materialism, the more is it a challenge to our manhood to attack and ever attack in the same bulldog spirit with which Foch faced the German lines.'[50]

Both Doyle's and Stead's 'sublime self-certainty' in their spiritualist writings, Brandon speculates, is a reflection of imperial domination (p. 193). But they frequently express fears about foreign rivals and British slippage in the real world, so the self-certainty of their spiritualism must be largely compensatory. In any event, Brandon reports that three weeks after Stead drowned in the *Titanic*, 'he appeared in his inner sanctuary in Mowbray House, where his daughter, his secretary and other devoted ladies were waiting. His face (so they said) shone out; and as it faded his voice rang through the room saying: "All I told you is true" ' (p. 205). Stead's ghost showed up a few years later, at one of the Doyle family séances, announcing that he had 'looked into the eyes of Christ with Cecil Rhodes by my side and he said tell Arthur that his work on Earth is holy and divine – that his Message is Mine' (quoted by Brandon, p. 220). This message came after the death of Doyle's son Kingsley, who had been wounded in combat during the world war and, while recovering, contracted the pneumonia that killed him.

Doyle's path to spiritualism was much like the one traversed by many late Victorians and Edwardians. In his *Memories and Adventures* (1924), he writes that his youthful education had trained him in 'the school of medical materialism,' formed by 'the negative views of all my great teachers' (p. 77). At first he was generally skeptical about occultism:

> I had at that time the usual contempt which the young educated man feels towards the whole subject which had been covered by the clumsy name of Spiritualism. I had read of mediums being convicted of fraud, I had heard of phenomena which were opposed to every known scientific law, and I had deplored the simplicity and credulity which could deceive good, earnest people into believing that such bogus happenings were signs of intelligence outside our own existence. . . . I was wrong and my great teachers were wrong, but still I hold that they wrought well and that their Victorian agnosticism was in the interests of the human race, for it shook the old iron-clad unreasoning Evangelical position which was so universal before their days. For all rebuilding a site must be cleared. (p. 77)

From the 1890s onward, Doyle became increasingly interested in the spiritualist rebuilding of nothing less than world civilization. He engaged in psychic research, experimenting with telepathy and searching for poltergeists in haunted houses, at first with a skeptical air but later with growing belief in an invisible realm of spirits just beyond the boundaries of material reality. If it seemed evident that adventure was vanishing from the modern world, Doyle for one rebelled against the evidence.

True, his reinventions of adventure in fiction have about them the same compensatory quality that characterizes most late Victorian romance writing, which senses its inferiority to realistic narration. Romance writers indicate in a variety of ways that their adventure stories are for adolescents; and occultist pursuits are also somehow, even to occultists themselves, childish and subrational. As a young man, at least, Doyle perceived these difficulties but plunged ahead anyway, toward the blinding light (he thought) at the end of the long tunnel of world history.

In Doyle's 1911 novel *The Lost World*, the journalist hero Malone is told by his girlfriend that he must go adventuring and become a hero before she will marry him. The demand seems to him next to impossible because, as his editor exclaims, 'the big blank spaces in the map are all being filled in, and there's no room for romance anywhere.'[51] But there is room – or Doyle at least will make room – for romance in a fantasy version of the Amazon basin, where the British adventurers regress through a Darwinian nightmare to the days of the dinosaurs. The characters in the story, including the atavistically apelike Professor Challenger, reappear next in *The Poison Belt* of 1913, where adventure shrinks: they watch the end of the world from the windows of an airtight room in Challenger's house. But the world does not end, the poisonous cloud lifts, people revive, and Doyle's band of fantasy adventurers live on to appear in a third novel, *The Land of Mist*, published in 1925, the same year as Yeats's *A Vision*. Challenger and the rest are now participants in what Doyle believes to be the greatest adventure of all, beyond the borders of the material world. Exploration and invasion metaphors abound. Lord John Roxton's newspaper ad sets the tone: Roxton is 'seeking fresh worlds to conquer. Having exhausted the sporting adventures of this terrestrial globe, he is now turning to those of the dim, dark and dubious regions of psychic research. He is in the market ... for any genuine specimen of a haunted house.'[52] While the crumbling of the Empire quickened after World War I, Doyle himself turned obsessively to haunted houses, séances, lands of mysticism and mist. The skeptical Challenger exclaims that the 'soul-talk' of the spiritualists is 'the Animism of savages,' but Doyle himself was no longer skeptical (p. 19). He believed in magic, he believed in fairies, he believed in ectoplasmic projections. He believed Spiritualism with a capital S was the successor to Christianity, the new advent of the City of God after the fall of the City of Man. The creator of that great incarnation of scientific rationalism Sherlock Holmes devoted himself to the spiritualist movement, becoming one of its leaders, and it became for him a substitute for all other causes – for imperialism itself. Just as his friend Stead felt that he had received a call from God, so Doyle after the world war felt that the meaningful part of his life had begun. He had received the call; it was his duty to save the world. 'In the days of universal sorrow and loss [after World War I], when the voice of Rachel was heard throughout the land, it was borne in upon me that the knowledge which had come to me thus was not for my own consolation alone, but that God had placed me in a very special position for conveying it to that world which needed it so badly (*Memories*, p. 387).

Doyle's version of 'Heaven was rather like Sussex, slightly watered down,' says Brandon (p. 222), but his plans for the future of the world were somewhat larger than Sussex. He believed the spirit world was arranged in a marvelous, infinite bureaucratic hierarchy very much like the British Raj in India.[53] In 1923 an 'Arabian spirit' named Pheneas began to communicate with him through his wife's automatic writing, telling him that the old world would end soon and a glorious new one dawn. Doyle was no doubt reassured to learn that 'England is to be the centre to which all humanity will turn. She is to be the beacon light in this dark, dark world. The light is Christ, and all humans will strive to get to that light in the great darkness' (*Pheneas Speaks*, p. 79). Sherlock Holmes cannot tolerate a mystery without solving it, nor can Doyle: the darkness of this world will soon disperse, and light, radiating especially from England and Sussex, will be universal. Doyle experienced a glimmer of embarrassment toward the end of the decade, shortly before his death, when Pheneas's predictions did not seem to be coming true on schedule, but it was only a minor setback. Material adventure in the material Empire might be on the wane, but over the ruins was dawning the light of the great spiritualist adventure.

As far as geopolitical arrangements were concerned, Doyle believed, the programs of all governments would have to be revised. In spiritualist armor, slaying the dragons of Bolshevism and materialism, Doyle sometimes felt that the future was his. Like the souls of the dead, the glories of the imperialist past would be reborn, purified or rarefied, for they were eternal. In his *History of Spiritualism*, Doyle writes: 'I do not say to [the] great and world-commanding . . . powers . . . open your eyes and see that your efforts are fruitless, and acknowledge your defeat, for probably they never will open their eyes . . . but I say to the Spiritualists . . . dark as the day may seem to you, never was it more cheering . . . never . . . more anticipatory of ultimate victory. It has upon it the stamp of all the conquering influences of the age.'[54] But the ultimate victory of spiritualism was prefigured for Doyle in the demise of the empires of this world, the precondition for the invasion and reconquest of reality by the realm of spirit, or perhaps of our transubstantiation – a kind of psychic emigration and colonization – into the world beyond reality, an invisible, even more glorious empire rising ghostlike out of the corpse of the old.

As cultural formations, both imperialism and spiritualism have roots in 'the dark powers of the subconscious, [and call] into play instincts that carry over from the life habits of the dim past. Driven out everywhere else, the irrational' seeks refuge in imperialism, Schumpeter contends (p. 14), and, I would add, in late Victorian and early modern occultism. Imperial Gothic expresses the atavistic character of both movements, shadowing forth the larger, gradual disintegration of British hegemony. Doyle's phantom empire – and the imperial Gothic themes of regression, invasion, and the waning of adventure – express the narrowing vistas of the British Empire at the time of its greatest extent, in the moment before its fall.

Notes

1. Bithia, M. Croker, *The Old Cantonment; with Other Stories of India and Elsewhere* (London: Methuen, 1905), pp. 48–63.
2. See Brooks Wright, *Interpreter of Buddhism to the West: Sir Edwin Arnold* (New York: Bookman Associates, 1957).
3. A brief account of the development of late-Victorian romanticism in conjunction with occultism appears in Tom Gibbons, *Rooms in the Darwin Hotel: Studies in English Literary Criticism and Ideas, 1880–1920* (Nedlands: University of Western Australia Press, 1973), pp. 1–24. See also Ruth Brandon, *The Spiritualists: The Passion for the Occult in the Nineteenth and Twentieth Centuries* (New York: Knopf, 1983); Janet Oppenheim, *The Other World: Spiritualism and Psychical Research in England, 1850–1914* (Cambridge, Cambridge University Press, 1985); and Frank M. Turner, *Between Science and Religion: The Reaction to Scientific Naturalism in Late Victorian England* (New Haven: Yale University Press, 1974).
4. Oppenheim, *Other World*, p. 160.
5. J. A. Cramb, *The Origins and Destiny of Imperial Britain* (New York: Dutton, 1900), p. 230.
6. Carroll, V. Peterson, *John Davidson* (New York: Twayne, 1972), p. 82.
7. John Davidson, 'St. George's Day,' in *The Poems of John Davidson*, ed. Andrew Turnbull, 2 vols (Edinburgh: Scottish Academic Press, 1973), vol. 1, p. 228.
8. Rudyard Kipling, 'Recessional,' in *Works*, 36 vols, Pocket Edition (London: Methuen, 1923), vol. 34, p. 186.
9. Jerome Hamilton Buckley, *William Ernest Henley: A Study in the 'Counter-Decadence' of the 'Nineties* (Princeton: Princeton University Press, 1945), p. 134. See also John Lester, *Journey through Despair, 1880–1914: Transformations in British Literary Culture* (Princeton: Princeton University Press, 1968), p. 9: both the imperialism and the socialism of the turn of the century 'became charged with an overplus of fervor which exalted each at times almost to religion.'
10. Erskine Childers, *The Riddle of the Sands: A Record of Secret Service* (1903: New York: Dover, 1976), p. 15.
11. Both White and Shaw are quoted by Lester, *Journey through Despair*, pp. 50n and 5.
12. Lester (*Journey through Despair*, p. 3) notes that this quotation from 1 Corinthians 10:11 'crops up recurrently in the literature of the time.'
13. Lewis S. Wurgaft, *The Imperial Imagination: Magic and Myth in Kipling's India* (Middletown: Wesleyan University Press, 1983), p. 57.

14. EDGAR WALLACE, *Sanders of the River* (1909; Garden City, N.Y.: Doubleday, Doran, 1930), p. 277.

15. For these and other examples see *The Best Supernatural Tales of Arthur Conan Doyle*, ed. E. F. Bleiler (New York: Dover, 1979). An interesting variant is W. SOMERSET MAUGHAM's *The Magician* (1908), based on the career of Aleister Crowley.

16. ANDREW LANG, 'Realism and Romance,' *Contemporary Review* 52 (November 1887), p. 684. Page numbers are given parenthetically in the next two paragraphs of the text. See also JOSEPH WEINTRAUB, 'Andrew Lang: Critic of Romance,' *English Literature in Transition* 18:1 (1975), 5–15.

17. Sir EDWARD BURNETT TYLOR, *Primitive Culture*, 2 vols (1871; New York: Harper & Row, 1970), vol. 1, pp. 155, 142.

18. Quoted by WESLEY D. SWEETSER, *Arthur Machen* (New York: Twayne, 1964), p. 116.

19. DAVID PUNTER, *The Literature of Terror: A History of Gothic Fictions from 1765 to the Present Day* (London: Longman, 1980), pp. 62, 241.

20. See PATRICK BRANTLINGER and RICHARD BOYLE, 'The Education of Edward Hyde: Stevenson's "Gothic Gnome" and the Mass Readership of Late-Victorian England,' in *Jekyll and Hyde after 100 Years*, ed. William Veeder (Chicago: University of Chicago Press, 1987).

21. JUDITH WILT, 'The Imperial Mouth: Imperialism, the Gothic and Science Fiction,' *Journal of Popular Culture* 14 (Spring 1981), 618–28.

22. BRAM STOKER, *Dracula* (Harmondsworth: Penguin, 1979), p. 41. Punter (*Literature of Terror*, p. 257) calls Dracula 'the final aristocrat.'

23. See NORMAN ETHERINGTON, *Rider Haggard* (Boston: Twayne, 1984), p. 47.

24. H. RIDER HAGGARD, *Three Adventure Novels: She, King Solomon's Mines, Allan Quatermain* (New York: Dover, 1951), pp. 192–3.

25. NINA AUERBACH, *Woman and the Demon: The Life of a Victorian Myth* (Cambridge: Harvard University Press, 1982), p. 37. See also SANDRA M. GILBERT, 'Rider Haggard's Heart of Darkness,' *Partisan Review* 50 (1983), 444–53, and CAROL A. SENF, '*Dracula*: Stoker's Response to the New Woman,' *Victorian Studies* 26 (Autumn 1982), 33–49.

26. Quoted by BRIAN ALDISS, *Billion Year Spree: The True History of Science Fiction* (New York: Schocken, 1976), pp. 8–9.

27. See I. F. CLARKE, *Voices Prophesying War, 1763–1984* (London: Oxford University Press, 1966), pp. 227–39. See also SAMUEL HYNES, *The Edwardian Turn of Mind* (Princeton: Princeton University Press, 1968), pp. 34–53.

28. P. G. WODEHOUSE, *The Swoop! and Other Stories*, ed. David A. Jasen (New York: Seabury, 1979).

29. See DAVID A. T. STAFFORD, 'Spies and Gentlemen: The Birth of the British Spy Novel, 1893–1914,' *Victorian Studies* 24 (Summer 1981), 489–509.

30. FREDERIC HARRISON, *Memories and Thoughts* (London: Macmillan, 1906), p. 233.

31. ROBERT M. BALLANTYNE, *The Coral Island* (London: Nelson, n.d.), p. 22.

32. Quoted by ETHERINGTON, *Rider Haggard*, p. 66.

33. JOSEPH CONRAD, 'Geography and Some Explorers,' in *Last Essays* (London: Dent, 1926), p. 17.

34. ANDREW LANG, 'The Supernatural in Fiction,' in *Adventures in Books* (1905; Freeport, N.Y.: Books for Libraries Press, 1970), pp. 279–80.

35. ANDREW LANG, *Cock Lane and Common Sense* (London: Longmans, Green, 1894), p. 2.

36. ANDREW LANG, 'Psychical Research,' *Encyclopedia Britannica*, 11th edn, vol. 22, pp. 544–7.

37. See L. S. Hearnshaw, *A Short History of British Psychology, 1840–1940* (New York: Barnes & Noble, 1964), especially chaps 9 and 10, and Ed Block, Jr., 'James Sully, Evolutionist Psychology, and Late Victorian Gothic Fiction,' *Victorian Studies* 25 (Summer 1982), 443–67.

38. Sigmund Freud, *The Future of an Illusion*, trans. James Strachey (New York: Norton, 1961), p. 28.

39. Quoted by Oppenheim, *Other World*, p. 132.

40. Rudyard Kipling, 'The Sending of Dana Da,' in *Works* vol. 6, p. 307.

41. Charles Carrington believes that 'They' contains a warning against engaging in 'psychical research,' and J. M. S. Tompkins thinks Kipling grew less rather than more interested in the supernatural. But 'They' clearly describes a supernatural experience. Perhaps all that Kipling quit doing was writing 'ghost stories' of the skeptical, frivolous, 'Phantom Rickshaw' variety. Carrington, *Rudyard Kipling, His Life and Work* (London: Macmillan, 1955), p. 373; Tompkins, *The Art of Rudyard Kipling* (London: University of Nebraska Press, 1965), p. 204. See also Elliot L. Gilbert, *The Good Kipling: Studies in the Short Story* (Manchester: Manchester University Press, 1972), p. 80.

42. See Sir H. Rider Haggard, *The Days of My Life: An Autobiography*, 2 vols (London: Longmans, Green, 1926), vol. 1, pp. 37–41. Hereafter volume and page numbers are given parenthetically in the text.

43. Saintsbury quoted in *Rudyard Kipling to Rider Haggard: The Record of a Friendship*, ed. Morton Cohen (London: Hutchinson, 1965), p. 4.

44. Alan Sandison's contention in *The Wheel of Empire: A Study of the Imperial Idea in Some Late Nineteenth and Early Twentieth-Century Fiction* (London: Macmillan, 1967) that Haggard in *King Solomon's Mines* 'as in every other [book] he wrote on Africa . . . repudiates without fuss the whole arrogant notion of the white man's burden' (p. 31) is misleading. Haggard's frequent criticisms of the behavior of white settlers – especially Boers – toward black Africans lead to arguments for strengthening rather than weakening imperial authority. Haggard was a keen admirer of Theophilus Shepstone and Sir Charles Buller, and he patterned his imperialist thinking after theirs.

45. Theodor Adorno, 'Theses against Occultism,' in *Minima Moralia: Reflections from Damaged Life*, trans E. F. N. Jephcott (London: Verso, 1978), p. 240.

46. Joseph Conrad, *Heart of Darkness*, ed. Robert Kimbrough (New York: Norton, 1963), p. 58.

47. George Gissing, *The Whirlpool* (Hassocks: Harvester, 1977), p. 16.

48. *The Last Will and Testament of Cecil John Rhodes*, ed. W. T. Stead (London: Review of Reviews Office, 1902), p. 190.

49. W. T. Stead, *After Death: A Personal Narrative* (New York: George H. Doran, 1914), p. 50.

50. Sir Oliver Lodge, *Phantom Walls* (New York: Putnam's, 1930), p. xi; Sir Arthur Conan Doyle, *Memories and Adventures* (Boston: Little, Brown, 1924), p. 390.

51. Sir Arthur Conan Doyle, *The Lost World* (New York: Review of Reviews, 1912), p. 13.

52. Sir Arthur Conan Doyle, *The Land of Mist* (New York: Doran, 1926), p. 132.

53. Sir Arthur Conan Doyle, *Pheneas Speaks: Direct Spirit Communication in the Family Circle* (London: Psychic Press, n.d.), p. 10.

54. Sir Arthur Conan Doyle, *The History of Spiritualism*, 2 vols (New York: Doran, 1926), vol. 1, p. 173.

12 The Content and Discontents of Kipling's Imperialism*

BENITA PARRY

Benita Parry has written extensively on the subject of literature and imperialism. She is the author of *Conrad and Imperialism*, and *Delusions and Discoveries* (see Further Reading). In the essay reprinted here Parry reworks the view of Kipling as the consummate artist of empire which she offered in her chapter on Kipling in *Delusions and Discoveries*. She also returns to the question of the broader cultural significance of Kipling's critical reputation. In *Delusions and Discoveries* she had argued that the history of Kipling criticism 'reproduces the history of western attitudes to the modern imperial experience'.† In the later, more politicised, essay she offers a more vigorous critique of both Kipling and his apologists. In her later reading Parry's Kipling becomes the 'exemplary' artist of imperialism; one who textually colonised India and created an imperialist construct which has subsequently been reproduced (or, alternatively, deconstructed) by succeeding generations of critics (see Introduction, p. 17).

Imperialism's Scribe

Kipling's writings moved empire from the margins of English fiction to its centre without interrogating the official metropolitan culture. In cataloguing a lifelong devotion to dominant beliefs and values in *Something of Myself*, an autobiography written in old age, he had no occasion to repent youthful indiscretions of opinion. The Club, the Mess and the Freemasons Lodge are prized, while the 'perversions' and 'unclean microbes' infecting male communities are deplored; there

*Reprinted from *New Formations*, 6 (1988), pp. 49–63.
†*Delusions and Discoveries*, p. 203

is hostility to liberals, socialists, and the labour movement, xenophobia towards Jews and contempt for blacks. Such predilections would be a matter for biography, were it not that they are written into the authoritative discourses of the texts, put there by a writer who conceived his function as teacher, prophet, and public voice. Pointing out that both his grandfathers had been Wesleyan ministers, Kipling recalls an early ambition to tell the English 'something of the whole sweep and meaning of things and effort and origins throughout the Empire'. Later, when an established author and a pillar of the establishment, political conviction inspired him to write his Boer War verses and tributes to Joseph Chamberlain, Cecil John Rhodes, and Lord Milner. It was passion for the expansion of empire which moved him to offer his gift with language to Rhodes, the architect of a plan for territorial aggrandizement whose imagination of conquest encompassed annexing the planets to England: 'he said to me apropos of nothing in particular: "What's your dream?" I answered that he was part of it. . . . My use to him was mainly as a purveyor of words; for he was largely inarticulate.'[1] In the story 'On the city wall', Kipling has the narrator, himself a word-*wallah*, decry the uselessness of books and scorn the lying proverb which says that the pen is mightier than the sword.[2] This is the stratagem of a dissembling writer who, having committed his own books and pen to political causes, feigns disbelief in the power of writing and directs attention instead to 'the line of guns that could pound the City to powder'.

Kipling's writings were not confined to fictions 'about empire', but it was his fiction of empire which, aided by the enthusiasm of the popular periodical press, made him the uncrowned laureate.[3] To gauge his role in the invention of an imperialist English identity requires the study of how reader responses were catalysed over many decades as forms of consciousness, social conduct, and political behaviour. What is immediately available to critical attention is the address of instructional and inspirational writing delivered from the heartland of an imperialist culture. Directed at a readership positioned as a racially homogeneous and masculine community, unfissured by class allegiances, Kipling's imperialist writings articulate a new patriotism purged of the radicalism in its earlier forms, and fabricate a linear narrative of England's 'undefiled heritage' beginning with the inheritance of the imperial flame as it passed from their conquerors into English hands, and consummated in the British Empire. Through blandishment and prophecy the cautionary verses urge the English to curb the unruly in themselves (as in 'The children's song' and 'If') if they are to realize their natural aptitude for ruling others. In 'A song of the English' (1893), he wrote:

> Fair is our lot – o goodly is our heritage!
> (Humble ye, my people, and be fearful in your mirth!)
> For the Lord our God Most High
> He hath made the deep as dry,
> He hath smote for us a pathway to the ends of all the Earth!
> . . .
> Hold ye the Faith – the Faith our Fathers sealèd us;
> Whoring not with visions – overwise and overstale.
> . . .
> Keep ye the Law – be swift in all obedience –
> Clear the land of evil, drive the road and bridge the ford.

Here the syntax of the sermon and the metre of the hymn regenerate the terms of imperialist propaganda into the notion of empire as a divinely appointed duty devolving on the English. Even as the mode shifts from the declamatory to the lyrical, and the stern call to imperial expansion and recall to ancestral belief is replaced by an indulgent longing to voyage beyond the constraints of metropolitan existence, Utopia is made instantly manifest in the colonial venture:

> We were dreamers, dreaming greatly, in the man-stifled town;
> We yearned beyond the sky-line where the strange roads go down.
> Came the Whisper, came the Vision, came the Power with the Need,
> Till the Soul that is not man's soul was lent us to lead.

Although Kipling has been hailed as a visionary, his mystique of empire more properly belongs to that worldly imperialist aspiration which imbued a predatory project with a revelational quality. In *Nostromo*, Conrad identified this compound as 'the misty idealism of the Northerners who at the smallest encouragement dream of nothing less than the conquest of the earth'.

Where the address of the imperialist verse is solemn and portentous, that of the stories idolizing the British as colonial rulers joins the briskly exegetical with the gallantly sentimental. Since the language of European ascendancy and Anglo-Indian conceit remains uncontradicted, the narrative structure of such tales is sealed against any interrogation of the Raj's self-presentation. On those occasions when the Indians do appear to speak, they are the mouthpieces of a ventriloquist who, using a facile idiom that alternates between the artless and the ornate, projects his own account of grateful native dependency. The monologism of these fictions is not Kipling's only mode, however. In those texts which call attention to their own fictional nature and stage the multivalencies of language, the pretence to authentic representation and the imparting of truths is caricatured. The playful posture towards words and writing of the narrator in 'On the city wall', who even as he presents himself in the process of composing his chronicle, distinguishes between 'living the story' and 'writing it', produces uncertainties in the proffered report of events. This ambiguity is sustained when the regulation reiteration of British discipline, fortitude, and devotion to duty, delivered in a diction which values social order and the exercise of stern political control, is undercut by the flamboyance of metaphor and the banter of puns:

> Lalun has not yet been described. She would need, so Wali Dad says, a thousand pens of gold and ink scented with musk. She has been variously compared to the Moon, the Dil Sagar Lake, a spotted quail, a gazelle, the Sun on the Desert of Kutch, the Dawn, the Stars, and the young bamboo. . . . One song . . . says the beauty of Lalun was so great that it troubled the hearts of the British Government and caused them to lose their peace of mind. That is the way the song is sung in the streets; but, if you examine it carefully and know the key to the explanation, you will find that there are three puns in it – on 'beauty', 'heart', and 'peace of mind' – so that it runs 'By the subtlety of Lalun the administration was troubled and it lost such and such a man.' (pp. 326, 323)

When Kipling sports with the referential mode which he so ably used to prescribe codes of conduct and instil ways of seeing, he puts in question the very predications which elsewhere he so aggressively articulated. The absent subject of 'To be filed for reference' (*Plain Tales from the Hills*, 1890) is 'The Book' compiled by an educated English drunkard gone native, and reputed to contain the truths about the people of the country concealed from the British. Allusions to its substance suggest the sensational ethnography of an excited Western imagination – it is coyly referred to by the Anglo-Indian narrator as in need of expurgation, an opinion proudly shared by its author – and not the text of an alternative system of meanings. Nevertheless, 'The Book' does function to contest the colonialist claim of 'knowing the Real India', a boast made sometimes archly and sometimes not, in other stories. Here the reader is invited to believe that the official British version is indeed faulty, even though the potential counter-knowledge is strategically suppressed. In these self-reflexive tales, the univocal pronouncements of the polemical writings are undermined or countermanded, and these departures from the dominant mode are a reminder of just how firmly such doubts are elsewhere quelled. If 'To be filed for reference' both intimates and averts a challenge to British knowledge, then *Kim* (1901) confidently reaffirms its validity. It is the English curator of a museum, 'with his mound of books – French, and German, with photographs and reproductions' and his acquaintance with 'the labours of European scholars', who communicates new learning about his own heritage to the amazed lama. It is through collecting and collating information about India's roads, rivers, plants, stones, and customs that the Ethnological Survey makes available to the government that intelligence which is essential to the proper exercise of British power. And it is Kim, the sahib who can pass as any one of India's many peoples, who has access to the secrets of all India and puts these at the disposal of a benevolent Raj.

Coercion, Desire and Fear in Kipling's India

Kipling's India raises the problem posed by Edward Said in *Orientalism* as to 'how one can study other cultures and peoples from a libertarian, or a non-repressive and non-manipulative perspective'.[4] More specific questions are: can a writer immersed in and owing allegiance to a master culture, construe the radical difference of another and subordinated culture as yet another conceptual order within a multiverse of diverse meanings? Are Kipling's fabrications of India, as has been claimed, testimony to the possibility of such ideologically unfettered constructions? It is *Kim* which critics call upon to argue that in his representation of India's uniquely multiple being, Kipling did indeed transcend the boundaries of his own ethnocentric vision.[5] While this is not the position taken by Edward Said, who criticizes Kipling's fiction of an immutable and immobile India, he does in his generous essay on *Kim* credit Kipling with giving India a positive identity: 'We can watch a great artist blinded in a sense by his own insights about India, confusing the reality before him, which he saw with such colour and ingenuity, with the notion that these realities were permanent and essential.'[6] The implication is that despite a crucial flaw in its composition, this India is the product of a non-coercive perspective. It could be argued, however, that because Kipling's India is reified under Western eyes as a frieze or a pageant, and romanticized as an object of sensuous and voluptuous pleasure to be enjoyed by Europe, it is an invention which colonizes the space of India's own significations with Western fantasies. Moreover, this 'Orientalized India of the imagination ... an ideal India, unchanging and attractive, full of bustle and activity, but also restful ... even idyllic' is not Kiping's only India[7] and within this larger, heterogeneous configuration, India can signify nullity as well as plenty, and its difference can be variously constituted as deviant, menacing, or magnetic.

Kipling's journalism made a major contribution to the text of the Raj, working within and extending existing representations by vilifying the customs and manners of contemporary India and ridiculing its ancient literary heritages.[8] A glorious past was reconstructed by nineteenth-century European Indologists, who like their predecessors saw their role as making India's traditional learning known to the West and returning a noble legacy to peoples whose religious life had fallen into debased practices. This project was anathema to the architects of an absolute government in the metropolis and their agents in India. Their scorn was eagerly reiterated by an Anglo-Indian community outraged at Max Müller's postulate of an Indo-European family of languages and cultures – this was the source of the witticisms about 'our Aryan brothers', who so clearly were not.

Enunciations of India's otherness are never absent, but in those writings which project India as the incarnation of what a European self is constrained to exclude, alienation is intercepted by identification. A regret at the necessary ending of intimacy is registered in 'The native born' where India is characterized as the lost object of desire that must be relinquished for entry into the patriarchal law:

> To our dear dark foster mothers,
> To the heathen songs they sung –
> To the heathen speech we babbled,
> Ere we came to the white man's tongue.

A different specification of lack is inscribed in those fictions which, reproducing colonialist fantasy, transfigure India as the provider of libidinal excitation. The embrace of that which the European self denies becomes enmeshed with the colonialist appetite for possession and control. Such multiple exigencies are dramatized in the love stories 'Beyond the pale' (*Plain Tales*) and 'Without benefit of clergy' (*Life's Handicap*, 1891), where native subordination and Oriental passion, those staples of colonial discourse, come together in the ecstatic and ceremonial yielding of the native as female to the dominating presence of a masculine West. In the battle between creative man and castrating woman fought on English ground in *The Light That Failed* (1890), the figure of a hybrid alien is invoked to represent a notion of woman's Manichaean nature: 'she was a sort of Negroid–Jewess–Cuban – with morals to match [serving] as a model for the devils and the angels both' (p. 155). In the tales of the white man's sexual encounters with the native woman, however, the Indian female, who must enact a double subjugation, is all innocence and ardent acquiescence. Ameera's obeisance to her English lover in 'Without benefit of clergy' stages the total abjection of India as colonized and female, the abasement of her address to the white man, 'My king, for all thy sweet words, well I know that I am thy servant and thy slave and the dust under thy feet' (p. 163) culminating in a deathbed blasphemy of her Islamic faith: 'I bear witness – I bear witness . . . that there is no God – but – thee – beloved' (p. 178).

Michael O'Pray has argued in *New Formations* for recovering Kipling as a key figure in a marginalized English tradition 'where romanticism merges with nostalgia . . . and an exoticism and quasi-mysticism that have a complex relationship to the British Empire'.[9] But because, as O'Pray recognizes, the fantastical is condensed with the colonizing spirit, the effect is to invest domination with libidinal intensities – Conrad's 'insatiable imagination of conquest'. A central trope of Kipling's other Indian novel, *The Naulahka* (1892), is an erotically charged urge for colonialist acquisition. The necklace of the title joins a sign of the East's fabled wealth with a symbol of woman's body, and the narration of the quest for the priceless and sacred jewel mimicks a bellicose act that is both an imperialist invasion and a sexual assault. A desolate landscape is transformed into a meaningless social space, giving the West a moral right to usurp its wasted resources: 'miles of profitless, rolling ground . . . studded with unthrifty trees . . . this abyss of oblivion. . . . The silence of the place and the insolent nakedness of its empty ways . . . the vast, sleeping land' (pp. 59, 78, 164). But an overweening white confidence enunciated in disdain for India – 'Standing there, he recognized . . . how entirely the life, habits and traditions of this strange people alienated them from all that seemed good and right to him' (p. 212) – is undermined by articulations of the panic afflicting the conquering imagination. The holy well where the jewel is secreted has an intolerable smell of musk and is 'fringed to the lips with rank vegetation'; the surrounding rock is 'rotten with moisture'; from the stagnant waters rears 'the head of a sunken stone pillar, carved with monstrous and obscene gods'; the pool, overhung by a fig tree buttressing the rock 'with snake-like roots', is inhabited by an alligator, 'a long welt of filth and slime' (pp. 155–6, 165–6). From these signs of a rank and corrupting sexuality and of original sin, the white assailant flees in horror.

Sometimes a source of guilty lust, India elsewhere is constructed as the negation of reason, order, and coherence so that the anxiety induced by difference is dispelled by moral censure. At its crudest, as in 'The enlightenments of Pagett M.P.',[10] this is articulated as an uninterrupted calumniation of Indian social existence: 'the foundations of their life are rotten – utterly and bestially rotten. . . . In effect, native habits and beliefs are an organized conspiracy against the laws of healthy and happy life.' Contempt for custom can be conflated with anger at India's climate, both standing in the way of implementing British purpose: 'storm, sudden freshets, death in every manner and shape . . . drought, sanitation . . . birth, wedding, burial, and riot in the village of twenty warring castes' ('The bridge-builders', p. 5). Where disquiet at India's otherness is not allayed by reproof, its particularities was perceived as a hostile presence threatening to overwhelm the white community:

> There was neither sky, sun, nor horizon – nothing but a brown purple
> haze of heat. It was as though the earth was dying of apoplexy. . . .
> The atmosphere within was only 104°. . . and heavy with the foul

smell of badly-trimmed kerosene lamps; and this stench, combined
with that of native tobacco, baked brick, and dried earth, sends the
heart of many a strong man down to his boots, for it is the smell of
the Great Indian Empire when it turns itself for six months into a
house of torment . . . a tom-tom in the coolie-lines began to beat with
the steady throb of a swollen artery inside some brain-fevered skull.
('At the end of the passage', *Life's Handicap*, pp. 183, 198)

India's incomprehensible menace serves also to displace the colonialist
nightmare of native vengeance, itself the verso of that fantasy where the
country and its people are willingly held in the Raj's embrace. 'The mark
of the beast' (*Life's Handicap*) uses the conventions of the horror story to
narrate an act of native retribution that is 'beyond any human and
rational experience' (p. 251): the lurid circumstances effectively screening
the import of colonial resentment. 'The strange ride of Morrowbie Jukes'
(*The Phantom Rickshaw*, 1892), Kipling's most potent tale of European
dread, veils this secular fright in the incertitude of hallucination. In
detailing the ride of a delirious engineer with a head for plans but
without imagination, 'over what seemed a limitless expanse of moonlit
sands', the narration transforms the physical terrain into a metaphysical
landscape. Accidentally plunged by his horse into a crater, Jukes finds
himself trapped in a grotesque community of pariah Indians who, having
recovered from trance or catalepsy after being presumed dead, have been
confined to conditions of appalling deprivation and degradation. Here
Jukes, who no longer commands the deference due to a sahib, suffers the
'nervous terror' of being immured amongst hostile Indians. His rescue by
a loyal servant both mimicks the relief of awakening from a bad dream,
and acts therapeutically to restore British confidence in the
invulnerability of a position undermined by the central narrative event.

Strategic Boundaries, Native Marginalization

Within the specification of India as other, the figures of the alluring
exotic and the minatory alien stand out, on the one hand, as the signs of
the sensual temptations impeding the exercise of British rule and, on the
other, of an unintelligible danger to its hegemony. Notably absent is
India incarnate as political opponent to the Raj. Edward Said has
proposed that Kipling studiously avoided giving us two worlds in
conflict because for him '*there was no conflict* . . . it was India's best
destiny to be ruled by England'. This confidence Said attributes to the
defining context in which he wrote: 'There *were* no appreciable deterrents
to the imperialist world-view held by Kipling. Hence he remained
untroubled.'[11] But potent counters *did* exist both in India's traditional

system of knowledge and in emergent nationalist discourses and if Kipling was serenely unaware that these transgressed imperialist principles, then his writings were not, as attention to those strategies which silence voices able to interrogate the British Empire as cultural text and political concept will show.

Parataxis is a favoured procedure for organizing incommensurable discourses in ways that conceal an antagonism of ideas. The road, the river, and the wheel in *Kim* serve dual and opposing functions within the narrative. While Kim 'flung himself whole-heartedly upon the next turn of the wheel', the lama strives to free himself 'from the Wheel of Things' (pp. 210; 13). Whereas for Kim the Grand Trunk Road is a river of life, to the lama it is a hard path to be trodden in his search for a mythic river that will cleanse him from the sin of material being. Between Kim's pursuit of action, the life of the senses, and personal identity, and the lama's quest for quietism, ascetism, and the annihilation of self, there is no dialogue. Hence disjunctive goals, the one valued and the other denounced by imperialism's tenets, easily cohere as the mutual venture defined by the lama who in his studied indifference to the temporal, accepts Kim's recruitment into the Secret Service as yet another insignificant action: 'he aided me in my Search. I aided him in his. . . . Let him be a teacher, let him be a scribe – what matter? He will have attained Freedom at the end. The rest is illusion' (p. 407). This happy end, which allows Kim to have his nirvana and eat it, prompts another agent, the pragmatic Mahbub Ali, to say, 'Now I understand that the boy, sure of Paradise, can yet enter Government Service, my mind is easier' (p. 407). There is a reprise of this expedient ending in the ceremonial healing of the crisis precipitated by the irreconcilable roles Kim must play as apprentice spy and *chela* to a holy man; his recovery is effected without any engagement with the competing commitments and it acts to abolish conflict.

The contradictory ideological imperatives of etching the division between imperialist self and native other at the same time as re-presenting colonialist/colonized hostility as British/Indian collaboration, engenders the invention of boundary situations inscribing both exigencies. In a territory signalled in the titles – 'Beyond the pale', 'Without benefit of clergy', 'On the city wall' – and which is literally out of bounds to the English in colonial conditions, the frontiers drawn up by the imperial power can be crossed without endangering the relationship dependent on the policing of borders. This liminal space thus neither constitutes a zone liberated from the Raj, nor is the positioning of master/native displaced. Instead it is construed as a peripheral district licensed by the centre for the episodic transgression of colonialist interdicts. The movement between the languages of Law and Desire, the one enunciating the light of Anglo-India, the other the dark of

India, reinstalls the chasm even as the protagonists from across the divide meet in intimacy. 'By day Holden did his work. . . . At nightfall he returned to Ameera' ('Without benefit of clergy', p. 165). 'In the daytime Trejago drove through his routine of office work . . . At night when all the City was still came the . . . walk [to] Bisesa' ('Beyond the pale', p. 175). When Holden has performed 'the birth-sacrifice' to protect the son born to Ameera, by slaughtering goats and 'muttering the Mahomedan prayer', he is 'eager to get to the light of the company of his fellows' (p. 157); and if Trejago's passion is an endless delight, it is also a folly and a madness.

The exclusions of the colonialist code are thus ambivalently displayed as necessary deprivation. The ecstasy which Englishmen find in Bisesa's room and Ameera's house, or the pleasures afforded by Lalun's salon on the city wall, none of which is available in the bungalow or the Club, are articulated in rhapsodic vein. But if the lucid world of Anglo-India inhibits sensual gratification, it also preserves reason and order. This demands that the poesy of the illicit crossings is disrupted by the prose of censure: in one case disobedience is punished by disease and death, in another by mutilation. After Ameera and her son have died, the house which Holden had taken for her is torn down 'so that no man may say where [it] stood', presaging her mother's prophecy that 'He will go back to his own people in time' (pp. 182; 137). 'Beyond the pale' opens with an ironic admonition:

> A man should, whatever happens, keep to his own caste, race and breed. Let the White go to the White, and the Black to the Black. Then, whatever trouble falls is in the ordinary course of things – neither sudden, alien, nor unexpected. (p. 171)

Although this is contradicted by the 'Hindu Proverb' which serves as the story's epigram ('Love heeds not caste nor sleep a broken bed. I went in search of love and lost myself' [p. 171]), its wisdom is confirmed by the ending. If the love stories are both eulogistic and censorious about the transgression of frontiers, the allegorical 'The bridge-builders' whole-heartedly applauds that passage through which the British donate and the Indians receive technological progress, for there is no encroachment on colonialist divisions. The gulf between the British doctrine on the conquest of nature and a deferential Indian stance towards the integrity of the physical environment is momentarily traversed by the British engineer's opium-induced vision of the gods in conclave. On awakening, however, he banishes all memory of what he has seen: 'in that clear light there was no room for a man to think dreams of the dark' (p. 41). An alien perspective on the universe and time is made known and dispelled; once again the status quo is entrenched.

Representations which neutralize or elide the challenge to the British world-view, and which ensure that the positioning of master and native is not disturbed, close the space for a counter-discourse authored by the colonized as historical subject and agent. Yet in the act of muting these utterances, the texts reveal a knowledge of their existence and their danger. If we follow Fredric Jameson's proposition that the hegemonic discourse implies a dialogue with a dissenting voice even when this is disarticulated,[12] then Kipling's imperialist writings can be read as a pre-emptive reply to Indian opposition. What is heard instead is the idiom of grateful dependence from villagers and servants, of proud compliance from sepoys and war-like tribesmen, and of insolent malcontent from Western-educated 'babus'. When the language of legend or religion is spoken, this is not permitted to contest imperialist teaching; nor does it confront European ascendancy on the political ground staked out by the text of the British Empire.

It is such suppressions which make the interlocution of voices in 'On the city wall' noteworthy, for in this fiction the Indians *are* autonomous and oppositional speaking subjects. Characteristically, the story moves between disjunctive modes. The Indian scene is represented in a vocabulary of parodic romanticism, its ironic effusions alternating with the pompous diction of British rule:

> Year by year England sends out fresh drafts for the first fighting-line, which is officially called the Indian Civil Service. These die, or kill themselves by overwork, or are worried to death, or broken in health and hope in order that the land may be protected from death and sickness, famine and war, and may eventually become capable of standing alone. It will never stand alone, but the idea is a pretty one, and men are willing to die for it, and yearly the work of pushing and coaxing and scolding and petting the country into good living goes forward. (p. 324)

But there is another and uncharacteristic arrangement of discourses. As always the might of the Raj is proclaimed loud and clear:

> Hugonin, the Assistant District Superintendent of Police, a boy of twenty, had got together thirty constables and was forcing the crowd through the streets. . . . The dog-whip cracked across the writhing backs, and the constables smote afresh with baton and gun-butt. (pp. 343–4)

Now, however, Britain's right to rule, whether projected as benevolent tutelage or brute force, is contested. Indian refusal is here spoken both in English, which was commonly used in the emergent nationalist writings and speeches, and also in the vernaculars, for once transcribed without coy and cloying archaisms. Opposition to colonialist claims thus joins

Hindu, Muslim, and Sikh in a chorus of dissident voices. The Western-educated Wali Dad, exceptionally speaking an impeccable 'standard' English, recounts the consistent anti-British record of the unrepentant old Sikh warrior, Khem Singh, and also spurns on his own account the rewards offered by the Raj to the subaltern Indian:

> I might wear an English coat and trouser. I might be a leading Muhammadan pleader. I might be received even at the Commissioner's tennis parties where the English stand on one side and the natives on the other, in order to promote social intercourse throughout the Empire. (p. 338)

In a quite different style, Lalun, the courtesan from whose house a rebellion is being planned, voices her disaffection in a song which joins the memory of war against the Moghul invaders with the hope of a present struggle against the British. This is intended for, and heard by, the imprisoned Khem Singh; he in turn speaks of his old hatred against the government and his wish to engage in further battle. Such utterances of enmity against the Raj are ironically compounded by the reversion of the agnostic Wali Dad to his ancestral religion during the Mohurran festival. Represented by the English narrator as proof of Indian fanaticism, communalism, and traditionalism, his action can also be read as a gesture of cultural resistance. This story imposes no formal rapprochement of opposites. The seditious plot is of course foiled, but without the instigators becoming reconciled to their subjugated condition – at the end Khem Singh is to be heard suggesting plans for the escape of other fighters jailed by the British administration. Still inchoate as an insurgent discourse, the speech of Indians confronting and rejecting British authority points up what Kipling's writings elsewhere effaced.

Kipling is an exemplary artist of imperialism. The fabrications of England's mysterious imperialist identity and destiny, reiterated in the Indian writings and carried over into the later English fictions; homilies on the development of character in the metropolitan population, hymned in one of the verses as adherence to a code of Law, Order, Duty and Restraint, Obedience, Discipline; the celebrations of a triumphalism extending from the conquest of the physical environment to autocratic relationships within the domestic society and between Britain and the colonies; the projection of the white race as the natural rulers of a global space created and divided by imperialism; the positioning of the other hemisphere as peripheral to a Western centre – these inscriptions of an outlook constructed in an historical moment continue to offer rich pickings to a militant conservatism seeking sanctions for authoritarianism, social conformity, patriotism, and Britain's commanding world role by references back to a splendid imperial past. To a criticism concerned with mapping the exclusions and affirmations of an imperialist culture whose legacy has still not been spent, these same texts can be made to reveal both imperialism's grandiloquent self-presentation and those inadmissible desires, misgivings, and perceptions concealed in its discourses.

Notes

1. RUDYARD KIPLING, *Something of Myself* (London: Macmillan, 1937), pp. 90–1, 173–4.
2. 'In black and white', from a volume including *Soldiers Three, The Story of the Gadsbys and In Black and White* (London: Macmillan, 1895). Page references to the uniform Macmillan edition are given in the text.
3. See ANN PARRY, 'Reading formations in the Victorian press: the reception of Kipling 1888–1891', *Literature and History*, 11, 2 (Autumn 1985), 254–63.
4. EDWARD SAID, *Orientalism* (London: Routledge & Kegan Paul, 1978), p. 24.
5. See, for example, MARK KINKEAD-WEEKES, 'Vision in Kipling's novels', in Andrew Rutherford (ed.), *Kipling's Mind and Art* (Edinburgh and London: Oliver & Boyd, 1964), and NIRAD CHAUDHURI, 'The finest story about India – in English', in JOHN GROSS (ed.), *Rudyard Kipling: The Man, His Work and His World* (London: Weidenfeld & Nicolson, 1972).
6. EDWARD SAID, introduction to *Kim* (Harmondsworth: Penguin, 1987), p. 45.
7. Ibid., pp. 28, 24, 40–1.
8. See *From Sea to Sea*, vols I and II (London: Macmillan, 1899).
9. MICHAEL O'PRAY, 'Radical visionaries: Powell and Pressberger' (a review of IAN CHRISTIE's *Arrows of Desire*), *New Formations*, 1 (Spring 1987), 155–9.
10. *Contemporary Review*, LVIII (September 1890).
11. SAID, introduction to *Kim*, p. 24.
12. *The Political Unconscious* (London: Methuen, 1981), p. 85.

13 Conrad's *Heart of Darkness* and the Histories of Empire*

EDWARD SAID

Edward Said is the author of *Orientalism* (see Further Reading) a seminal book on Western constructions of the East through literary representations, travel writing, and such forms of knowledge as Egyptology, anthropology and philology. In his later book *Culture and Imperialism* (from which the extracts below are taken) Said extends his thinking about the interrelationships of culture and empire, both geographically and in terms of the forms of representation which are analysed. The later book focuses on acts of narration and on the novel as one of the central cultural forms in the history and culture of empire. Said's method in *Culture and Imperialism* is to look at particular novel texts first as products of the creative imagination and secondly as illustrative of the relationship between culture and empire. He self-consciously distances himself from a mechanistically determinist model which sees authors and texts as produced by class, ideology, or the economic structure, preferring instead a view of the author/text as both shaped by and shaping social and cultural history. In the extracts below Said engages with what he sees as the paradox of Conrad – a 'great' writer who was both an anti-imperialist and an imperialist: 'progressive when it came to rendering fearlessly and pessimistically the self-confirming, self-deluding corruption of overseas domination, deeply reactionary when it came to conceding that Africa or South America could ever have had an independent history or culture't (see Introduction, pp. 17–18).

[The] imperial attitude is, I believe, beautifully captured in the complicated and rich narrative form of Conrad's great novella *Heart of*

*Reprinted from EDWARD SAID, *Culture and Imperialism* (London: Chatto and Windus, 1993), pp. 24–34 and 79–82.
tCulture and Imperialism, p. xx

Darkness, written between 1898 and 1899. On the one hand, the narrator Marlow acknowledges the tragic predicament of all speech – that 'it is impossible to convey the life-sensation of any given epoch on one's existence – that which makes its truth, its meaning – its subtle and penetrating essence . . .We live, as we dream – alone'[1] – yet still manages to convey the enormous power of Kurtz's African experience through his own overmastering narrative of his voyage into the African interior towards Kurtz. This narrative in turn is connected directly with the redemptive force, as well as the waste and horror, of Europe's mission in the dark world. Whatever is lost or elided or even simply made up in Marlow's immensely compelling recitation is compensated for in the narrative's sheer historical momentum, the temporal forward movement – with digressions, descriptions, exciting encounters, and all. Within the narrative of how he journeyed to Kurtz's Inner Station, whose source and authority he now becomes, Marlow moves backward and forward materially in small and large spirals, very much the way episodes in the course of his journey up-river are then incorporated by the principal forward trajectory into what he renders as 'the heart of Africa'.

Thus Marlow's encounter with the improbably white-suited clerk in the middle of the jungle furnishes him with several digressive paragraphs, as does his meeting later with the semi-crazed, harlequin-like Russian who has been so affected by Kurtz's gifts. Yet underlying Marlow's inconclusiveness, his evasions, his arabesque meditations on his feelings and ideas, is the unrelenting course of the journey itself, which, despite all the many obstacles, is sustained through the jungle, through time, through hardship, to the heart of it all, Kurtz's ivory-trading empire. Conrad wants us to see how Kurtz's great looting adventure, Marlow's journey up the river, and the narrative itself all share a common theme: Europeans performing acts of imperial mastery and will in (or about) Africa.

What makes Conrad different from the other colonial writers who were his contemporaries is that, for reasons having partly to do with the colonialism that turned him, a Polish expatriate, into an employee of the imperial system, he was so self-conscious about what he did. Like most of his other tales, therefore, *Heart of Darkness* cannot just be a straightforward recital of Marlow's adventures: it is also a dramatization of Marlow himself, the former wanderer in colonial regions, telling his story to a group of British listeners at a particular time and in a specific place. That this group of people is drawn largely from the business world is Conrad's way of emphasizing the fact that during the 1890s the business of empire, once an adventurous and often individualistic enterprise, had become the empire of business. (Coincidentally we should note that at about the same time Halford Mackinder, an explorer, geographer, and Liberal Imperialist, gave a series of lectures on imperialism at the London Institute of Bankers:[2] perhaps Conrad knew about this.) Although the almost oppressive force of Marlow's narrative leaves us with a quite accurate sense that there is no way out of the sovereign historical force of imperialism, and that it has the power of a system representing as well as speaking for everything within its dominion, Conrad shows us that what Marlow does is contingent, acted out for a set of like-minded British hearers, and limited to that situation.

Yet neither Conrad nor Marlow gives us a full view of what is *outside* the world-conquering attitudes embodied by Kurtz, Marlow, the circle of listeners on the deck of the *Nellie*, and Conrad. By that I mean that *Heart of Darkness* works so effectively because its politics and aesthetics are, so to speak, imperialist, which in the closing years of the nineteenth century seemed to be at the same time an aesthetic, politics, and even epistemology inevitable and unavoidable. For if we cannot truly understand someone else's experience and if we must therefore depend upon the assertive authority of the sort of power that Kurtz wields as a white man in the jungle or that Marlow, another white man, wields as narrator, there is no use looking for other, non-imperialist alternatives; the system has simply eliminated them and made them unthinkable. The circularity, the perfect closure of the whole thing is not only aesthetically but also mentally unassailable.

Conrad is so self-conscious about situating Marlow's tale in a narrative moment that he allows us simultaneously to realize after all that imperialism, far from swallowing up its own history, was taking place in and was circumscribed by a larger history, one just outside the tightly inclusive circle of Europeans on the deck of the *Nellie*. As yet, however, no one seemed to inhabit that region, and so Conrad left it empty.

Conrad could probably never have used Marlow to present anything other than an imperialist world-view, given what was available for either Conrad or Marlow to see of the non-European at the time. Independence was for whites and Europeans; the lesser or subject peoples were to be ruled; science, learning, history emanated from the West. True, Conrad scrupulously recorded the differences between the disgraces of Belgian and British colonial attitudes, but he could only imagine the world carved up into one or another Western sphere of dominion. But because Conrad also had an extraordinarily persistent residual sense of his own exilic marginality, he quite carefully (some would say maddeningly) qualified Marlow's narrative with the provisionality that came from standing at the very juncture of this world with another, unspecified but different. Conrad was certainly not a great imperialist entrepreneur like Cecil Rhodes or Frederick Lugard, even though he understood perfectly how for each of them, in Hannah Arendt's words, to enter the maelstrom of an unending process of expansion, he will, as it were, cease to be what he was and obey the laws of the process, identify himself with anonymous forces that he is supposed to serve in order to keep the whole process in motion, he will think of himself as mere function, and eventually consider such functionality, such an incarnation of the dynamic trend, his highest possible achievement.[3]

Conrad's realization is that if, like narrative, imperialism has monopolized the entire system of representation – which in the case of *Heart of Darkness* allowed it to speak for Africans as well as for Kurtz and the other adventurers, including Marlow and his audience – your self-consciousness as an outsider can allow you actively to comprehend how the machine works, given that you and it are fundamentally not in perfect synchrony or correspondence. Never the wholly incorporated and fully acculturated Englishman, Conrad therefore preserved an ironic distance in each of his works.

The form of Conrad's narrative has thus made it possible to derive two possible arguments, two visions, in the post-colonial world that succeeded his. One argument allows the old imperial enterprise full scope to play itself out conventionally, to render the world as official European or Western imperialism saw it, and to consolidate itself after World War Two. Westerners may have physically left their old colonies in Africa and Asia, but they retained them not only as markets but as locales on the ideological map over which they continued to rule morally and intellectually, 'Show me the Zulu Tolstoy', as one American intellectual has recently put it. The assertive sovereign inclusiveness of this argument courses through the words of those who speak today for the West and for what the West did, as well as for what the rest of the world is, was, and may be. The assertions of this discourse exclude what has been represented as 'lost' by arguing that the colonial world was in some ways ontologically speaking lost to begin with, irredeemable, irrecusably inferior. Moreover, it focuses not on what was shared in the colonial experience, but on what must never be shared, namely the authority and rectitude that come with greater power and development. Rhetorically, its terms are the organization of political passions, to borrow from Julien Benda's critique of modern intellectuals, terms which, he was sensible enough to know, lead inevitably to mass slaughter, and if not to literal mass slaughter then certainly to rhetorical slaughter.

The second argument is considerably less objectionable. It sees itself as Conrad saw his own narratives, local to a time and place, neither unconditionally true nor unqualifiedly certain. As I have said, Conrad does not give us the sense that he could imagine a fully realized alternative to imperialism: the natives he wrote about in Africa, Asia, or America were incapable of independence, and because he seemed to imagine that European tutelage was a given, he could not foresee what would take place when it came to an end. But come to an end it would, if only because – like all human effort, like speech itself – it would have its moment, then it would have to pass. Since Conrad *dates* imperialism, shows its contingency, records its illusions and tremendous violence and waste (as in *Nostromo*), he permits his later readers to imagine something other than an Africa carved up into dozens of European colonies, even if, for his own part, he had little notion of what that Africa might be.

Let us return to what I have been referring to as the second, less imperialistically assertive possibility offered by *Heart of Darkness*. Recall once again that Conrad sets the story on the deck of a boat anchored in the Thames; as Marlow tells his story the sun sets, and by the end of the narrative the heart of darkness has reappeared in England; outside the group of Marlow's listeners lies an undefined and unclear world. Conrad sometimes seems to want to fold that world into the imperial metropolitan discourse represented by Marlow, but by virtue of his own dislocated subjectivity he resists the effort and succeeds in so doing, I have always believed, largely through formal devices. Conrad's self-consciously circular narrative forms draw attention to themselves as artificial constructions, encouraging us to sense the potential of a reality that seemed inaccessible to imperialism, just beyond its control, and that only well after Conrad's death in 1924 acquired a substantial presence.

This needs more explanation. Despite their European names and mannerisms, Conrad's narrators are not average unreflecting witnesses of European imperialism. They do not simply accept what goes on in the name of the imperial idea: they think about it a lot, they worry about it, they are actually quite anxious about whether they can make it seem like a routine thing. But it never is. Conrad's way of demonstrating this discrepancy between the orthodox and his own views of empire is to keep drawing attention to how ideas and values are constructed (and deconstructed) through dislocations in the narrator's language. In addition, the recitations are meticulously staged: the narrator is a speaker whose audience and the reason for their being together, the quality of whose voice, the effect of what he says – are all important and even insistent aspects of the story he tells. Marlow, for example, is never straightforward. He alternates between garrulity and stunning eloquence, and rarely resists making peculiar things seem more peculiar by surprisingly misstating them, or rendering them vague and contradictory. Thus, he says, a French warship fires 'into a continent'; Kurtz's eloquence is enlightening as well as fraudulent; and so on – his speech so full of these odd discrepancies (well discussed by Ian Watt as 'delayed decoding'[4]) that the net effect is to leave his immediate audience as well as the reader with the acute sense that what he is presenting is not quite as it should be or appears to be.

Yet the whole point of what Kurtz and Marlow talk about is in fact imperial mastery, white Europeans *over* black Africans and their ivory, civilization *over* the primitive dark continent. By accentuating the discrepancy between the official 'idea' of empire and the remarkably disorienting actuality of Africa, Marlow unsettles the reader's sense not only of the very idea of empire but of something more basic, reality itself. For if Conrad can show that all human activity depends on controlling a radically unstable reality to which words approximate only by will or convention, the same is true of empire, of venerating the idea, and so forth. With Conrad, then, we are in a world being made and unmade more or less all the time. What appears stable and secure – the policeman at the corner, for instance – is only slightly more secure than the white men in the jungle, and requires the same continuous (but precarious) triumph over an all-pervading darkness, which by the end of the tale is shown to be the same in London and in Africa.

Conrad's genius allowed him to realize that the ever-present darkness could be colonized or illuminated – *Heart of Darkness* is full of references to the *mission civilisatrice*, to benevolent as well as cruel schemes to bring light to the dark places and peoples of this world by acts of will and deployments of power – but that it also had to be acknowledged as independent. Kurtz and Marlow acknowledge the darkness, the former as he is dying, the latter as he reflects retrospectively on the meaning of Kurtz's final words. They (and of course Conrad) are ahead of their time in understanding that what they call 'the darkness' has an autonomy of its own, and can reinvade and reclaim what imperialism had taken for *its* own. But Marlow and Kurtz are also creatures of their time and cannot take the next step, which would be to recognize that what they saw, disablingly and disparagingly, as a non-European 'darkness' was in fact a non-European world *resisting* imperialism so as one day to regain sovereignty and independence, and not, as Conrad reductively says, to reestablish the darkness. Conrad's tragic limitation is that even though he could see clearly that on one level imperialism was essentially pure dominance and land-grabbing, he could not then conclude that imperialism had to end so that 'natives' could lead lives free from European domination. As a creature of his time, Conrad could not grant the natives their freedom, despite his severe critique of the imperialism that enslaved them.

Conrad's Africans, for example, come from a huge library of *Africanism*, so to speak, as well as from Conrad's personal experiences. There is no such thing as a *direct* experience, or reflection, of the world in the language of a text. Conrad's impressions of Africa were inevitably influenced by lore and writing about Africa, which he alludes to in *A Personal Record*; what he supplies in *Heart of Darkness* is the result of his impressions of those texts interacting creatively, together with the requirements and conventions of narrative and his own special genius and history. To say of this extraordinarily rich mix that it 'reflects' Africa, or even that it reflects an experience of Africa, is somewhat pusillanimous and surely misleading. What we have in *Heart of Darkness* – a work of immense influence, having provoked many readings and images – is a politicized, ideologically saturated Africa which to some intents and purposes was the imperialized place, with those many interests and ideas furiously at work in it, not just a photographic literary 'reflection' of it.

This is, perhaps, to overstate the matter, but I want to make the point that far from *Heart of Darkness* and its image of Africa being 'only' literature, the work is extraordinarily caught up in, is indeed an organic part of, the 'scramble for Africa' that was contemporary with Conrad's composition. True, Conrad's audience was small, and, true also, he was very critical of Belgian colonialism. But to most Europeans, reading a rather rarefied text like *Heart of Darkness* was often as close as they came to Africa, and in that limited sense it was part of the European effort to hold on to, think about, plan for Africa. To represent Africa is to enter the battle over Africa, inevitably connected to later resistance, decolonization, and so forth.

Works of literature, particularly those whose manifest subject is empire, have an inherently untidy, even unwieldy aspect in so fraught, so densely charged a political setting. Yet despite their formidable complexity, literary works like *Heart of Darkness* are distillations, or simplifications, or a set of choices made by an author that are far less messy and mixed up than the reality. It would not be fair to think of them as abstractions, although fictions such as *Heart of Darkness* are so elaborately fashioned by authors and so worried over by readers as to suit the necessities of narrative which, as a result, we must add, makes a highly specialized entry into the struggle over Africa.

So hybrid, impure, and complex a text requires especially vigilant attention as it is interpreted. Modern imperialism was so global and all-encompassing that virtually nothing escaped it; besides, as I have said, the nineteenth-century contest over empire is still continuing today. Whether or not to look at the connections between cultural texts and imperialism is therefore to take a position *in fact taken* – either to study the connection in order to criticize it and think of alternatives for it, or not to study it in order to let it stand, unexamined and, presumably, unchanged. One of my reasons for writing this book is to show how far the quest for, concern about, and consciousness of overseas dominion extended – not just in Conrad but in figures we practically never think of in that connection, like Thackeray and Austen – and how enriching and important for the critic is attention to this material, not only for the obvious political reasons but also because, as I have been arguing, this particular kind of attention allows the reader to interpret canonical nineteenth- and twentieth-century works with a newly engaged interest.

Let us return to *Heart of Darkness*. In it Conrad offers an uncannily suggestive starting point for grappling at close quarters with these difficult matters. Recall that Marlow contrasts Roman colonizers with their modern counterparts in an oddly perceptive way, illuminating the special mix of power, ideological energy, and practical attitude characterizing European imperialism. The ancient Romans, he says, were 'no colonists; their administration was a squeeze and nothing more'. Such people conquered and did little else. By contrast, 'what saves us is efficiency – the devotion to efficiency', unlike the Romans, who relied on brute force, which is scarcely more than 'an accident arising from the weakness of others'. Today, however,

> the conquest of the earth, which mostly means the taking it away from those who have a different complexion and slightly flatter noses than ourselves, is not a pretty thing when you look into it too much. What redeems it is the idea only. An idea at the back of it; not a sentimental pretence but an idea; and an unselfish belief in the idea – something you can set up, and bow down before, and offer a sacrifice to . . .[5]

In his account of his great river journey, Marlow extends the point to mark a distinction between Belgian rapacity and (by implication) British rationality in the conduct of imperialism.[6]

Salvation in this context is an interesting notion. It sets 'us' off from the damned, despised Romans and Belgians, whose greed radiates no benefits onto either their consciences or the lands and bodies of their subjects. 'We' are saved because first of all we needn't look directly at the results of what we do; we are ringed by and ring ourselves with the practice of efficiency, by which land and people are put to use completely; the territory and its inhabitants are totally incorporated by our rule, which in turn totally incorporates us as we respond efficiently to its exigencies. Further, through Marlow, Conrad speaks of redemption, a step in a sense beyond salvation. If salvation saves us, saves time and money, and also saves us from the ruin of mere short-term conquest, then redemption extends salvation further still. Redemption is found in the self-justifying practice of an idea or mission over time, in a structure that completely encircles and is revered by you, even though you set up the structure in the first place, ironically enough, and no longer study it closely because you take it for granted.

Thus Conrad encapsulates two quite different but intimately related aspects of imperialism: the idea that is based on the power to take over territory, an idea utterly clear in its force and unmistakable consequences; and the practice that essentially disguises or obscures this by developing a justificatory regime of self-aggrandizing, self-originating authority interposed between the victim of imperialism and its perpetrator.

We would completely miss the tremendous power of this argument if we were merely to lift it out of *Heart of Darkness*, like a message out of a bottle. Conrad's argument is inscribed right in the very form of narrative as he inherited it and as he practised it. Without empire, I would go so far as saying, there is no European novel as we know it, and indeed if we study the impulses giving rise to it, we shall see the far from accidental convergence between the patterns of narrative authority constitutive of the novel on the one hand, and, on the other, a complex ideological configuration underlying the tendency to imperialism.

Notes

1. JOSEPH CONRAD, 'Heart of Darkness' in *Youth and Two Other Stories* (Garden City: Doubleday, Page, 1925), 82.
2. For MACKINDER, see NEIL SMITH, *Uneven Developments: Nature, Capital and the Production of Space* (Oxford: Blackwell, 1984), 102–3. Conrad and triumphalist geography are at the heart of FELIX DRIVER, 'Geography's Empire: Histories of Geographical Knowledge,' *Society and Space*, 1991.
3. HANNAH ARENDT, *The Origins of Totalitarianism* (1951; new ed., New York: Harcourt Brace Jovanovich, 1973), 215. See also FREDERIC JAMESON, *The Political Unconscious: Narrative as a Socially Symbolic Act* (Ithaca: Cornell University Press, 1981), 206–81.
4. IAN WATT, *Conrad in the Nineteenth Century* (Berkeley: University of California Press, 1979), 175–9.
5. JOSEPH CONRAD op. cit., 50–1. For a demystifying account of the connection between modern culture and redemption see LEO BERSANI, *The Culture of Redemption* (Cambridge, Mass.: Harvard University Press, 1990).
6. Theories and justifications of imperial style – ancient versus modern, English versus French, and so on – were in plentiful supply after 1880. See as a celebrated example EVELYN BARING (Cromer), *Ancient and Modern Imperialism* (London: Murray, 1910). See also C. A. BODELSEN, *Studies in Mid-Victorian Imperialism* (New York: Howard Fertig, 1968), and Richard Faber, *The Vision and the Need: Late Victorian Imperialist Aims* (London: Faber & Faber, 1966). An earlier but still useful work is KLAUS KNORR, *British Colonial Theories* (Toronto: University of Toronto Press, 1944).

Further Reading

General studies

BOWLBY, RACHEL *Just Looking* (London: Methuen, 1985).

DJIKSTRA, BRAM *Idols of Perversity: Fantasies of Feminine Evil in the Fin de Siècle* (New York: Oxford University Press, 1986).

DOWLING, LINDA *Language and Decadence in the Victorian Fin de Siècle* (Princeton, New Jersey: Princeton University Press, 1986).

FLETCHER, IAN (ed.) *Decadence and the 1890s* Stratford upon Avon Studies no. 17 (London: Edward Arnold, 1979).

JACKSON, HOLBROOK *The Eighteen Nineties* [1913] (Brighton: Harvester, 1976).

LEDGER, SALLY and MCCRACKEN, SCOTT *Cultural Politics at the Fin de Siècle* (Cambridge: Cambridge University Press, 1995).

SHOWALTER, ELAINE *Sexual Anarchy: Gender and Culture at the Fin de Siècle* (New York: Viking, 1990 and London: Bloomsbury, 1991).

STOKES, JOHN *In the Nineties* (Hemel Hempstead: Harvester Wheatsheaf, 1989).

STOKES, JOHN (ed.) *Fin de Siècle, Fin du Globe: Fears and Fantasies of the Late Nineteenth Century* (London: Macmillan, 1992).

TEICH, MIKULAS and PORTER, ROY *Fin de Siècle and its Legacy* (Cambridge: Cambridge University Press, 1990).

Gender and sexuality

ARDIS, ANN *New Women, New Novels: Feminism and Early Modernism* (New Brunswick, New Jersey: Rutgers University Press, 1990).

BJORHOVDE, GERD *Rebellious Structures: Women Writers and the Crisis of the Novel, 1880–1900* (Oxford, Oxford University Press, 1987).

BOUMELHA, PENNY *Thomas Hardy and woman: Sexual Ideology and Narrative Form* (Brighton: Harvester, 1982).

COHEN, ED *Talk on the Wilde Side: Towards a Genealogy of Discourse on Male Sexualities* (London: Routledge, 1993).

COHEN, ED 'The double lives of man: narration and identification in late nineteenth-century representations of eccentric masculinities', in LEDGER, SALLY and MCCRACKEN, SCOTT *Cultural Politics at the Fin de Siècle* (Cambridge: Cambridge University Press, 1995).

CRAFT, CHRISTOPHER 'Kiss Me With Those Red Lips: Gender and Inversion in Bram Stoker's *Dracula*' in Elaine Showalter (ed.), *Speaking of Gender* London: Routledge, 1989), pp. 216–42.

CUNNINGHAM, GAIL *The New Woman and the Victorian Novel* (London: Macmillan, 1978).

FOUCAULT, MICHEL *History of Sexuality* (Vintage Books, 1978) Vol. 1.

GILBERT, SANDRA and GUBAR, SUSAN *No Man's Land: the Place of the Woman Writer in the Twentieth Century* (New Haven: Yale University Press, 1989). Vol. 2 *Sexchanges.*

KOESTENBAUM, WAYNE *Double Talk: The Erotics of Male Literary Collaboration* (London: Routledge, 1989).

PYKETT, LYN *The Improper Feminine: The Women's Sensation Novel and the New Woman Writing* (London: Routledge, 1992).

PYKETT, LYN *Engendering Fictions: The English Novel in the Early Twentieth Century* (London: Edward Arnold, 1995).

ROTH, PHYLLIS 'Suddenly Sexual Women in Bram Stoker's *Dracula*', *Literature and Psychology*, 17 (1977), pp. 113–21.

SEDGWICK, EVE KOSOFSKY *Between Men: English Literature and Male Homosocial Desire* (New York: Columbia University Press, 1985).

SEDGWICK, EVE KOSOFSKY *Epistemology of the Closet* (Berkeley: University of California Press, 1990).

SENF, CAROL A. '*Dracula*: Stoker's response to the New Woman', *Victorian Studies* 26 (1982).

SINFIELD, ALAN *The Wilde Century* (London: Cassell, 1994).

STUBBS, PATRICIA *Women and Fiction: Feminism and the Novel, 1880–1920* (London: Methuen, 1979).

TUCHMAN, GAIL *Edging Women Out: Victorian Novelists, Publishers and Social Change* (London: Routledge, 1989).

VEEDER, WILLIAM 'Children of the Night: Stevenson and Patriarchy', in William Veeder (ed.) *Doctor Jekyll and Mr Hyde After One Hundred Years* (Chicago: University of Chicago Press, 1988).

WALKOWITZ, JUDITH *City of Dreadful Delight: Narratives of Sexual Danger in Late-Victorian London* (London: Virago, 1992).

WEEKS, JEFFREY 'The Late-Victorian Stew of Sexualities', *Victorian Studies* 35 (1992), pp. 409–15.

Degeneration

CHAMBERLIN, J. E. 'An Anatomy of Cultural Melancholy', *Journal of the History of Ideas* 42 (1981), pp. 691–705.

CHAMBERLIN, J. E. and GILMAN, SANDER (eds) *Degeneration: the Dark Side of Progress* (New York: Columbia University Press, 1985.

GREENSLADE, WILLIAM *Degeneration, Culture and the Novel, 1880–1940* (Cambridge: Cambridge University Press, 1994).

PICK, DANIEL *Faces of Degeneration: A European Disorder, c, 1848–c.1914* (Cambridge, Cambridge University Press, 1989).

Imperialism

BIVONA, DANIEL *Desire and Contradiction: Imperial Visions and Domestic Debates in Victorian Literature* (Manchester: Manchester University Press, 1990), pp. xi and viii.

CHRISMAN, LAURA 'The Imperial Unconscious? Representations of Imperial Discourse', *Critical Quarterly* 32 (1990), pp. 217–55.

CHRISMAN, LAURA 'Empire, "race" and feminism at the *fin de siècle*: the work of George Egerton and Olive Schreiner', in LEDGER, SALLY and McCRACKEN, SCOTT *Cultural Politics at the Fin de Siècle* (Cambridge: Cambridge University Press, 1995).

DAVIN, ANNA, 'Imperialism and Motherhood', *History Workshop*, 5 (1978).

HYAM, RONALD *Empire and Sexuality: The British Experience* (Manchester: Manchester University Press, 1990).

PARRY, BENITA *Delusions and Discoveries: Studies on India and the British Imagination, 1880–1930* (London: Allen Lane, 1972).

PARRY, BENITA *Conrad and Imperialism: Ideological Boundaries and Visionary Frontiers* (London: Macmillan, 1983).

RICHARDS, JEFFREY (ed.) *Imperialism and Juvenile Literature* (Manchester: Manchester University Press, 1989).

SAID, EDWARD *Orientalism* (London: Routledge and Kegan Paul, 1978).

Index

Adams, Francis 52
Adorno, Theodor 208–9
adventure fiction 193–216
aestheticism 11
Africa 239–40
Allen, Grant, *The Woman Who Did*
    51, 56, 62
anti-essentialism 139, 148
anti-humanism 136
anti-semitism 165, 208, 209
Ardis, Ann L., *New Women, New*
    Novels 7, 8
Arendt, Hannah 236
Arnold, Edwin, *The Light of Asia*
    194
Arnold, Matthew 90, 138
    Culture and Anarchy 136
Arnold, Thomas 89
atavism 193–216
    Athenaeum, The 66, 111
Auerbach, Nina 5, 200

Baldick, Chris 145
Balfour, Arthur J. 97, 194
    Defence of Philosophic Doubt 205
    Foundations of Belief 205
Ballantyne, R.M., *Coral Island* 202
Barlas, John 52
Barry, W.F. 53
    The New Antigone 50, 51, 55
Barthes, Roland 4, 9, 66, 148
Beardsley, Aubrey 27, 95
    The Story of Venus and
      Tannhäuser 62
Beerbohm, Max 56
Belgian colonialism 240–1
Bernhardt, Sarah 31

Besant, Annie 194
bisexuality 85
Bivona, Daniel 16
Bjorhovde, Gerd, *Rebellious*
    Structures 7
Blackwood's Magazine 94, 201
Blavatsky, Madame 206
    Isis Unveiled 45, 194
Boer War 168, 222
Bonnard, Pierre 95
Borrow, George 61
Boumelha, Penny 6
    Thomas Hardy and Women 7, 99
boundary situations 229
Bradfield, Thomas 53
Bradley, A.C. 25
Brandon, Ruth 211, 213, 215
Brantlinger, Patrick 17
    Rule of Darkness 16, 193
Breuer, Josef, *Studies on Hysteria* 24,
    28, 30
Brooke, Emma Frances, *A*
    Superfluous Woman 52, 54, 61,
    62
Buchan, John 196
    Greenmantle 194
    Thirty-Nine Steps 201
Butler, Josephine 90, 177

Caird, Mona 179
    The Daughters of Danaus 50, 57
capitalism 11, 146–7
Carpenter, Edward 94, 116
    Civilisation: Its Cause and Cure 14,
    165
Carson, Edward 94
    Century Magazine, The 79

Chamberlin, Edward 13
Chapman, Elizabeth 50, 51
Charcot, Jean Martin 28, 35, 161
Charlesworth, Barbara, *Dark
     Passages: The Decadent
     Consciousness in Victorian
     Literature* 2
Chesney, George, *The Battle of
     Dorking* 201
Childers, Erskine, *Riddle of the
     Sands* 195, 201
Chrisman, Laura 40
Christian manliness 88–9
civilisation 79, 208
Clarke, I.F., *Voices Prophesying War*
     201
Cleveland Street scandal 84, 91, 93,
     96
Cohen, Ed, 'Writing Gone Wilde:
     Homoerotic Desire in the
     Closet of Representation' 10,
     11, 12, 13, 93
Collins, John Churton 99
     Talk on the Wilde Side 108
colonialism 235, 240–1
compulsory heterosexuality 83–102
Conrad, Joseph 203, 238
     Heart of Darkness 18, 47, 203, 210,
          234–42
     Nostromo 223, 238
     Personal Record, A 239
Contagious Diseases Acts 5, 175,
     177
Cramb, J.A., *Origins and Destiny of
     Imperial Britain* 194
criminal anthropology 163–4
Criminal Law Amendment Act
     (1871) 91
     Critical Quarterly 40
Croker, Bithia 193–4
Cultural Materialism 3, 12
Cultural Studies 3–4
Cunningham, Gail, *The New
     Woman and the Victorian
     Novel* 6, 7
Curzon, George 86

dandyism 89, 93, 111
Darwin, Charles 162
Davidson, John 52, 195

decadence 2, 6, 111
     and New Woman 48–63
degeneration 13–16, 155, 165–8, 196
Delay, Jean 133, 134, 141
Dellamora, Richard, 'Homosexual
     Scandal and Compulsory
     Heterosexuality in the 1890s'
     10–11, 12, 13, 83–102
Derrida, Jacques 145
Dickens, Charles, *Hard Times* 136
Dixon, Ella Hepworth, *The Story of
     a Modern Woman* 52, 60
Dollimore, Jonathan 10, 12
     *Sexual Dissidence: Augustine to
          Wilde, Freud to Foucault* 132
     Don Leon 87
Doolittle, Hilda ('H.D.') 35–6
     Helen in Egypt 36
     Tribute to Freud 36
Dostoevsky, Fedor 197
Douglas, Alfred 94–7, 109, 132, 134
Dowie, Ménie Muriel 180
     Gallia 56
Dowling, Linda, *Language and
     Decadence in the Victorian Fin
     de Siècle* 2, 8
Dowson, Ernest 48–50, 60–2
Doyle, Arthur Conan 194, 196, 197,
     212–15
     History of Spiritualism 215
     Land of Mist, The 214
     Lost World, The 214
     Memories and Adventures 213
     Pheneas Speaks 215
     Poison Belt, The 214
dreams 70, 155
du Maurier, George, *Trilby* 5, 25–7
duality 70, 71

Eagleton, Terry 146–8
Egerton, George 52, 57
     Discords 52, 55
     Keynotes 55, 179
     Spell of the White Elf, The 1
Eliot, George 25, 62, 95, 188, 197
     The Mill on the Floss 180
Eliot, T.S., *The Love Song of St
     Sebastian* 44
Ellis, Havelock 54, 59, 85, 101, 116,
     187, 188

Sexual Inversion 101
Studies in the Psychology of Sex 75
Ellmann, Richard 93, 97, 134
Elmy, Elizabeth Wolstenholme 100
essentialism 139, 147, 148

femininity, myths of 5
feminism 99–100, 179
feminist literary history 3, 4, 5
Fletcher, Ian, *Decadence and the
    1890s* 2
Foucault, Michel 8, 15, 16, 83, 109,
    144
    The History of Sexuality 175
French Revolution 50, 51, 135
Freud, Sigmund 5, 6, 10, 23, 47, 73,
    75
    Civilization and its Discontents
        78–9
    'Civilized sexual morality and
        modern nervous illness' 14
    Dora 32–5, 178–9
    Future of an Illusion, The 204
    on Haggard's *She* 46–7
    Interpretation of Dreams 34, 68
    Studies on Hysteria 24–5, 28, 30–3
    theory of sexuality 76
    *Three Essays on the Theory of
        Sexuality* 168
    Totem and Taboo 156–7, 158
Froude, J.A., *The Two Chiefs of
    Dunboy* 137

Gagnier, Regenia 11, 89, 93, 96, 111
gay studies 13, 83
gender definition 8
gender differences 85
gender politics 4
gender roles 10, 84
general paralysis of the insane 175
gentleman, status of 86–90, 93, 98
Gide, André 111, 139–42
    Corydon 139
    Counterfeiters, The 134
    encounters with Wilde 13, 132–6,
        148–9
    Immoralist, The 134, 140, 142
    Oscar Wilde 132
    Si le grain ne meurt (*If It Die*) 132,
        133, 134, 140

Gilbert, Sandra 5, 40
    No Man's Land 40
    Sexchanges 40
Gilman, Charlotte Perkins, *Herland*
    179
Gilman, Sander 13
Gilmour, Robin 88, 89–90
Gissing, George 52, 196
    The Whirlpool 210
Gladstone, William Ewart 85, 91,
    95, 211
Gosse, Edmund 72, 79, 98–9, 186
Grand, Sarah, *The Heavenly Twins*
    51, 180, 181
Greenslade, William 13
Gubar, Susan 40
    No Man's Land 40
    Sexchanges 40
Guthrie, T.A., *The Seizure of the
    Channel Tunnel* 201

Haggard, H. Rider
    Allan Quartermain 209–10
    Dawn 207
    Days of My Life, The 207
    interest in occultism 207–8
    King Solomon's Mines 194, 209
    She 5, 9, 30, 40–7, 181–2, 188,
        200, 209, 210
    Witch's Head, The 207
Hamer, D.A. 85
Hamilton, Cecily 177, 179
Hansson, Laura Marholm 58
Harcourt, Sir W.V. 95, 96
Hardy, Thomas 28, 52
    Jude the Obscure 11, 52, 57, 72, 84,
        86, 92, 98, 100–1, 185–8
    Mayor of Casterbridge, The 186
    Tess of the D'Urbervilles 28
    Woodlanders, The 186
Harker, Jonathan 27, 163
Harrison, Frederic 202
Harvie, Christopher, *The Lights of
    Liberalism* 89
Heath, Stephen
    'Psychopathia sexualis:
        Stevenson's *Strange Case*' 6,
        9, 10, 14, 66
    Sexual Fix, The 66
Henley, William Ernest 93, 195

Hilliard, David 95
Hobson, J.A., *The Psychology of Jingoism* 201
homoerotic desire 108–26
  in *Picture of Dorian Gray, The* 116–26
  in *Teleny* 112–16
homosexuality 3, 10, 83–102, 144
Hopkins, Gerard Manley 67, 83, 188
Hughes, Thomas 89
Huysmans, J.K. 54
hypnosis 24–6, 161
hypocrisy 71, 74
hysteria 72, 76, 78, 161, 162

Ibsen, Henrik 182
  Ghosts 185, 187
imperial Gothic 194–202, 209, 210, 216
imperialism 3, 16–18, 40, 193–205, 209, 234–42
India 225–33
individualism 136–8
invasion-scare stories 199, 201
inversion 86, 101, 144, 145
'Iota', *A Yellow Aster* 57
Ireland 91, 137

Jackson, Holbrook, *The Eighteen Nineties* 1, 2–3
James, Henry 87, 197
Jameson, Frederic 16, 146, 231
Jefferies, Richard, *After London* 196
Jeffreys, Sheila 85, 102
Jews 165, 208, 222
John, Augustus 61
Jouvenot, F. de 1
Jowett, Benjamin 89

Keats, John 42, 47
Kermode, Frank 24
Kingsley, Charles 89
Kipling, Rudyard 17, 52, 196
  death of daughter 206
  Debits and Credits 207
  ghost stories 206
  imperialism 221–33
  on India 225–8
  Kim 201, 224, 225, 229

Life's Handicap 226, 228
Light That Failed, The 226
'Mark of the Beast' 195
Naulahka, The 227
Phantom Rickshaw, The 228
Plain Tales from the Hills 224, 226
'Recessional' 195
Something of Myself 221
Kleinpaul, Rudolf, *Die Lebendigen und die Toten in Volksglauben, Religion and Sage* 157
Krafft-Ebing, Richard von 96
  Psychopathia Sexualis 10, 76, 77, 79, 110

Labouchère, Henry du Pré 91, 92, 93, 96
Lacan, Jacques 108
Lang, Andrew 49, 194, 197–8, 203–4, 208
  Cock Lane and Common Sense 204
Lankester, Edwin, *Degeneration: A Chapter in Darwinism* 13, 164
Lawrence, D.H. 54, 60, 62, 145, 187
  The Woman Who Rode Away 44
Le Fanu, J. Sheridan, *Carmilla* 159
Le Gallienne, Richard 51, 54, 60
Le Queux, William, *The Great War in England* 201
lesbians 84, 85, 96, 97, 101–2
Lester, H.F., *The Taking of Dover* 201
Levi-Strauss, Claude 9
Liberalism 87, 91
  Lippincott's Monthly Magazine 111, 113
literary periodisation 7
Lockwood, Sir Frank 94, 97
Lodge, Oliver 194, 205
  Phantom Walls 212
Lombroso, Cesare 163
lust-murder 77

MacDonald, George 42, 47
  Lilith 44
Machen, Arthur 198
McMillan, Margaret 91
Marcus, Steven 33
  The Other Victorians 112
masculinity 9, 66, 84, 87, 88
Mattos, Katherine de 68–9, 78, 79

Meyers, F.W.H. 28
Micard, H. 1
Mill, John Stuart 99
  On Liberty 87
Miller, Henry 44
Millgate, Michael 98
  mission civilisatrice 239
Mitchell, Juliet 78
modernism 3, 40, 50, 146, 148
morality 71
Morrison, Arthur 52
Myers, F.W.H. 205
myths
  of *fin de siècle* 9
  of womanhood 23–36

neurosis 71, 73, 74
New Realism 6
New Woman 5–8, 11, 15, 29, 41
  critique of marriage 99
  and decadence 48–63
Nietzsche, Friedrich 71
  Thus Spake Zarathustra 141
Noble, James Ashcroft 53
Nordau, Max, *Degeneration* 1, 14,
  58, 163

occultism 17, 158, 194, 197, 198,
  204, 211–16
  Adorno on 208–9
  Haggard's interest 207–8
  Kipling's scepticism 206
Oliphant, Mrs 53, 56, 98
Oppenheim, Jane 194
O'Pray, Michael 226

Pankhurst, Christabel, *The Great
  Scourge and How to End It*
  189
parataxis 229
Parry, Benita 17
  Conrad and Imperialism 221
  Delusions and Discoveries 221
pastoralism 60
Pater, Walter 42–3
Pearson, Norman Holmes 36
perversion 73, 76–8, 144
physiognomy 164
Pick, Daniel 13
  Faces of Degeneration 155

' "Terrors of the Night": *Dracula*
  and "Degeneration" in the
  Late Nineteenth Century' 15
Pittock, Murray, *Spectrum of
  Decadence* 2, 18–19
Plarr, Victor 48
Poggioli, Renato 59, 61
Polidori, *The Vampyre* 159
pornography 94, 112, 125
post-structuralism 4, 9, 146
postmodernism 13, 143–9
Praz, Mario 5, 24
  The Romantic Agony 40
procreative sex 57
Propp, Vladimir 9
prostitution 92, 96, 175–8
psychic research 158, 204, 205, 213
psychoanalysis 6, 146, 158
psychology 14
public schools 86, 88, 93–4
  Punch 27, 51, 53, 56, 61

Quarterly Review 99
Queensberry, Marquis of 94, 97,
  109, 149

Reade, Brian 94
reconstruction of *fin de siècle* 18–19
Reed, John, *The Decadent Style* 2
reincarnation 206–7
representation 77, 78, 230
  Revue Blanche, La 95, 96
Rhodes, Cecil 210–11, 222, 236
Rich, Adrienne 10, 83–4, 85
Richards, I.A. 145
Rieff, Philip 30
Rolfe, Harvey 210
Romans, ancient 241
Rosebery, Lord 95–6, 97
Ross, Robert 99, 133

*Sack of London in the Great French
  War of 1901, The* (Anon.) 201
Said, Edward 228
  Culture and Imperialism 234
  Orientalism 17, 18, 225, 234
Salisbury, Lord 92
Savage, Sir George 175, 186
scandal 83–102
Schreiner, Olive 179, 180

The Story of an African Farm
45–6, 48, 49, 58, 60–2
Schwabe, Maurice 94
Schwob, Marcel 75
sciolism 55
Sedgwick, Eve Kosofsky
*Between Men: English Literature
and Male Homosocial Desire* 8,
9, 10, 12, 83, 87, 110
Epistemology of the Closet 9
sexology 77, 78, 84, 100
sexual politics 4, 10
sexuality 3, 66, 168
female 72, 186
male 71–4, 76, 109, 186, 187
medicalisation 10, 76
psychologisation 10, 34
Shaw, George Bernard 196
Shelley, Mary, *Frankenstein* 9, 159
Showalter, Elaine 15, 95
Literature of Their Own, A 6, 7,
174
Sexual Anarchy 19, 174
Siegel, Sandra 14
Sinnett, A.P.
Esoteric Buddhism 194
Occult World, The 194
Smith, Barbara Herrnstein 7
social attitudes 71
socialism 91, 135, 137, 138
Society for Psychical Research 28,
158, 204, 205
Sontag, Susan, *Illness as Metaphor*
174, 175
Speaker 52
spiritualism 17, 45, 198, 203, 205,
211–15
Spivak, Gayatri 7, 17
spy stories 201
Stafford, David 201
Stansky, Peter 85
Stead, W.T. 91, 96, 211, 213
Borderland 211
*Last Will and Testament of Cecil
John Rhodes* 210–11
Stevenson, Robert Louis
Beach of Falesa, The 203
death 75
Ebb-Tide 203
Kidnapped 197, 198

*Strange Case of Dr Jekyll and Mr
Hyde, The* 9, 10, 14, 66–80, 87,
182–3, 198
Treasure Island 73, 197, 198
Wreckers, The 203
Stoker, Bram
Dracula 5, 9, 14–15, 25, 27–30, 44,
155–70, 180–1, 199
Jewel of Seven Stars, The 29, 30,
200
Lady of the Shroud, The 29
Lair of the White Worm, The 29,
30
Man, The 168, 169
Stubbs, Patricia, *Feminism and the
Novel* 6, 7
Stutfield, Hugh E.M. 51, 55, 59
Swinburne, Algernon Charles 42,
47, 83, 187
Swiney, Francis 100, 178
Symbolism 19
Symonds, J.A. 61, 75, 94, 99, 116
Symons, Arthur 2, 54, 60
syphilis 15, 32, 174–85

taboos 157–8
Talbot, Eugene, *Degeneracy, Its
Signs, Causes and Results* 164
Teleny 11, 94, 112–16, 125–6
Tennyson, Alfred Lord 89
'Lotos Eaters' 203
Princess, The 46
theosophy 45, 203, 206
Thornton, R.K.R., *The Decadent
Dilemma* 2
Thornycroft, Hamo 99
Titanic (liner) 211, 213
transgression 139–41
transitional status of *fin de siècle* 3
Trilling, Lionel 8, 50
Troll-Borostyani, Irma von 58
Tylor, Edward Burnett 198

vampires 156, 158, 160, 163, 180
Vance, Norman 88
Verlaine, Paul 49, 58
Victoria, Queen 188
Victorianism 2, 3
violence 67

Wallace, Edgar, *Sanders of the River*
196
'Walter', *My Secret Life* 176
Walton, Frank 48
Ward, Mrs Humphrey, *Marcella* 53
Weeks, Jeffrey 8, 83, 87, 92, 100
Coming Out 110
Wells, H.G.
Time Machine, The 184
'Truth about Pyecraft, The' 197
War of the Worlds 199, 200
Westminster Review 52, 179
White, William Hale, *Mark
Rutherford's Deliverance* 196
Whitechapel murders 79
Whitman, Walt 61
Wilde, Oscar
advocacy of transgression 141–3
aesthetic 138–9
encounters with Gide 13, 132–6,
148–9

*Phrases and Philosophies for the
Use of the Young* 142, 143, 144
Picture of Dorian Gray, The 12, 60,
84–95, 111–13, 116–26, 177,
183–4, 199
'Portrait of Mr. W. H.' 94
Salome 44
Soul of Man Under Socialism, The
12, 135, 146
trials 11, 84–7, 93–7, 99, 109, 116,
144
Williams, Raymond 3, 4, 12, 126
Wodehouse, P.G., *The Swoop...A Tale
of the Great Invasion* 201
working-class 91, 92
Wurgaft, Lewis 196

Yeats, William Butler 60, 61, 194
A Vision 214

Zola, Emile 181